ROOTS AND REALITIES
AMONG EASTERN AND CENTRAL EUROPEANS

CEESSA and CEESAC gratefully acknowledge grants from the Secretary of State (Multiculturalism) and the Alberta Department of Culture without whose support this publication could not have materialized.

ROOTS AND REALITIES
AMONG
EASTERN AND
CENTRAL EUROPEANS

Martin L. Kovacs, editor

Committee:

Robert L. Busch
University of Alberta,
associate editor

Alan Anderson
University of Saskatchewan

Maurice Williams
Okanagan College, B.C.

Tova Yedlin
University of Alberta

Central And East European Studies Association of Canada

Edmonton, Alberta
Canada
1983

To order this book write:

CEESAC
c/o Central & East European Studies Society of Alberta
#7 Noble Building
8540 – 109 Street
Edmonton, Alberta, Canada   T6G 1E6

ISBN 0-9691091-0-5

Kovacs, Martin Louis
University of Regina
Regina, Saskatchewan
Canada

Canadian Cataloguing in Publication Data

Main entry under title:
Roots and realities among Eastern and Central
        Europeans.

        Based on papers and panel reports presented at
a conference at the University of Alberta, March
13-15, 1980.
        Includes index.
        ISBN 0-9691091-0-5

        1. Canada – Population – Ethnic groups – Congresses.* 2. Slavs – Canada – Congresses. 3. Germans – Canada – Congresses. 4. Finno-Ugrians – Canada – Congresses. 5. Europe, Eastern – Social conditions – Congresses. 6. Central Europe – Social conditions – Congresses. I. Kovacs, Martin L. (Martin Louis), 1918–. II. Central and East European Studies Association of Canada.
FC104.R66 _1980_   971'.004   C82-091385-5
F1035.A1R66

37,340

TABLE OF CONTENTS

I. ROOTS: EAST AND CENTRAL EUROPE

iii

II. REALITIES: THE COMMUNITY

III. THE WHOLE

FOREWORD

The Central and East European Studies Association of Canada was privileged to have had the opportunity to sponsor a national conference which provided the stage for the presentations included in this volume.

The papers vividly illustrate the diversity of viewpoints in the academic and ethnocultural communities and point to the need for establishing vehicles for dialogue between these two groups, both provincially and nationally.

The third national conference of CEESAC held in Edmonton, Alberta, March 13-15, 1980, provided the opportunity for members of academic and ethnocultural communities to exchange views and information and, in general, to participate in a scholarly forum. The papers are consonant with our main objectives, namely: to stimulate greater understanding among Canadians of diverse cultural heritages; and to support the writing of contemporary histories on Canadians of Central and East European origin.

While we commend all the contributors to this volume, special appreciation and thanks must be directed to Dr. Martin Kovacs, Editor, and his team of Dr. R. Busch and Dr. T. Yedlin of the Division of East European Studies, University of Alberta. Finally, it is important to thank Alberta Culture for its generous funding which helped to make this publication possible.

N. Spillios, President
Central and East European
Studies Association of Canada

PREFACE

The contents of this publication are based on papers and panel reports presented to the "Central and East European Community in Canada: Roots, Aspirations, Progress and Realities" conference at the University of Alberta, March 13-15, 1980. The event was sponsored by the Central and East European Studies Association of Canada (CEESAC), the Central and East European Studies Society of Alberta (CEESSA) and the Division of East European Studies, University of Alberta.*

As one of the contributors to this volume has pointed out, not too much attention is directed as a rule by researchers and historians of general Canadian history to the backgrounds, individually or collectively, of Canadians of Central or East European origin, and their attainments in contributing to the advancement of Canada in the past or the present. One objective of this volume is to attempt in some measure to narrow that gap in public awareness.

Another important task of the book is to represent the work of academics and Central and East European community representatives from across Canada. The common tie for all these is their avowed interest in Central and East European Studies.

At times, questions are asked about the difference between this discipline and Ethnic Studies. These are queries not easily answered, yet there are differences between the two. An obvious one is that, while Ethnic Studies claims all ethnic groups as its province, CEES prefers to deal with topics related to Canadians of Central and Eastern European extraction, or Central and East Europe in respect of their present and past.

Fittingly, much material in this volume is devoted to "Roots" and addresses itself mainly to the ethnocultural past, the immigration and settlement, as well as the Central and East European scene. The "Realities" section chiefly reflects feelings, plans, ambitions and achievements as seen in various ethnic communities.

The Edmonton community, which includes a wide variety of ethnic groups, has played an important part in the crystallization of what is usually referred to as multiculturalism. The 1970s in particular witnessed an important part of that development. A significant contribution to the start of a new decade was made by the joint conference in March 1980 of the Central and East European Studies Society of Alberta and the Central and East European Studies Association of Canada. Both groups enjoyed the sponsorship and active

---

* Both the participants and the organizers of the conference greatly appreciate the financial support provided by the Multicultural Directorate, Department of the Secretary of State, and the Alberta Department of Culture.

support of the Division of East European Studies at the University of Alberta.

Owing to his untimely death, Professor Metro Gulutsan, the former Director of the Division and President of both the Society and the Association, could not participate in the Conference. However, his memory and former activities very much permeated official speeches and private conversations. Through his help in promoting and establishing the entities mentioned above, Metro Gulutsan appreciably contributed to the sociocultural change which was a chief characteristic of the past decade and constituted both the background and a recurrent theme of the community papers.

The great success of the Conference derived in large part from the efforts of the CEESAC executive, headed by Nicholas Spillios, the President of CEESSA and CEESAC, and the interest of the membership.

The editor is greatly indebted to his Advisory Committee — Professors Tova Yedlin, Alan Anderson, Robert Busch and Maurice Williams — both for their valuable assistance in the reading and correction of the papers and for their many suggestions. Besides, special thanks are due to Tova Yedlin and, particularly, Robert Busch, who arranged for and supervised the "photoreadying" of the manuscript and acted for the editor during his absence.

Of course, the views expressed by contributors to this volume do not necessarily reflect the opinions of the sponsoring societies, the committee and the editor.

M.L. Kovacs

ROOTS: EAST AND CENTRAL EUROPE

THE MENNONITES IN THE UKRAINE, 1789–1917

Roy Vogt,
University of Manitoba

The Significance of the South–Russian Experience for the Mennonites of Western Canada: Introduction.

Though no exact figures are available, it can be said with considerable assurance that of the approximately 100,000 Mennonites now living in western Canada, more than 80% trace their roots to that area of the Soviet Union which we refer to as the Ukraine, but which, before 1917, was known as New Russia or South Russia. Most of the other less-than-20 per cent either migrated directly from northern Europe (the Danzig area) to Canada, or from Switzerland via the eastern United States and Ontario. The concern of this paper is with the south-Russian roots of the majority. Many of the basic attitudes and practices of the Mennonites in western Canada cannot be understood — so it will be argued here — without consideration of the long developmental process of the Mennonite people in South Russia.

Mennonite life in western Canada is characterized by deep-seated ambivalence about the nature and purpose of the Mennonite community. The most frequent doubts reduce to one question: to what extent ought Mennonites to participate in the surrounding culture?

The facts themselves are clear. Mennonites are active participants in almost every segment of Canadian life. Without going into detail it can be noted that hundreds of businesses in western Canada, particularly in construction, real estate, transportation, and in retail trades of various types, are owned and run by Mennonites. The medical and teaching professions in some western regions are heavily infused with Mennonites. More surprising, perhaps, is the fact that in the last federal election at least sixteen persons with roots in the Mennonite community ran for political office.

Despite this substantial involvement strong doubts persist about its propriety. In many ways the Mennonite community remains an insular one. Social relations are still predominantly intra-Mennonite. In 1976, the last year for which data are available, in more than 60% of the Mennonite marriages performed in Manitoba both of the partners were Mennonite.[1] Numerous taboos and moral codes are still employed to limit participation in "worldly" activities. There are alternating waves of relaxation and reinforcement. The net result is that for a large number of Mennonites in western Canada active participation in Canadian culture is accompanied by much more self-doubt and

3

hesitation than the actual degree of participation would suggest.

At the same time Mennonite life is also made ambiguous by the wide range of social attitudes found within the community. This is well illustrated by the party allegiance of those Mennonites who participated in the last election. Five were Conservative, four Liberal, three Independent, two NDP, and one Marxist-Leninist. Within the Mennonite community there are strong critics of established Canadian traditions, as well as stout defenders. A majority of Mennonites favour capital punishment for murderers, but a substantial minority are vigorously opposed to it. Most Mennonite young people and professionals are conscientiously opposed to participation in war, but the older generation, and most workers and businessmen, are in favour of some form of military defence.[2]

The tensions and ambiguities just described are undoubtedly related to a basic dilemma which the Mennonites face in defining themselves. This dilemma is largely the product of their sojourn in South Russia, and it is for this reason that peculiar practices and attitudes of Mennonites in western Canada can be attributed to their south-Russian experience.

The dilemma involves the coexistence in Mennonite consciousness and experience of two different constitutive elements, religion and ethnicity. Mennonitism was originally a religious movement arising out of the Anabaptist wing of the Protestant Reformation. The chief characteristic of this movement was a radical biblicism, out of which grew a radical commitment to even the strictest ethical demands of Jesus. In this vision there was no room for compromise with the sub-Christian standards of the world. What developed very early on, therefore, was a deep sense of non-conformity with the world. This in turn laid the basis for a separated, isolated, and distinctive religious group, unified in its defiance of a compromising world. There is a link, then, between the original conception of the faith and the emergence of a unique, identifiable group. The cultural and racial characteristics acquired by this group later in its history represent important additions to the group's identity, but they are additions made possible by the faith itself. In other words, Mennonite ethnicity has some basis in Mennonite religion. Mennonite faith created distinctiveness, and it was on this distinctiveness that later generations built a Mennonite commonwealth in South Russia. The process, however, was not inevitable. It was made so by special circumstances in South Russia.

The Creation of a Mennonite Commonwealth in South Russia

The Mennonites migrated to Russia from the Province of West Prussia and the Free City of Danzig in three waves: 1777-1796, 1804-1840, and 1855-1873.[3] Their ancestors had originated in the Netherlands where they had become adherents of a new Christian movement whose most forceful leader was an ex-Catholic priest named Menno Simons. Persecution drove both Simons and many of his followers to the various free cities of northern Europe, and particularly to the Vistula-Nogat Delta area where they could utilize their experience in the Netherlands to reclaim and settle marshy lands. Documents mention Dutch Anabaptists in that area as early as 1540. While the Polish Crown remained faithful to Rome, Protestant congregations of various types were tolerated. Indeed, special privileges were granted to Mennonites as a distinctive religious group, including the right to worship in their own churches and to control their educational system. Their unique religious beliefs and privileges separated them from other settlers with a Dutch-Germanic background. Their language — which remained Dutch for about a century, until gradually being replaced by the West Prussian Platt — separated them from their Polish neighbours. While these conditions furthered their social cohesiveness and the development of a folk-identity, their landholdings were interspersed with those of numerous other groups, and they were prohibited by law from consolidating their holdings into larger and more cohesive units. Such legislation became especially onerous under Prussian rule after the Partition of Poland in 1772. Because of this, and because of growing threats to privileges such as exemption from military service, they became receptive to invitations to settle in other countries.

Such an invitation was extended by the Russian Czarina, Catherine II (1762-1796). As a result of expansionary thrusts into territories bordering on the Black Sea and the Sea of Azov, sparsely populated by hostile nomadic tribes and marauding bands like the Zaporozhian Cossacks, Catherine developed an aggressive colonization policy to secure and develop the new regions. A predecessor, Czarina Elizabeth (1741-1762), had sought to secure the new frontiers with military settlements. These, however, failed to attract enough settlers and therefore proved to be inadequate in terms of both military security and economic development. Catherine initiated a new settlement policy enunciated in a series of manifestos and special decrees and laws between October 1762 and March 1764, and in 1785.[4] The basic purpose of the policy was to attract colonists from outside Russia, who could be counted on to develop the new territories and provide an ideological counterbalance to dissident minority groups in those areas.

Catherine's colonization policies were modelled closely on policies developed in Prussia and Austria. This involved considerable assistance to immigrants by the host government, including the granting of free land, economic subsidies, temporary suspension of taxation, and a range of special privileges appropriate to each colonizing group. The recruitment machinery also resembled western models. Crown agents were appointed to woo colonists, and they in turn appointed special recruiting agents or procurers (vyzyvateli) whose income depended on the number of colonists they attracted. The first formal manifesto inviting foreigners, except Jews, to immigrate to Russia was issued on December 4, 1762, based on an Ukase of October 14 of that year.

The first manifesto produced no results. A number of countries, including Prussia, expressly prohibited emigration of their subjects and the circulation of such manifestos. Where it was circulated the first Manifesto proved ineffectual because it contained only vague promises and guarantees. Subsequent changes to the law, in July 1763, extended the following rights and privileges to prospective colonists:[5]

1. Free board and transportation from the Russian boundary to the place of settlement.
2. The right to settle in any part of the country and to pursue any occupation.
3. A loan for the building of houses, the acquisition of farm implements, the establishment of factories, etc.
4. Perpetual exemption from military and civil service.
5. Exemption from taxes for a varying period ot time, depending on the place of settlement and type of occupation.
6. Free religious practice and, to those founding agricultural colonies, the right to build and control their own churches.
7. The right to proselytize among the country's Mohammedan population, even to "enserf" them, but under no condition to proselytize among other Christian subjects.
8. The right of local self-government for those establishing agricultural communities.
9. The right to those who established factories at their own expense to buy serfs and peasants.
10. The right to send delegates to Russia to negotiate specific terms with the government prior to colonization.

In March, 1764, several additional provisions were enacted which were later of great significance to the Mennonites. These included the allotment of thirty dessiatine of land per immigrant family, the requirement that different faiths were to settle in separate districts, the stipulation that only the youngest son could inherit the land, and that the land was the inalienable property of the whole village, which the individual colonist could own in inheritable form but which neither he nor his descendants could ever sell, mortgage, or subdivide. Lands opened for colonization by foreign colonists and native Russians were situated on the Lower Volga and in the area north of the Black Sea.

The various provisions of these laws were promulgated in a new manifesto issued in July, 1764. It again met with opposition in countries like Austria and

Prussia, but thousands of persons from the western and southern states of Germany responded. During 1765-1766 nearly 23,000 migrated to the Volga where they subsequently established 104 colonies on both banks of the Volga River.[6]

Because of restrictions in Prussia, it is unlikely that any Mennonites were contacted by Russian immigration agents in the 1760s. It was the famous Count Potemkin who, as viceroy of New Russia, initiated steps which brought the Mennonites to Russia. Disparate groups of Greeks, Armenians, Swedes, Italians, Bulgarians, French, Germans, and English were induced to settle in lands under Potemkin's control. Through these endeavours Potemkin also heard of the economic achievements of the Mennonites in Danzig and in West Prussia, and of their growing resentment of increased tax burdens, and land restrictions, placed on them by the Prussian government. In 1786-1787 he therefore dispatched on his own authority a special envoy to negotiate with Mennonites in Danzig and in the surrounding areas. Subsequently two Mennonite delegates travelled to Kherson, at the Russian government's expense, to meet personally with Potemkin to negotiate conditions for immigration and to choose potential sites for a settlement. On July 5, 1787, the two Mennonite delegates, Höppner and Bartsch, concluded an agreement with Potemkin, ratified by Catherine II, which became an official act of the Russian government and formed the basis for Mennonite emigration from Prussia to Russia.

The site agreed upon for a large Mennonite settlement was on the Lower Dnieper near Berislav, and close to the city of Kherson. The conditions were based on the laws of 1763 and 1764. Essentially the Mennonites received privileges available to all other groups. Unique items in the agreement with Potemkin concentrated on detailed specifications regarding actual loans, travel provisions, and other types of assistance which had been described in general terms in the laws.

Both the economic and religious provisions of the Russian laws appealed to the Prussian Mennonites, because it was difficulties in both these areas that frustrated them in Prussia. Indeed, the two areas were often interrelated. For example, special taxes had been imposed on Mennonites to frustrate their economic advancement and to provide for the military build-up of the state. However, they could be exempted from these taxes if they were willing to render military service. Similarly, landholdings could be enlarged only by Mennonites who gave up membership in their church. To the Mennonites it appeared that they were being punished economically for their religious convictions. It is not surprising that the religious and economic freedom promised them in the Russian colonization laws proved to be tremendously appealing.

When the Mennonite delegates returned to Danzig in the fall of 1787 the news of their agreement with the Russian government was greeted with enthusiasm by most Mennonites. Many made immediate plans to emigrate. However, authorities in Danzig and Prussia did their best to prevent any mass exodus of Mennonites. In Prussia persons with property were prevented outright from leaving. In Danzig property could be sold, but there were long delays in issuing exit permits. The result was that when the first small group of Mennonites was finally able to leave for Russia in 1788 it consisted almost entirely of propertyless and poor tradesmen and craftsmen, and no religious leaders.

By early 1789 slightly more than 1,000 emigrants had proceeded by land or sea to Riga, and from there to one of Potemkin's estates in the Moghilev province. After several months they moved on to New Russia, only to discover, to their extreme anger and dismay, that the land promised to them near Kherson would not be made available to them. Instead they were sent to a new site along the Dnieper River, near the small military fort of Alexandrovsk, since then submerged in the city of Zaporozhe. In fact, the land granted to them was Potemkin's personal estate at the Chortitza tributary.

Despite strong misgivings about the quality of the land and a series of broken promises, the new settlers began to lay the foundations for what became known as the Chortitza colony. The settlement contained 21,460 dessiatines of arable land, 987 in hay land, 240 wooded, and 1,293 of waste lands. The 228 families established eight colonies in 1790. Between 1793 and 1796, 118 more families arrived and a ninth colony was established.

In 1803 a second major settlement was founded on the Molotschna River in the province of Taurida. By this time wealthier Mennonites, including many economic and spiritual leaders, were able to leave Prussia so that the new settlement prospered much more quickly than the old. From 1788 to 1810 between 15,000 and 18,000 Mennonites left Danzig and Prussia for these two Russian settlements. In 1855 and 1859, additional colonies were established to accommodate new immigration, and to ease population pressures in the older colonies, at places called Am Trakt and Old Samara on the Volga. On the eve of World War I there were approximately 104,000 Mennonites in Russia, concentrated in four mother colonies, in about fifteen daughter colonies and in large numbers of hamlets and communities. The closed communities numbered about 400, each with its own village government, and independent congregation. They were scattered through most of the provinces in South Russia, the Northern Caucasus, in Central Russia from west of the Volga to the foot of the Ural mountains, and in Siberia from the steppes of the West almost to Lake Baikal in the East. Sizable pockets of Mennonites were also to be found in cities, towns, river ports, and at railroad junctions throughout most of these areas.[7] Most of them were farmers, specializing in grain production, dairying, and stock-breeding, but by World War I they had also achieved unusual success in various branches of industry, particularly in the manufacture of farm implements.[8] In the process of achieving success as a virtually autonomous, well-organized commonwealth, they also forged a new kind of identity, which proved to be problematic for them in South Russia and has continued to plague them in places like western Canada. To understand this it is necessary to examine the nature of this Russian-Mennonite community more closely.

The Mennonite Community in South Russia

There are many factors which explain the development of a unique, ethnic-type Mennonite commonwealth in Russia. First, the Mennonites saw in the unusual freedoms granted to them by the Russian government a God-given opportunity to establish the utopian community suggested by their religion. It was not merely fear that drove them from Prussia to Russia, but religious zeal and a firm commitment to the construction of a unique community life.[9]

Second, they were in fact allowed an unusual degree of autonomy by the Russian colonization laws, and by later concessions given to them. No group of Mennonites has ever been granted greater freedom to develop its own institutions of self-government. Each colony in Russia formed a separate unit of government, consisting of the community or village assembly, composed of one representative from each farm. This assembly in turn elected both the village and district officials and decided on all matters of taxation, education, land distribution, and other matters affecting the economic, social and spiritual life of the community. Churches had autonomous structures but the village assembly had a hand in the selection of ministers. Russian governmental reforms in 1870 and in years following officially set aside all the distinctive rights and privileges of the colonists, and placed the colonies under the regular district, provincial and central agencies of the government.[10] However, the Mennonites retained the right to engage in alternative forms of service to military service, and they were allowed to continue to operate their autonomous units of local government. Merely the name of such units was changed to "volost" to conform to the new nomenclature. All official transactions had now to be carried out in Russian, but otherwise they were treated with benign neglect.

Third, groups like the Mennonites, as seen previously, were deliberately separated from other colonizing groups and from Russian natives. The various religious and cultural groups on the frontier were kept neatly compartmentalized. The fact that few Russians lived in Mennonite colonies was due not so much to Mennonite exclusiveness as to the fact that at the time of the initial settlements the Russian government expressly prohibited anyone but members of the colonizing group from settling there. This provision was vigorously enforced, with the co-operation of the Russian Orthodox Church. When, later,

Russians began to work on Mennonite farms and in Mennonite households and factories, the government and the state church insisted that the children of such families had to be trained in special factory schools by Russian teachers. In addition, Orthodox Churches were established in almost every Mennonite colony which had a substantial number of Russian inhabitants.[11]

The method of land tenure further contributed to the creation of closed, exclusive Mennonite communities. Regardless of its size, each Mennonite family received a separate land allotment of sixty-five dessiatines, consisting of arable land, meadow, pasture, and woodland, as well as a house and garden lot. This was granted as a perpetually inheritable possession, not personally to any one colonist but to each colony as a whole. In order that the land should never fall into the possession of outsiders not even a small part of the allotment could be sold, divided, or mortgaged. Under the initial inheritance laws only the youngest son could inherit land received from the crown, but in 1800 the Czar Paul expressly permitted the Mennonites to use their own rules of inheritance. Under their system the eldest son took over the farm and financially compensated the other members of the family for it. As colonies grew, surplus land initially set aside for this purpose was allocated to those without an inheritance, though quite early this proved to be insufficient and for decades a bitter struggle took place between landowners and the landless peasants. Provision was finally made to establish daughter colonies with financial assistance from the mother colonies. Thus the Mennonites expanded their holdings through the creation of a series of closed communities.

As one scholar summarizes these developments:

> Basic to the Mennonite identity in Russia was the fact that initial coloniza-
> tion as well as later expansion was economically and socially a closed
> process ... As a result, new environments with their inevitable economic
> pressures did not bring about any loss of identity. During the century-long
> sojourn in Russia almost every area of Mennonite experience was
> continuously protected from external interference or alteration.[12]

The unusual success of the Mennonites undoubtedly made them feel superior to many other groups around them, and contributed to their sense of social, economic, political, and religious exclusiveness.

All these developments, however, created a fundamental dilemma for the Mennonite community. How was the original Anabaptist vision, with its stress on social justice, religious zeal, and compassion for the underdog and the outsider, to be squared with the growth of a powerful, exclusive ethnic community intent on preserving social stability and autonomy? The tension appears to have been resolved fairly quickly in favour of ethnic solidarity and social stability, though not without struggle, and never completely.

The new situation required a redefinition of the relationship between religious and non-religious elements in the Mennonite community. It is this problem which the Mennonite experience in South Russia accentuated, and which remains a central, unresolved problem among the descendants of those Mennonites in western Canada today.

The nature of this problem is poignantly portrayed in a recent Mennonite short story in which a Mennonite religious leader in Russia of the 19th century reflects upon the life and objectives of Johann Cornies, who, more than anybody else, helped the Mennonites to achieve prosperity in Russia.

> In my long friendship with Cornies I saw a few things in him that I never told anyone. I could never get him to talk much about religion or his own faith, although he was a good church man. But once — that was in the later years already — he said something to me which I have never forgotten. 'Ohm Fast,' he said, 'I've read the Bible as much as the next man, and my favorite chapter in God's Word is still the first one and His first words: 'Let there be light.'
>
> Something clicked in my head when Cornies said that . . . It wasn't power that Cornies was hungering for. I never felt that in him . . . He was in love with order. And progress . . . A Mennonite society here on the steppe that would be an extension of his own clear mind and will . . . What he really wanted was to transform the whole Molotschna into one big efficient, progressive estate . . .
>
> But the changes Cornies made were not all good. By changing the instruction in our schools, he was letting the world into the classroom. The Bible had always been our book of instruction. Cornies brought in other books – worldly books . . . And that's where the danger came in. I tried to tell him that once, but he only looked past me and said that the church could not always control everything . . . [13]

12

FOOTNOTES

[1]Mavis Reimer, "Marriage and Divorce Among Mennonites of Manitoba," *Mennonite Mirror*, 9 (1980) 5, p. 8.

[2]This is documented and discussed in Roy Vogt, "New Forms of Withdrawal From the World by Urban Mennonites" published as part of an anthology of Mennonite writers, *Mennonite Images* (edited by Harry Loewen, University of Winnipeg).

[3]The basic sources used for this section are as follows:

David G. Rempel, "The Mennonite Commonwealth in Russia, A Sketch of Its Founding and Endurance, 1789-1919," *Mennonite Quarterly Review (MQR)*, 47 (1973), 259-308 and 48 (1974), 5-54. (Referred to here as "Rempel").

David G. Rempel, "An Introduction to Russian Mennonite Historiography." *MQR*, 48 (1974), 409-46.

P. M. Friesen, *The Mennonite Brotherhood in Russia (1789-1910)*, Fresno, California, 1978. Tr. from *Alt-Evangelische Mennonitische Bruderschaft in Russland (1789-1910)*, Halbstadt, Raduga, 1911.

Adolf Ehrt, *Das Mennonitentum in Russland von seiner Einwanderung bis zur Gegenwart*, Berlin-Leipzig, 1932.

Karl Lindeman, *Von den deutschen Kolonisten in Russland*, Stuttgart, 1924. I am indebted to Professor E. E. Reimer of the University of Winnipeg for making these hard-to-obtain documents available to me from his personal library.

E. K. Francis, *In Search of Utopia, the Mennonites in Manitoba*, Altona, Man., 1955. See also the same writer's, "The Mennonite Commonwealth in Russia, 1789-1914. A Sociological Interpretation," *MQR*, 25 (1951), 173-82, and "The Russian Mennonites: From Religious Group to Ethnic Group," *American Journal of Sociology*, 54 (1950), 101-107.

[4]Rempel, 266.

[5]Ibid., 269. This list is not comprehensive.

[6]Ibid., 271-72.

[7]Ibid., 49.

[8]For independent evaluations of Mennonite material and cultural success in Russia see Ehrt, Lindeman, and Francis.

[9]This point is emphasized by E. K. Francis, 20.

[10]Rempel, 9ff.

[11]Ibid., 49.

[12]John B. Toews, "The Russian Mennonites," *MQR*, 47 (1974), 403-404.

[13]E. E. Reimer, "Daniel Fast and the Mennonite Czar," *Mennonite Mirror*, 6 (1977), 28-30.

DOUKHOBORS, MOLOKANS AND SKOVORODA'S TEACHINGS

Victor O. Buyniak,
University of Saskatchewan

The Doukhobors, who came to this country just over 80 years ago, are one of the original religious groups that had its roots in Russia. Although Doukhoborism was officially mentioned under this name for the first time in 1785, the sect was already in existence much earlier.[1] These sectarians represented a Cathar tradition, probably that which in the middle ages among the Balkan Slavs was known as Bogomilism.[2] Many reformatory and dissident movements in Europe between the 9th and the 18th centuries had something to do with this tradition, e.g., the Anabaptists, the Mennonites and the Bohemian Brethren. The movement of religious dissent penetrated into Russia in the 17th century and added to the general upheaval and discord accompanying Patriarch Nikon's reforms of 1654-56, and resulting in the Raskol (Split) within the Russian Orthodox Church. In such an atmosphere the ground was fertile for the appearance in Russia of numerous sects in the 18th century. The Subbotniki (Sabbatarians, Sabbath Keepers), the Shchelniki (Cave Dwellers), the Pryguny (Jumpers), and the Molokane (Milk Drinkers) were among the more important of these sects.

It is generally believed that Doukhoborism (Spirit Wrestling) also originated then. The religious tenets of the Doukhobors were close to those of the Molokans. The two sects coexisted in friendly relations. But in the latter part of the 1770s an internal split occurred within the Doukhobor group provoked by the excesses of one of their leaders who, among other things, rejected the authority of the Bible itself.[3] The dissenting faction joined the Molokans as their closest counterpart, and from that time on the Molokans would continue to absorb the Doukhobors aside from other sectarians. Another feature that distinguished them from a number of religious groups was that the tenets of their philosophy were not written down but were contained in oral tradition — they were enshrined in the memory and the hearts of the Faithful. In time, the collection of Doukhobor beliefs became known as the *Book of Life*.[4] Some individuals were very influential upon the formulation of these creeds. Such a person was Hryhory Savych Skovoroda.[5]

To Skovoroda man was the greatest riddle in life, and self-knowledge the most important means for its solution. His philosophical system embraces three aspects: the ontological, the cognitive, and the ethical. According to him, man is a microcosm reflecting the macrocosm. In order to get to know the universe one must first know oneself. Self-knowledge was for Skovoroda the first aim of philosophy which he approached with the Socratic maxim "know thyself."[6]

Like Socrates, Skovoroda travelled on foot from village to village and taught his philosophy in market places and homes of his friends and people who wished to listen to him. His personality may be compared with that of Leo Tolstoy (a great admirer of his), in their common striving for a simple life, in the midst of common folk, as well as their strong moralizing tendencies. Skovoroda was known to carry all his worldly possessions in a bag, among them the Bible and a flute, both of which he was very fond. It was this unorthodox style of preaching and travelling which had a profound impact on the peasant masses in the Ukraine and which endeared him to them.[7] Since Skovoroda was known to visit a large number of localities not only in the Ukraine proper but also in the southern part of Russia, he may have come in contact with dissidents and sectarians in those parts, who would have been exposed to his teachings. Undoubtedly, the significance of Skovoroda's instruction had implications considerably far beyond the Ukraine proper.[8]

It was, apparently, this early absence of documented information regarding the life and precepts of Skovoroda and the origins of the Doukhobor and the Molokan sects and their philosophical tenets that gave rise to speculation concerning his impact on their beliefs. Since Skovoroda disseminated his philosophy mainly by means of discourses, and since the beliefs of the sectarians, especially those of the Doukhobors, remained for a long time in oral form, passed from generation to generation, some later investigators of Doukhoborism were inclined to see similarities between Skovoroda's teachings and the Doukhobors' practices. Even some contemporary researchers and authors, studying both philosophies, were led to believe in Skovoroda's significant role in the development of Doukhoborism.

It is significant that Skovoroda's *Katekhyzys* (Catechism), which he compiled in 1766, outlines some rudimentary principles of Christianity similar to the ones which early Doukhobors and Molokans held dear.[9] Both Skovoroda and the sectarians believed in a simple pure life and in abstinence — a life characterized by meekness and humility vis-à-vis their neighbours in the biblical sense. They denounced individual property and did not view favourably the amassment of material goods. The Doukhobors and the Molokans were courteous in their dealings with strangers but they did not recognize ranks or offices.[10]

Thus, in the second half of the 18th century, when Skovoroda was engaged in his wanderings and teaching, the people who were to become known as the Doukhobors toward the end of that century were residing on the same territory (the eastern part of the Ukraine) where he was preaching. Mutual contacts and interaction of the two are not excluded, although there is no definitive written documentation in proof of such relations. Nevertheless, the very probability of personal contacts contributed to the spreading of certain myths and suppositions regarding Skovoroda and the Doukhobors. These myths occasionally made their way into the published works of various researchers. Let us consider one such account presented in a book by a Canadian author:

> A bearded pilgrim named Gregory Skovoroda, born in Kiev in 1722, appeared among them carrying a Hebrew Bible in one hand and a flute in the other, claiming that he had been led to them by God. The Doukhobors touched their heads to the ground before him and wept with joy.
>
> He told them he had trained for the priesthood, but his brilliance had confused and frightened the theologians and he had been obliged to feign insanity to escape the monastery. The Doukhobors believed him and adored him.
>
> Gregory's songs enchanted them and they committed them to memory. According to the legend, ten years after he arrived, Skovoroda put down his flute and Bible and told them: 'I am going home.'
>
> Chanting their sorrow, they buried him in a mountain tomb beside Sylvan Kolesnikoff.[11]

Aylmer Maude, who was involved in the negotiations with the Canadian authorities concerning the immigration of the Doukhobors into this country in 1899, had the following to say in this regard:

> That, under the circumstances of the time, this peasant sect should have been able to formulate such reasonable and coherent views / . . . / seems wonderful; but what we know of the life of the philosopher, Gregory Skovoroda, who, reports say, drew up for the Doukhobors the confession of faith they supplied to the Governor of Ekaterinoslav, throws some light on this manner in which such ideas were formulated.[12]

Maude adds that a man of the type of Skovoroda could perform a great service for the peasant masses. Among other things, Skovoroda was a musical composer whose verses and tunes were still popular with the Molokans in the first decade of the 20th century.[13]

The first reliable researcher on the Doukhobors and Doukhoborism, Orest Novitskii, says that there are no positive proofs indicating Skovoroda's connection with the sect.[14] However, he admits that the above-mentioned "Confession of Faith," compiled in 1791,[15] indicates Skovoroda's authorship: his profound knowledge of the Bible, his acquaintance with foreign languages, an elaborate, polished style and, finally, the Ukrainian words and expressions which occasionally appeared in it.[16]

It was Novitskii's critic, G. Varadinov, who, while reviewing the former's book in an article entitled, "O dukhobortsakh" (About the Doukhobors), published in *Istoria ministerstva vnutrennikh del* (History of the Ministry of the Interior), 1863, advanced the theory that Skovoroda had a pronounced influence on the Doukhobors and the Molokans. He criticized Novitskii for not mentioning it in his book on the Doukhobors.[17] Varadinov was convinced that Skovoroda contributed greatly to the dissemination of the Doukhobor beliefs in the Province of Kharkov, and that the Molokans copied his works, used his verses, and sang the psalms adapted by him.[18]

Later students of Skovoroda's philosophy and biography, in addition to sharing or refuting the points of view of Novitskii or Varadinov pertaining to this subject, advanced some new hypotheses. For example, V. Ern, a Skovoroda biographer, believed that in the person of the philosopher there was the make-up of a potential sectarian, and, moreover, that Skovoroda was the initiator of the Russian Slavophile movement.[19] Another prominent Skovoroda scholar, D. Bahalii, admits, like Ern, that the philosopher stood in some form of silent opposition to the official Orthodox Church, without, however, being its enemy in principle.[20] But he was as much against the dogmatism and intolerance of any established Church as he was against the superstitions and the fanatical beliefs of the sectarians.[21] Skovoroda was opposed in general to all sets of philosophical rules which compelled a man to follow a rigid interpretation of faith.[22]

Similarly, nineteenth-century students of Russia sectarianism speculated on the possibilities of Skovoroda's influence on the spiritual beliefs of the Doukhobors and the Molokans. Thus, F. V. Livanov, in his works, "Molokane i dukhobortsi v Ukraine i Novorossii 18-go veka" (Molokans and Doukhobors in the Ukraine and New Russia in the 18th Century), in *Vestnik Evropy*, October, 1868; "Ukrainskii filosof G. S. Skovoroda sredi molokan i doukhobortsev" (G. S. Skovoroda, the Ukrainian Philosopher, among Molokans and the Doukhobors), in *Novoe Vremya*, 1869, No. 168; and in *Raskol'niki i ostrozhniki* (Dissenters and Convicts), St. Petersburg, 1870, v. II, pp. 288-99, came to the conclusion that in all the archival material which he had used in his research he could not find corroboration that Skovoroda might be, on some basis, considered as the philosopher of one of these sects. Livanov concluded that some attitudes of the sectarians appealed to Skovoroda, as, for example, the Molokans contempt for objects made of gold or silver, but there was no general convergence of his views and theirs.[23] What the researcher found was a document listed as No. 32, Case of 1802, Archives of the Ministry of the Internal Affairs, which mentioned that the Molokans, especially those residing in the South, had been using some of Skovoroda's adaptations of psalms and melodies, in particular his "Vsiakomu horodu," (To Every City) on certain festive occasions.[24] Another researcher, A. S. Lebedev, in his work, "Dukhobortsy v slobodskoi Ukraine" (The Doukhobors in Eastern Ukraine), *Istorichesko-*

Filologicheskoe Obshchestvo (The Historico-Philological Society), 1803, mentions an 1801 criminal case against the Doukhobors, where the name of a witness was Skovoroda. Obviously, this must have been another person with the same name, since Hryhory Skovoroda had died in 1794.[25]

Paul M. Miliukov, a historian of Russian culture, says the following on the subject:

> It is significant that the ardent and popular preaching of the famous Ukrainian mystic and philosopher, Gregory Skovoroda, dates from that period (between the sixties and nineties of the eighteenth century) in which the sect of the Doukhobors was founded. Gregory Skovoroda, while not a member of any sect, was a Sectarian in spirit, except for the doctrine on reincarnation, his views were identical with those of the Dukhobors, and he frankly called himself an 'Abrahamite' /a Bohemian sect similar to the Dukhobors/ in his letters to friends. 'Let everyone else do as he pleases,' he wrote, 'I have devoted myself wholly to seeking the divine wisdom. We were born to that end, and I live by it, think of it day and night, and by it I shall die.' In all Skovoroda's works, so highly praised by Russian Sectarians, Spiritual Christianity is ardently propagated.[26]

And, certainly, such axioms as "compared to faith the ceremonies are as husk to the grain or compliments to true kindness,"[27] could only endear Skovoroda to people like the Doukhobors who rejected the external rituals of religion.

The official confession of faith written by the Ekaterinoslav Doukhobors and presented to Governor Kakhovsky during their imprisonment in 1791, bears close similarity to the ideas of Skovoroda, although a direct influence is impossible to prove. The most probable inference is that when the confession was prepared the same ideas had been more or less adopted by all Spiritual Christians. From this confession, however, it is evident that the writers were possessed of natural eloquence and skilful literary expression. In spite of defects in the exposition, the ideas presented make up a complete and harmonious system, possessing a philosophical basis similar to that of ancient Gnosticism.[28]

From the above exposition it becomes evident that the speculations or suppositions of various Skovoroda biographers, students of Russian philosophy or of Russian sectarianism may have persuaded later scholars that Skovoroda really was a founder or philosopher of this or that religious movement. These scholars included Vladimir Dmitrievich Bonch-Bruevich (1873-1955), the well-known Marxist, a former co-worker of Lenin on *Iskra*, writer, historian, ethnographer, and student of Russian sectarianism. Because of his political and scholarly prestige, his theories concerning the role of Skovoroda in the formation of various Russian sects (including that of Doukhoborism) were widespread.

In searching for a prototype of communal living among the Russian peasant class, Bonch-Bruevich became interested in various sects, among them, the Doukhobors. His belief was that the Doukhobors lived on the basis of a communal system and as such were the closest, among the Russian peasants, to the tenets of Communism. He came with the Doukhobors to Canada in May 1899, and lived with them in this country until the end of January 1900.[29] He also visited those who remained in the Caucasus, together with members of the New-Israel sect, in the spring of 1910.[30] His interest, and that of other researchers in the life and the beliefs of the Russian sectarians culminated in a project to publish a number of works dealing with this subject, entitled, *Materiaux pour servir à l'histoire des sectes russes*. The editor of this series, Bonch-Bruevich, appealed to those interested to send material about the sects either to himself or to Vladimir Chertkov's Publishing House in England. Unfortunately, owing to adverse circumstances at the time, Bonch-Bruevich was able to publish only a small number of the projected volumes, among them, *The Doukhobor Living Book* and one volume of Skovoroda's *Collected Works*.

It was in this latter book that he expressed the idea that the philosophical views and opinions of Skovoroda resembled those of the sect known as New Israel. He wrote:

> Already in 1900, when I began to study systematically the *Weltanschauung* of the Russian Spiritual Christians — the Israelitans, I also became acquainted with the works of Skovoroda. His ideas were similar to the socio-religious views widespread at that time in Russia, which were contemptuously called 'khlystovstvo' by the clergy. We are firmly convinced that Skovoroda was one of the main theoreticians of the Russian 'Spiritual Christians.' His works represent a revealing exposé of all that was discussed around him clandestinely by the peasant masses. We are convinced that he added to these views and further developed them, thus exerting an enormous influence on the formation of thought which kept circulating among the members of these socio-religious groups, ever growing in strength in spite of all the preventive measures /by the authorities/. If anyone wishes to learn and to understand the ancient teachings of the 'Spiritual Christians' which have reached our times he should study thoroughly the works of Skovoroda.[31]

Bonch-Bruevich planned to give detailed proofs of Skovoroda's spiritual relationship with the Russian sectarians in the second volume of his publication which was to be dedicated to an exposition of the thinker's philosophy. Again, unfortunately, this sequel never appeared in print.[32] A number of later Skovoroda scholars criticized Bonch-Bruevich's edition of Skovoroda's works with regard to his subjective attempt to connect him with the world of the Russian sectarians.[33]

M. Red'ko, who seems to reflect in his work the present Soviet point of view in the evaluation of Skovoroda's philosophy, denies any possibility of the philosopher's having been a founder or spiritual mentor of any Russian or Ukrainian religious sect. He considers as groundless the attempts by Miliukov and Bonch-Bruevich to mould Skovoroda into a latent sectarian.[34] He rejects Bonch-Bruevich's endeavours to equate the philosopher with the Russian Spiritual Christians — especially in considering him one of the chief theoreticians of the New-Israel sect.[35] According to Red'ko's interpretation, Bonch-Bruevich exaggerated the importance of sectarians in peasant movements before the Revolution of 1905. Bonch-Bruevich considered them mistakenly as the most progressive, best educated rural element. However, Red'ko assures the reader that toward the end of his life Bonch-Bruevich had already changed his previous opinions and did not insist on Skovoroda being the theoretician of the Doukhobor sect.[36]

Red'ko discounts also as inconclusive the fact that some of Skovoroda's verses, psalms and works were current among the Doukhobors and the Molokans during the 19th century, as attested by G. Varadinov and F. V. Livanov. This did not prove in itself that their author belonged to these sects or was consciously involved in shaping their philosophical tenets.[37] Similarly, Red'ko denies the credibility of the data contained in M. Arendarenko's book, *Zapiski o Poltavskoi gubernii* (Notes on the Province of Poltava), 1852, where the latter indicates the connection between the formation of the Doukhobor sect and the philosopher's role in it.[38] On the other hand, the Soviet researcher lists the testimony of E. Shmurlo, a student of the life and works of the Metropolitan Evgenii, in his book, *Mitropolit Evgenii kak uchonyi* (The Metropolitan Evgenii As Scholar), St. Petersburg, 1888. This Metropolitan, who was considered by official clerical circles to be an authority on the history of Doukhoborism, did not link Skovoroda with this sect in any way.[39]

Thus, the extant written evidence does not provide positive proof of Skovoroda's involvement with the sectarians. In his own opinion, he viewed sectarianism as still another spiritual vehicle for the development of superstition and for the limitation of religious freedom.[40] He always objected strongly when anyone tried to accuse him of belonging to any sectarian or heretic movement. He would say: "The love of one's neighbour is non-denominational and non-sectarian."[41] The philosopher, in his long and fruitful life, did show at times some unorthodox tendencies and beliefs with regard to the official Church of the day. Nevertheless, he never severed relations with this Church. Any influence that his works or teachings might have exerted on the religious philosophy of the Doukhobors or other similar sects were coincidental and, apparently, non-intentional. Nowhere in the documents can one find any direct indications of his being consciously involved in establishing or actively supporting such sects. Nor is there any sound indication of his being indebted in the formation of his own *Weltanschauung* to any ideas or beliefs of the Doukhobors or other Spiritual Christians of the time.

FOOTNOTES

[1]See, e.g., Orest Novitskii, *Dukhobortsy* (The Doukhobors) (Kiev, 1832), 4; Orest Novitskii, *Dukhobortsy, ikh istoriia i verouchenie* (The Doukhobors, Their History and Their Doctrine) (Kiev, 1883), 1-5; Frederick C. Conybeare, *Russian Dissenters* (New York, 1962), 264.

[2]P. N. Malov, *Dukhobortsy, ikh istoriia, zhizn' i bor'ba* (The Doukhobors, Their History, Life and Struggle) (Winnipeg, 1948), 14.

[3]George Woodcock and Ivan Avakumovic, *The Doukhobors* (Toronto, 1968), 30.

[4]See: Vladimir Bonch-Bruevich (ed.), *Zhivotnaia kniga dukhobortsev* (Winnipeg, 1954); *The Book of Life of Doukhobors*, transl. by V. O. Buyniak (Saskatoon, 1978).

[5]Hryhory Savych Skovoroda was born on December 3, 1722, into a Ukrainian Cossack family of the Poltava region. He studied at the Kiev Academy and later abroad, in Vienna, Munich and Breslau. He is generally known as the "Ukrainian Socrates," who composed his works in the form of dialogues, and who made a profound anthropologism the source of his philosophical contemplation. The philosopher died on November 9, 1794, in the village of Ivanivtsi, not far from Kharkov.

[6]The universe had two aspects for him, one visible and material, which was worthless, and the other invisible and spiritual, which was of inestimable value and to which alone man's life should be dedicated. However, the search for truth is not an end in itself, but only a means which prompts man to exercise his will and to use his heart. The significance of Skovoroda's philosophy lies not in theoretical speculations, but in a practical quest for happiness. The aim of human life is happiness — however, only the kind of happiness which comes to man when he fulfills his inner quest and, through it, God's will, and not the happiness which results from material satisfaction. Thus the major premises of Skovoroda's philosophy are self-knowledge, and living one's life according to the natural order and, therefore, in accord with God.

[7]Dmytro Ivanovych Bahalii, *Ukrains'kyi mandrovanyi filosof, Hryhorii Savych Skovoroda* (The Ukrainian Travelling Philosopher) (Kharkov, 1926), 188-89.

[8]V. V. Zenkovskii, *Istoriia Russkoi Filosofii* (Paris, 1948), v. I, 65.

[9]See: H. S. Skovoroda, *Katekhyzys*, Detroit, Ukr. Yevanh, Obyedn., 1963; Hryhorii Skovoroda, *Tvory v dvokh tomakh* (His Works in Two Volumes) (Kyiv, 1961), v. I, 14-26; Hryhorii Skovoroda, *Povne zibrannia tvoriv u dvokh tomakh* (Complete Collection of His Works in Two Volumes) (Kyiv, 1973), *passim.*

Information on the early religious philosophy of the Molokans and the Doukhobors can be obtained from a variety of sources, among them: Orest Novitskii, *Dukhobortsy* (The Doukhobors) (Kiev, 1832), *passim*; T. I. Butkevich, *Molokansto* (Molokanism) (Kharkov, 1909); F. V. Livanov, "Molokane i dukhobortsy v Ukraine i Novorossii (Molokans and Doukhobors in the Ukraine and New Russia) (XVIII vek)", *Vestnik Evropy*, (St. Petersburg, 1862), v. 5, 673-701, v. 6, 809-36; John D. Buhr, *The Origin of the Doukhobor Faith* (Vancouver, n.d.).

[10]This was precisely Skovoroda's attitude. One could quote the well-known incident when Skovoroda refused to recognize the Governor Shcherbinin so long as the latter insisted on being addressed by his official title, but accepted him as his equal on the basis of his first name and patronymic. Similarly, Peter Verigin, the Doukhobor leader, while dispatching to

the Empress his letter-petition, addressed her simply as — 'Sister.' There are many other similar points of convergence in philosophies and beliefs of the Doukhobors and of Skovoroda.

[11]Simma Holt, *Terror in the Name of God* (Toronto, 1964), 11.

[12]Aylmer Maude, *A Peculiar People. The Dukhobors* (London, 1905), 115.

[13]Ibid., 116 and 117.

[14]Novitskii, 179.

[15]Published in *Chteniia v Imperatorskom obshchestve istorii i drevnostei rossiiskikh pri Moskovskom Universitete* (Readings in the Imperial Society of Russian History and Antiquities at Moscow University) in 1871.

[16]Ibid., 211.

[17]Ibid., 178.

[18]Ibid.

[19]V. Ern, *G. S. Skovoroda. Ego zhizn' i uchenie* (His Life and Teaching) (Moskva, 1912), 325.

[20]Ern, 325; Bahalii, 147.

[21]Bahalii, 148.

[22]Ibid., 148.

[23]See: M. Red'ko, *Svitohliad H. S. Skovorody* (The World View of H. S. Skovoroda) (Lvov, 1967), 236-37, cf. Georges Roussov, "G. S. Skovoroda et sa lutte contre le materialisme," in *Etudes Slaves et Est-Européennes*, v. II, Part I, 1957, 15-30.

[24]Bahalii, 338.

[25]See: Malov, 51; Red'ko, 236.

[26]Paul Miliukov, *Outlines of Russian Culture* (Philadelphia, 1942), Part I, 94.

[27]Miliukov, Part I, 98.

[28]See: Novitskii, 211.

[29]See: Bonch-Bruevich, *Zhivotnaia kniga dukhobortsev*, 6.

[30]See: Vladimir Bonch-Bruevich, *Iz mira sektantov* (The World of Sectarians) (Moskva, 1922), 41-77.

[31]*Matériaux pour servir à l'histoire des sectes russes*. Livraison 5, rédigé par V. Bontch-Bruievitch, St. Petersburg, 1912. *Sobranie sochinenii G. S. Skovorody*, v. I, VII-VIII.

[32]Bahalii, 337.

[33]See: Bahalii, 225; Red'ko, 237-38.

[34]Red'ko, 238.

[35]Ibid.

[36]Ibid., 239.

[37]Ibid., 240.

[38]Ibid., 237.

[39]Ibid.

[40]Bahalii, 148.

[41]Ibid., 339.

24

POLICY OR PRACTICE: CANADA AND AUSTRIA 1938-1948*

Robert H. Keyserlingk
University of Ottawa

Just as we know a tree by its fruit, so must a policy be judged by the practice which grows from it. Canada's policy on the 1938 Anschluss of Austria with Germany (and the consequences of that act) was a good deal more enlightened than that of the other major members of the Commonwealth. The United Kingdom collapsed almost immediately in the face of Hitler's forcible take-over of Austria in 1938. By requesting German permission to exchange a consul general for its minister in Vienna, Britain extended *de jure* recognition to the annexation. It later deemed its 1939 declaration of war against Nazi Germany to have included Austria as well.[1] After the war Britain, together with the other major members of the Commonwealth, decided that a state of war had existed with Austria. As a result, these countries formally ended their state of war by declaration or proclamation during 1947 and 1948.[2]

Canada, on the other hand, preferred to assume a much more principled stand, one closer to that of the United States.[3] The official Canadian position on Austria was made public in 1948. It spoke of steady Canadian opposition to the Anschluss over the past decade and of Austria as a friendly state never at war with Canada.

> Canada never recognized, *de jure*, German sovereignty over Austria, although *de facto* recognition of German sovereignty was accorded. Austria is now recognized as an autonomous State, liberated from German occupation. Canada was never at war with the political entity of Austria, nor with any Austrian predecessor to the present government.[4]

Certainly this statement was unique within the Commonwealth. It clearly stated the history of the case and the obligations of practice which should flow from it. Austria had not ceased to exist in Canadian eyes, but had continued to exist as a nation friendly to Canada.

Did not Canada and Austria also share many of the same major interests in the postwar world? A good deal of the east-west struggle in which Canada

* Sources are mainly from the archives of the Canadian Department of External Affairs, Ottawa (DEA), and the Public Archives of Canada, Ottawa (PAC). Prime Minister W. L. Mackenzie King was his own Secretary of State for External Affairs. O. D. Skelton was his Under-Secretary until 1941, when Skelton died and N. A. Robertson took his place.

was implicated took place over the Austrian body politic. Increasing Russian pressure on Czechoslovakia, which led to its take-over, was almost as direct a threat to Canada as it was to Austria. Certainly most Canadian statesmen seemed to understand that the emerging Cold War involved both Canada and Austria in its quickening progression. As Lester Pearson wrote at the time, "it is advisable for us to do what we can to help Austria strengthen the ties with the West."[5] Austria too, reported a Canadian diplomat at the time following an official visit to Austria, "desires by all possible means to strengthen its position vis-a-vis the West."[6] One would then have expected that Canadian policy and practice towards Austria would have reflected a serious intent to demonstrate support for Austria, and that the Austrians would be grateful for this.

It would therefore appear to be inappropriate to label the bold 1948 Canadian statement mere rhetoric. Yet it is usually wise to look behind principles. Great efforts are made to write the history of events from the principles enunciated, when in fact practice often staggers down more crooked paths. Historical development is rarely static, and practice does not always unerringly move in step with principles. The high-principled is occasionally found not to be practicable.

Certainly, official Austrian reaction to the 1948 Canadian statement on Austria lacked the enthusiasm and graciousness one might have expected. The Austrian ministers in Washington and London were informed of the Canadian position, as there was at that time no Austrian diplomatic representative in Canada. Both treated the news somewhat laconically. The Washington representative of Austria dryly acknowledged "the statement that it had been decided that Canada has never been at war with the political entity of Austria," adding maliciously, "which ceased to exist after the annexation by Germany."[7] His London colleague took two weeks to generate an answer for his Canadian counterpart in the same city. He was clearly not moved by the information concerning "the general legal position in which your country considers itself towards Austria."[8]

In order to understand the restrained Austrian reaction to the Canadian position enunciated in 1948, it is necessary to review Canada's Austrian policy and practice over the previous decade. Austria had not loomed large in Canadian concerns after the First World War. Trade between the two countries was minimal.[9] Although far more Austrians than Germans became naturalized in Canada between the wars, Austria never assumed the importance of Germany in Canadian eyes.[10] Diplomatic relations between the two countries were non-existent. Although an Austrian consul general was stationed in Ottawa in 1930, he was recalled again the following year for financial reasons.[11] Thereafter an honorary Austrian consul general of Irish nationality functioned in Montreal until the Anschluss.[12]

Thus at the time of the Anschluss, Canada's financial or legal interests in Austria were almost non-existent. This permitted Canada to adopt a passive stance on the Anschluss, although Canadian officials were shocked by the manner of small Austria's demise.[13] Canada's delegate to the League of Nations wrote of a "flagrant violation of German and Austrian international engagements," from which it was not clear whether the two countries had colluded or not in the act.[14] The Canadian government decided that, although the act was clearly illegal, because the Germans had not officially notified them of it, they were not bound to make an official reply or public protest. It was decided quietly to deplore the Anschluss and make the necessary "administrative adjustments" in Canada so that the corresponding German treaties would be applied in place of the Austrian treaties.[15] No problem was thought liable to arise from this. If the Germans did make problems in matters of extradition, for instance, and "if the German authorities insisted upon keeping the Canadian criminal in Vienna, the loss to this country would not be great."[16]

Principle and practice began almost immediately to diverge. When asked by a firm of Montreal lawyers whether "the German-Austrian Anschluss had been recognized by Canada" and consequently whether Nazi decrees were enforcible here, the government clearly stated that it had "recognized *de facto*, but not *de jure*, the union of Germany and Austria."[17] Yet, when domestic interests were at stake, practice changed. The chief of Canada's naturalization branch enquired how to classify Austrians resident in Canada before the Anschluss, who applied for naturalization. The answer back was that "in so far as the former Austrians are concerned, it seems to me that the only possible course is to treat them as being German nationals."[18]

When war broke out in September 1939, it therefore appeared probable that Austrians in Canada would be treated as Germans. About 12,000 Austrians, including many refugees from Hitler's Europe, were resident in Canada at the time.[19] When the Defence of Canada Regulations were proclaimed in September 1939, which described the government's programme for control of enemy aliens and disloyal elements within Canada, Austrians appeared to fall under the definition of enemy aliens. Under the regulations, an enemy alien was "not a British subject, possessing the nationality of a state at war with His Majesty."[20] Did this include Austrians? Registration was proclaimed shortly afterwards for everyone over sixteen "of German nationality or born in territories under the control or sovereignty of the German Reich on 3rd September 1939, who are not naturalized British subjects."[21] This clearly included Austrians. In December 1939 an Order-in-Council was made public prohibiting entry to Canada of "enemy aliens and nationals of any country now occupied by an enemy country." The Defence of Canada Regulations also spoke of "persons of German (and later Italian) national origin," which could have included even Mennonites in Canada and personnel of the Swiss consulate.[22] In 1940, registration was made obligatory for British subjects since 1939 (later extended backwards to 1922) who had been German or Italian nationals at the time of naturalization. This latter category was unique, for it lifted Canadian citizenship (strictly, British subjects still) from persons possessing it. The confusion was compounded because persons compelled to register had to do so with the registrars of enemy aliens and would be issued Enemy Alien Documents. This elicited passionate protests from refugees and governments-in-exile, especially from the Czechs, with the result that the document issued was renamed a Certificate of Exemption.[23]

The public could therefore be excused for blurring the distinction between registrants and enemy aliens, and putting them all in the same basket. Even the Commissioner of the RCMP, who was chief Registrar of Enemy Aliens, and high officials of other government departments were guilty of this.[24] Norman Robertson, Under-Secretary for External Affairs, attempted to keep the distinction alive, but even he admitted the resulting muddle might have been avoided.

> As should have been made clear when the (Registration) Order was issued, its scope embraces numerous persons who are not in any sense of the word enemy aliens, as well as many persons of German nationality who can only be regarded as enemy aliens in the technical sense of the term.[25]

Speaking specifically of Austrians, Poles and Czechs, he admitted the numerous territorial transfers, both legal and illegal, in Central Europe before the war "had complicated and confused the legal position of persons who have emigrated to Canada in recent years," and that loyal registrants should not be considered or treated as enemy aliens.[26] Throughout the press and public, however, these distinctions remained obscure.[27]

Although Austrians in Canada appear to have fallen "technically" within the enemy alien category during the war, there certainly existed some recognition that Austrians were different from Germans. Austrians were permitted to register as Austrians, and most did. By mid-1941 about 780 Germans were interned in Canada, but the statistics do not differentiate between German nationals and those of German territorial or "racial" origin.[28] Ten Austrians were interned by the Canadians during the war, although it appears not for nationality but security reasons. Three were interned as leaders in the *Deutsche Arbeitsfront*, a branch of the NSDAP. All but two were released before 1945, and only one, a leader in the *Kraft durch Freude* movement before the war, was termed an "obnoxious Nazi."[29] Many more Austrians were interned in Canada after transportation from Britain, but these remained the responsibility of the British government. The British had interned all male, adult Germans and Austrians in Britain during the Fifth Column scare of 1940, and about three thousand of these were sent to Canada in 1940.[30] About a thousand were sent back to Britain by late 1940. The rest were kept in refugee camps in Canada for varying lengths of time until 1943, while about nine hundred were released in Canada and granted immigrant status at the end of the war.[31] In the United States, Austrians were classed as enemy aliens, but were exempted from registration and were not interned because of their Austrian background.[32]

But the exact status of Austrians in Canada was not clear. In early 1942 this matter was referred to the Prime Minister, and External Affairs and the RCMP agreed to begin a study of the problem.[33] At the same time, Austrian exiles in Canada put pressure on the government to make a distinction between Austrians and Germans.[34] Officials seemed to be impressed by the British and American treatment of Austrians, for in both countries the Austrians technically remained enemy aliens, but were granted administrative privileges and exemptions not available to Germans. Canadian practice up to this time had also been somewhat discriminating, for the RCMP had been more ready to hand Certificates of Exemption to Austrians rather than to Germans. As an official of External Affairs wrote to his Under-Secretary: "It is clear that Austria was one of the earliest victims of German aggression, and that our failure to distinguish between Austrians and Germans so far as enemy alien status is concerned, is difficult to justify."[35] In none of these discussions did Canada's non-recognition of the 1938 Anschluss emerge as either a point in favour of more lenient treatment for Austrians or a legal justification of it. Norman Robertson felt it might be going too far to exempt Austrians "as a class (of enemy aliens) from the Defence of Canada Regulations," but perhaps some administrative measures could be found to differentiate their situation from that of the Germans.[36] It would probably not be possible to drop them from the enemy alien category like the Czechs, as there existed no Austrian government-in-exile, nor were the British or Americans interested in the formation of one, largely because of the deep political rifts evident among Austrian exiles.[37]

As the war entered its third year, Canadians became convinced that most "enemy aliens" were essentially loyal to Canada and deserved some relief from the original restrictions placed upon them in 1939-40. In October 1942 all enemy aliens except for the Japanese were permitted to volunteer for Canadian military service if they had taken out 'first papers' for Canadian naturalization.[38] In November, the Cabinet War Committee specifically mentioned Austrians as a group to be studied with a view to improving their treatment.[39] By the end of December a new policy could be announced loosening the restrictions on several classes of people coming under the Defence of Canada Regulations. British subjects of ex-enemy nationality, except for the Japanese, were removed from "the restrictions imposed upon enemy aliens." Italians and Austrians were specifically exempted from the registration regulations. Italians were termed not allies, but unwilling vassals of Germany, while Austrians were described as solid anti-Nazis. "Consideration has also been given to the case of Austrians," the press release read, "most of whom have shown their hostility to the Nazi regime and loyalty to Canada."[40] But Italians and Austrians were not removed from the category of enemy aliens.

While this more lenient treatment was in part a recognition of Italian and Austrian anti-Hitlerism, a good deal of it had to do with psychological warfare against Germany as well.[41] The United States Office of War Information agreed that this new policy "would be of much value to us in our propaganda to enemy countries."[42] Austrian exiles in Canada were encouraged to organize anti-Nazi activities to boost the Canadian public's morale by fostering the belief that large pockets of anti-Nazi sentiment existed in Europe. A Dr. Klein, who supported the Austrian monarchist cause, was permitted to put out an English-language magazine in Ottawa called *The Voice of Austria*, while other Austrians were free to give public talks and organize anti-Nazi groups. Ex-Empress Zita of Austria lived in Quebec City as a political refugee, while the widow of Austrian chancellor Dolfuss spent the war in Montreal with her two children. Archduke Otto, as he was always referred to in official Canadian correspondence, and his brothers entered Canada easily on their Belgian passport from the United States to visit their mother or to have interviews with the Prime Minister.[43] There is no evidence that their counsel carried any weight with Canadian officials; certainly less so than in the United States.[44]

At the same time, the squabbles between the Austrian exile groups diminished their value as both pressure groups on the government and as propaganda instruments. Both the British and the Americans refused officially to support any one Austrian group, as the Austrians could not transcend the deep political differences which had split them before the Anschluss.[45] Canadians were again informed by the British in 1943 of their negative view of Austrian exiles' bickering, and were asked their opinion. Canadian officials were quick to concur.[46] A violent altercation between two Austrians of differing views had become so boisterous and public during 1942 that the matter was raised in Parliament. The two were called into External Affairs and chastised.[47] As one External Affairs officer put it, "we have in Canada, Zita and the headquarters of the Austrian monarchist organization, and some experience of the difficulty of getting any two free Austrians to be civil to each other."[48]

During 1943 and after, the Canadian government was more concerned with Austria itself as a target for psychological warfare than with Austrians in Canada. Information received through both British and American sources in 1943 indicated that unrest was growing within Austria itself, and that this might be tapped for propaganda warfare purposes.[49] Canada was rather late entering this whole field, and never developed a very effective or professional approach to it, as the government admitted after the war. The weak interdepartmental committee was riven with problems of jealousy, unclear lines of authority and only received a separate budget in the last year of the war.[50] Two papers were prepared within External Affairs in late 1943 analyzing psychological warfare possibilities in Austria, and concluded that these were at present excellent.[51] When the October 1943 Moscow Declaration on Austria, with its promise to re-establish an independent Austria and its call to Austrians to assist in their own liberation, became known in Canada, it was viewed mainly as an effective propaganda war tool against Germany.[52] Canada's effort in this regard was small. A few radio programmes by Austrians in Canada were put together to be beamed by the British and Americans to the Austrian troops in Norway.[53]

Canada's postwar planning was also commenced late in the war, lagging considerably behind that of the British or Americans. Postwar planning only got underway in 1944, and depended almost exclusively upon British information and views regarding postwar Austrian policy.[54] Inclined mainly to protect Canada's desire not to become implicated in postwar occupation or control of Europe, especially of Central Europe, no purely Canadian policy on Austria was developed.[55]

Thus, as the war neared its end, Canada trailed far behind both the Americans and the British in both propaganda work and planning. When in late 1944 the British suggested that Canada follow their lead in segregating Austrian from German Prisoners of War (POWs), mainly for propaganda reasons, the Canadians studied the idea leisurely and found much to recommend it.[56] But in early 1945, before anything in this line could be implemented, they decided instead to divide all POWs for re-education purposes according to degree of disaffection with Nazism into separate camps rather than by national lines.[57]

When the war ended, there was no change in the Austrians' situation. Austrians continued to be categorized as enemy aliens, despite pressure from Canadians to recognize Austrians as friends. The Canadian Friends of Austria, a Canadian group organized in Toronto and chaired by B. K. Sandwell, editor of the influential national weekly *Saturday Night*, approached the Prime Minister at the end of 1945 to drop the appellation "enemy aliens" for Austrians and to initiate diplomatic relations with the new and struggling republic.[58] The Prime Minister, however, found that "no useful purpose would be served" by this, and turned the suggestion down.[59] Several months later in 1946 the United Church of Canada adopted a resolution calling for the same change of policy towards Austria, but again with no result.[60] The public was unaware that as early as April 1945 the Canadian government had decided to continue to class Austrians as enemy aliens and to pass a special Order-in-

Council if necessary making both Germany and Austria "proscribed territory."[61]

In January 1946 the Big Four extended official recognition to the new Austrian republic, despite past recognition of the Anschluss or technical state of war with Austria. The Prime Minister of Canada refused to follow suit. When several options were suggested to him, he wrote opposite the one suggesting mere "noting" of the re-establishment of an independent Austrian government: "This is, I think, good enough." He also scratched out a paragraph in the draft press release, which recalled Canada's non-recognition of the Anschluss in 1938.[62] In his mysterious manner Mackenzie King gave no reason for this, but he clearly liked the idea of delaying a decision for the time being. For passport purposes, Austrian nationality was again recognised, but all Austrians as enemy aliens were forbidden entry into Canada under several Orders-in-Council.[63]

Canada needed a few more years to formulate another policy towards Austria, and several more before it was willing to establish diplomatic relations with it. Two reasons can be given for the 1948 definition of policy reflected in the statement with which this paper began; the delay and unacceptable procedures in procuring an Austrian peace, and Austrian pressure on Canada to open diplomatic relations.

Canada had no strong feelings against Austrians, considering that eventual signature of an Austrian peace treaty would solve its problem of recognition of and relations with Austria.[64] But this peace treaty appeared impossible to procure due to Russian intransigence, while at the same time the major powers seemed unwilling to allow Canada and the other smaller allies any active role in the German and Austrian peacemaking process. Most of the Canadian thinking on Germany and Austria in this period had to do with the unacceptable procedures employed by the Special Deputies on Austria of the Council of Foreign Ministers rather than with substantive matters. In the meantime, Canada did assist Austria through UNRRA aid for the large population of displaced persons in Austria. When invited to present Canadian views on Austria in 1947, Canada at first refused to do so until it be given an active role in peacemaking.[65] Finally, and begrudgingly, a short memorandum was submitted to the Special Deputies, which outlined in very general terms Canada's concerns that Austria remain free and democratic, and that Nazi influences and Anschluss tendencies be guarded against.[66] When asked in late 1947 by the United Kingdom whether it would end its state of war with Austria, Canada decided, in its disappointment with the peacemaking process, to issue its own policy on Austria.[67]

Another reason why it put out this 1948 statement was that the Canadian government was unable or unwilling, generally for financial reasons, to open diplomatic relations with Austria. It hoped through this statement to deflect from itself some of the Austrian pressure for diplomatic relations. In this, it was not successful. Both the Canadian High Commissioner in London and the Canadian ambassador in Washington, who bore the brunt of repeated Austrian requests for diplomatic relations between the two countries, passed on with mounting embarrassment these pleas to Ottawa, and included their own positive recommendations.[68] Officials in External Affairs agreed with them, and several times from as early as 1946 tried to convince their minister and cabinet that this should indeed be done.[69] However, the minister and cabinet proved intractable. They were more interested in opening diplomatic relations with Italy (1948), Germany (1951) and even Finland than with Austria, extending western defence through NATO, and limiting the External Affairs budget for foreign representation.[70] As a result, it was hoped that a noble statement on Canada's non-recognition of the Anschluss and continued peace between the two countries would act as a sop for wounded Austrian feelings.

Three times during 1948, and after the statement was issued, External officials tried for cabinet agreement to diplomatic relations with Austria, and each time they were turned down. The first answer used lack of finances as the reason. The second hinted at something like NATO, while the third even turned down the notion of a non-reciprocal Austrian consul general in Ottawa.[71] The last refusal was accompanied by an instruction to Canada's diplomats to plead "special circumstances" to their Austrian counterparts, thereby leaving the impression that the decision may have had something to do with the lack of an Austrian peace treaty.[72] Finally, at the end of the year, cabinet relented as little as possible by extending permission to the Austrians to send a tourist representative to Canada.[73]

Is there any wonder that the Austrians received the 1948 policy with some scepticism? Canada continued to drag its feet in the matter of extending Austrians the international recognition and support so dearly desired for their embattled country.[74] In 1949 an Austrian consul general was allowed into Canada, but this did not constitute diplomatic recognition. To the consternation of the Austrians, diplomatic recognition was granted to two ex-enemy states, Italy and Germany, before Austria. A deeply disappointed Austrian consul general in Ottawa wrote the Department of External Affairs that he was "stunned" by the latter news regarding Germany. He felt himself to be in "great distress" at the "grave hurt" done to Austria by Canada's recognition of Germany before Austria. Austria deserved more consideration as "the first victim of German aggression" and as a result of its "bitter fight against communism."[75]

Finally, in 1952, diplomatic relations were established between Austria and Canada, but only on the basis of dual representation from Bern and Washington. In 1955 the Austrian State Treaty was signed, but it took Canada years — until 1959 — to sign it. In 1956 a separate Canadian ambassador presented his credentials in Vienna, while Austria did not raise its Canadian mission to an embassy until 1958.

Looking back over this period, it is possible to conclude that the Austrians were right to be unhappy in 1948 with what appeared on the surface to be a unique and courageous Canadian policy statement on Austria. In the decade before this statement, Canada had remained passive on the Anschluss, while Austrians had been classified as enemy aliens, even though their actual treatment was improved. Until 1948, Austrians continued to be regarded legally by Canadians as enemy aliens. Before and after the 1948 statement, Canada consistently refused repeated Austrian requests to establish diplomatic relations between the two countries, despite similar pressures from members of the Canadian public and officials within External Affairs to do so. For the Austrians, this refusal could understandably be interpreted as a lack of interest in or support for Austria in its struggle against the Russians. Indeed, in this case Canadian principle and practice often moved in different directions.

FOOTNOTES

[1] United Kingdom Secretary of State for Dominion Affairs, London, (hereafter SSDA) to Canadian Secretary of State for External Affairs, Ottawa, (hereafter SSEA), 16.3. and 25.3.1938 : PAC RG 25. G1, v.1781. Also SSDA to SSEA, 9.11.1946 : DEA 7-Ps.

[2] Dates of termination of state of war : United Kingdom – 16.9. 1947 ; South Africa – 18.2.1948 ; Australia – October 1948 ; India – February 1949.

[3] R. W. Flournoy to Green H. Hackworth, Legal Adviser, US Secretary of State, Washington, 17.4.1945 : RG 59 (Secretary of State), National Archives, Washington, DC : 711.63/4-1745. R. Langer, *Seizure of Territory. The Stimson Doctrine and Related Principles in Legal Theory and Practice* (New York, 1947 and 1969), 163 and 285.

[4] SSEA to J. A. Glan, Minister of Mines and Resources, Ottawa, 22.1.1948. DEA 8447-40.

[5] Memorandum from L. B. Pearson to SSEA, 14.5.1948 : PAC RG 25. A12, v. 2094.

[6] Quoted in L. B. Pearson memorandum to the Minister for External Affairs, 17.4.1948 : DEA 8447-40.

[7] H. H. Wrong to Austrian Ambassador Ludwig Kleinwaechter, Washington, 12.4.1948, and reply quoted in part, 13.4.1948 : DEA 8447-40.

[8] Fredrick Hudd to Austrian Minister Heinrich Schmid, London, 27.4.1948, and reply quoted in part, 10.5.1948 : PAC RG 25.A12, v. 2094.

[9] In 1934-1938, Canada exported $254,000 worth of goods to Austria, and imported only $24,000 worth. Memorandum for Under-SSEA, "Austrian Treaty," 14.5.1948 : PAC RG.25.A12, v. 2094.

[10] 22,204 "Austrians" as against 14,507 Germans. Table 12, memorandum to N. A. Robertson from the Dominion Statistician, 13.3.1939 : PAC RG 25.G1, v. 1964.

[11] Austrian Consul General Ludwig Kleinwaechter to O. D. Skelton, Ottawa, 28.4.1930 ; Canadian High Commissioner, London to SSEA, 22.10.1931 ; Austrian Minister, London to Marquess of Reading (Foreign Office), 24.10.1931 : PAC RG 25. G1, v. 1556.

[12] Hon. Austrian Consul General Thomas Guerin to O. D. Skelton, Montreal, 19.3.1938. PAC RG 25.G1, v. 1556.

[13] "Note to His Excellency the Governor General in Council," 8.4.1938 : PAC RG 25.G1, v. 1556 ; SEEA to SSDA, 19.1.1939 : PAC RG 25.G1, v. 1876.

[14] H. H. Wrong, Geneva to SSEA, 28.3.1938 : PAC RG 25.G1, v. 1781.

[15] "Summary of the Note Concerning Position of Austria," 7.4.1938 : PAC RG 25.G1, vol. 1876.

[16] JER memorandum, 6.3.1939, p. 4. : PAC RG 25.G1, v. 1876.

[17] Philip F. Vineburg to O. D. Skelton, 16.8.1939, and reply, 4.9.1939 : PAC RG 25.G1, vol. 1876.

[18]O. Coderre, Department of Secretary of State to SSEA, 12.1.1939, and reply 13.1.1939 : PAC RG 25.G1, v. 1876.

[19]*Hamilton Spectator*, 24.3.1943 "Austrians Wish to Fight at the Side of the Allies," by A. C. Cummings, *Spectator's* London News Bureau. 2,000 Austrians in Britain were in the Pioneer Corps.

[20]*Defence of Canada Regulations* (Ottawa, 1939), p. 13.

[21]N. A. Robertson memorandum, 27.10.1939 : PAC RG 25.G1, v. 1964.

[22]D. Toews to W. A. Tucker, M.P., 16.7.1940 ; N. A. Robertson to W. A. Tucker, 24.7.1940 ; N. A. Robertson to Coleman, Department of Secretary of State, 15.8.1940 ; also PC. 2653 (14.9.1939), quoted in full in O. D. Skelton to F. C. Blair, Director of Immigration : PAC RG 25.G1, v. 1964.

[23]O. D. Skelton to RCMP Commissioner S. T. Wood, 1.11.1939 ; O. D. Skelton to the Czech Consul General, Montreal, 3.11.1939 : PAC RG 25.G1, v. 1964.

[24]RCMP Commissioner S. T. Wood, in N. A. Robertson to D. C. Saul, RCMP, 14.9.1939 : PAC RG 25.G1, v. 1964.

[25]N. A. Robertson memorandum, 27.10.1939 : PAC RG 25.G1, v. 1964.

[26]Ibid.

[27]*Hamilton Spectator*, 15.9.1939, "Appeal Court." Also *Toronto Globe and Mail*, 28.10.1939, "Protect Rights of Loyal Aliens."

[28]1940 and 1941 statistics on PAC RG 25G1, v. 1964. For the Canadian internment policy during the war, see John Kelly, "The Prisoner-of-War Camps in Canada 1939-1947," unpublished M.A. Thesis, University of Windsor, 1976, chapters 1-4.

[29]RCMP Commissioner to SSEA, 20.8.1947 : SSEA to British High Commissioner, Ottawa, 24.10.1947 : DEA 8008-A.

[30]N. A. Robertson to the Prime Minister, 6.6.1940. PAC MG 26.J4. v. 324. Paula Draper, "The Accidental Immigrants," two parts, *Canadian Jewish History*, 1978.

[31]Memorandum to cabinet and attached Order-in-Council, October 1945 : DEA 8008-A-40C.

[32]United States Department of Justice Press Release, 23.2.1942 : DEA 2915-40C. See also Franz Goldner, *Die oesterreichische Emigration 1938 bis 1945* (Wien-Muenchen, 1972). For Great Britain, see Helene Maimann, *Politik in Wartesaal. Oesterreichische Exilpolitik in Grossbritanien 1938-40* (Wien-Koeln, 1975).

[33]S. F. Rae (DEA) to D. C. Saul, RCMP, 20.3.1942 : PAC RG.25.G1, v. 1964. Registration figures for 1940-1941 were: 30,000 Germans, 31,000 Italians, 21,500 Czechs and Austrians. Certificates of Exemption for unquestioned loyalty to Canada were granted to 21,175 of these. *Hamilton Spectator*, 14.2.1942, "List of Aliens Reaches 82,500."

[34]SEEA to Canadian High Commissioners, London, 30.3.1942 : DEA 773-F-40.

[35]S. F. Rae memorandum to N. A. Robertson, 15.4.1942 : DEA 773-F-40.

[36]N. A. Robertson to RCMP Commissioner S. T. Wood, 21.4.1942 : DEA 773-F-40.

[37]Ibid. For United Kingdom views on free Austrian movements, see Foreign Office print, 18.6.1941 : PAC MG 26.J4, v. 358. Canada agreed, see S. F. Rae memorandum, 15.1.1942 : DEA 3241-40C.

[38]Conference Bulletin, Department of External Affairs, 17.10.1942 : PAC MG 26.J4, v. 249.

[39]N. A. Robertson to the Prime Minister, W. L. Mackenzie King, 17.11.1942 : PAC MG 26.J4, v. 348.

[40]Department of External Affairs Press Release, 24.12.1942 : DEA 2915-40C.

[41]N. A. Robertson memorandum to Prime Minister W. L. Mackenzie King, 24.12.1942 : PAC MG 26.J4, v. 310.

[42]Elmer Davis, Director, Office of War Information, Washington to L. B. Pearson, 24.12.1942 : PAC RG 25.G1, v. 1965.

[43]For instance, Belgian Ambassador de Silvercruys to A. D. P. Heeney, 28.3.1940 : PAC MG 26.J4, v. 310.

[44]N. A. Robertson to Prime Minister W. L. Mackenzie King, 24.12.1942 : PAC MG 26.J4, v. 235. Otto Hapsburg to Prime Minister (re Quebec conference), 20.8.1943; HW memorandum for Prime Minister, 23.8.1943 : DEA 7-Ps. Otto Habsburg to F. D. Roosevelt, 1.6.1943 : US State Department, 863.01/779.

[45]SRF memorandum, 8.9.1942 : DEA 3421-40C. Office of Strategic Services, "The Austrian Scene," 30.6.1943 : US Secretary of State, RG 59, National Archives, Washington, DC, 863.01/782. Also A. A. Berle memorandum, 19.10.1943, US Secretary of State, 863.01/807.

[46]SEEA to SSDA, 14.12.1943 : DEA 7-Ps.

[47]Dr. Klein, editor of *Voice of Austria* was attacked by Dr. Redlich, a censorship employee. N. A. Robertson to Prime Minister, W. L. Mackenzie King, 11.5.1942 : PAC MG 26.J4, v. 235.

[48]N. A. Robertson to H. H. Wrong, 13.12.1943 : DEA 7-Ps.

[49]For instance, "News from Austria," memorandum, 3.8.1943 : DEA 5353-S-40C.

[50]"Psychological Warfare," 23 pp., 3.7.1946 : DEA 5353-40C (Part 2).

[51]MG memorandum, 25.8.1943 ; T. A. Stone memorandum, 11.9.1943 : DEA 5353-S-40C.

[52]"Psychological Warfare Directed to Austria," 18.12.1943 : DEA 5353-S-40C. Also British print "Germany," 31.12.1943 : DEA 5874-40C.

[53]Scripts on DEA 5353-E-40C ("Canadian Political Intelligence Against Germany").

[54]Memorandum to Cabinet War Committee, 24.11.1943 : PAC RG.25.D1, v. 823 ; HW memorandum 23.2.1944 : PAC MG 26.J4, v. 370. For British articles, see DEA 7-CAS, 5404-40C.

[55]HW memorandum to Under-SSEA, 7.11.1944 : DEA 22-Ss.

[56]Psychological Warfare Committee Minutes, 14.4.1944 and 16.3.1945 : DEA 5353-A-40C. The pressure also came from several exile Austrian organizations.

[57]Psychological Warfare Committee Minutes, 29.11.1945 : DEA 5353-A-40C.

[58]B. K. Sandwell to Prime Minister W. L. Mackenzie King, 4.12.1945 : DEA 8447-40.

[59]Prime Minister W. L. Mackenzie King to B. K. Sandwell, 12.12.1945 : DEA 8447-40.

[60]*Toronto Globe and Mail*, 1.4.1946, "Ottawa Asked to Re-classify Enemy Aliens."

[61]Memorandum to Ignatieff, 26.4.1945 : DEA 855-E-39.

[62]N. A. Robertson memorandum to Prime Minister W. L. Mackenzie King, 18.1.1946 : PAC MG 26.J4, v. 235.

[63]H. H. Wrong to the Director of Immigration, 13.3.1946 ; the last Order-in-Council applying to Austrians as enemy aliens was PC 2908 (31.7.1947), DEA 8447-40.

[64]New Zealand, for instance, expressed very strong negative opinions about Austria. "Austria has not deserved, nor can she legally claim, a treaty more favorable that that applied to other active supporters of Germany." Ministry of External Affairs, New Zealand to SSEA, 12.6.1946 : DEA 7-DGs.

[65]SSEA to Canadian High Commissioner, London, 10.1.1947 : PAC RG 25.A12, v. 2087. Department of External Affairs Press Release, 16.1.1947 : St. Laurent draft statement, 6.2.1942 ; text of cabinet recommendation, SSEA to Canadian Ambassador, Washington, 10.3.1947 : DEA 7-DGs.

[66]SSEA to Canadian High Commissioner, London, 25.2.1947 : PAC RG 25.A12, v. 2087.

[67]SS Commonwealth Relations (ex-SSDA) to SSEA, 26.8.1947 : DEA 7-DGs.

[68]H. H. Wrong to SSEA, 5.3.1948 : E. Reid to SSEA, 19.4.1948 : PAC RG 25.A12, v. 2094.

[69]The first Austrian letter in a long series on file is from Ludwig Kleinwaechter (once Consul General in Canada, 1930-31) to the Canadian Ambassador, Washington, 21.6.1946 : PAC MG 26.J4, v. 235.

[70]L. St. Laurent remarks, 14.2.1942 ; memo for SSEA, 17.4.1948 ; memorandum for SSEA and handwritten remarks, 14.5.1948; H. H. Wrong to E. Reid, 28.5.1948 : DEA 8447-40.

[71]Ibid.

[72]L. B. Pearson to N. A. Robertson, Ottawa, 29.7.1948 : DEA 8447-40.

[73]European division to Mr. Maynard, 23.8.1948; memorandum for SSEA, 25.8.1948 : DEA 8447-40.

[74]A memorandum to SSEA stated that "it would appear to be in the interests of western solidarity to make any gesture of sympathy to Austria which lay in our power." 20.12/1949 : DEA 8447-40.

[75]F. O. Ried, Austrian Consul General to A. D. H. Heeney, DEA 8447-40. The state of war between Germany and Canada ended on 10.7.1951, and a Canadian ambassador presented his credentials in Germany on 16.8.1951. Department of External Affairs Press Release No. 34, 10.7.1951 : DEA 10194-L–40.

STRUCTURAL CHANGES IN EAST CENTRAL EUROPEAN SOCIETIES AND THEIR CONSEQUENCES: POLAND AND HER NEIGHBOURS[1]

Alexander J. Matejko,
University of Alberta

The Polish Scene

The events in Poland during 1980-81 almost certainly will have some meaningful consequences for Comecon* as a whole, and especially for Poland's immediate neighbours. There has for years been considerable traffic between Poland, East Germany and Czechoslovakia; in the second half of the 1970s around 10 million people per year visited Poland — 60 per cent from East Germany and about 15 per cent from Czechoslovakia.** Also, around 10 million Poles a year visited other Comecon countries, mainly East Germany and Czechoslovakia.[2] Even a complete closure of the state boundaries will not prevent the spread of the "Polish trade-union disease" when taking into consideration the availability of mass media. Radios are common and the Polish TV programs are widely watched across the borders in the densely populated frontier areas. The one-sided emphasis in the whole Soviet Bloc on industrial expansion has had evident negative effects in Poland by leading to mass dissatisfaction, food shortages, and inflation. In this respect, Poland shares her fate with all her neighbours, but thanks to local circumstances (tradition of resistance to partitions, independence of the Church, liberalism of the intelligentsia), the economic and structural difficulties of Soviet state socialism have become social and political to a greater extent in Poland than in other Comecon countries.

Family life there has a long tradition of being intensive and emotionally satisfying and goes together with religiosity. Under state socialist modernization there have been great changes also in this respect. First of all, the high level of female employment, including mothers of small children, has caused severe

---

* Council for Mutual Economic Assistance. For a brief summary, see *The Europe Year Book: A World Survey* (London, 1981), vol. 1, 165-168.

** All statistical data utilized in this study (also for drawing inferences) — unless otherwise indicated — derive from *Rocznik Statystyczny 1980* (Warsaw, 1980) and *Kraje RWPG 1980* (Warsaw, 1980). The publication in the present context of an "Appendix" comprising 28 Tables connected with this study had to be omitted owing to lack of space.

strains within the family. These have been compounded by the inadequate supply of consumer goods, poor housing conditions,[3] great congestion in public transportation, very limited opportunities for part-time employment[4] and an inadequate contribution by various family members to the household chores. Besides, among the newly-married, 90 per cent of the men and 50 per cent of the women have jobs. The concept of housewives outside the labour force has become nearly obsolete, especially in the white-collar segment of society.

Divorces doubled in Poland during the 1960s and 1970s, achieving the equivalent of more than one-tenth of the marriage rate (though the figure is a third of the Swedish and Soviet rates), and it is four times more frequent in urban than in rural areas. While in the non-socialist countries the increase in divorce is mainly related to consumerism and a good-time orientation in hedonistic societies, under Soviet state socialism it has roots in the discordant nature of everyday life — as, for instance, difficulties in household maintenance.

As to the phenomenon of Polish mass opposition to the political status quo, it is necessary to refer not only to the unique Polish national heritage (well-rooted Catholicism, the gentry tradition, nationalism and struggle for independence), but also to the perspective of structural transformations happening in East-Central Europe.[5] Substantial economic and social changes have been prompted there by Soviet-style state socialist industrialization. However, the changes did not necessarily follow the direction expected and accepted by their sponsors.

The Marxist model of socioeconomic transformation, as understood by the ruling local élite and by the Soviet power centre in Moscow, had reached its limits. It had proven unable to handle adequately the latent contradictions within the system. It is not accidental that the reform movement in Poland came from outside party ranks, even when these ranks had grown considerably during the 1960s and '70s — from 16 to 26 per cent of all employed in the nationalized economy.

The ruling élite in Poland has to deal with a population becoming, in many respects, more sophisticated.[6] For example, the share of adults and youths (aged 15 and over) with at least secondary education was up to 26 per cent in 1978, from half that in 1960;[7] and the segment of the population with less than full elementary education dwindled to 13 from 45 per cent.[8] During the 1970s, the number of people with post-secondary education increased by 84 per cent (to 1.2 million), even faster than the number with secondary education (65 per cent). Educational growth is even more pronounced among the labour force employed in the nationalized economy, and much effort was made to upgrade the educational standards of this segment of workers.

The general image of Polish society is altered under the impact of educational and cultural modernization, even if several gaps and contradictions cause signs of mass dissatisfaction e.g., resistance to the government policy of atheism, anger over shortages of meat and some other foodstuffs and over the use of political leverage as a key factor in hiring and promotion. From a structural perspective, we see that present-day Polish society has at its disposal a large, well-educated, but consumption-hungry labour force, and it is impossible for the system to avoid increasing pressure to deliver more and better — something state socialism just cannot do.

Impact of Full Employment

The growing grass-roots pressure exerted on the traditional state socialist system in Poland comes, amongst other things, from the fast growth of employment. In the last 20 years the population has risen by one-fifth, but employment in the nationalized economy has increased by three-quarters; in science and technology it has quadrupled; in agriculture, foreign trade and education it has at least doubled. The number of industrial blue-collar workers has increased to four million from two-and-a-half million.

The percentage of wage and salary workers in the Polish labour force has also grown between 1960 and 1979 from 58 to 74 as a result of the numerical decline in private agriculture (to 3.3 million from 4.9 million farmers). At the same time, employment in socialized agriculture has risen by 230 per cent and in total for the socialized economy, by 170 per cent.

Only 22.5 per cent of the population in 1979 derived their living from agriculture, as compared with 47 per cent in 1950. In the last 30 years the contribution of agriculture to the national income has declined to 14 per cent (1979) from 52 per cent, and that of industry has doubled, achieving slightly more than agriculture's old share. This change is due mainly to much greater accumulation than consumption. The ratio between them has changed in the period 1950-1978 from 24:76 to 31:69, and the share of capital investments in GNP has grown to 26 per cent from 11 per cent. This investment effort has developed together with a considerable labour mobilization of the whole population, including women.

Over the same period, the total employment rate has gone up from 41 to 47 per cent. The percentage of those employed in industry has grown from 8 to 15, in construction from two to four. Only the ratio of those employed in agriculture has diminished. Investment and industrial production per capita have had a tenfold increase, but agricultural production has expanded by only one-and-a-half times.

The Issue of Consumption

Rising income in Poland during the 1970s was not paralleled by the availability of consumer goods, especially in the case of food. Meat supply, for one, lagged behind income by one-third during the second half of the 1970s. Furthermore, the distribution of food was highly uneven, varying per head in different regions of the country from 90 Kg to 17 Kg of (red) meat (average 36 Kg), from 13 Kg to 3 Kg of poultry, from 8.5 Kg to 3.5 Kg of butter (average 7.6 Kg), from 5.1 Kg to 1.5 Kg of animal fat, from 19 Kg to 3 Kg of fish. Among all 49 regional districts, the 12 most urbanized were privileged; in the remaining 37, food deliveries were infrequent and irregular.

Since 1960, consumption of material goods has trebled in Poland, and the demand for various leisure goods and services has grown even faster.

Though in terms of consumption, food still plays the major role, alcohol and housing needs have gone up since 1960 particularly quickly. They now constitute each about one-eighth of all consumption expenditures. Over the last 20 years alcohol consumption (per person) has more than doubled, partly due to the fact that liquor is always available and plays the role of a siphon for the money in circulation. Poles consume more milk and meat than do the people in several other Comecon countries. They have fewer automobiles; in 1978, 5 per cent of Poles had cars as compared with more than 10 per cent of East Germans, Czechs and Slovaks, and the percentage is larger in Hungary and Bulgaria.[9]

The popularity of motor vehicles has become a problem in Poland because of the rising world oil prices. The number of cars had grown by 1978 to 1.7 million from 117,000 in 1960, and should the standard of one car per family be achieved (in 1978 there was one car for every six families), this number would stand at 10 million in the year 2000. The demand for cars imposes an additional pressure on the communist system in Poland. With the much underdeveloped infrastructure of the automotive industry and the very high level of car cost (a small Fiat 126 costs the equivalent of 30 average monthly incomes), as well as with the rise in oil prices, there are strong reasons for irritation, especially when there is an evident gas shortage.

The inadequacy of consumer goods has become a major cause of tension between the party and the blue-collar masses. Workers are vitally interested in pursuing higher standards of living and in this respect they seem to be pushing the meagre capacity of state socialism beyond its limits. The situation has become really dramatic in this respect since 1981.

The prolonged confrontation between new trade unions and the Polish government since 1980 has been rooted, to a large extent, in consumer dissatisfaction, as well as in the growing awareness among trade unionists of how effectively they can use organization as a weapon. The difficulty in 1981 in reaching an agreement about free Saturdays has been significant in this respect. The claim of the government that the Polish economy is unable to allow people not to work on Saturdays does not seem very convincing when one considers that approximately one-fourth of working time is regularly wasted anyway due to poor organization, late deliveries electricity shortage, or just laziness.

Blue-Collar Workers as Social Power

The number and influence of blue-collar workers have expanded rapidly with the progress of Polish industrialization: from around 600,000 in the early 1930s (one-third of them agricultural workers) to around seven million in the late 1970s with a large part of them in modern industrial plants. They are mainly young workers; more than half are below 29 and two-thirds not yet 40. One-third are of peasant origin. Also, one-third still reside in the rural areas and commute; some 12 per cent cultivate their land on top of working in industry. Women constitute 44 per cent of industrial blue-collar workers. Two-thirds of all blue- and white-collar workers are concentrated in enterprises that employ between 500 and 5,000 persons and a quarter are in enterprises with 5,000 or more personnel.

The blue-collar stratum in Poland is much diversified, but its members have several things in common: vivid interest in such objectives as social and cultural upgrading, which goes beyond reading. They pursue higher material standards, Roman Catholic traditions, a sense of patriotism, and such qualities as a negative attitude to bureaucrats and bureaucracy in general, practicality, pride in the industrialization of the country, and mindfulness of the nature of economic and structural crises. Their new trade unions are genuinely committed to the common national cause and are ready to make compromises and even sacrifices so long as there is a chance for economic improvement. Of course, these unions, in order to remain popular, have to show their members some specific achievements. This is why free Saturday has become such a heated bargaining issue. On the other hand, the bread-and-butter demands have generally remained relatively modest due to the awareness, on the part of the union leadership, that the current poor state of the Polish economy does not allow for much more. The situation has deteriorated dramatically in this respect with the introduction of martial law in December 1981.

Under pressure of the working masses, the Polish establishment was forced, in the 1970s, to raise the incomes of blue- and white-collar workers. Real wages and salaries grew during the period 1970-1979 by 49 per cent, but this figure does not take into consideration the shortage of some basic goods (which have been rationed since 1981) and the exorbitant black-market prices of meat and similar items. Absenteeism, high labour turnover and low productivity in Poland have had at least the same negative impact on the economy as the strikes and demonstrations of 1956, 1970-71, 1976 and 1980-1981.

Between 1970 and 1979 the ratio of blue-collar earnings to the incomes of technical personnel (graduate engineers and technicians) diminished to 10:13 from 10:15 (10:18 in 1950). In 1979 an average industrial worker earned 17 per cent more than the average employee of the industrial administration, but 29 per cent less than an average technician or engineer. Professional white-collar workers usually moonlight much more than do blue-collar ones. Bonuses sometimes (e.g., among architects) play a bigger role in their earnings, yet during the 1970s the income of blue-collar workers in industry grew faster than that of white-collar ones.

Instead of diminishing, income inequalities have risen in Poland during the 1970s. The minimum income[10] declined in that decade from almost one-half to one-third of the average earnings. Occupational groups, strong due to their strategic position in the economy (miners excavating coal precious for export, skilled construction workers, experts), have been able to apply more pressure than other groups. Women, stuck mainly in the less rewarding work positions, are in a worse situation, for the most part, than men. At the end of the 1970s, a full 83 per cent of women's wages, but only 43 per cent of men's, fell below average.

The great importance of various bonuses in the work income is an additional factor contributing to earning inequalities. The bonuses constitute two-fifths of the average income from work in the nationalized economy, and at least some of them are of a discretionary nature; more bonuses accrue in positions of responsibility than at the bottom of the hierarchy.

In the distribution of employees among various income groups, there is not much difference between blue-collar and white-collar workers. However, there are differences among various branches of the nationalized economy. Thus, there are better paid blue-collar workers in construction, where the labour shortage has remained for many years one of the most critical factors. Additionally, earnings among white-collar workers are definitely higher in industry than in health, culture and education.

The internal differentiation of income within the blue-collar category is quite important: a worker in the power industry, usually a male, earns more than twice as much as a textile operator (usually a female). Highly skilled and better paid workers are generally more in favour of a substantial wage differentiation than the semiskilled and unskilled ones, and the growing educational level of the labour force[11] reinforces the acceptance of income inequality.

Social Selection

At the end of the 1970s, one-third of the labour force and one-half of the women workers had secondary education, while this qualification had been rare at the beginning of the period. This development is momentous and means the gradual overcoming of traditional educational and cultural barriers between the various strata. Very significant in this respect is the substantial numerical growth of vocational-school graduates, originating mainly from the blue-collar category.

The educational and occupational upgrading has had weighty consequences, directly for the income level and the household budget (more white-collar wives have paying jobs). However, its segregational impact also shows. To name the more obvious areas: in housing congestion (one or more persons per room is typical for more than half the blue-collar workers, but only for around a quarter of the white-collar ones), in living conditions, cultural consumption (less creative leisure among blue-collar workers), social life (close so-called contacts among the intelligentsia) in tourism and sport activities.

The educational system and hiring procedures in Poland have functioned right from the beginning as selective devices throughout the process of gradual socialization. Starting at the nursery school level, there are limited places available (half the children aged three to six remain outside these schools) and those children not admitted, frequently from lower strata, are handicapped in their intellectual and social development.

At the secondary-school level there is also a selection process and the lower class children gain admission to better schools well below their numerical share among the total population.[12] On the one hand, a high percentage of lower-strata offspring attend some kind of secondary school, but among the graduates of secondary general schools and the mainstream post-secondary schools, their quota is relatively much lower than the share of the intelligentsia. Among first-year students of the post-secondary schools, the portion of registrants of blue-collar origin has grown in the period 1960-1979 only to 37 per cent from 26 (far below the 42 per cent figure representing blue-collar workers in the social structure), while the percentage of students of white-collar origin has remained at the level of about 50 per cent. If one considers the allocation of educational funds at the post-secondary level in 1970, one sees that the blue-collar worker stratum shared 30 per cent of the allocation while representing 42 per cent of labour; the farmers were apportioned 17 per cent while constituting 36 per cent of the workforce, and the white-collar stratum received 53 per cent while representing only 22 per cent of the working population.[13]

There is a tendency among the youth from the traditionally lower strata to take extension courses instead of a regular course that does not allow one to hold a job and study simultaneously. Learning outside the main stream, chiefly by taking evening courses, has gained in popularity.

The selection applied at various levels of education is particularly disadvantageous for the lower strata offspring who are culturally and financially handicapped. Immediately after the Second World War the communist party was vitally interested in the promotion of blue-collar workers to responsible positions. From 1945 to 1959, about 63,000 blue-collars were promoted to white-collar jobs. Now, 57 per cent of the party intelligentsia is of blue-collar origin. On the other hand, blue-collar workers are less influential in the party than are several white-collar professions. While 25 per cent of industrial blue-collars have membership in the party, 85 per cent of army officers, 28 per cent of engineers and technicians, 40 per cent of school teachers and 31 per cent of the academic staff are party members.[14] Even if blue-collar workers constitute 46 per cent of the total party membership, their bargaining power is much lower than that of some of the organized professional groups.

Blue-collar workers can exert collective pressure, as a rule, only under the exceptional circumstances of a major price rise in consumer goods, when the top party leadership is internally split or the existing working conditions endanger a large number of people. Under the circumstances, traditional trade unions sponsored by the ruling party proved of little use to blue-collar workers (even with a membership of around 90 per cent of the workers) because of the subservience of the trade union bureaucracy to the state and party apparatus.

The dissatisfaction of blue-collar workers had already been in evidence for years, as indicated by the labour turnover rates, particularly in construction. These rates tended to be higher among men than among women, who had less choice in employment, due to the fact that employers were not eager to spend funds on maternity leave or tolerate absence for the care of sick children. In industries with three work shifts (coal, steel, textiles), simulated sickness became a device for obtaining relief from the heavy work schedule. Beginning in 1980, Polish blue-collar workers started collective protests against working weekends. Miners particularly objected to Sunday work and, therefore, promoted, with determination, a demand for free weekends.

Private Farmers in Poland

Most Poles (77 per cent) work within the socialized economy, but the non-socialized sector remains quite a substantial part of the total economy thanks to the private ownership of farms — which occupy 53 per cent of the whole land and employ around 80 per cent of the agricultural working population. Most of the private farms are small — 5.3 hectares on an average. Three-fifths of all private farms are below this average and very small farms of 0.5 to 2 Ha constitute 30 per cent of all private farms; only 14 per cent have an area of 10 Ha and over.

The role of agriculture in the national income formation diminished between 1960 and 1979 to 14 per cent from 34 per cent. The socialized agricultural economy (state and collective farms) represents only a fifth of the working agricultural population and of the total agricultural production, but almost half the land. Its labour force grew in the last twenty years more than twice as fast as that of the private sector. This increase is due, among other things, to the fact that young people do not want to stay on private farms. The farmers are old and the farms remaining after they die are often taken over by the state. Many young people have been discouraged from staying in the countryside by differences between the standard of living and their expectations, as well as by the boredom of village life.

Probably even more important is the fact that private agriculture has only very limited chances of growth under the Soviet state socialism that features poor financing, and great dependence on the state party bureaucracy. From 1960 to 1978, the gross production of private farms rose by 33 per cent, in comparison with the tripling of production in the heavily subsidized socialized agriculture. In the same period, the amount of land given over to private agriculture decreased to 53 per cent from 63 per cent.[15]

Agriculture has been neglected in state budgets for many years. In the late 1970s, only one-fifth of all investment was allocated for agriculture; two-thirds of that was set aside for nationalized agriculture, even when the latter delivered only one-third of the total agricultural production. While means of producing capital goods expanded by only 40 per cent in the private sector from 1970 to 1978, they increased by six times in nationalized farming. Fertilization in the latter has been twice as high as in the former, and the difference between the two sectors has been even more evident in the supply of seeding grain and seed potatoes.

Besides the discriminatory state policy, private farming has to contend with occurrences of bribery, over-dependence on the state, shortages of basic requirements for production, as well as with the relative decline of private farmers' incomes to about 70 per cent of the average in the nationalized economy. Consequently, the late 1970s were to witness a steady decline in private farming. The area cultivated by private farmers diminished in the period 1970-78 by 11 per cent. This decline also derived from the somewhat lower yields per hectare of major crops produced by the private farmers as compared to those in the nationalized agriculture, this being due to the fact that the former still depended mainly on human and animal power. There were 13 horses for every 100 hectares of farming area in 1978. Very few tractors were used in private farming; the three tractors for every 100 Ha compared poorly with the 11 in nationalized agriculture. Besides, private farms use 50% less chemical and lime fertilizers than the state or collective farms.

There still remain striking differences in prosperity between urban and rural areas in Poland. The peasant households are far behind urban households in terms of owning refrigerators (respectively, 59 and 93 per 100 households), vacuum cleaners (32 and 88), TV sets (82 and 104) and cars (11 and 18). The contrast is even more noticeable in the lower average income of the rural population (around 30 per cent less than in urban areas), compounded by poorer housing conditions (in 1974 only 20 per cent of rural houses had running water and 10 per cent had toilets inside), limited educational opportunities and less chance for promotion.

A shrinking number of people has become committed to agricultural production even in the countryside. In 1978, from the private farm population, 27 per cent worked on farms only part time, gaining their living mainly from other sources. Among those working chiefly on the farm 29 per cent were aged 60 or more, and 52 per cent 50 or more. In the age group 19-30, one-third left the countryside and moved to the cities to study or work. Most former farm workers do not return to farming because of the long hours, difficulty in obtaining investment credit, few comforts of life in rural areas, limited prospects to succeed as a private farmer, and the general boredom associated with rural life. Besides, housing conditions remain consistently worse in the countryside than in urban areas.

The Failure of Polish Modernization

The growing dependence of Poland during the 1970s on western loans and technological imports financed from them has not led to the expected advantages because the bureaucratic economy did not capitalize fast enough on the investments. In March 1980, 45 per cent of the imported machines and other pieces of equipment were stored unused for more than one year; in total, 50 billion zlotys were frozen in idle capital equipment.

Polish debt to the West had grown during the 1970s to 28 per cent from 11 per cent of the total indebtedness of Comecon. It was four times the value of the Polish export to "first world" (non-socialist developed countries), much higher than in any other Comecon country.

It is significant that, from all the western purchases made by Poland during the 1970s, capital investment products represented one-third and food one-fifth. The negative balance of food exchange with the non-socialist countries trebled during the second half of the decade and Poland, in order to feed her more and more restless population, gradually had to divert foreign credit from fixed assets to consumer goods, mainly imported food.

From the middle of the 1970s onward, western credit has been used mainly for consumption while, at the same time, Poland's chances to sell goods in the West did not improve accordingly. The share of food in Polish exports diminished to 16 per cent from 29 per cent during the 1970s. Thus, there is little hope in the forseeable future for Poland to improve its trade balance by exporting more food. Coal and food already constitute half the Polish exports to the non-socialist countries, technological products making up only 15 per cent (60 per cent of the exports to socialist countries).

With the progress of industrialization and modernization of production, Poland is becoming more and more dependent as it imports various sophisticated technical devices from the West — spare parts and even some raw materials, not available in Comecon countries. This process would be profitable if only foreign technology could be adapted fast enough to local conditions. However, in reality, adaptation has become very difficult or even impossible in several cases. The local production of new articles based on foreign licences has been delayed and, in some instances, reliance for years on expensive imports has made the whole business unprofitable. This was the case, amongst others, with the manufacture of Massey-Ferguson tractors, colour television sets and buses based on American and French licences respectively.

One of the major problems in the relatively high cost of industrial production in Poland is waste. For each unit of production, three times more energy, cement and steel are wasted than in the non-socialist developed countries. According to 1977 data, exports constituted 13 per cent of the GNP, but they consumed 25 per cent of all expenditures. Owing to high costs deriving partly from waste, Poland has to invest relatively much more to be able to export goods than do her more sophisticated western competitors. Polish industry uses too much energy, transport, raw materials and labour. These are, in addition to red-tape, the main sources of the inefficiency.

Raw materials and fuels make up half of Poland's imports; their cost per head rose during the 1970s fivefold to US $250 from $50. The import of natural gas quadrupled and imports of oil grew by two-and-a-half times. The import of wheat and barley also increased considerably: threefold in the first case and ninefold in the second. Poland depends on foreign imports for all her oil, for one-third of her wheat and barley, for a third of her leather, to mention some of the more important items. The country relies to a very large extent on the USSR as a supplier of raw materials. All natural gas, four-fifths of all petroleum, 70 per cent of iron ore, chromium, magnesium, cotton and potash fertilizers in Poland come from the Soviet Union.

The Polish economy, in order to overcome its crises, has, no doubt, to count on external help, but at the same time, it requires a thorough remodelling. What remains to be seen is the extent of remodelling possible without provoking direct Soviet intervention similar to that in Hungary (1956) and Czechoslovakia (1968). The USSR is well aware of the burdens and dangers related to such a venture and, therefore, is acting with caution. Any considerable deterioration of relations between the new trade unions and the Polish government may provoke the Russians to move in. This was readily appreciated by both sides until the sudden imposition of martial law in December 1981.

Perspectives of a New Model in Poland

Before December 1981 Poland was the only member of Comecon in which opposition is more or less tolerated by the communist authorities and a kind of accommodation between the ruling establishment and various non-communist political groups had emerged. Poland was gravitating towards a new political model of a semi-pluralistic system under the rule of communists, but with the acknowledged input of several independent centres of public opinion that articulated non-communist orientations and criticisms. This was different from the token pluralism of the "People's Democracy" model with the political groups steered clandestinely by the communist party. This new model resulted not so much from the pressure exercised by the growing Polish opposition as from the economic difficulties of communist Poland.

The ruling establishment relies largely on the status- and power-seekers who have gained substantially from the massive upgrading of the lower classes. The upgrading has been achieved, as shown above, through industrialization, the spread of government-sponsored education (lower-class offspring have some priority in admittance to secondary and post-secondary education), through recruitment to the party and state apparatus and through promotion within it. According to 1972 data, there are in Poland well over a million people in managerial and other powerful positions; their survival depends primarily on the preservation of the status quo. They are often in favour of tough methods in dealing with opposition and do not hesitate to act brutally when they see occasion for it. It is not only, perhaps, the pressure coming from Moscow, but also tension within party ranks, that encouraged the establishment to take much more severe measures against its opposition in December 1981.

On the other hand, the risk is enhanced mainly by the constant shortage of food, by hidden inflation, and the internal struggle for power. As long as opposition is tolerated, some kind of scapegoat is always available and the ruling clique is insecure enough to appreciate the device. It is interesting to note that various groups and orientations within the party do not hesitate to develop contacts among the opposition in order to use them in their power struggle, should the need arise. From time to time there are official or semi-official pronouncements that the establishment will not remain indifferent to those who denigrate its polices and that the anti-communist forces will be resolutely opposed. The arrests of oppositionists follow, but after a few days or weeks they are released and they resumed their semi-clandestine activities.[16] This practice ended, at least temporarily, with the introduction of martial law in 1981.

The opposition and the establishment continually accuse each other of a lack of realism and of disloyalty. But the situation does not change much as long as the licensed mass media are scarcely available to the critics of the status quo. The blue-collar workers limit themselves to local strikes, the economic situation remains unfavourable, the intelligentsia complains, but does not act much, and the shakey power balance within the party ranks makes impossible any decisive policy either of far-reaching reforms or suppression. *Apparatchiks* opposed, in effect, any reforms against their vested interests. On the other hand, Poland's heavy dependency on Western loans, does not allow sufficient room for oppressive policy. No action can be taken in either of the two opposing directions and the atrophy of problem-solving results.

The chasm separating the establishment and most of the citizenry derives mainly from the rigid and callous nature of Soviet state socialism[17] which makes any substantial reform very difficult. It would be necessary to abandon the externally imposed model of society which remains intact and is guaranteed by Soviet dominance. Even the leading Polish communists are not quite happy with present conditions and would like to see some changes. Before December, 1981, the opposition and the communist establishment in Poland gradually learns how to coexist, and this is a very important factor in the transformation process. In this respect Poland differs profoundly from East Germany and Czechoslovakia, but shows some similarity with Hungary. The developments in Hungary and Poland seem to have gained sympathy among Eurocommunists. They are vitally interested in a democratized version of state socialism. As long as there is a dearth of democracy in eastern Europe, there is little chance for Eurocommunists to come to power in their own countries, except in the case of an occupation by Soviet military groups ("Panzerkommunismus").

As long as the Polish opposition had an opportunity (prior to Dec. 1981) to take an active part in the reconstruction of the Polish economy, its influence remained limited. The traditional establishment was much more willing to tolerate general criticism, even open attacks against the USSR, than to share power with the new socio-political forces: free trade unions, independent intellectuals and experts, noncommunist politicians, etc. This is the real drama of present-day Poland. It is in the best interest of bureaucrats to retain full power. And so, the political opposition is unable to develop beyond a limited circle of academic youth and intellectuals as long as it does not have the opportunity to organize itself openly, gain its own mass media, and appeal publicly to the electorate. The free trade union movement managed to gain temporarily substantial power but was crushed in December 1981.

The Neighbours of Poland

The East Central European (ECE) group of Soviet allies consists of countries diverse not only in territory and population, but also in levels of socioeconomic growth, culture and tradition. Of 109 million people living there in 1979, a third were in Poland and a fifth in Rumania; the rest were split among Hungary, East Germany, Czechoslovakia and Bulgaria. From the whole Comecon — which includes, in addition to the aforementioned countries, the USSR, Cuba, Mongolia and Vietnam — the ECE nations constitute altogether around 30 per cent of the total population, but their economic share in many fields is much higher than that.

The individual ECE countries play a major role in the foreign trade of Comecon as a whole. Their share of Comecon foreign trade turnover from 1960 to 1980 has remained around 60 per cent. In this trade, the exchange with other Comecon countries represents a half of their respective foreign trade totals in the cases of Poland and Hungary, two-fifths for Rumania, and more than half for all remaining members.

In 1960 the per capita export rate in Comecon was worth US $43 (equal to the world export rate) and represented less than one-third the rate for the developed non-socialist countries; in the period from 1960 to 1979, the ratio between these rates grew from 10:32 to 10:45.[18] This means Comecon has lagged behind the international development of foreign trade and this factor limits considerably the dynamics of economic growth. Only in Rumania, Poland and Hungary do exchanges with First-World countries constitute a considerable part of foreign trade: around 40 per cent of imports and around 30 per cent of exports (1978 data). In other East-European countries, interdependence within Comecon plays the dominant role.

The share of animal and plant products and raw materials considerably diminished as a part of overall Comecon exports during the period 1960-1978; to 10 per cent from 27 per cent in the USSR, to 20 per cent from 36 per cent in Rumania, to 11 per cent from 23 per cent in Poland, to 27 per cent from 56 per cent in Bulgaria. In the same period the role of machines and other technical equipment in the total value of imports increased: to 42 per cent from 31 per cent in the USSR, to 38 per cent from 34 per cent in Rumania, to 35 per cent from 27 per cent in Poland, to 37 per cent from 22 per cent in Czechoslovakia, to 34 per cent from 13 per cent in East Germany, to 34 per cent from 28 per cent in Hungary.[19]

This structural transformation of foreign trade exchanges would be profitable and socially beneficial in the long run only in the case of Comecon being able to compete effectively on the world market. However, industrial products offered by Comecon on the world markets are quite often not of competitive quality.

In some fields Comecon has tallied considerable achievements, even if the official data have to be taken with a grain of salt. In the period 1950-1979 the share of Comecon in world production increased to 30 per cent in steel from 19 per cent, to 25 per cent in cement from 14 per cent, and to 21 per cent from 14 per cent in electric energy. However, production of food and other consumer goods remained far behind the growth rate of heavy industry. In the whole Comecon bloc during 1950-1978, overall industrial production grew 1,200 per cent, but agricultural production only 250 per cent and its share in the export market increased only from 7 to 8.5 per cent. In Eastern Europe almost everywhere industry represents from 50 to 60 per cent of the national income and from 30 to 40 per cent of the working population.

There are differences between various ECE countries in their socioeconomic potential, but all the countries have achieved a high level of industrialization and urbanization. At the end of the 1970s, between 50 and 60 per cent of each country's population lived in urban areas; in Czechoslovakia, the figure was even as high as 67 per cent, and in the German Democratic Republic (GDR) 76 per cent, but these two countries are traditionally urbanized. The growth of gross industrial production during the 1950s, 1960s and 1970s was particularly high in Bulgaria and Rumania (around 10 per cent per year). With the achievement of a higher developmental level, the trend shows a general tendency to slow down. The high level of accumulation (25 to over 30 per cent of national income) is typical for the ECE countries. Total capital investment in Poland grew by five times between 1960 and 1977, making this the second-highest rate in Comecon after Rumania. In comparison with industry and construction taken together, total capital means and investments in agriculture and forestry in 1978 represented much less. This is one of the reasons why the gross agricultural production from 1960 to 1977 at best doubled (in Rumania), and in the remaining countries grew by less than half, while gross industrial production rose by several times.

In the national income of all ECE, industry constituted in 1977 from 50 to 60 per cent and construction around 10 per cent. The share of agriculture and forestry has diminished substantially since 1950, except in Czechoslovakia, where it was relatively low in the first place. This decline was, in Bulgaria, from almost a half to less than a fifth, in the GDR from about one-third to one-tenth, and so on. The progress of industrialization seemed closely related to the dramatic transformation of occupational structures.

The number of wage earners and salaried workers has grown dramatically after 1950: by fivefold in Bulgaria, by threefold in Rumania, by more than twofold in Hungary and Poland. This process resulted from the socialization of agriculture and the promotion of state-owned economics. Self-employment is almost negligible in the ECE countries, except in the case of Polish private farmers who, together with their families, constitute almost a quarter of the population.

Under state socialism, the factors mentioned above meet in the processes of mass mobilization and collectivization, which may become bearable only in a highly sophisticated and efficient system.

Changing Social Structures in Eastern Europe

The gradual equalization of social structures in various ECE countries comes as a result of industrialization and urbanization, both following the Soviet pattern oriented mainly towards heavy industry. From 1960 to 1979, employment outside agriculture and forestry doubled in the USSR, Rumania and Bulgaria and grew considerably in all the ECE countries except East Germany (which experienced a 22 per cent growth). The fact that in all ECE countries — except for Poland with her private agriculture — almost the whole workforce consists of wage and salary earners (the collective farmers do not differ much in real status from the wage earners) creates a great similarity of problems. The main ones among them are limitations and internal contradictions in the bureaucracy.[20]

The rising educational and cultural level of ECE populations is the key determinant of some major transformations. The scope of general education is substantial in all Comecon countries: from not much over 100 (Hungary, Bulgaria) to around 300 (Cuba) pupils per 1,000 population. Differences are much related to the age structure.

The Soviet system prescribes rigid selection of candidates to higher levels of education and consequent tough competition among the various families and strata to secure future advancement for their offspring. The authorities assign priority to the children of blue-collar workers, but in reality, the intelligentsia have more leverage and, therefore, especially in day courses, they enjoy the upper hand, as seen from Polish data.

The availability of books and mass media is already sizable in all ECE countries, leading to greater expectations, with respect to living standards than is achievable in the framework of rigid state socialism. Television licence holders constitute around 29 per cent of the total population on an average, which breaks down to 33 per cent in East Germany, 26 per cent in Czechoslovakia, 24 per cent in Hungary and 15 per cent in Rumania. Public libraries are popular. The average number of books available per citizen grew between 1960 and 1977 from one or two to over five in the USSR (6.6) and Bulgaria (5.1). An average of 160 newspaper copies per capita are read by East Germans in a year and Soviet citizens read 120. Annual book production varies from 10 per inhabitant in Hungary, 8 in East Germany and 7 in the Soviet Union, to only 4 in Poland and Rumania.

The basic structural differences between various ECE countries are indicated by the levels of employment in agriculture and forestry taken together. These comprise from 20 to 33 per cent of the work force in Bulgaria, Hungary, Poland and Rumania, but less in the GDR (11 per cent) and Czechoslovakia (14 per cent).

Among the economically active population, blue-collar workers constitute between 40 to 50 per cent in Poland, Rumania and Bulgaria, and around 60 per cent in Czechoslovakia, Hungary and the GDR. From the total East Central European labour force in 1976 of 55 million people, workers in industry and construction constituted around 20 million (35 per cent).

Contrary to the situation in developed Western countries, the third sector in ECE remains relatively small and contains 30 to 35 per cent of all wage earners, i.e., half the rate typical for the First World.

The predominance of blue-collar workers under state socialism does not mean they have much to say and that their problems and life perspectives influence the whole society. White-collar workers constitute around a fourth of the economically active population in Bulgaria, Hungary and Poland, less in Rumania (14 per cent), but more in Czechoslovakia (28 per cent) and East Germany (34 per cent).[21] Within the bureaucratic setup of Soviet state socialism, white-collar characteristics prevail over the blue-collar values,[22] except for present-day Poland with her strong free trade unions. Even recruitment into the ranks of the ruling party for years has been much more oriented towards the white-collar workers, especially experts, than to their blue-collar counterparts.

All ECE countries have followed a policy of enforced industrialization based almost exclusively on internal mobilization of resources, which apart from other factors, has entailed the limitation of labour mobility, application of piece rate (on the dysfunctions of the latter see Haraszti[23]), widespread worker training and manipulation of their motivation (the "socialist emulation"). Under Soviet state socialism, Eastern European labour did not have any other way to articulate its anxieties and demands, until the Polish mass unrest in 1980, except by informal restraint of productivity, absenteeism, turnover etc.[24]

Since in all Comecon countries but Cuba and Rumania[25] women constitute almost half (and more) of the work-force, the state takes responsibility for much of the upbringing of pre-school children. Institutions look after 80 per cent of the children up to 6 years old in East Germany and around half of such youngsters in most of the other East European countries.

Social consumption, governed directly by the state and associations controlled by it, makes up 5 (in Bulgaria and Mongolia) to 20 per cent (in

Czechoslovakia and Hungary), of the general consumption. It consists of pensions (from a third to a half of the total), education and culture (from one-fifth to one-quarter), health and sport (from one-sixth to one-fourth), and scholarships.

The considerable growth of health services is assured by the government budget. However, this does not necessarily mean that good quality and availability of these services are guaranteed. The unequal distribution of health services, and very inadequte housing become major causes of dissatisfaction for the population.

Difficulties in daily life have a negative impact on natural increase, and lead to tensions between marriage partners. People even have sufficient money but are dissatisfied because good are not available on the open market. The fact that social consumption plays a major role in Eastern Europe does not help in this respect, because the public sector is inefficient in satisfying the needs of the population. One obvious example is the underdevelopment of the communications network while the needs of the population are rapidly growing in this field due to higher levels of education and mobility.

There are substantial differences in the allocation of various leisure facilities in individual Comecon countries. For example, the rate of guest nights in the government-subsidized holiday facilities per 100 people is greater than 10 in East Germany, Hungary and Poland (in this last case 13) but below 4 in Czechoslovakia, and only 2 in the USSR. TV-set ownership per 100 people is more than 25 in Hungary, Czechoslovakia, and East Germany (33), but less than 20 in Rumania and Bulgaria. In the availability of radio sets there are also differences per 100 population: more than 20 in Czechoslovakia, Poland, Hungary, the Soviet Union and East Germany (37.5), but less than 15 in Bulgaria and Rumania. Attendance at the movies is popular in the USSR (1,600 viewers per 100 population in a year) and Bulgaria, but much more limited in Poland (331 viewers), East Germany (480) and Czechoslovakia (560). Attendance at stage theatre plays, operas and operettas, per 100 population, compared with some Comecon countries, is low in Poland (36), Rumania (38) and the USSR (45).

Differences in the standard of living amongst various countries as well as amongst various strata still remain quite substantial in East Central Europe. According to data from the middle 1970s, food consumption (a reliable indicator of relative well-being) comprised around 40 per cent of the household expenditures of blue-collar, as well as white-collar workers in Bulgaria, Hungary and Poland, but only 25 to 30 per cent in the GDR and Czechoslovakia. Polish and Hungarian farmers spend more of their household expenditures on food (40 to 45 per cent) than their blue-collar (around 40 per cent) or white-collar compatriots (30 to 35 per cent) and more than

Czechoslovakian farmers (around 25 per cent).[26]

Until the Polish crisis in 1980-81, differences in the standard of living of various ECE countries were not great enough to lead to major problems in relations among them, so long as the Pax Sovietica dominated, progress through forced industrialization brought about unification. The mass media, mass culture and education have been widely used by the authorities to indoctrinate the population with official policy, which includes "fraternal" ties with the USSR and other communist countries. On the other hand, under the impact of the Polish example, people of East Central Europe are gaining new inspirations and insights that definitely go beyond the rigid limits of an ossified official creed.

Interstrata Relations

The liaison between the blue-collar workers and the intellectuals has been weak in all ECE countries except Poland, where the link was started in 1976 through the establishment by intellectuals of an effective and influential committee for "defense of blue-collar workers." Even in Czechoslovakia and Hungary during the 1968 and 1956 takeovers, there was relatively little contact and understanding between the two groups.[27] However, in Poland, intellectuals have become very much involved in organized activities on behalf of blue-collar workers and their trade unions.

There are several reasons why in East European countries interstrata contacts have remained weak, even if most of the new intelligentsia are of blue-collar or peasant origin. First of all, the bureaucratic apparatus has set itself up as effective insulation between various strata. Almost all interstate social contacts are arranged and effectively controlled by state and party functionaries. Second, vital interests are not the same for intellectuals as for blue-collar workers, for example: civil rights versus economic improvement, self-expression versus security, moral principles versus consumerism. Third, the political-freedom movements, articulated by intellectuals, originate mostly in élitist circles (as, for instance, the Writers' Union). These acquire power from the well-established status of the élite members, while the blue-collar workers rely mainly on their numbers, spontaneous organization and the strategic location of their workplaces for any level they may attain. For example, female textile workers in Lodz (Poland) won a legal battle at the start of 1971, mainly because to handle this big industrial city would have been too heavy a task for the authorities in the event of a mass revolt. A similar situation occurred on a much larger scale during the summer of 1980 on the Baltic coast.

The communist élites governing East Europe have a common interest in preventing the development of a liaison between intellectuals and blue-collar workers. As long as the articulation of dissatisfaction remains contained within each separate layer of society, the intellectuals fail to acquire mass appeal, and blue-collar demands do not become generalized and upgraded to the level of a specific political program. Until the 1980-81 events in Poland the mass media have remained under the full control of the governments and cannot be used by dissidents as a platform for program formulation. Illegal media, even under circumstances most favourable for the opposition, remain tied mainly to one particular class and do not upset, to any major degree, the equilibrium favoured and sponsored by the élite. Since 1980 this difficulty in expressing grievances and demands has been overcome in Poland at least, thanks to a strong alliance between the leaders of independent trade unions and free intellectuals who do not hesitate to act as advisers to, and even spokesmen for labour.

Z. Bauman is right in emphasizing the "myth" of a socialist consumer society as undermining the solidarity of those working people who potentially are oriented towards the transformation of the existing political system.[28] People, some of whose conditions were significantly improved during the period of socialist industrialization and urbanization, so far have had enough opportunity to learn the advantages of collective action independent of state and party authorities. With the exception of Poland, most countries that have risked such an action have failed (e.g., Rumania in 1977), because the authorities were strong enough to put down the organizers. However, also in Poland at the end of 1981 the ruling elite managed to gain back their control.

The relative youth of the blue-collar stratum is a fact of life in ECE countries.[29] At the end of the 1970s, for the first time the majority of blue-collar workers originated from the same background, and not, as had previously been the case, from the peasant stratum. The educational level has changed considerably and exposure to outside influences has grown rapidly. Particularly in Poland, blue-collar workers, until the end of 1981, had an opportunity to travel outside their own country, thanks mainly to no-visa agreements between Poland and her socialist neighbours, as well as Sweden and Austria. The number of tourist departures from Poland increased during the 1970s to more than 11 million from 871,000 (and to countries outside Comecon, to almost half a million from slightly in excess of 100,000). Since 1980 this traffic has been curtailed by Poland's socialist neighbours who fear the dissemination of the "Polish disease".

Income Differences

Income differences among various job holders remain significant in ECE countries. In Bulgaria the top ranks of administration, army and police earn from 10 to 12 times what the average worker does. Differences among various blue-collar categories range in Bulgaria from 1 to 7. On the one hand, there are relatively prosperous construction workers, miners, and metallurgists; on the other, women earn very little in trade and other services. In commerce, and in other job categories occupied mostly by women, average incomes are 30 per cent lower than in construction. If one takes the average monthly blue-collar income as having been around 1,250 leva per person in 1976, then 47 per cent of blue-collar families, 56 per cent of collective farmer families and 39 per cent of white-collar families had below average incomes. Less than half the 1,250 leva level was earned by 7 per cent of peasant and 4 per cent of blue-collar families.[30]

In Hungary, according to 1973 data, among blue-collar families 45 per cent had per person monthly incomes below the national average of 1,300 forints and only around 15 per cent had more than one-and-a-half times that amount.[31] In Hungary, as in other ECE countries, a considerable part of the additional income in the blue-collar families comes either from overtime and moonlighting or from working small plots of land that provide much of the nation's fruits, vegetables and meats. Of Hungarian semi-skilled and unskilled workers, almost two-thirds live in the countryside,[32] which gives them an opportunity to farm, at least on a small scale. The average blue-collar family with a plot of land spends from 20 to 25 hours a week working on this "farm."[33]

There is a tendency in ECE countries to narrow the gap between income levels of the traditional strata of blue-collar workers, white-collar ones and peasants. A reduction of the difference has been achieved between the first two, but peasant incomes are well behind. For example, in Bulgaria in 1976, peasant families in the collective farms had average incomes lower by a quarter than those of blue-collar or white-collar families.[34]

The Selection of Elites

The ruling élites in central and eastern Europe are products of bureaucracies (the generation of revolutionaries is already on pension) and depend for their survival mainly on the administrative positions they occupy. The institution of a suitable *nomenclature* of leading positions allows the members of the élite to circulate in them, and to keep under strict control any new candidates to the hierarchy. In all ECE countries there is growing pressure from various classes to be admitted to the élite circle through educational channels and a party career. With the gradual decline — except in Poland — of the former opposition to the establishment (accompanied by a similar decline in religious beliefs, and an obsolescence of the pre-communist ideologies), status seekers pushing upwards from the bottom positions treat party affiliation more and more as just a rational solution to status ambiguity. Most technically educated people know that, in order to last any length of time in managerial postings, they have to be admitted to the party. Whatever their attitude toward Marxism, people who treat party membership as an ideological issue are thought, in this light, to be

62

simply irrational.

The process of selection to the élite has been, in this respect, approximately the same in all ECE countries and has led to the virtual separation between ideology and party ranks, especially in the higher positions. In addition, the principle of co-operation, characteristic of the party élite, has lent a certain neo-aristocratic character to internal relationships, more evident in some countries — Bulgaria and Rumania, for instance — than in others. Whereas bureaucrats and technocrats prevail at the lower and middle levels of the apparatus, in the top positions "partocrats" dominate. They know one another very well, are personally free from economic worries, can afford to participate in political games, and are widely influential. A personal affiliation with the Soviet upper ranks plays a major role but, at the same time, local pressures and collective ambitions are much "closer to home" and more vital. Contingent on the way power is reshuffled, leaders change, but the principle of their arbitrary appointment remains the same.

With the growing economic modernization of ECE countries and the increasing influence of technocrats, some changes occur. For example, in Bulgarian agriculture during the 1970s the big agribusiness enterprises became crucial and their managers have grown considerably in importance. The same thing happened with the big industrial corporations in Poland that absorbed, during the 1970s, many smaller nationalized enterprises. However, it would be naïve to assume that the reorganization of economic life is genuinely justified mainly because of rational and technological considerations. Power struggles within bureaucracies are very often ends in themselves. For example, Poland's expensive administrative reform in the mid-1970s was mainly dictated by the interests of the top leadership in destroying the power of regional party secretaries. By moving from relatively few to many administrative regions, it was possible for the party leadership to eliminate the potential threat coming from strong, local party bosses.

The meaning, image and identity of the intelligentsia in Central and East European countries have changed greatly and at the same time, its numbers have increased considerably. The ability of the intelligentsia to exercise some influence is greater or smaller, depending on the strength and will power of the party élite. For example, this ability has been conspicuous in Poland and Hungary, but less so in Rumania, Bulgaria and the GDR. Czechoslovakia's intelligentsia during the late 1960s had become very influential, but during the 1970s this was no longer the case. In all these countries there is a permanent problem: who really represents the national interest — the ruling party élite or the intelligentsia? After the death of Stalin the universal character of communism became a thing of the past. Now, to gain some support from the masses, these ruling élites make a show of their national commitment.

The highly artificial character of economic relations inside and outside these lands tends to lead to a high level of ambiguity. In many cases it is difficult to say who gains and who loses in the mutual foreign trade relationships. This uncertainty inspires tensions and reciprocal distrust. The ruling élites have a vested interest in creating the impression among the local population that there is no alternative to their rule and that they effectively defend the national interest against intrusion by the Soviet Union and other ECE countries. The danger of direct Soviet military intervention is widely used to justify the exclusion of other choices. This propagandistic weapon was widely used in Poland in 1980-81 but with very limited success. And all this distrustful backbiting takes place between various Comecon partners behind an official façade of "fraternal love."

Structural Characteristics of Individual Societies

The basic structural differences among ECE societies are related to the relative roles of the peasantry and intelligentsia. In all these countries — even in Czechoslovakia and the GDR — the rural tradition is still alive in the minds of a considerable number of blue-collar workers as well as, to some extent, among the new white-collar stratum, emerging from the massive political, social and educational upgrading under state socialism. The collectivization of the peasantry everywhere but in Poland, or its recruitment to work in the public sector, prompted it to abandon traditions, but its characteristic way of thinking and acting has greatly influenced the internal style of state socialism. Many peasants found themselves elevated to various vital posts and subconsciously they had their self-importance enhanced as quasi-landlords, or at least managers of estates. Loyalties originating from class and village traditions play a major role in power struggles and in the choice of values. A distrust of the traditional intelligentsia, a trait of East Central European political leaders and bureaucrats, probably derives not so much from divergent vested interests as from a divergence in their view of the world. The "limited good" principle[35] that prevents economic bosses from appreciating the creative value of entrepreneurial imagination, is deeply lodged in the peasant mentality.

The traditional role of the intelligentsia has been particularly pronounced in Poland and Hungary, as well as, to some extent, in Czechoslovakia and Rumania. The idea of a whole social stratum devoted to the spiritual leadership of a nation is peculiar to East Central Europe, and even after a holocaust like the Second World War, it has remained quite powerful.[36] Soviet-style communism never represented in East Central Europe a cultural and moral power that could ever challenge effectively the appeal of the intelligentsia. On the other hand, many members of the new intelligentsia, recruited from the peasant and blue-collar classes, have shown respect for the intelligentsia's ethos, which they needed to shape their own identities. Even the gentry tradition has been conveyed by the intelligentsia to those social climbers who took advantage of promotional opportunities offered them by state socialism. This is particularly true for Poland and Hungary, and in some measure, also for Czechoslovakia and Rumania, but much less so for Bulgaria and the GDR.

In Bulgaria the blue-collar stratum is particularly new and still rooted in the peasantry. The share of the urbanites in the labour force grew during 1946-1976 to 63 per cent from 27 per cent. The percentage of agriculture in the total employment diminished to 26 from more than 80, and that of industry and construction increased to 42 from around 10. Bulgarian blue-collar workers constituted in 1976 almost half the workforce, in comparison with only 17 per cent 20 years earlier. It is perhaps significant that, with the development of state-owned agricultural estates, the allocation of blue-collar workers has changed considerably: just two-fifths are in industry now — as opposed to 58 per cent in 1948 — and almost one-third are involved in agriculture (only six per cent in 1948). The share of women among the blue-collars grew to 45 per cent from 27 per cent in 1957-1976, and they definitely prevail in textile and leather factories; in industry as a whole they constitute half the workforce, and the same condition exists in the state-owned agriculture industry.[37]

In Bulgaria the social potential of the intelligentsia was weak before the communist seizure of power, and, under an authoritarian regime such as the present one, there has been no opportunity for intellectuals to establish a clearly defined identity. A state ruled by a privileged establishment closely tied to the USSR keeps a very tight rein on all high-ranking white-collar workers and does not offer any chance for independence. Rumania's situation is similar to Bulgaria's with the difference that contacts with the West are somewhat closer and the ruling establishment has gained popular appeal by preserving independent political philosophies not necessarily in step with the USSR's. Of the ECE countries, Rumania has had the highest share of foreign trade with the developed capitalist countries: 43 per cent of her imports and 31 per cent of her exports in 1977.

Before the Second World War, 80 per cent of Rumania's population was to be found in villages, but in the urban areas, already almost one-fourth of the labour force was employed in secondary industry. In 1950-1980 the rural population diminished to 55 per cent from 75 per cent and the secondary sector grew to 43 from 14 per cent of the labour force (the primary sector having decreased to 32 from 74 per cent). As in other ECE countries, in Rumania there is little difference in average income between blue- and white-collar workers, and the earnings of the former are based on bonus rates closely tied to productivity.

The social structure of Rumania changed rapidly following enforced industrialization (subsequently it will have the highest production growth in Eastern Europe) at the expense of mass consumption. From 1950 to 1977 the portion of agriculture and forestry in the national income decreased to 17 from around 40 per cent, and the share of industry increased from 43 to 62 per cent.[38] Accordingly, the number of wage and salary earners expanded in the period to 6.7 million from 2.1 million.

Inflation, poor management, ossified bureaucracy and the hesitancy of the Rumanian state to allocate enough money for social needs have led to difficult conditions. Significantly, Rumania is the only Comecon country in which the number of newly-built apartments did not grow, but diminished between 1960 and 1977 to 67 from 137 per 10,000 population. This annoying condition led to disturbances among miners in 1972, 1975 and 1977.[39]

In Hungary, the number of blue-collar workers had been on the increase already before the First World War: from 400,000 in 1880 to a million in 1910; 70 per cent of the industrial workers were skilled. From 1920 to 1946, the blue-collar class grew by two-and-a-half times. Still, the size of the rural proletariat was around four-fifths that of the blue-collar workers.[40] However, only during the 1950s, under conditions of forced socialist industrialization, have basic economic priorities been changed to any great degree. The share of industrial employment more than doubled between 1950 and 1977 (to 35 per cent of the labour force) while employment in agriculture and forestry diminished by half (to 21 per cent). Whereas the gross industrial production grew by 800 per cent, gross agricultural production merely doubled. With a threefold per capita consumption growth, it is clear how far Hungarian agriculture lags behind.

Though growth of blue-collar employment in industry was rapid during the 1950s, it slowed down later. The rural population in Hungary (21 per cent in 1970 were collective farmers and 3 per cent were private farmers or artisans) produced a considerable percentage of new blue-collar workers. In the early 1960s, 68 per cent of labourers, 60 per cent of semi-skilled workers and 36 per cent of skilled workers were of peasant stock.[41] Of the more highly-placed white-collar workers, no fewer than half are of blue-collar origin.

At the start of 1977, 70 per cent of Hungarian wage and salary earners were blue-collar workers; the unskilled among them constituted not much more than a fifth, and the remainder were evenly divided between skilled and semi-skilled. A steady educational upgrading in the lower strata of Hungarian society has been taking place. The relative number of people receiving secondary vocational education more than doubled from 1960 to 1977; the same happened with the relative number of students in higher education. However, in both cases these rates are far below the Soviet or even Polish rates.[42]

Of the Hungarian population aged 15 or more the percentage with at least secondary education grew in the period 1960-1975 to 18 from eight per cent.[43]

Hungary has a relatively large white-collar class (27 per cent of the labour force in 1970) that remains under the strong influence of the traditional intelligentsia; it is perhaps worth mentioning that part of this intelligentsia was leftist even before the seizure of power by the communists. The political establishment since the late 1950s has promoted a policy of consumerism. In the 1960s comparatively more money was devoted to mass consumption in Hungary than in Poland, Bulgaria or the USSR. Food consumption decreased relative to total consumption from 39 to 30 per cent between 1960 and 1977, while the buying of durable goods and other industrial products increased to 18 from 12 per cent.[44]

East Germany has gone far in implementing Soviet state socialism, as is evidenced by its social structure. Approximately 90 per cent of the labour force consists of blue- and white-collar workers employed in the nationalized economy, mostly in big enterprises, and 9 per cent are collective farmers. The share of private-sector employment sank below 2 per cent in the 1970s from 19 per cent in 1955. There is little differentiation of incomes among various economic branches (from -13 per cent to +10 per cent on the two sides of the average).[45] The seemingly permanent labour shortage has stimulated the mobilization of female workers and the promotion of mechanization in work to a greater extent than in other ECE countries. In the period 1950-1978 the share of women in the labour force advanced to 50 from 40 per cent.[46] Labour participation of both sexes does not vary in any great degree, but at the same time the birthrate went down from 16.5 per 10,000 in 1960 to 14 in 1978 and is the lowest in East Central Europe. Gross production in East German industry grew by more than 8 times between 1950 and 1978. The share of the labour force in industry increased to 38 from 29 per cent, while that in agriculture and forestry declined to 11 from 28 per cent.

The establishment understood the message provided by the blue-collar workers' mass strikes in 1953 and followed a policy of securing for people a fairly high standard of living, even if it was lower than in West Germany. The food segment in the average household budget decreased in the period 1960-1978 to 23 from 33 per cent (if drinks are included, then to 31 from 41 per cent) and the share of expenditure on culture and education almost doubled (from 9 to 15 per cent).[47] Equipment per 100 households improved between 1963 and 1978 as follows: automobiles, from 4 to 40; TV sets, from 42 to 95; refrigerators, from 16 to 92; washing machines, from 18 to 87.[48]

The decline to 77 from 82 per cent in the share of national income devoted to consumption in East Germany between 1960 and 1977 in the share of national income devoted to consumption in East Germany to 77 from 82 percent must necessarily have had some effect on the style of life. Still, the standard of living there has remained the highest in the whole of Comecon — perhaps, in exchange for obedience to the state.

The GDR relies on other Comecon countries for two-thirds of its foreign trade, and on the USSR for half of this. Therefore, economic difficulties faced by these countries must reflect on the East German economy. However, the departures of GDR citizens for foreign countries remained on the same level during the 1970s at around 13 million trips per year. The destinations were generally Czechoslovakia, Poland and Bulgaria.

East Germany is a bureaucratic state with a relatively efficient administrative apparatus that manipulates the rest of society to make it behave according to governmental expectations. This manipulation is much more effective than in other ECE countries and its success can be attributed to East German gains on world markets and the threat of direct Soviet interference, should there be any trouble. As long as these factors remain, the present power structure of the GDR is probably in no danger of changing.[49] However, transformations in Poland are evidently viewed as a threat.

In Czechoslovakia, the last 30 years have seen structural changes mainly with respect to farmers and their families. They have become collectivized and their number has declined between 1950 and 1976 to 9 per cent from 20 per cent. The position of the white-collar workers and their families also changed; their number rose to 28 per cent from 16 per cent (9 per cent in 1930). The percentage of blue-collar workers in the Czechoslovakian economy increased to only 61 from 56.

Industrial output grew threefold from 1960 to 1977, but agricultural production during that time increased by just 47 per cent. In order to secure a work force adequate to the task, it was necessary both to transfer a large number of people from the agricultural sector (particularly in Slovakia) and to mobilize women. From 1948 to 1976, the labour force grew by one-third and the share of women in the labour force rose to 46 per cent. In the Czech part of the country, employment among working-age women increased during the period 1950-1973 to 79 from 34 per cent.

In Czechoslovakia, just as in the GDR, there has been a trend towards the equalization of incomes and living conditions. More than one-and-a-half times the average income was characteristic in 1976 for 18 per cent of the households, but only four per cent received less than half the average.[50] There are only very small differences in the average income of blue- and white-collar workers and collective farmers; given a base of 100 for blue-collar workers, white-collar workers have wages set at 119 and collective farmers stand at 109. There is a pay range variation from +16 to -23 among the sectors. Under state socialism some categories of blue-collar workers in Czechoslovakia have lost in terms of relative income level (printers, for example), but other categories such as miners have gained. Relatively, the white-collar group has lost and blue-collar workers have gained income. Moreover, there has been a steady approach towards parity not only in incomes, but also in living standards. The portion of the average household budget taken up by food diminished between 1955 and 1976 to 29 per cent from 51 per cent in blue-collar and to 26 per cent from 49 per cent in white-collar households.[51]

The standard of living in Czechoslovakia is relatively high — similar to that in the GDR — and much higher than in the other Comecon countries. In the period 1960-1977, the use of household appliances increased; the number of washing machines went up to 118 from 54 per 100 households; refrigerator use soared to 86 from 11; radio sets to 178 from 89 and automobiles to 34 from 2.[52] The consumption of meat per person also increased in this period, from 57 Kg to 81 Kg per person per year, and is at the same level as in the GDR — 31 per cent higher than in Bulgaria and 42 per cent higher than in the USSR. A similar high level prevails in the consumption of eggs.[53] Housing conditions in Czechoslovakia fall below Western standards, but they are good compared to East European standards.

Upgrading in Czechoslovakian society is limited mainly to the educational system (the number of post-secondary students rose between 1960 and 1977 to 119 from 69 per 10,000 population), but it also affected political leverage. In the period 1948-1953 between 200,000 and 400,000 workers were transferred by the communist authorities to white-collar jobs. By the end of the 1960s many "unreliable" people were being demoted and replaced by candidates carefully gleaned by the authorities from the lower ranks.

Conclusion

Poland plays a vital role within the Soviet Bloc not only because of her geopolitically strategic position, but also thanks to her economic potential. One-tenth of Comecon's economic potential as well as one-tenth of its employment in industry are provided by Poland. Poland produces more than half of the Soviet Bloc's sulphur, a third of its ships and potatoes, and a quarter of its bituminous coal, cranes and sophisticated engines. In all these fields Poland's contribution is larger than its share of the Comecon population (10 per cent). Poland's exports within Comecon are approximately the same as her imports.

Poland, more than other ECE countries, is familiar with the good and bad sides of accelerated industrial growth and this fact is probably the major cause of repeated internal tension which was acutely manifest in the years 1956, 1970, 1976, 1980-81. It explains the eagerness of Poles to question "the system" or even to challenge it actively. In the past, as long as Poland remained a mostly peasant society, it was easy for the authorities to keep the population subservient. During the whole interwar period, the urban population was in the minority, but under state socialist industrialization and urbanization, the influence of the village, that is, the agricultural population, declined considerably. The decrease occurred simultaneously with a large, prolonged investment in heavy industry and construction at the expense of agriculture, mass consumption, housing and services. A third of Poland's working population is still involved in agriculture and forestry — and this amount is sizable compared with First-World statistics — but this is only about half the figure typical for interwar Poland. At the same time, almost two-fifths of the work force have jobs in industry and construction — much more than, for example, in Canada.

The slow growth of agriculture and services created more problems for Poland than for other Comecon countries, due mainly to the exposure of Poles to the higher standard of living found in the West. The centralized, highly bureaucratized Soviet-style Polish economy retarded a modernization effort based on Western loans during the 1970s. On account of this failure, for which the Polish Communist Party and state establishment publicly took responsibility, the political opposition managed to broaden its appeal; as well, the free union organizers were able, as a result of the government's gaffe, to promote their cause very successfully at least until December 1981.

Because most wage and salary workers joined the new independent trade unions, the ruling establishment in Poland became formally bound by an agreement between the government and the *Solidarity* trade union federation on August 31, 1980, to recognize free unionization and to implement several important concessions. With the ruling Communist Party (PUWP) in internal turmoil, and public officials losing much of their power, present-day Poland had become *de facto* a pluralist society for at least 15 months. However, the pluralist structure was only partly developed and liberalization of the economy still was far from being implemented. Free unions, as well as the establishment — the latter being the only legitimate power in Poland officially recognized by the USSR — confronted each other regularly in a series of power contests. There was always a threat of direct Soviet intervention. The Polish economy suffered not only because of shortages, but also from work stoppages. There was considerable mistrust between the ruling élite in Poland and the new "grass-roots" leaders who are gaining wide popular support. The situation has dramatically changed with the introduction of martial law in December 1981.

What are the chances of the "Polish disorder" spreading to neighbouring countries and undermining the Soviet-style status quo? Inasmuch as events in Poland occur mainly as consequences of systemic disruption in progress, the internal conflicts can be expected to show up sooner or later in other ECE countries — especially where food shortages, price increases and government indolence abound. Of course, arbitrary rule, as practised all over eastern Europe, might temporarily postpone the public manifestation of internal tensions. However, negative conditions similar to those now found in Poland are latent in all East Central European countries. The Soviet System is loaded with tension because, while it supposedly welcomes fulfilment of human aspirations, it really presents only illusions of justice, well-being, growth in mass education, sociocultural upgrading and egalitarian ideology; at the same time it displays a strong conservative bias in economic and administrative fields.

In Poland, many present-day reformers hope that by making nationalized enterprises more autonomous and by encouraging shop-floor self-government by workers, it will be possible in the long run to encourage collective entrepreneurship, improve productivity and inspire people with enthusiasm. The Polish government wants the new trade unions to take joint responsibility for improvement in efficiency. The union leadership has had good reasons to avoid such a far-reaching commitment, claiming unions should not involve themselves in tasks that might divert them from the main purpose — to defend the basic occupational interests of their members.

It is likely that in the democratized model of socialism currently advocated by oppositionists in Poland (involving autonomous work groups and other forms of management participation) the apolitical unions will play a vital role apart from the state. The Poles might represent an attractive model for other ECE countries wanting to attempt democratization under favourable circumstances. Such a development would mean the gradual collapse of Soviet-style state socialism in East Central European countries, an eventuality that would have a profound effect on relationships between these countries and the USSR.

This is probably the main reason why an intervention "by proxy" took place at the end of 1981, precisely in order to stop the growth of a democratic grass-roots movement.

FOOTNOTES

[1]This is a completely revised version of the study as read at the CEESAC Conference in March 1980. Another version was presented at the 1981 annual meeting of the Pacific Sociological Association in Portland, Oregon.

[2]Poles are very mobile within as well as outside their country. Domestic tourist traffic grew by five times from 1960 to 1978 and travel outside Poland increased 1,300 per cent during the 1970s alone. There are many Poles outside Poland, and many emigrants still maintain contacts with the motherland. It is significant that the development of political opposition in Poland was not only welcomed, but also financially and morally supported by many emigrants. Polish political lobbying outside Poland has made some impact on public opinion in the West. An indication of this effect can be seen in the setting up of the North American Study Centre for Polish Affairs, in Ann Arbor, Michigan.

[3]At the end of the 1970s, only one in five newlywed couples had a new dwelling to themselves; 600,000 young couples were still waiting for dwellings. Seventy per cent had to be materially assisted by their parents.

[4]Part-time work even among women is exceptional. In 1979 only 4 per cent of all employed women worked part-time; the figure for women in commerce was 7 per cent.

[5]Changes in the Polish population structure have also to be taken into consideration. From 1950 to 1977, the share of children (less than 14 years old) in the population diminished to 24 from 30 percent, equalling the average for Europe and falling just short of the North American average. The percentage of people 60 and over grew to 13 from 5. Life expectancy increased from 60 to 67 years for males and from 65 to 75 years for females. It is the same length of age as in First World countries, and somewhat higher than that in most Comecon nations. Infant mortality decreased to one-fifth its former size, but on the other hand, the average number of children has stabilized at a maximum of three per family.

[6]From 1960 to 1979 the number of graduates grew by four times at the secondary level and the figure was the same for post-secondary graduates.

[7]Among only women, to 26 per cent from 11 per cent.

[8]Among women, to 15 per cent from 47 per cent.

[9]*Wiadomosci Statystyczne*, 9 (1979), 10.

[10]In 1980, 2,000 zlotys. Only 2.5 per cent of wage and salary earners had such an income, but 37 per cent of pensioners received less than this amount (60 per cent less than 2,500 zlotys).

[11]In the late 1970s, workers who had only elementary or even less education accounted for 48 per cent of the Polish labour force as a whole (in industry, the figure stood at 80 per cent; in construction and trade, 94 per cent; and in collective farming, 97 per cent), while those with at least secondary education made up 31 per cent of the total work force (industry, 9 per cent; trade and construction, each 3 per cent; agriculture, 2 per cent).

[12]Jan Szczepanski, et al., *Raport o stanie oswiaty w Polsce* (Warsaw, 1973).

[13]Micheline de Felice and G. Mink, *Egalité et inégalités en Europe de l'Est* (Paris, 1979), 45.

[14]Georges Mink, *Structures sociales en Europe de l'est: Notes et études documentaires.* 2. *Transformation de la classe ouvrière* (Paris, 1979), 106.

[15]*Poland. Statistical Data* (Warsaw, 1979), 39.

[16]Leszek Moczulski, *"Rewolucja bez rewolucji,"* *Droga* (1979), 7. Moczulski suggested that Poles would respond with a general strike to any attempt by authorities to start mass suppression. The events of December 1981 have shown that he was wrong. The opposition's tactics consisted in the gradual development of a counterstructure of groups and institutions to duplicate official structures, but having much more appeal for the general public through their greater authenticity. However, opposition has also been retarded by a general feeling of despair and apathy. Some opposition leaders — J. Kuron, for instance — wanted to find some accommodation with government authorities in order to avoid a bout of massive violence that might be disastrous for Poland.

[17]Maria Hirszowicz, *The Bureaucratic Leviathan: A Study in Sociology of Communism (Oxford, 1980).*

[18]*Kraje RWPG* (Warsaw, 1980), 10.

[19]*Rocznik Statystyczny* (Warsaw, 1980), 566.

[20]Alexander Matejko, "The Obsolescence of Bureaucracy," *Relations Industrielles*, 35 (1980).

[21]Mink, 1979, 15.

[22]Hirszowicz, *passim.*

[23]Miklos Haraszti, *Salaire aux pièces: ouvrier dans un pays de l'Est* (Paris, 1976).

[24]Z. Bauman, "La classe ouvrière dans les pays de l'Est: Tendance du developpement et hypothèses," in *Structures sociales en Europe de l'Est*, ed. by G. Mink, 19-31; 24.

[25]One-third of all employed persons are women in both these countries.

[26]Mink, 16.

[27]Bauman (1979), 24-25.

[28]Ibid., 27.

[29]Matejko, *passim.*

[30]Mink, 53.

[31]Ibid., 70.

[32]Ibid., 71.

[33]Ibid., 68.

[34]Ibid., 50-51.

[35]G. M. Foster, *Traditional Societies and Technological Change* (New York, 1973).

[36]A. Matejko, *Social Change and Stratification in Eastern Europe* (New York, 1974); A. Gella, "The Life and Death of the Old Polish Intelligentsia," *Slavic Review*, 30 (1971) 30,

1-27 and *idem*, ed. *The Intelligentsia and the Intellectuals: Theory, Method and Case Study* (Beverly Hills, California, 1976).

[37]Mink, 45-48.

[38]*Statistisches Jahrbuch der DDR* (Berlin, 1979), 4.

[39]Mink, 155-57.

[40]Ibid., 63.

[41]Ibid., 65.

[42]*Statistical Yearbook* (Budapest, 1979), 412, 414.

[43]*Statistical Yearbook* (Budapest, 1977), 49.

[44]Ibid., 48.

[45]*Statistisches Jahrbuch der DDR* (Berlin, 1979), 106.

[46]Ibid., 91.

[47]Ibid., 271.

[48]Ibid., 276.

[49]Mink, 136-37.

[50]*Cisla pro kazdeho 1978* (Prague: SNTL, 1978), 162.

[51]Mink, 174.

[52]*Cisla*, 275.

[53]*Statistical Yearbook of Member States of the Council of Mutual Economic Assistance* (Moscow, 1979), 50.

74

THE STUDY OF CONTEMPORARY RUSSIAN LITERATURE IN CANADIAN UNIVERSITIES: AN ASSESSMENT

Teresa Polowy,[1]
University of British Columbia

Two questions must be posed: How much do we Canadians know about Soviet Literature? How much will we *allow* ourselves to know about this literature? The former question will be answered within the course of this presentation and indeed forms the basis of the discussion. The latter question flows from my assessment and must be left to the end in order to be given objective, thoughtful treatment.

Most reasonably well-read individuals are familiar with the writers who are commonly called the "masters" of Russian literature — Pushkin, Tolstoy, Dostoevsky, Chekhov; perhaps Gorky, Sholokhov, and Solzhenitsyn are also known to them. The titles of the major works by each of these authors are easily recalled and discussions centred around them are diverse.

The lack of knowledge about important writers within the Soviet Union is hardly the fault of the layman, who is at the mercy of the popular media — newspapers, magazines, and collections of translated works — which promote the stereotype of an impoverished, dreary, primitive, and utilitarian literature in the USSR. There is perpetuated a strong image of Soviet literature as little more than politics.

It is a common complaint of critics and scholars in North America, that the Soviet Union evaluates its literature by criteria which are extra-aesthetic, namely by its social and political content. It is my contention that our books as well as scholarly articles place their emphasis on soviet literary politics, but relatively little attention is paid to the analysis of the literature per se. Few attempts at a sound analysis of individual works and trends in Soviet fiction have been made.

For the purposes of the present discussion, the period toward which most of my comments shall be directed will be from 1956 to the present. It appears from the information I collected that a strong political bias governs the perception of Russian literature written since the mid-1950s and that the existence of such a bias is very marked in the content of courses in Russian literature offered at our universities. Thus, my remarks will be concentrated on the assessment of the present state of post-Stalin Russian literature within the undergraduate courses in Russian and Slavic Studies departments at Canadian universities. I will address basic, yet ultimately revealing, questions concerning the course content of offerings in modern Russian literature, describe the literature selected for study, and examine reasons as to why certain choices are made while others are not. Based on this information it will be safe to make some assumptions regarding the way students are trained attitudinally and intellectually to approach contemporary Russian works, as compared with how they approach the literature of the 19th and early 20th centuries, particularly the rich writings of the 1920s and 1930s. Finally and most vitally, in such an examination lie deep-seated implications concerning the apparent declining interest in Russian language and literature in many of the departments throughout the country.

The data for my assessment were collected by requesting outlines, descriptions, and reading lists for courses covering the area of 20th century Russian literature at fifteen Canadian universities. I chose to concentrate on courses in Russian prose rather than poetry, mainly because the scope and comprehensiveness of poetry courses varied among universities even more than those in prose genres. With the information gathered, it was possible to isolate for deeper analysis certain facets of the study of Russian literature which were relevant to the purpose of my investigation. Firstly, it was possible to get a sense of the type of exposure to Russian literature that students received prior to a study of the most contemporary literature. Second, the bias of courses offered in contemporary literature was evident from the works selected for the reading lists. Third, the general bias and scope of the various programmes in Russian literature offered at Canadian universities was outlined in course offerings and reading lists. I would like to deal with each of these three areas individually.

It may be said that the exposure of students to Russian literature written before the post-Stalin (1953) period is remarkably consistent among various departments. Naturally, variations in materials encompassed result from objective considerations: does the course run for one or two semesters? Does it focus on a particular genre, be it the novel, the short story, the anecdote, etc.? Is the format of the course lecture, seminar, or discussion? Are the works read in translation or in the original?

I found courses dealing with pre-1956 Russian literature are basically wide in scope and provide the student with the opportunity to be exposed to a reasonably balanced fare of modern Russian writing. One feature, however, is outstanding. Such courses are most frequently given titles which might lead a student to believe that the content is more comprehensive than in fact it turns out to be. Thus, many departments offer courses entitled '20th Century Russian Literature,' 'Russian Writing of the 20th Century,' 'Studies in 20th Century Russian Literature,' and 'Russian Literature after the Revolution,' embracing authors from Chekhov to Solzhenitsyn. These courses share a common reading list to a certain point, for present on all are at least one work each of pre-revolutionary and war-time writers. Solzhenitsyn is consistently selected as representative of contemporary Russian literature. As variants of the possible works to be studied, some courses offer selections from the poetry of Akhmatova and Mandel'shtam and from the prose works of Belyi, Pilniak, Platonov, Paustovskii and A. N. Tolstoy. The socialist realist construction literature, which falls within the scope of such courses may often be presented in such a way as to diminish its literary significance, and usually, the student is given the option of reading one out of four or five works. Within these courses the only writers belonging to the post-Stalin period are, besides Solzhenitsyn, Andrei Siniavskii and the poet Evgenii Evtushenko.

Thus, it is evident that despite the appellation, most Russian departments utilize courses in 20th century literature to emphasize the innovative works of the 1920s and 1930s but downplay or ignore the writings of subsequent decades. The generally practised approach of overviewing 20th century prose and the extremely small representation of post-war literature illustrates the existence of a possible bias against new Soviet literature. A student who, after completing such a course, plans to continue his reading in Russian literature independently, will have acquired no information as to the best writings of the present day.

It is the examination of the content of courses dealing with Soviet literature after the mid-1950s that offers the strongest support for the contention that the treatment of Soviet literature in Russian departments needs to be re-examined. Very few departments offer a comprehensive course with a representative selection of works. The most commonly discussed authors of recent Soviet literature courses include Pasternak, Solzhenitsyn, Siniavskii, Voinovich, Tvardovskii, Paustovskii, Erenburg, Kazakov, Evtushenko, Sholokhov and Akhmadulina. The two authors always examined in the greatest detail are Pasternak and Solzhenitsyn.

The selection of actual reading material for courses in contemporary Soviet literature varies, but it does correspond to the broader outlines of the course and the bias found within it. For example, if the course covers a two-decade period with a view to representing various authors and trends, then the reading material is fairly comprehensive. If however, the course focuses on the works of the late 1950s and early 1960s, the material is narrower and the selection almost predictable.

At times, judging by the choices made, courses do not present the most mature, developed fiction, but rather select those works which can be interpreted to confirm prejudices of various types. Common in content selection is a preference for works with "oppositionist leanings." It seems that too often

78

the selection of reading material is influenced by political considerations. For example, the Siniavskii work *The Trial Begins* and the Daniel story "This is Moscow Speaking" are very often included on the reading lists. That works selected by these criteria may not be the best for literary analysis appears to be irrelevant in many courses. But in reading such works, many students will be persuaded to perceive Soviet literature as political documentation.

Pasternak's *Dr. Zhivago* and Solzhenitsyn's *One Day in the Life of Ivan Denisovich* are being studied faithfully in each course. Preference seems to be afforded those works which deviate from the norms of Socialist Realism as the West perceives them to be at a given time. Because of this selection criterion, many interesting authors are omitted from study due to the focus on "discordant" voices and themes in Soviet literature.

More fruitful is the approach taken by some departments to move through trends and literary schools in a roughly chronological order. Courses might, for example, deal with the literary schools of Symbolism, Imagism, Futurism, the doctrine of Socialist Realism, and several of the trends in prose which have emerged, such as an interest in science-fiction, in utopian and anti-utopian prose, in the psychological novel, etc.

Secondary reading material used to supplement and augment the original literature is also often strongly biased toward the politics of literature. Since 1956, numerous books have been published on this subject, not to mention countless articles discussing similar themes. Texts commonly used in literature courses on 20th-century and Soviet literature bear titles which signal the bias of the content. These include M. Slonim's *Soviet Russian Literature: Writers and Problems* (1977) as well as the outdated *Soviet Russian Literature: From Chekhov to the Present* (1954) by the same author. G. Struve's *Russian Literature under Lenin and Stalin* (1971) is often recommended, as is E. Brown's *Russian Literature Since the Revolution*. It is also interesting to take note of the Soviet sources recommended, the most recent of which was published twenty years ago.

What lies behind the refusal of many of our Russian departments to expand their contemporary literature courses to include a comprehensive study of Soviet Russian writers of the 1970s? Perhaps a large factor is that these works, with their lyrical, psychological, and ethical depictions of life, cannot be related directly to the political scene, and thus do not fit into the prevalent bias. Another consideration may be that an acknowledgement would be required as to some of the positive changes which have occurred in the demands of Socialist Realism since its introduction in 1934. Statements such as the following from a 1975 article in *Literaturnaia gazeta* are representative of the changes in doctrine:

... socialist realism does not in the least require that the author should state his position in a declarative form. In a political poem or novel depicting sharp class conflicts, the blunt expression of the author's view is natural and necessary; but in works such as love lyrics, a psychological tale, or in literature describing the so-called "byt," such forms may be out of place.[2]

In an article by T. Motyleva in *Voprosy literatury*, the suggestion is made that:

The meaning of heroic characters ... is exceedingly important. Art, however, can influence the minds and hearts of people not only with the help of positive but also with the help of negative examples, thus heightening the ethical vigilance of the reader to the types and views alien to socialism.[3]

One Russian department in particular is direct in its bias: it offers an entire course entitled "The Literature of Contemporary Soviet Dissent" which examines the movement from World War II to the present and dwells on the movements of dissent amongst the various nationalities and their concerns.

From the information which I gathered, there would appear to be a consensus amongst some Russian/Slavic departments in our universities that there should be a cautious approach to the literature being produced in the Soviet Union today. Recent articles in journals of Eastern European studies demonstrate that the tendency toward extra-aesthetic criticism of Soviet literature is prevalent, especially in regard to discussions of theme and characterization. For example, an article on Iurii Kazakov's theme of isolation in his stories interprets this as grounds to classify them as works of escape.

Do Kazakov's characters strive for isolation because it is the *sine qua non* for certain positive values ordinarily unworthy of serious consideration in Soviet literature, or is the theme of isolation merely an attempt to escape from the official problems of Soviet literature and life?[4]

The heroes of Iurii Trifonov are assessed in relation to the reforms which have taken place in the Soviet system and society since the Twentieth Party Congress in 1956: "Trifonov has turned to a kind of literature in which there are few positive heroes, but in which there is a hidden call to self-perfection. This is a call for Soviet man to preserve his human face and dignity."[5] Even critical comments on stylistic devices and particularly on lyricism, which is one of the notable features of much contemporary literature, frequently deprive them of their literary dimension and interpret them as devices for social protest.

By omitting works of excellent prose writers from the content of courses on Soviet Russian literature, students may be deprived of an opportunity to understand some of the important trends and attitudes prevalent in the Soviet

Union today – phenomena and concerns which form the basis of much of the current literature. While some of these are typically Soviet and even typically Russian concerns, many others are universal in nature. For example, A. Bitov concentrates on levels of human consciousness in his prose, V. Aksenov on the possibilities of fantasy and the grotesque in the depiction of present reality, V. Shukshin on man's moral searchings and requirements in technological and highly atomized societies, and V. Rasputin on the portrayal of strong-willed men and women acting in everyday situations. Given the opportunity to read and discuss such works objectively and intelligently, the student will get a sense of the character of contemporary Soviet man and of his desires, needs, concerns, ethics and values. In the course of such reading, he will also come to realize that the best traditions of Russian literature — of Dostoevsky, Gogol, Chekhov, Tolstoy — have continued to evolve and now exist in the content, style, and form of many of the best contemporary Russian writers.

There is much positive work to be accomplished in the field of Russian literature, but this can only occur if a sincere re-evaluation of ideological presuppositions and political prejudices is undertaken by Western scholars and critics.

Currently, it is a fact that Russian programmes in Canada are experiencing a constant decline in enrollment. Some claim that this is the natural result of the public unpopularity of the Soviet Union. If the textbooks and reading lists could be updated and the material taught with a greater attempt at objectivity, Canadian students would be more likely to find relevance in the need to study the language, history, culture, and literature of one of the world's major countries.

Students must be presented with options and be permitted to make their judgments and choices through comparison and contrast, using the kinds of scholarly tools and training that a university should instill in its students. If this environment and atmosphere for learning is introduced and pursued, it will to a great extent revitalize and enrich the entire area of Slavic Studies.

FOOTNOTES

[1]Ms. Polowy is a Ph.D. candidate in Philology at the University of British Columbia.

[2]Quoted in N. N. Shneidman, "Soviet Prose in the 1970's: Evolution or Stagnation?" *Canadian Slavonic Papers*, XX (1978), 64.

[3]T. Motyleva, "Vsmatrivaias' v novoe," *Voprosy literatury*, (1972), 58.

[4]Quoted in P. Meyer, "Hoisted by the Socialist-Realist Petard: American Interpretations of Soviet Literature," *Russian Literature Triquarterly*, (1971), 422.

[5]N. N. Shneidman, "Iurii Trifonov and the Ethics of Contemporary Soviet City Life," *Canadian Slavonic Papers*, XIX (1977), 349.

82

ATTITUDES TO LANGUAGE AMONG GERMAN/SLAVIC BILINGUALS IN SOUTHERN AUSTRIA

Tom Priestly,
University of Alberta

"Language is not merely a *carrier* of content, whether latent or manifest. Language itself *is* content, a referent for loyalties or animosities, an indicator of social statuses and personal relationships, a marker of situations and topics as well as of the societal goals and large-scale value-laden arenas of interaction that typify every speech-community" [J. A. Fishman, *Sociolinguistics* (Rowley, Mass., 1970)].

Introduction*

Along the southern edge of Austria, where the Carnic Alps and the Karavanken delimit the present-day border with Italy and Yugoslavia, lives a numerically small but culturally vigorous Slavic minority. This minority numbers some 40,000 (perhaps much more[1]) and is in a number of respects subject to certain pressures from the German-speaking majority in the province (Carinthia, Kärnten). My paper will not discuss these pressures, but a modest description — one which may be minimally acceptable to extremes of opinion, in a province where opinions often do run to extremes — is in order. Briefly, then: the number of native speakers of Slavic dialects, which are variously called Slovene, Windisch, or (the local term) *swej*, has noticeably decreased during the 20th century, and the number of native German-speakers has correspondingly increased; in most parts of Carinthia it is now economically and socially advantageous to speak German in public, whereas to be known as a speaker of a Slavic dialect is generally (but not universally) regarded as a sign of a status that is, in some respects at least, inferior.[2] My own interest in *swej* dates back to 1973, when I first visited Southern Carinthia, but I did not begin to come to grips with the linguistic problems until I began field-work in one of the Carinthian villages in the Fall of 1978. My main aim was to learn and analyze the dialect spoken in that particular village; but any linguistic analysis in a multilingual community is bound to be incomplete unless certain aspects of that multilingualism are properly assessed, and since Southern Carinthia is

* My research in Carinthia was made possible by a grant from the Social Sciences and Humanities Research Council of Canada, to whom I express my gratitude.

83

essentially quadrilingual, I could not ignore these aspects. The four language-varieties involved are the following: *Dialect Slovene*, or *swej̃*, in its various dialectal forms from Hermagor (Šmohor) in the West to Bleiburg (Pliberk) in the East; *Standard Slovene* which is spoken over the border to the south (3 Km. from the village where I stayed), can be heard on the radio and is used in some of the churches and taught in a few of the schools; the German dialect, *Kärntnerisch*, spoken by most Carinthians whose native language is not *swej*; and *Standard German*, the official language of the province (these will be abbreviated henceforward as, respectively, DS, SS, DG and SG).[3]

One problem — not the subject of this paper — was the assessment of the extent to which each speaker knew and used each of these four language-varieties. A second problem — the one to be discussed here — concerns the ATTITUDES of the various speakers to each of the four; the influence of each language-variety upon each speaker's way of speaking, and ultimately on the village dialect as a whole and the Carinthian dialects as a greater whole, must depend to a considerable extent upon these attitudes. It is clear (to put the matter simply) that a language or dialect that enjoys any kind of prestige will normally have a greater influence than one that does not: one has only to look at the mutual influence of Russian and Ukrainian in Soviet Ukraine, or the mutual influence of French and English in Québec, to see that, although in each case a two-way street is involved, the traffic is much heavier in the direction of the language-variety carrying lesser status.

The "Matched Guise Technique"

When I was in Carinthia in 1978-79, I decided to attempt an experiment which is designed to reveal speakers' attitudes to different language-varieties; namely, the experiment known as the "matched guise technique." It is now exactly twenty years since the first experiment of this nature was reported in the technical literature;[4] and it is now generally accepted that this kind of experiment is "particularly valuable as a measure of group biases in evaluative reactions."[5] The experiment, which involves a little harmless trickery, is as follows.

Subjects listen to a number of tape-recorded voices reading the same text in two or more dialects or languages, and are asked to evaluate the personality characteristics of each of the speakers. They are reminded of the common tendency to try to assess personality from voice cues alone, e.g., over the telephone. They are told that each voice belongs to a different speaker, and herein lies the catch; for in fact they hear each speaker reading the text in two or more of the language-varieties involved. If, for example, two dialects are involved, they may hear what they are told are ten different speakers when in fact there are only five different voices. If, then (as normally happens) they judge the personality of any one speaker differently depending on the dialect or language used, the theory is that these differences in their assessment reveal true attitudes towards the dialects or languages themselves. Under the conditions of this experiment, there is none (or at least a minimum) of the "pain [of being] caught in the influence-spheres of two or more ethnic groups and [of being] tested [with the demand] that you show your true colors."[6]

The experiment has been much refined over the twenty years of its existence and has been tried in multilingual and multidialectal situations in Canada, the U.S.A., Britain, the Philippines, Peru and Egypt. To the best of my knowledge, it has not been tried out before in continental Europe (see however DISCUSSION below). It has also only seldom been attempted in what amounts to a quadrilingual community.[7]

Text

First, I had to choose a text which would be NEUTRAL; i.e., the choice of text should not entail any particular association with any one of the four language-varieties (DS, SS, DG, SG) rather than any other. A text with political overtones, for example, was definitely ruled out, given the often tense linguistic politics in Carinthia. An ecclesiastical text (such as a prayer) might be associated with the language-variety used by the subjects in Church or in private prayer. A weather forecast or a news article would belong to a standard language rather than to one of the two dialects. A casual conversation would be more 'at home' in a dialect rather than one of the two standards. A text with technical or predominantly modern vocabulary would have a number of borrowings from German in the DS texts, but conversely very few or no Slavic borrowings in the DG text. Further, the text had to be short — of about two minutes' duration.

Eventually, with the assistance of Dr. Erih Prunč of the University of Graz, a folk text was selected and translated from its original SS into the other three language varieties. The folk-tale (which is provided in the appendix to this paper) does admittedly have religious features, but clearly belongs outside the normal ecclesiastical setting, and could with equal likelihood be either German or Slavic in origin and occur either in an orally-transmitted dialectal form or in a written standardized language, e.g., in a printed collection of folk-tales.[8]

Next, I recorded a selection of speakers who were fluent in all four language-varieties. Here two drawbacks must be reported. First, (with the exception of the odd linguist) only native speakers of DS are in any way fluent therein; and very few native DS-speakers are at the same time really fluent in DG — by the nature of things in Carinthia, many people whose first language is DS learn SG (and in many cases SS) actively and DG only passively. Further, they are most unlikely to see many texts written in DG (with the exception of short humorous paragraphs in newspapers). They are therefore naturally hesitant when they try to read it. I gave the speakers time, before recording them, to rehearse each text in turn, and extra time for the DG text. In the event, judgments with respect to the *clarity* with which the DG texts were read (see GRAPH I below) are not markedly out of line with expectations or with the pattern of other judgments.

The second drawback is the following. The speakers who were competent and fluent enough for my purposes came from different parts of Southern Carinthia, and thus spoke different DS varieties: the dialects of Slovene being notorious for local variability. It is possible these regional differences have a bearing upon the individual assessments. It has been shown[9] that degrees of accentedness affect judgments in these experiments; and any one dialect speaker will probably have different perceptions about the 'accentedness' of other dialects in Carinthia. Under the circumstances of my experiment, however, this disadvantage was however unavoidable.

From my recordings, I finally selected three male and three female speakers, all students in their late teens or early twenties from Klagenfurt and Graz Universities. This choice resulted in my avoiding an appreciable age-range among my speakers, and thus avoiding inter-speaking judgment differences which could result from age-differences. The choice of subjects (see below) in fact meant that there was very little age-distinction between speakers and listeners; future experiments will have to involve the question of age differences.[10]

I then re-recorded my 24 recordings (six speakers, four texts each) in such an order that no one speaker is heard speaking two different language-varieties except with a minimum of three intervening other voices. Male and female voices are ordered randomly; and so were the different language-varieties.

Questionnaire

I prepared a questionnaire booklet for the subjects to fill out. The first page had questions about the individual's personal details, language knowledge and language use. The remainder of the booklet consisted of sets of five-point rating scales for assessment of personality characteristics. Each set had six different scales; each was labelled in SS, since I was dealing with Slovene-speaking subjects; here again, there is a possibility that the actual choice of language for the labels could affect the results — ideally, another run should be made with SG labels. Questionnaire samples are appended.

Following comments in the available literature (and in particular Elyan, Smith, Giles and Bourhis),[11] I chose two scales which come under the general heading of PERSONAL COMPETENCE, namely, *intelligent/unintelligent* and *self-confident/unself-confident*; two scales which relate to SOCIAL ATTRIBUTES, namely *likable/unlikable* and *sociable/unsociable*; and one scale on the PERSONAL INTEGRITY dimension, *reliable/unreliable*. As a sixth scale, I included *clear/unclear*, a trait relating to COMMUNICATIVE COMPETENCE.[12] This latter scale was included because it was clear from the literature that the clarity of the spoken text affects attitudinal judgments; by including this question, I hoped (and my hope was confirmed in practice) to be able to make statistical allowances for this interfering factor.

Subjects

I originally intended to administer this text in the Carinthian village in which I was living. After trying it out on three villagers, I found however that it was simply too long for this purpose. I had also arranged to visit the Slovene Gymnasium in Klagenfurt, and decided to restrict my experiment — in this preliminary form, at least — to a class in that school.[13]

The class chosen for the purpose was a senior class with average age of 17 years 1 month. There were 18 pupils all told, 10 girls and 8 boys. I myself conducted the experiment. The explanations were in SS, since it was a specifically Slovene school.

To make a break in the possibly tedious business of marking 144 scales, I arranged a pause after the twelfth recording, which the students used for filling out the first page of the questionnaire. At the end of the experiment, I explained the real purpose behind it. The students generally evinced surprise; this meant of course that they had not suspected the 'trick' behind the whole procedure. A few, however, said that they had at least suspected they were hearing the same voice more than once. To this extent, the results may be suspect, although it is hard to judge whether, or in which way, or to what extent this realization would substantially affect the individual assessments.

The Slovene High School (*Slowenische Gymnasium, Slovenska gimnazija*) in Klagenfurt is unique in Carinthia. It was officially opened in 1957 (following the enabling legislation of the *Staatsvertrag* of 1955) but did not move into its own school building until 1975. "This school provides academic university preparatory education for ethnically conscious Slovene students, many of whom continue their studies and become doctors, lawyers, teachers and university professors, thereby providing the nucleus for an activist young intelligentsia."[14] Many students come from Carinthian villages which cannot easily be reached by daily public transport, and therefore they board in Klagenfurt and visit their homes at weekends; the sacrifice involved — which may be both monetary and familial — is evidence of a high degree of ethnic consciousness among the parents, at least. Even if only few become ethnically 'activist,' the students — and especially the oldest class — can be expected to have a degree of ethnic pride not typical of Carinthian Slovene high school students in general.

Analysis[15]

Assessments were tabulated and two analyses made. First, an analysis of variance of the subjects' ratings was computed for each of the six rating scales. Second, because of the probable interference upon other judgments from attitudes concerning clarity (see below), the same data were subjected to an analysis of co-variance with respect to the *clarity* scale. In the graphs presented below, the means for each scale have been standardized with respect to individual error terms with the visual effect that the relative heights of mean scores on the different graphs are directly comparable. The graphs show relative mean assessment values on either side of zero in each instance.

Results

The findings for each scale appear in Table I with F values and associated significance levels as indicated.

There were no significant evaluative differences with respect to either the sex of the listener (8 males, 10 females) or the sex of the speaker (3 males, 3 females). The result was a disappointment: preliminary hypotheses had been made, for example, concerning the ratings of male and female dialect varieties on the reliability and/or sociability scales.[16]

CLARITY: It appears generally accepted that "speakers who are hesitant or whose speech contains a relatively high number of speech non-fluencies . . . are perceived less favourably, particularly with regard to competence, than more fluent speakers."[17] The unadjusted results must therefore first of all be contrasted with the results after adjustment with respect to *clarity* by the co-variance analysis. The differences between each set of figures suggest that there is indeed a considerable (but varying) amount of interference of this nature, and that the adjusted levels of significance are the more acceptable.

An additional argument is involved. Inspection of the individual speaker means on the clarity scale shows that one of the female speakers was very aberrant; while each of the other five speakers was rated as *'clearer'* when speaking a standard language (viz., SS and SG) than when speaking a dialect (DS and DG), this one speaker was rated *'least clear'* when speaking one of the two standard languages, SG. One answer to this problem would be to expunge this one speaker's data from the whole analysis; but not only would this mean losing one-sixth of the total data, which are not extensive to begin with; it would also involve getting rid of a real voice which could well be representative

TABLE I.
F VALUES AND ASSOCIATED SIGNIFICANCE LEVELS FOR EACH SCALE

Scale	Unadjusted		Adjusted w.r.t. CLARITY	
	Language X Speaker	Language	Language X Speaker	Language
INTELLIGENT	2.815**	14.646**	1.63	7.84**
SELF-CONFIDENT	3.627**	4.426**	2.58**	2.65
RELIABLE	1.870*	2.915*	1.44	1.71
LIKABLE	1.894*	4.442**	1.08	4.23**
SOCIABLE	0.730	4.738**	0.80	3.69*
CLEAR	3.560	12.314*	—	—
	**p<.01	*p<.05		

of a section of the Slavic Carinthian population. Examination of the individual speaker means with respect to the other five scales shows no comparable aberrance, however; and the adjustment for clarity is proposed as a method of obviating this particular speaker's individualistic treatment of the SG text.

The chance remains that an over-compensation may be achieved by making this adjustment; i.e., that factors involved in the five judgments which are of greatest interest may have been eradicated from the analysis along with the assessments of clarity. One might suppose, in particular, that assessments of a speaker's *self-confidence* may be based, inter alia, upon some of the characteristics of clarity of delivery. Further, it may well be that standard languages are normally *expected* to be clearer because they are vaunted as official, ideal norms. Relative mean assessments of clarity are presented in GRAPH I; do the higher assessments for SG and SS reflect actual fluency, or linguistic expectations, or other attitudes?

In what follows, the adjusted levels of significance from Table I are assumed to be more representative, if only because they suggest a greater rigour as far as *language-effect* results are concerned; and indeed, while the speaker x language effects are of little interest, it is the *language effects* — i.e., the statistical importance of the various attitudes to the different languages regardless of speaker — that are particularly interesting.

RELIABILITY as a scale does not appear to be of significance in this study; even without the adjustment for clarity, the level of confidence (.044) is unacceptable with such a small number of subjects.

SELF-CONFIDENCE deserves little attention, for the same reason; after adjustment, the level of confidence is unacceptable (.06). The unadjusted level (.008) is, however, suggestive, and for this reason the relative unadjusted assessment means are presented in GRAPH II. Note here that SS receives a much higher, and DS a rather lower, evaluation than either of the two varieties of German.

After adjustment for *clarity*, the other scales all have levels of confidence that are respectively close to, at and beyond the .01 level. It is on these three scales (see GRAPHS III, IV, V) that the main conclusions are based.

Inspection of the three graphs shows that each of the three scales evoked different mean responses from the subjects. The ratings for INTELLIGENCE show that Slovene-speakers were rated higher than German-speakers, and Standard-language-speakers higher than speakers of dialects. The assessments for LIKABILITY and SOCIABILITY, on the other hand, clearly show speakers of dialects being assessed more favourably than speakers of the corresponding standard language. On the LIKABILITY scale, the two Slovene varieties are a little higher than the two German ones; on the SOCIABILITY scale, DG is upgraded to the extent that it is rated more favourably than SS.

To summarize the assessments on these three scales: in every case the assessment for a variety of Slovene is higher than for the corresponding variety of German (i.e., SS is always higher than SG; DS is always higher than DG). In almost every case, moreover, both Slovene varieties rank higher than either German variety; the exception here being SS being ranked as 'less sociable' than DG. For teenagers in the Slovene Gymnasium in Klagenfurt, these high ratings for the minority language should come as no surprise, because of their high degree of ethnic consciousness and ethnic pride. This result suggests only that it is imperative to compare these assessments with those from Carinthian Slovene students who study in a German-language school and whose ethnic consciousness and pride — to the extent that it exists — will be probably more covert.

We may now turn to the distinctions between dialect and standard. Ignoring, then, the German/Slovene dichotomy, we can note that the standard is rated as 'more intelligent' than the dialect, but less 'likable' and much less 'sociable.' Indeed, as we saw earlier, sociability is associated with dialect speakers so much that the otherwise clear preference for Slovene over German breaks down on this scale.

Discussion

At about the same time as my experiment in the Slovene High School, the 'matched guise technique' was applied in a class in the University of Klagenfurt. This class was composed of students all of whose first language was German; the two language varieties used were SG and DG. The scales were as follows: *Sprechfertigkeit* (linguistic preparedness), *Klarheit* (clarity), *Intelligenz* (intelligence), *Unabhängigkeit* (independence), *Beruflicher Status*

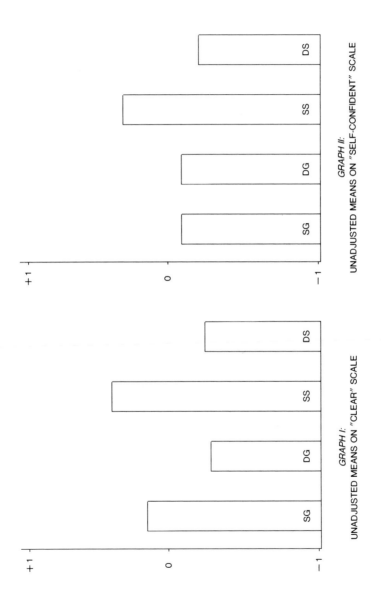

GRAPH I:
UNADJUSTED MEANS ON "CLEAR" SCALE

GRAPH II:
UNADJUSTED MEANS ON "SELF-CONFIDENT" SCALE

92

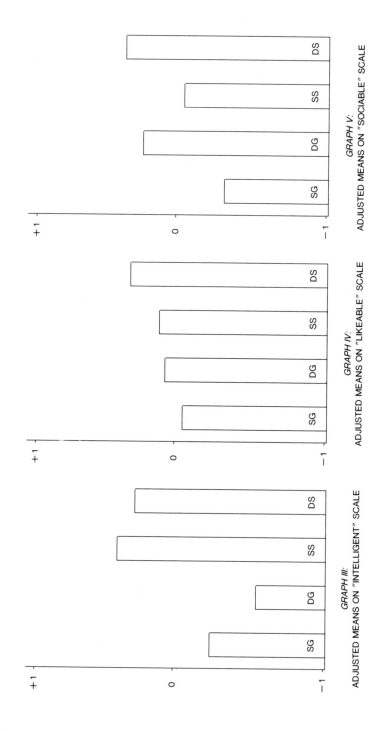

GRAPH III:
ADJUSTED MEANS ON "INTELLIGENT" SCALE

GRAPH IV:
ADJUSTED MEANS ON "LIKEABLE" SCALE

GRAPH V:
ADJUSTED MEANS ON "SOCIABLE" SCALE

(professional status), *Selbstbewusstsein* (self-confidence), *Aggressivität* (aggressiveness), *Egoismus* (egotism), and *Vertrauenswürdigkeit* (reliability); many of these being directly comparable (as far as the Standard:Dialect dichotomy is concerned) with my own scales.

On nearly all scales, SG was upgraded and DG downgraded. No significant results were obtained with respect to *intelligence*. *Linguistic preparedness* and *clarity* ($p < 0.5$ and $< .01$ respectively) showed a higher rating for SG; this is the same result as in my experiment. The *self-confidence* scale also showed a higher rating for SG ($p < .01$), a result in conflict with mine (see GRAPH II). DG, on the other hand, was upgraded with respect to *reliability* ($p < .01$), a scale where my own results were not significant. Finally, SG speakers were judged more *aggressive* ($p < .01$) and more *egotistic* ($p < .01$); perhaps this is to be linked to my own findings that DG speakers were rated as slightly more likable than SG speakers (see GRAPH IV).

In general, the upgrading of Slovene over German by the Slovene High School students may be interpreted as evidence of a favourable ethnic self-image; we may compare the position in Wales, where Welsh is upgraded at the expense of English,[18] and contrast the situation in Québec, where English has been rated as generally more acceptable than French.[19]

The elevated judgments for standard languages as compared with dialects on the *intelligence* scale are comparable to the findings of El-Dash and Tucker (1975) and Tucker (1968)[20] from Egypt and the Philippines, namely that the "superposed" language-variety (respectively, Classical Arabic and American English) is upgraded with respect to other language-varieties (see also Carranza and Ryan 1979 concerning the relative assessments of American and Mexican-American English varieties). The reverse of this coin — the relative upgrading of dialects over standard language on scales involving *social attributes* — finds echoes in studies in, for example, Britain and Peru.[21]

Further research is required to correlate these findings with educational, social and political factors in Carinthia. In particular, it would be desirable to run the "matched guise technique" in the more ordinary schools in Southern Carinthia, with populations of students ranging from those who are ethnically conscious and speak the Slovene dialect as their first language (and thus resemble the students in the Slovene Gymnasium in Klagenfurt) to those who are ethnically conscious and speak a German dialect as their mother tongue. It is dubious, however, whether the self-reporting about first- and second-language use would be fully reliable in the present day situation.

Finally, a word or two about the relevance of this kind of study to the multilingual situation in Alberta. We have in the last few years seen the introduction of bilingual education in Ukrainian, German, and Hebrew; and some twenty languages are taught in "Saturday schools" and are possible future candidates for bilingual classes.[22] In this context, I can do no better than quote the following:

> "Unfortunately, little background research information is available about the critical matter of attitudes in the communities concerned toward the introduction of ethnic language or bilingual programs, the attitudes of the ethnic minority or majority groups. Information of this nature would seem to be vital in determining whether a bilingual program will have the social climate to enable it to survive, let alone flourish"[23]

FOOTNOTES

[1]Census reports are unfortunately unreliable; first, because it is never easy to define degrees of linguistic assimilation; second, because significant numbers of not-fully assimilated Slovenes report themselves as "Windisch" rather than "Slowenisch," and the former term is interpreted in various, often detrimental, ways; and third, because some Slovenes boycotted the most recent census. On the size of the Slavic population, see D. Stermole, "Some Factors Affecting the Maintenance of Bilingualism in Carinthia," in R. M. Susel, ed., *Papers in Slovene Studies* (New York, 1977), 40-50 and A. Brumnik, T. Domej, A. Malle and F. Velik, *Die Slovenen in Kärnten/Slovencia na Koroskem* (Klagenfurt, 1974).

[2]On the minority situation in Carinthia, see e.g., Lilyan A. Brudner, "The Maintenance of Bilingualism in Southern Austria," *Ethnology* 10 (1972), 39-54; T. Veiter, "Die Kärntner Slowenen in Geschichte und Gegenwart," *Europäische Rundschau*, 3 (1975), 63-72; Stermole, 40-50; T. M. Barker, "The Carinthian Slovene Question in the Light of Recent German Austrian Scholarship," *Nationalities Papers*, 7 (1979), 138-46; R. P. Čuješ, "Minorities: Methodological Questions in Relation to Slovene in Carinthia," *Nationalities Papers* 7 (1979), 125-37. For another kind of sociolinguistic investigation in a multilingual district of Austria, see S. Gal, *Language Shift: Social Determinants of Linguistic Change in Austria* (New York, 1979).

[3]For descriptions of one DS dialect, see A. V. Isačenko, *Narečje vasi Sele na Rožu* (Ljubljana, 1939) and T. M. S. Priestly "Consonant Alterations in the Dialect of Sele Fara," in R. L. Lenček, ed., *Papers in Slovene Studies* (New York, 1976). The Carinthian German dialects have not been adequately described; see e.g., H. Kurath, *Die Lautgestalt einer Kärntner Mundart und ihre Geschichte* (Wiesbaden, 1965) and H. J. Simon, "Italienisch-Österreichisches and Französisch-Deutsches," *Klagenfurter Beiträge zur Sprachwissenschaft* 3 (1977), 69-70.

[4]W. E. Lambert, R. C. Hodgson, R. C. Gardner, S. Fillenbaum, "Evaluational Reactions to Spoken Languages," *Journal of Abnormal and Social Psychology*, 60 (1960), 44-51.

[5]W. E. Lambert, "The Social Psychology of Bilingualism," *Journal of Social Issues*, 23 (1967), 337.

[6]W. E. Lambert, H. Giles, D. Picard, "Language Attitudes in a French-American Community," *International Journal of the Sociology of Language*, 4 (1975), 127-52.

[7]For a summary of matched guise technique experiments since their inception, of the main methodological problems, and of the most important conclusions, see H. Giles and P. F. Powesland, *Speech Style and Social Evaluation* (London, 1975).

[8]On problems in choosing a reliable text, see e.g., W. Wölck, "Attitudes toward Spanish and Quechua in Bilingual Peru," in R. W. Shuy and R. W. Fasold, eds., *Language Attitudes: Current Trends and Prospects* (Washington, D.C., 1973), 129-47.

[9]E. B. Ryan, "Subjective Reactions toward Accented Speech," in Shuy and Fasold, 60-73.

[10]On age as a variable, see e.g., W. E. Lambert, H. Giles and G. Albert, "Language Attitudes in a Rural Community in Northern Maine," *La monda lingvo-problemo*, 5 (1973), 130 and M. A. Carranza and E. B. Ryan, "Evaluative Reactions of Bilingual Anglo and Mexican American Adolescents towards Speakers of English and Spanish," *International*

Journal of the Sociology of Language, 6 (1975), 85.

[11]O. Elyan, P. Smith, H. Giles and R. Y. Bourhis, "RP-Accented Female Speech," in P. Trudgill, ed., *Sociolinguistic Patterns in British English* (London, England, 1978).

[12]On the categorization of scales, see e.g., Carranza and Ryan, 91.

[13]The visit was arranged through the good offices of *Hofrat* Dr. Valentin Inzko, to whom I hereby express my gratitude.

[14]Stermole, 47.

[15]For invaluable assistance with statistical analyses and their interpretation, I wish to thank Dr. W. J. Baker, Department of Linguistics, University of Alberta.

[16]E. B. Ryan and M. A. Carranza, "Ingroup and Outgroup Reactions to Mexican American Language Varieties," in H. Giles, ed., *Language, Ethnicity and Intergroup Reactions* (London, 1979), 59-81 and Elyan, Smith, Giles and Bourhis on differences involving sex. In fact, some non-significant results in my own experiment do point to the possible interaction of the sex of the hearer with the sex of the listener; this must receive attention in further studies in Carinthia.

[17]Giles and Powesland, 4.

[18]R. Y. Bourhis, H. Giles, and H. Tajfel, "Language As a Determinant of Welsh Identity," *European Journal of Social Psychology*, 3 (1973), 447-60.

[19]See Giles and Powesland, *Speech Style and Social Evaluation* for references and discussion and A. d'Angeljan and G. R. Tucker, "Sociolinguistic Correlates of Speech Style in Quebec," in Shuy and Fasold, 1-27.

[20]L. El-Dash and G. R. Tucker, "Subjective Reactions to Various Speech Styles in Egypt," *International Journal of the Sociology of Language*, 6 (1975), 33-55.

[21]For Britain, see Giles & Powesland, and for Peru, Wölck, "Attitudes toward Spanish and Quechua . . . "

[22]See F. Pelech, "Heritage Language Programs in Alberta," pp. 267-286 in this volume.

[23]Lambert, Giles and Albert, 129.

Appendix I: Texts

Warum nicht alle Bäume ihr Laub verlieren (SG).
Die Teufel fragten Gott, wann sie denn in den Himmel kommen könnten. Gott antwortete ihnen: Dann, wenn alles Laub von den Bäumen gefallen sein wird. Die Teufel warteten und warteten. Doch von allen Bäumen fiel das Laub ab, nur von der Eiche nicht. Die Teufel aber waren zu ungeduldig. Deshalb fielen sie uber die Bäume her und wollten alles Laub von ihnen reissen. Doch sie hatten zu ungeschickte Krallen und konnten nicht alles Laub herunterreissen. Und so sind die Teufel bis heute noch nicht in den Himmel gekommen.

Barum nit ale pama das laab faliern (DG).
Die tajfl hom den liabn hergot gfrogt, wan sie bern in den himel kuman kenen. Da hergot hot inen zur antbort gebn: Don, ben ales laab fon den paman gfoln biart. Die tajfl hom gbortet un gbortet. Fon aln paman is das laab gfoln, nur fon da ajchn nit. So sans holt iba da ajchn hergfoln un hom fasuacht, das gonze laab fon ir obezureissn. Abe sie boarn z'ungschickt un hom nit das gonze laab obereissn kenan. Un so san die tajfl pis heite nit in den himel kuman.

Zakaj vse listje ne odpade (SS).
Hudiči so vprašali Boga, kdaj bodo smeli v nebesa priti. Bog jim je rekel: Tedaj, ko bo vse listje odpadlo. Hudiči so čakali in čakali. Toda z vseh dreves je padlo listje, samo s hrasta ne. Bili pa so preveč neučakani in so se spravili na hraste in skušali spraskati vse listje z vej. Toda imeli so preveč nerodne kremplje in zato niso mogli strgati vsega listja. Tako hudiči še do danes niso prišli v nebesa.

Zaqaj da vsi listje dow qne pade (DS).
Zwodiji so boha baral, qdaj boj w nebiese prišl. Buəh pa jim je requ: təda, qəbo wse listje dow padu. Zwodiji s čaqal pa čaqal. Z useh drewi je padu listje, z doba pa naq. Pa so bil cweč neučaqan pa so se sprawil na dobe pa squšal wse listje dow strhat. Mel s pa cweč nerodne qremple pa zatu ni s mohl wse listje dow strhat. Zwodiji pa še do nešneha dnu qniso pršl u nebiese.

Why it is that not all trees lose their leaves.
The devils asked God when they could get to heaven. God replied: When all the leaves have fallen from the trees. The devils waited and waited. The leaves fell from all the trees, but not from the oak. The devils were too impatient, however, and so they leapt on to the oak trees and tried to pull off the leaves. But their claws were too clumsy and they were not able to pull off all the leaves. So the devils have to this day not yet got to heaven.

98

Appendix II: Questionnaire

APPENDIX II: QUESTIONNAIRE

(page one)

1. roj.:	v:	spol:	
sedanje bivališče:		od:	
prejšnja bivališča:		od:	do:
		od:	do:

2. poklic: od: delovno mesto
prejšnji poklic(i)
(v oklepaju dodaj leta):
poročen(a): da - ne   od leta:
poklic moža / žene: roj.:
rojstni kraj: kraj bivanja
                    pred poroko:

oče:	roj.:	mati:	roj.:
rojstni		rojstni	
kraj:		kraj:	
kraj pre-		kraj pret.	
težnega biv.:		bivanja:	
poklic:		poklic:	

3. Jezikovni izbor (po subjektivni oceni): (1-slov., 2-nem.)

	nikoli	redko	v enaki meri	pretižno	samo
govori	_____	_____	_____	_____	_____
bere	_____	_____	_____	_____	_____
pise	_____	_____	_____	_____	_____

4. Sposobnost dvojezičnosti: (1-ne, 2-slabo, 3-dobro)

	1. slov.		2. nemško	
	narečje	knjižno	narečje	knjižno
razume	_____	_____	_____	_____
govori	_____	_____	_____	_____
bere	_____	_____	_____	_____
piše	_____	_____	_____	_____

(page two)

A. razumen - nerazumen	5	4	3	2	1
B. samozavesten - nesamozavesten	5	4	3	2	1
C. zanesljiv - nezanesljiv	5	4	3	2	1
D. simpatičen - nesimpatičen	5	4	3	2	1
E. družaben - nedružaben	5	4	3	2	1
F. govori jasno - nejasno	5	4	3	2	1

etc. etc.

EDMONTON'S RECENT SOVIET-JEWISH IMMIGRANTS

Robert L. Busch,
University of Alberta

Introduction

Soviet-Jewish immigration to North America became numerically quite signifi-cant in the 1970s. According to information from the Central Office of the Jewish Immigration Aid File, Canada received 5,424 Soviet immigrants between 1973 and 1979. Approximately 40% have settled in Metropolitan Toronto while the remainder have largely chosen cities in Ontario, Quebec and Manitoba.[1] However, Edmonton, too, has become the home for a sizable number of recent Soviet immigrants. Once again, according to the Central Office of the Jewish Immigrant Aid File, individual and family arrivals amounted to 286 and 122 respectively:

YEAR:	1973	1974	1975	1976	1977	1978	1979	1973–1979
Individuals	7	10	47	55	39	43	85	286
Families	3	5	25	21	17	15	36	122

The latest wave of immigrants from the USSR has been the subject of a number of studies.[2] Although several of these papers contain highly pertinent information about the experience of recent Soviet émigrés in the West, no study focuses primarily on the adaptation of the heads of households to North American life. The present paper, which concentrates on recent Soviet im-migrants in Edmonton, is intended to contribute to the understanding of their adaptation.

Identification

There were problems involved in locating recent Soviet immigrants. Were there enough of them to constitute a meaningful sample? If so, how was one to find and approach them? Friends among the immigrants helped with addresses, and the Jewish Community Telephone Directory assisted in finding numerous others. By mid-December 1979, 135 names had been gathered. These were believed to represent adult men and women, living together or separately. Both young dependents (from children through university students) and elderly dependents were excluded. In the second half of December questionnaires were mailed with instructions to return them no later than the end of January. Some potential respondents had moved, others were improperly identified. All in all, the eligible sample group numbered 126 at most. From that number, 57 responded, thereby yielding a return rate of 45.23%.

Approaching the Immigrants

The questionnaire and all communications were in Russian. The author identified himself and explained that the goal of the questionnaire was to study the experience and adaptation of Russian immigrants in Edmonton in the hope that some of the information gathered could be broadly useful. The respondents were assured of anonymity. Thus, a self-addressed envelope for returning the questionnaire was included and no writing was required, although there was a place for optional comments at the end. Very few used it, but several parties, responding to an invitation in the covering letter, phoned or arranged interviews to discuss the study. Four wrote in comments at the end, including one especially terse remark: "Excuse me"/Izvini.

Questionnaire Design

There were 73 questions involving:

1. Relative age.
2. Gender.
3. Family situation.

4. Residence in the USSR.
5. Reasons for leaving the Soviet Union.
6. Reasons for choosing Canada.
7. Route to Edmonton, i.e., via Israel? via a Canadian City?
8. Length of stay in Canada.
9. Contact with social agencies.
10. Use of English.
11. Educational level.
12. Professional experience.

13. Employment in Canada.
14. Housing.
15. Attitude toward leaving Edmonton.
16. Transportation.
17. Continued interest in the USSR.

18. The press.
19. Electronic media.

20. Leisure.
21. Interest in Canada.
22. Religion.
23. Anti-Semitism.
24. Fulfillment of expectations.

Respondents were encouraged to check off more than one response to a question where appropriate. The following section of the paper provides a discussion of the responses. Appended to the study is a translated copy of the original questionnaire, along with a statistical breakdown of responses to each question.

Age

In age, 86% of the respondents are distributed fairly evenly among four categories ranging from under 30 to 40-45 years old.

	M	F	(N)	TOTAL	%
Under 30	4	9		13	22.80
31–35	9	3		12	21.06
36–40	3	7		10	17.54
41–45	11	2	(1)	14	24.57
. . . . .					
46–50	4	2		6	10.53
51–55	0	0		0	–
56–60	0	1		1	1.75
60 & over	0	1		1	1.75
	31	25	(1)	57	100.00[3]

Gender

Approximately 55% (31) of the respondents were male (M). Approximately 44% (25) were females (F). There was one neuter (N).

Family Situation

Some four-fifths (80.7%/46–21M-1N-24F) came together with families, while most others, 15.78% (9 — 6M,3F) came with relatives. A few (3 — 2M,1F) arrived alone. One party reported coming both with family and relatives. With respect to children in the family, approximately 43.85% (25-13M,12F) report one child, 40.35% (23-13M-1N-9F) report two children. In other words, for families reporting children, there are roughly 1.5 per family. The children run to all ages, but the 6-10 years category is by far the largest.

	M	(N)	F	TOTAL
under 5 yrs.	5		4	9
6–10	13	(1)	9	23
11–15	7		5	12
16–20	6		3	9
over 20	3		5	8

Residence in the USSR

The Ukraine was home to 71.9% (41 — 21M,19F), Russia to some 28% (16-9M-1N-6F), Belorussia to 5.26% (3-2M,1F), and one respondent gave the Caucasus and a Republic other than the ones listed.[4] Several respondents gave more than one Republic as being the place from which they hailed.

Reasons for Leaving the USSR

There were 42 multiple responses to this question, 71.9% (41 — 24M,17F) giving nationality, i.e., their Jewishness, as being a reason for leaving the USSR; 61.4% (35 — 20M,15F) left for political reasons; 54.38% (31 — 18M,13F) listed economic factors and only 14.03% (8 — 5M,3F) mentioned religion as a factor for leaving.

The high response for Jewishness is ambiguous. It could refer to anti-Semitism, which most respondents encountered frequently. However, it could simply refer to the fact that, in keeping with Soviet emigration policy, which allows for ethnic reunification, being Jewish provided the opportunity to leave.

The Edmonton respondents have given emphasis to economic and political factors different from groups studied elsewhere. Gitelman and Markus have found that the reasons for leaving the USSR are essentially non-political.[5] For the Toronto group, Markus found "the three main reasons for departure in order of importance were: anti-Semitism (58.5%), lack of opportunities for the young (49.1%), and lack of economic opportunities (45.3%)."[6] While not negligible, economic factors were clearly not overriding for the Edmonton group. Indeed, many researchers attest to the solid economic situation left behind by Soviet immigrants in their homeland.[7]

Reasons for Choosing Canada

There were 21 multiple responses to this question. The reasons the respondents chose to come to Canada are obviously quite varied, and do not allow for meaningful generalization. One-third (19–10M-1N-8F) checked off the category "other reasons"; otherwise, the responses in ascending order of frequency were:

12.28% (7 — 4M, 3F)	"the presence of close friends";
24.56% (14 — 8M, 6F)	"the presence of close relatives";
28.07% (16 — 10M, 6F)	"the possibility of a job in a field of specialization";
40.35% (23 — 11M,12F)	"the possession of solid information about Canada."

Route to Edmonton

Nearly everyone 96.5% (55–30M-1N-24F) reported coming directly to Canada from Europe. Only one respondent mentioned living in Israel. Almost all (94.73% 54–29M-1N-24F) came directly to Edmonton once they had arrived in Canada. The failure to go to Israel reflected a growing trend since 1973.[8] The great majority (about 75%) stopped off in Rome and waited an average of eight months to receive a visa for Canada.[9]

Length of Stay in Canada

Nearly half, 47.36% (27 — 13M,14F) have been living in Canada for less than a year, nearly one-fifth or 19.29% (11–7M-4F) have lived here between one and two years; 10.52% (6 — 3M,3F) for two to three years; 22.8% (13–8M-1N-4F) have been living here for more than three years.

Social Agencies

The vast majority of Soviet immigrants received help from one or both of two agencies: 80.7% (46–26M-1N-19F) from Canada Manpower; 59.64% (34–22M-1N-11F) from Jewish Family Services (there were 28 who reported help from both). Only one other social agency was mentioned as having supplied aid — the Edmonton Immigrant Services Association. All but three respondents reported having received help from at least one agency. Assistance was required by 36.84% (21–11M-1N-9F) for less than three months, by 19.29% (11–8M,3F) for three to four months, and by 24.56% (14 — 7M,7F) for four to six months. Only two used the services for six months to a year, and 15.78% did not respond (9 — 4M,5F). That the immigrants turned to social agencies which transcend specific geographical-ethnic boundaries shows looser bonds between the ethnic community, as such, and the new immigrant. This probably serves to send most immigrants out into the community at large more rapidly, but it also could fragment and isolate the group. Indeed, responses show that after work only 26.31% (15 — 7M,8F) of the immigrants socialized regularly with one another, while 68.42% (39–21M-1N-17F) did so rarely. Comparable figures for socializing with Canadians show that 14.3% (8–5M,3F) seek, after work, the company of native-born Canadians while 56.14% (32–16M-1N-15F) seldom do.

Use of English

Canada Manpower provided English-language instruction for the immigrants which, judging from the questionnaire, was a much needed service. Approximately half — 49.12% (28 — 16M,12F) had not known English at all before leaving the Soviet Union and 42.1% (24 — 14M,10F) knew only a little English; therefore, more than 90% were in need of English-language training. Many immigrants who had come via Rome took the opportunity to study English there, but the quality of instruction was found wanting.[10]

The need to learn English was especially great, in that 77.19% (44-24M-1N-19F) viewed it as indispensable for their work and 15.78% (9 — 6M,3F) regarded it as useful. Approximately 70 to 75% attended day-time (47.35% [27–14M,13F]) or night-time (33.3% [19–14M,5F]) or both types of English courses. The English language courses were found very useful (43.85% [25 —

13M,12F]) or useful (26.31% [15 — 10M,5F]) by just over 70% of the respondents. A sizable number (43.85% [25–14M-1N-10F]) considered their English pretty good at that stage, about the same number (40.03% [23 — 14M,9F]) considered it poor. Obviously, length of stay in Canada played a role here. Of the 23 who said their English was poor, 47% (11 — 6M,5F) had been here less than a year; 34% (8 — 6M,2F) had been in Canada between one and two years. Correlation between age and a poor command of English was not significant since 91% fell within the age group from under 30 to 41-45:

Under 30	2	(1M,1F)	46–50	0	
31–35	6	(3M,3F)	51–55	0	
36–40	5	(1M,4F)	56–60	1	(1M)
41–45	8	(7M,1F)	Over 60	0	

Given this situation with English, it was not surprising that most of the respondents spoke only Russian with their children at home, although 19.29% (11 — 6M,5F) indicated that they utilized both Russian and English with their children. Nearly twice that number, 35.08%, reported that their children used English as well as Russian at home. Clearly, Russian remained the language of communication and 45 (78.94%) wanted their children to study Russian. Only three (all from Russia) showed opposition to their youngsters' studying Russian.

Ties with the culture of origin were obviously very strong and this was, no doubt, indicated by the fact that 82.45% (47–24M-1N-22F) would welcome the creation of a centre for Russian culture in Edmonton. This response, which represented the opinion of 85% of the 41 people hailing from the Ukraine, showed a remarkable orientation to Russian culture. This appears to be an anomaly since the Ukraine has its own language and culture. However, many would argue that the Russian language and culture have achieved predominance in the Ukraine, and therefore the Soviet Jews behave like most minorities which identify with the dominant culture and its language.[11]

Educational Level

The recent Soviet immigrants are on the whole a well-educated group: 28.07% (16 — 12M,4F) have undergone specialized technological training (*tekhnikum*); 17.54% (10 — 3M,7F) have completed college; 70.17% (40–22M-1N-17F) have graduated from a university or its equivalent. This is a significant figure and may reflect a tendency of the highly educated to respond to the questionnaire. Still, according to some studies, an advanced level of education among the respondents appears to reflect Soviet conditions, wherein 46.8% of the Jewish population have received higher education as compared with 6.5% for Russians.[12]

Professional Experience

With more than one response possible (64 total) the breakdown according to professional activity is listed in the following descending order of frequency:

Manufacturing	36.84%	(21 — 15M,6F)
Scientific research	17.54%	(10 — 8M-1N-1F)
Education	14.03%	(8 — 2M,6F)
Consumer services	14.03%	(8 — 4M,4F)
Arts	14.03%	(8 — 2M,6F)
Medicine	5.26%	(3 — 1M,2F)

Employment in Canada

More than two-thirds of the respondents had held jobs (71.9% [41–26M-1N-14F]) and two-thirds of them were currently employed (38–25M-1N-12F). Only 19 were out of work, 6 men and 13 women. Of the unemployed, 84.2% have been in Canada less than a year. Most respondents had found work quickly: 38.5% (22–16M-1N-5F) within a month; 14.03% (8 — 4M,4F) within three months; and another 21.5% (8 — 6M,2F) within six months. About half of those who reported being employed stayed with the same job (48.78% [20–12M-1N-7F]); 13 others, (7M,6F) or 31.7% of those who had been employed, reported changing their jobs once. The standard ways of finding employment were used; friends, advertisements in the paper, and Canada Manpower, with none of these particularly standing out.

Of those who were employed, 80.4% (33–20M-1N-12F) reported their job relations with Canadians to be good; 14.63% (6–5M-1F) rated them indifferent; 2.4% (1M) termed them poor. Of those who worked, 46.34% (19–13M,6F) were employed in their specialization; 31.7% (13–8M-1N-4F) worked close to their fields of specialization; 15.78% (9 — 5M,4F) had employment unrelated to their specialities.

Of those working in their areas of specialization or close to them, about 75% found employment within six months: 37.5% (12–8M-1N-3F) within one month; 15.62% (5 — 2M,3F) within three months; 21.87% (7M) within six months; 9.37% (3 — 2M,1F) took from six to twelve months; and 15.62% (5 — 2M,3F) took more than a year.

As one can see from the table, the best record, both in finding employment and in having that employment related to one's area of specialization is found among those involved in scientific research and in manufacturing. According to Markus, lawyers, poets, film directors, journalists, psychiatrists and teachers have the greatest difficulty practising their professions in Canada.[13]

JOB HOLDERS BY OCCUPATION

	MANUFACTURING (21--15M,6F)	SCIENTIFIC RESEARCH (10--8M-1N-1F)	EDUCATION (8--2M,6F)	CONSUMER SERVICES (8--4M,4F)	ARTS (8--2M,6F)	OTHER (6--3M,3F)	MEDICINE (3--1M,2F)
Employed	13M,3F	7M (1)	3F	1M, 2F	1M, 2F	2M, 1F	1M, 1F
In Specialization	7M, 1F	3M	2F	1F	1M, 1F	1M	—
Close to Specialization	3M, 1F	3M (1)		1M	—	1M, 1F	1F

Housing

Most of the Soviet immigrants were renting, 77.19% (44–24M-1N-19F). The remaining 13 were purchasing their homes, and for 12 of these it was a house. Understandably, there was a positive correlation between buying and length of stay: 61.53% of the buyers had been in Canada more than three years, 23.07% between two and three years, but two people (15.38%), likely a couple, were buying during their first year in Canada.

Some 77% (44–25M-1N-18F), of the respondents resided in three-room apartments or larger; 52.62% (30–17M,13F) were living in condominiums or private houses — accommodations which would be, for all practical purposes, unobtainable in a comparable Soviet city.

Most of the immigrants had moved at least once since their arrival in Edmonton: (75.42% [43–25M-1N-17F]). The pattern was, probably, to find affordable housing and then, once jobs had been obtained and the city was better known, to move to a preferable accommodation.

Slightly fewer than half, 47.36% (27 — 12M,15F) were planning to stay in their current homes, while 38.59% (22–13M-1N-8F) wanted to move; 14.03% (8 — 6M,2F) did not respond. Apparently, the North American dream of owning one's home had greatly affected the recent group of Soviet immigrants, for 64.8% (37 — 21M,16F) expressed a desire to own a home.

Leaving Edmonton

As indicated, nearly half of the respondents (47.36%) felt they would be staying for some time. In response to a question concerning moving, only 10.52% (6–3M-1N-2F) directly expressed a desire to leave Edmonton. Still, a number of questions involved the possibility of leaving Edmonton — as many Soviet immigrants have. Were this the case, 85.96% (49–26M-1N-22F) would prefer to live in a city larger than Edmonton. Recent Soviet immigrants were inveterate urbanites; none wished to live in the countryside. However, four respondents, perhaps showing some signs of dissatisfaction with Edmonton, did say they would not care where they moved. In reaching a decision to leave Edmonton, the following criteria, in descending order of importance, were considered:

54.38% / 31	(18M-1N-12F)	Chances for advancement at work
29.82% / 17	(7M,10F)	The presence of relatives or friends
29.82% / 17	(9M, 8F)	Climate
22.8% / 13	(7M, 6F)	Pay
15.78% / 9	(6M, 3F)	The type of work

It is interesting that prospects for advancement in one's work rated well ahead of, say, type of work. One might be somewhat surprised to see climate considered ahead of salary and type of work, but, then, the survey was taken in the middle of Edmonton's winter. More than half (8 — 3M,5F) who listed climate were "enjoying" their first Edmonton winter. Still, almost one-quarter (4–2M,2F) had been in Edmonton for more than three years and were, perhaps, ready for a change. In any case, somewhat more temperate parts of the world were given preference in a hypothetical move. Of the many options given, only the most popular are listed here:

Ontario:	36.84% / 21	(12M,9F)
Europe:	33.33% / 19	(9M-1N-9F)
U.S.A.:	21.05% / 12	(7M,5F)
B.C.:	17.54% / 10	(7M,3F)

Of the 19 who gave Europe as a choice in moving from Edmonton, almost half (9 — 3M,6F) had been in the city for less than a year and may well not have become accustomed to North American life. Still, roughly a quarter of those choosing Europe (5 — 4M,1F) had been in Canada for over three years.

Transportation

The questionnaire asked only about cars. Most respondents report having cars in the family — 71.9%/41. One car is the norm, but of those reporting car ownership, just over one-quarter (26.82%) report having two or more cars (8 report two cars, 3 report more than two). The latter almost always correlated with families having children of driving age, and this likely shows how quick

108

the youngsters of the Soviet immigrants are in adapting to North America's car culture. Most owners (85.36%/35) bought their automobiles within a year of arrival. Roughly one-third of these persons bought within three months of arrival and approximately another third (12) within three to six months. Thirty-five owners purchased large or mid-size cars; 41%/17 say they would buy smaller cars next time.

As in the case of housing, car ownership compared favourably with the situation in the USSR. In the Soviet Union, 28.8% of the Jews polled by Gitelman reported owning cars, (as compared with 4% for the total population).[14] One cannot make too much of the increased car ownership in North America, for here it is the norm, while in the USSR it is clearly the exception.

Continued Interest in Events in the Soviet Union

Interest in the Soviet Union remained with 80.7% (46–25M-1N-20F) of the respondents, while 15.78% (9 — 6M,3F) said they were not interested. Two did not respond.

The immigrants followed events in the Soviet Union largely through the Western press 70.17% (40–22M-1N-17F) and other media: TV 52.63% (30 — 19M,11F) and radio 40.35% (23 — 14M,9F). Just over half, 50.87% (29 — 16M,13F) said they kept in touch with events through letters from home, while only 12.28% (7 — 4M,3F) reported using the Soviet media to do so.

The Press

Most respondents, 61.4% (35–17M-1N-17F) reported reading the Russian émigré press in Russian, while the next largest number, i.e., 43.85% (25 — 15M,10F) read the Canadian press. While seven people, or 12.28%, reported following Soviet events in the Soviet press, only three said they read the Soviet press — an apparent discrepancy that may be explained by the sense of the question being interpreted as "you read regularly." Subscription to the Russian émigré press and the Canadian press ran about equal–36.84% (21–12M-1N-8F) and 33.33% (19 — 11M,8F) respectively. No respondents subscribed to the Soviet press, and this is perhaps somewhat surprising. The reasons for such a low readership of the Soviet press may be interpreted in a number of ways:
1. The Soviet press may be a psychological irritant;
2. The Soviet press may be viewed as an unreliable way of following events in the Soviet Union;
3. There may be worries that reading the Soviet press in Canada is as ill-thought-of as reading the Western press in the Soviet Union.

Electronic Media

Most of the immigrants reported owning TV sets, i.e., 77.19% (44–25M-1N-18F).[15] The largest number of TV viewers, 25 (17M,8F) watched TV one hour per day, while 12 (4M,8F) did so two hours daily. If one lists the programs from most watched to least watched one gets the following picture:

The news	(34 — 23M, 11F)	Sports	(11M)
Concerts	(17 — 8M, 9F)	Situation comedies	(8 — 4M, 4F)
"Cops 'n' Robbers"	(17 — 9M, 8F)	Soap Operas	(7 — 3M, 4F)
Specials	(12 — 8M, 4F)	Plays	(5 — 2M, 3F)

TV offers a good opportunity both to learn English and to learn more about life in Canada — or, more accurately, in North America. As for radio, which holds more promise in terms of Canadian content, two-thirds (38 — 23M,15F) reported listening to it, the great majority of these between one-half and one hour daily, (14–8M,6F and 18–12M,6F) respectively. A listing of the types of programming from most-listened-to downwards gives the following order:

News	(29 — 18M, 11F)
Music	(24 — 13M, 11F)
Weather	(22 — 13M, 9F)
Sports	(4 — 4M)

Leisure

The Soviet immigrants were not restaurant-goers: 43.52% (25–9M-1N-15F) did not go at all to restaurants. Another 42.09% reported going from once every two months to once every six months, 15.78% (9 — 6M,3F) and 26.31% (15 — 9M,6F) respectively.

Many more respondents went to the movies. Approximately one-fifth did not go 21.05% (12 — 5M,7F), but 42.1% did so from once per month to once every two months, 21.05% (12 — 7M,5F) and 21.05% (12 — 6M,6F) respectively. The picture for concert going was very similar, the difference being that slightly more (3) went once every six months and only half (6) attended every month. As for the theatre, a larger percentage, 31.57% (18 — 9M,9F) did not go to the theatre at all. Still, over one-third, 36.84% (21–11M-1N-9F) went once every six months and 10.52% (6 — 3M,3F) did so once a month.

During their vacations the immigrants did not roam far and wide:

22.8%	/ 13 — 7M,6F	travelled in Alberta
14.03%	/ 8 — 5M-1N-2F	went to B.C.
7.01%	/ 4 — 3M,1F	made trips to the U.S.
5.26%	/ 3 — 2M,1F	visited Ontario

One went to Quebec, another travelled to Europe. Many of the same people were taking these various trips (3 double and 3 triple responses) and a clear majority, 63.15% (36 — 18M,18F) reported no travel at all. Travel outside Alberta always correlated with a stay of two to three years and, usually, with more than three years (all but one case). Putting aside questions of the expense of travel and the need to devote financial resources to establishing homes, most immigrants had been on the road too long by the time they arrived in Edmonton, so they seemed quite ready to stay in one place for a while.[16]

Interest in Canada

The lack of travel does not indicate indifference to Canada, its geography, history or culture: 82.45% (47 — 26M,21F) had a strong desire to learn about these aspects of Canada, 14.03% more (8–4M-1N-3F) felt some interest, while one had no wish to do so, and there was one non-respondent.

Religion

Religion tends not to be practised in the Soviet Union, where it is discouraged as a so-called superstitious remnant of the past. Therefore, it is not surprising that only 14.03% (8 — 4M,4F) attended the synagogue while living in the Soviet Union. This figure did not include the person who went to Israel before coming to Canada, and it did not correlate with advanced age, in the way that attending religious services in the Soviet Union usually does (under 30: 3F,1M; 31-35: 1M; 36-40: 1M; 41-45: 1M; 56-60 1F). In Canada 77.19% (44 — 24M,20F) reported going occasionally to the synagogue, but only 7.01% (4 — 3M,1F) were going often. Three of the latter were people who did not go to the synagogue in the Soviet Union. Once again, there was no special correlation with age (31-35: 1M; 36-40: 1M; 41-45: 1M; over 60: 1F). There were 14.03% (8–3M-1N-4F) who never attend. The casual approach to worship attests to the fact that Jewishness in the Soviet Union has little to do with religion. In the Toronto group, 98.1% of the parents saw themselves as secular, and clearly, most felt they were only nominally Jewish.[17]

Anti-Semitism

Anti-Semitism was a fact of Soviet life for the great majority of respondents: 85.96% (49 — 30M,19F) reported encountering it frequently, another 12.28% (7–1M-1N-5F) seldom met with it.[18] No one reported not having any experiences with anti-Semitism, although there was one non-respondent. As the same question was applied to Canada, 56.14% (32–19M-1N-12F) claimed not to have found anti-Semitism here; however, 33-1/3% (19–10M,9F) mentioned coming across it occasionally. The occasions when prejudice was experienced by them were as follows:

USSR		Canada	
64.8% / 37 (23M,14F)	– In Society at large –	17.54% / 11 (6M,5F)	
63.15% / 36 (22M-1N-13F)	– Getting a job –	10.52% / 6 (3M,3F)	
57.89% / 33 (21M,12F)	– In school –	/ 0	
56.14% / 32 (19M,13F)	– At work –	5.26% / 3 (2M,1F)	
47.36% / 27 (16M,11F)	– At the institute –	/ 0	

Fulfilment of Expectations

When asked if they had found in Canada what they were looking for when they left the USSR, 77.19% (44–26M-1N-17F) reported finding the fullfilment of their material expectations, and just a little more than a third, i.e., 35.08% (20–15M,5F) claimed satisfaction in non-material ways. While no one regretted leaving the Soviet Union, 3.52%/2F, failed altogether to find what they were looking for. Whether for good or for ill, 15.78% (9 — 4M,5F) had a completely different idea about life in the West.[19]

The picture presented by the responses is, on the whole, positive. With time, one would expect that the already-high percentage of material satisfaction will go above 90%. While a satisfactory standard of living is commonly seen as a precondition of man's happiness, the dictum that "man lives not by bread alone" is well known to Soviet émigrés. One might hope that these one-third who have found what they desired in non-material ways will increase as the adaptation to a new life becomes more complete. Cause for optimism in the overall can be seen in the fact that 87.71% would like to be joined by relatives and friends who remained back in the USSR. While this figure can be viewed as a desire to see others get out of the Soviet Union, or the desire, through the nearness of loved ones, to attenuate some of the difficulties of the adaptation process, it can also be viewed as a basic vote of confidence in Canada. After all, the newcomers from the Soviet Union would not wish to share their lot with those dear to them unless their experiences were essentially positive.

112

FOOTNOTES

[1]See Roberta Lander Markus, *Adaptation: A Case Study of Soviet Jewish Immigrant Children in Toronto, 1970-1978* (Toronto, 1979), p. 13. Additionally, as of 1977, approximately 15,000 Soviet Jews had recently immigrated to the U.S. See Z. Gitelman's "Recent Emigres and the Soviet Political System: A Pilot Study in Detroit," *Slavic and Soviet Series, II* (Fall, 1977), p. 40.

[2]In addition to the previously cited, one can mention: Z. Gitelman's "Soviet Jewish Emigrants: Why Are They Choosing America?", *Soviet Jewish Affairs*, vol. 7, no. 1 (Fall, 1977); Z. Gitelman, "Soviet Political Culture: Insights from Recent Jewish Emigres," *Soviet Studies*, XXIX, 4 (1977); Gur Ofer, Aaron Vinokur, and Yechiel Bar-Chaim, "Family Budget Survey of Soviet Emigrants in the Soviet Union," *Rand Paper Series* P-6015 (Santa Monica, 1979).

[3]The statistics for the Metropolitan Toronto group, not restricted like the present study to heads of households, show 60.8% out of just over 2,054 are between 20-55; 24.6% are 19 or under. See Markus, pp. 13-14. *Cf.* Gitelman's "Recent Emigres . . . ," p. 43, where, 71.2% in a Detroit survey group of 132 people (restricted to 18 years and older) ranged in age between 18 and 50.

[4]*Cf.* Markus, p. 14, where Russia (Moscow and Leningrad) accounts for 26.3% of the Metropolitan Toronto group, and Ukrainian cities (Odessa, Kiev and Lvov) 62.3%; these figures closely resemble Gitelman's findings for his 1976 Detroit group; 63.4% from the Ukraine, 22.3% from RSFSR. See Gitelman's "Recent Emigres . . . ," p. 42. The somewhat larger percentage for Edmonton could be accounted for by its significant Ukrainian population, a possible attraction to many immigrants who, while predominantly of Russian cultural heritage, are often bi-cultural to a considerable degree.

[5]See Markus, p. 8 and Gitelman's "Soviet Jewish Emigrants . . . ," p. 39.

[6]Markus, p. 36. These reasons were seen to be significantly interrelated.

[7]Ibid., p. 29; See Ofer, Vinokur and Bar-Chaim, p. 39; Gitelman, "Recent Emigres . . . ," pp. 45 and 49. Gitelman's respondents gave low priority to economic factors, (p. 50).

[8]Ibid., p. 41.

[9]Markus, pp. 11, 13. According to her findings, 7.3% went to Israel before coming to Canada.

[10]See ibid., p. 36.

[11]In the Metropolitan Toronto group, 96.3% consider Russian to be their mother tongue, and 91.6% of the youngsters interviewed by Markus wished to preserve their Russian language and culture. See ibid., pp. 27 and 59.

[12]See Gitelman, "Recent Emigres . . . ," p. 44. *Cf.* Ofer, Vinokur and Bar-Chaim, pp. 21-23 for broader based statistics involving the Soviet Union and emigrants to Israel.

[13]Markus, p. 16.

[14]Gitelman, "Recent Emigres . . . ," p. 49.

[15]This is only slightly above figures for the Soviet population as a whole (70.5%) and well below an average figure of 97% for Soviet immigrants in general. See ibid.

[16]The average transit time for Soviet immigrants in the Metropolitan Toronto group was two to three years. See Markus, p. 35.

[17]Markus, pp. 44-45.

[18]The Edmonton figures for the Soviet Union are considerably higher than those reported elsewhere. As stated earlier, Markus, p. 8 found 58.5%, presumably parents, mentioning anti-Semitism as a reason for leaving the USSR. Happily, 56.1% of the children studied never experienced anti-Semitism in the USSR and half of those who did, experienced it seldom, one-fourth occasionally, and only one-fourth often (p. 28). This might indicate that anti-Semitism is on the wane. Cf. Gitelman's "Recent Emigres . . . ," p. 50, where only 19% of those who were dissatisfied with life in the USSR reported having experienced anti-Semitism "often" or "sometimes."

[19]Judging from the Markus study, the child's assessment of the immigration experience is a qualified "positive." Some 85% of the children had a positive attitude toward the USSR, where they viewed themselves as materially satisfied. The break with close friends and relatives, transit stresses and adaptation problems once in Canada caused anxiety. Still, 65.4% rated life in Canada better than in the USSR, 14% saw it as similar, and 20.5% viewed it as worse. See Markus, especially pp. 29-30 and 57-58.

114

Appendix: The Survey

Key: N.R. = No response
      M.R. = Multiple response
       (1) = "genderless" respondent

The number just prior to a slash is male, the one after female, thus the first set below reads 1 "neuter" 9 male six female totalling [16] bracketed or 28.07%

1. You lived for the most part
    28.07% [16]   (1)   9/6   in Russia
    71.9%   [41]   22/19   in Ukraine
    5.26%   [3]   2/1   in Belorussia
      –   –   0/0   in the Balkan countries
    1.75%   [1]   1/0   in the Caucasus
    3.5%   [2]   2/0   in another republic
    8.77%   [5]   4/1   M.R.

2. The reason for your leaving the USSR
    54.38% [31]   18/13   economic
    63.15% [36]   (1)   20/15   political
    71.9%   [41]   24/17   national
    14.03% [8]   5/3   religious
    10.52% [6]   1/5   other
    73.68% [42]   24/18   M.R.

3. Did you live in Israel before your arrival in Canada?
    1.75%   [1]   1/0   yes
    96.5%   [55]   (1)   30/24   no
    1.75%   [1]   0/1   N.R.

4. You arrived in Canada
    80.7%   [46]   (1)   21/24   with your family
    5.26%   [3]   2/1   alone
    15.78% [9]   6/3   with relatives
    1.75%/12.28% [1]/[7] 1/0 N.R.; 4/3 M.R.

5. The reason you came to Canada as opposed to another country
    24.56% [14]   8/6   close relatives
    12.28% [7]   4/3   close friends
    40.35% [23]   11/12   possession of good information about Canada
    28.07% [16]   10/6   possibility of finding work in your field of
                                         specialization

33.33% [19]   (1)   10/8   other reasons
3.5%/36.84% [2]/[21] 2/0 N.R.; 14/7 M.R.

6. Having come to Canada you settled first
   5.26% [3]   2/1   in another city
   94.74% [54]   (1)   29/24 in Edmonton

7. You have been living in Canada
   47.36% [27]   13/14 less than a year
   19.29% [11]   7/4   1-2 years
   10.52% [6]   3/3   2-3 years
   22.8% [13]   (1)   8/4   more than three years

8. How many children do you have in your family?
   14.03% [8]   5/3   0
   43.85% [25]   13/12 1
   40.35% [23]   (1)   13/9   2
   –   –   0/0   3
   –   –   0/0   more
   1.75% [1]   1/0   N.R.

9. Which organizations in Canada have helped you materially as well as in finding lodging,
work and instruction?
   15.78% [46]   (1)   26/19 Canada Manpower
   59.64% [34]   (1)   22/11 Jewish Family Services
   1.75% [1]   0/1   Edmonton Immigrant Services Association
                                        (EISA)
   –   –   0/0   Catholic Immigrant Services
   –   –   0/0   Others
   50.87% [29]   (1)   18/10 M.R.

10. You would like to be joined by your
    40.35% [23]   (1)   11/11 parents
    49.12% [28]   14/14 brothers and sisters
    26.31% [15]   11/4   other relations
    52.63% [30]   (1)   19/10 friends
    8.77% [5]   2/3   would not like this
5.26%/42.1% [2]/[24] 2/0 N.R.; (1) 13/10 M.R.

116

11. How long did you receive help from the aforementioned organizations
        36.84% [21]   (1)   11/9   less than three months
        19.29% [11]   8/3   3-4 months
        24.56% [14]   7/7   4-6 months
         3.5%   [2]   1/1   6-12 months
          –   –   0/0   over one year
        15.78% [9]   4/5   N.R.

12. Before leaving the USSR you knew the English language
        49.12% [28]   16/12   not at all
        42.1%   [24]   14/10   a little
         7.01% [4]   (1)   1/2   fairly well
         1.75% [1]   0/1   very well

13. You attended English courses
        47.36% [27]   14/13   during the day
        33.33% [19]   14/5   during the evening
        24.56% [14]   7/7   did not attend
    5.26%/10.52% [3]/[6] 1/2 N.R.; 4/2 M.R.

14. How long did you study English at daytime courses?
         5.26% [3]   0/3   less than a month
         7.01% [4]   3/1   1-2 months
        33.33% [19]   10/9   2-4 months
         7.01% [4]   1/3   4-6 months
          –   –   0/0   more than six months
        47.36% [27]   (1)   17/9   N.R.

15. Same for evening classes
         7.01% [4]   0/4   less than a month
        10.52% [6]   4/2   1-2 months
         5.26% [3]   3/0   2-4 months
        10.52% [6]   4/2   4-6 months
         8.77% [5]   3/2   more than six months
        57.89% [33]   (1)   17/15   N.R.

16. Courses in the English language you found
        43.85% [25]   13/12   very useful
        26.31% [15]   10/5   useful
         5.26% [3]   2/1   not very useful
         1.75% [1]   0/1   useless
        22.8%   [13]   (1)   6/6   N.R.

17. For your work a command of English
    1.75% [1]   1/0   does not matter
    1.75% [1]   0/1   is not very important
    15.78% [9]   6/3   is useful
    77.19% [44]   (1)   24/19   is indispensable
    3.5%   [2]   0/2   N.R.

18. Now, your command of English is
    7.01% [4]   1/3   very poor
    40.35% [23]   14/9   poor
    43.85% [25]   (1)   14/10   rather good
    7.01% [4]   2/2   good
    –   –   0/0   excellent
    1.75% [1]   0/1   N.R.

19. After finishing work, you visit with
— Soviet immigrants
    5.26% [3]   3/0   never
    68.42% [39]   (1)   21/17   rarely
    26.31% [15]   7/8   often

— immigrants from other countries who came to Canada long ago
    22.8% [13]   6/7   never
    68.42% [39]   (1)   21/17   rarely
    –   –   0/0   often
    8.77% [5]   4/1   N.R.

— native-born Canadians
    21.05% [12]   7/5   never
    56.14% [32]   (1)   16/15   rarely
    14.03% [8]   5/3   often
    8.77% [5]   3/2   N.R.

20. If you came with elderly relatives, their command of English is
    26.31% [15]   9/6   very poor
    8.77% [5]   2/3   poor
    1.75% [1]   (1)   0/0   rather good
    –   –   0/0   very good
    –   –   0/0   excellent
    63.15% [36]   20/16   N.R.

118

21. Are they/have they been studying English in school?
    17.54% [10]   5/5   yes
    21.05% [12]   (1)   6/5   no
     61.4% [35]   20/15   N.R.

22. With your children you speak
    66.66% [38]   (1)   20/17   almost exclusively in Russian
       –   –   0/0   almost exclusively in English
    19.29% [11]   6/5   both in Russian and in English
    14.03% [8]   5/3   N.R.

23. At home your children speak
    49.12% [28]   (1)   13/14   almost exclusively in Russian
       –   –   0/0   almost exclusively in English
    35.08% [20]   12/8   both in Russian and in English
    15.78% [9]   6/3   N.R.

24. Do you want your children to study Russian?
    78.94% [45]   (1)   24/20   yes
     5.26% [3]   2/1   no
    15.78% [9]   5/4   N.R.

25. Do you want your children to get a higher education?
    85.96% [49]   (1)   26/22   yes
       –   –   0/0   no
    14.03% [8]   5/3   N.R.

26. In the USSR you completed
     3.5%   [2]   1/1   high school
    28.07% [16]   12/4   technical school
    17.54% [10]   3/7   college
    70.17% [40]   (1)   22/17   institute, university, academy
    19.29% [11]   7/4   M.R.

27. In what field did you work in the USSR?
    14.03% [8]   2/6   pedagogical
    17.54% [10]   (1)   8/1   scientific research
    14.03% [8]   4/4   consumer service
    36.84% [21]   15/6   manufacturing
     5.26% [3]   1/2   medical
    14.03% [8]   2/6   artistic

10.52% [6]   3/3   other
1.75%/14.03% [1]/[8] 1/0 N.R.; 5/3 M.R.

28. Are you currently employed?
    66.66% [38]   (1)   25/12   yes
    33.33% [19]   6/13   no

29. How many times did you change your place of employment?
    35.08% [20]   (1)   12/7   did not change
    22.8%   [13]   7/6   changed once
    5.26%   [3]   2/1   changed twice
    7.01%   [4]   3/1   changed three times
    1.75%   [1]   1/0   more
    26.31% [15]   5/10   N.R.

30. Your first job in Edmonton you found
    38.59% [22]   (1)   16/15   within a month
    14.03% [8]   4/4   after looking 1-3 months
    14.03% [8]   6/2   after looking 3-6 months
    3.5%   [2]   0/2   after looking 6-12 months
    1.75%   [1]   0/1   after looking more than a year
    28.07% [16]   5/11   N.R.

31. Your first job in Edmonton you found
    17.54% [10]   8/2   through acquaintances
    22.8%   [13]   8/5   through an ad in the paper
    19.29   [11]   7/4   with the help of Canada Manpower
    8.77   [5]   5/0   with the help of Jewish Family Services
    33.33%/1.75% [19]/[1] (1) 5/13 N.R.; 1/0 M.R.

32. You work
    33.33% [19]   13/6   in your specialization
    22.8%   [13]   (1)   8/4   at a job close to your specialization
    15.78% [9]   5/4   at a job far from your specialization
    29.82%/1.75% [17]/[1] 5/12 N.R.; 0/1 M.R.

33. At work your relations with Canadians are
    57.89% [33]   (1)   20/12   good
    10.52% [6]   5/1   indifferent
    1.75%   [1]   1/0   poor
    31.57%/1.75% [18]/[1] 6/12 N.R.; 1/0 M.R.

34. If you are working in your specialization or close to it, how soon after your arrival in Edmonton did you find it?

21.05%	[12]	(1)	8/3	within a month
8.77%	[5]		2/3	after 1-3 months
12.28%	[7]		7/0	after 3-6 months
5.26%	[3]		2/1	after 6-12 months
8.77%	[5]		2/3	after more than a year

45.61%/1.75% [26]/[1] 11/5 N.R.; 1/0 M.R.

35. This work you found

17.54%	[10]	7/3	through acquaintances
14.03%	[8]	5/3	through an ad in the paper
8.77%	[5]	2/3	with the help of Canada Manpower
8.77%	[5]	4/1	with the help of Jewish Family Services
5.26%	[3]	3/0	having previously received information about all firms in your specialization to whom you sent a curriculum vitae

52.63%/5.26% [30]/[3] (1) 13/16 N.R.; 2/1 M.R.

36. Since settling in Edmonton, how many times have you changed your residence?

22.8%	[13]		6/7	0
49.12%	[28]	(1)	16/11	1
15.78%	[9]		4/5	2
8.77%	[5]		4/1	3
1.75%	[1]		1/0	more
1.75%	[1]		0/1	N.R.

37. Your lodging – you are

77.19%	[44]	(1)	24/19	renting
22.8%	[13]		7/6	buying

38. Currently you are living

–	–		0/0	in a room
10.52%	[6]		3/3	in a studio apartment
10.52%	[6]		3/3	in a two-room apartment
24.56%	[14]	(1)	8/5	in a three-room apartment
31.57%	[18]		10/8	in a condominium
21.05%	[12]		7/5	in your own house
1.75%	[1]		0/1	N.R.

39. You intend
38.59%	[22]	(1)	13/8	to move
47.36%	[27]		12/15	to remain at your present residence for a long time
14.03%	[8]		6/2	N.R.

40. If you moved, you would want to
–	–		0/0	rent a larger apartment
5.26%	[3]		2/1	buy a larger apartment
–	–		0/0	rent a condominium
1.75%	[1]		0/1	buy a condominium
1.75%	[1]		1/0	rent a house
64.8%	[37]		21/16	buy a house
5.26%	[3]		2/1	simply change neighborhoods
10.52%	[6]	(1)	3/2	move to a different city

14.03%/5.26% [8]/[3] 4/4 N.R.; 3/0 M.R.

41. If you moved from Edmonton you would prefer to live
85.96%	[49]	(1)	26/22	in a larger city
1.75%	[1]		1/0	in a smaller city
–	–		0/0	in the country
7.01%	[4]		2/2	does not matter

7.01%/1.75% [4]/[1] 2/2 N.R.; 0/1 M.R.

42. Which of the following criteria is the most important in a decision to leave or stay in Edmonton?
22.8%	[13]		7/6	salary
15.78%	[9]		6/3	type of work
54.38%	[31]	(1)	18/12	chance for advancement at work
29.82%	[17]		7/10	presence of relatives or friends
29.82%	[17]		9/8	climate

10.52%/35.08% [6]/[20] 4/2 N.R.; 13/7 M.R.

43. If you moved from Edmonton you would prefer
3.5%	[2]		2/0	the Maritimes
–	–		0/0	Quebec
36.84%	[21]		12/9	Ontario
–	–		0/0	Manitoba
–	–		0/0	Saskatchewan
17.54%	[10]		7/3	British Columbia
–	–		0/0	the Canadian North
21.05%	[12]		7/5	U.S.A.
–	–		0/0	Australia
1.75%	[1]		0/1	New Zealand
33.33%	[19]	(1)	9/9	Europe
–	–		0/0	Other countries/continents

14.03%/24.56% [8]/[14] 4/4 N.R.; 8/6 M.R.

122

44. The number of cars in your family
    28.07% [16]   9/7   0
    52.63% [30]   (1)   16/13   1
    14.03% [8]   4/4   2
     5.26% [3]   2/1   3
       –   –   0/0   more

45. Your first car you bought
    19.29% [11]   7/4   within 2-3 months after moving to Canada
    21.05% [12]   6/6   within 3-6 months after moving to Canada
    21.05% [12]   6/5   within 6-12 months after moving to Canada
     1.75% [1]   1/0   one year after moving to Canada
     3.5%   [2]   1/1   one year and a half after moving to Canada
       –   –   0/0   two years after moving to Canada
     1.75% [1]   1/0   more than two years after moving to Canada
    31.57% [18]   9/9   N.R.

46. Your car/cars is/are
     3.5%   [2]   2/0   sub-compact
    10.52% [6]   3/3   compact
    33.33% [19]   (1)   11/7   mid-size
    28.07% [16]   9/7   full-size
    29.82%/5.26% [17]/[3] 8/9 N.R.; 1/2 M.R

47. If you intend to change cars you would wish to buy
    29.82% [17]   8/9   a smaller one
     7.01% [4]   2/2   larger
    22.8%   [13]   10/3   the same
    40.35% [23]   (1)   11/11   N.R.

48. After moving to Canada are you still interested in what is happening in the USSR?
    80.7%   [46]   (1)   25/20   yes
    15.78   [9]   6/3   no
     3.5   [2]   0/2   N.R.

49. You follow events in the USSR by
    40.35% [23]   14/9   radio
    52.63% [30]   19/11   T.V.
    70.17% [40]   (1)   22/17   Western press
    12.28% [7]   4/3   Soviet press
    50.87% [29]   16/13   letters from the USSR
    8.77%/64.8% [5]/[37] 3/2 N.R.; 22/15 M.R.

50. You read
   43.85% [25]   15/10   the Canadian press
   24.56% [14]   9/4   all kinds of Western press material
   61.4%   [35]   (1)   17/17   the emigre press in Russian
   5.26%   [3]   2/1   the Soviet press
8.77%/40.35% [5]/[23] 3/2 N.R.; (1) 13/9 M.R.

51. You subscribe to
   14.03% [8]   5/3   some Western journals or newspapers
   36.84% [21]   (1)   12/9   to the emigre press
   33.33% [19]   11/8   to the Canadian press
     –   –   0/0   to the Soviet press
33.33%/17.54% [19]/[10] 9/10 N.R.; 7/3 M.R.

52. Do you have a T.V. set?
   77.19% [44]   (1)   25/18   yes
   22.8%   [13]   6/7   no

53. You watch T.V.
   43.85% [25]   17/8   around one hour per day
   21.05% [12]   4/8   around two hours per day
   8.77%   [5]   3/2   more than three hours per day
   15.78% [9]   (1)   5/3   I do not watch T.V.
12.28%/1.75% [7]/[1] 3/4 N.R.; 1/0 M.R.

54. On T.V. you regularly watch
   59.64% [34]   23/11   the news
   19.29% [11]   11/0   sports
   21.05% [12]   8/4   specials
   29.82% [17]   8/9   concerts
   8.77%   [5]   2/3   plays
   14.03% [8]   4/4   situation comedies
   12.28% [7]   3/4   soap operas, e.g., *Another World*
   29.82% [17]   9/8   cops 'n' robbers
31.57%/52.63% [18]/[30] (1) 7/10 N.R.; 18/12 M.R.

55. You listen to radio
   19.29% [11]   (1)   5/5   I do not
   24.56% [14]   8/6   about one half hour per day
   31.57% [18]   12/6   about one hour per day
   5.26%   [3]   2/1   about two hours per day
     –   –   0/0   about three hours per day
   5.26%   [3]   1/2   more than three hours per day
15.78%/1.75% [9]/[1] 4/5 N.R.; 0/1 M.R.

56. On radio you regularly listen to

38.59%	[22]	13/9	the weather forecast
50.87%	[29]	18/11	news
42.1%	[24]	13/11	musical programs
7.01%	[4]	4/0	sports

35.08%/49.12% [20]/[28] (1) 10/9 N.R.; 17/11 M.R.

57. You go to restaurants

26.31%	[15]		9/6	about once every six months
15.78%	[9]		6/3	about every other month
3.5%	[2]		2/0	at least once a month
1.75%	[1]		0/1	at least once a week
43.85%	[25]	(1)	9/15	I do not go to restaurants
8.77%	[5]		5/0	N.R.

58. You go to the movies

28.07%	[16]	(1)	9/6	about once every six months
21.05%	[12]		6/6	about every other month
21.05%	[12]		7/5	at least once a month
1.75%	[1]		1/0	at least once a week
21.05%	[12]		5/7	I do not go to movies
7.01%	[4]		3/1	N.R.

59. You go to concerts

33.33%	[19]	(1)	9/9	about once every six months
21.05%	[12]		7/5	about every other month
10.52%	[6]		3/3	at least once a month
3.5%	[2]		1/1	at least once a week
19.29%	[11]		6/5	I do not go to concerts
12.28%	[7]		5/2	N.R.

60. You go to the theatre

36.84%	[21]	(1)	11/9	about once every six months
10.52%	[6]		3/3	about every other month
1.75%	[1]		1/0	at least once a month
–	–		0/0	at least once a week
31.57%	[18]		9/9	I do not go to the theatre
19.29%	[11]		7/4	N.R.

61. Did you go to the synagogue in the USSR?

14.03%	[8]		4/4	yes
84.21%	[48]	(1)	26/21	no
1.75%	[1]		0/1	N.R.

62. In Canada you go to the synagogue

14.03%	[8]	(1)	3/4	never
77.19%	[44]		24/20	sometimes
7.01%	[4]		3/1	often
1.75%	[1]		1/0	N.R.

63. During your vacation you travelled

22.8%	[13]		7/6	in Alberta
14.03%	[8]	(1)	5/2	in British Columbia
–	–		0/0	in Saskatchewan or Manitoba
5.26%	[3]		2/1	in Ontario
1.75%	[1]		1/0	in Quebec
–	–		0/0	in the Maritimes
7.01%	[4]		3/1	in U.S.A.

63.15%/12.28% [36]/[7] 18/18 N.R.; 5/2 M.R.

64. Do you want to get to know Canada, its history, geography, culture, etc.?

82.45%	[47]		26/21	very much
14.03%	[8]	(1)	4/3	somewhat
1.75%	[1]		1/0	do not want to
1.75%	[1]		0/1	N.R.

65. You would welcome the creation of a centre for Russian culture in Edmonton

8.77%	[5]		3/2	I am indifferent
82.45%	[47]	(1)	24/22	yes
7.01%	[1]		1/0	N.R.

66. Having come to Canada, have you found that which you aspired to in leaving the USSR?

77.19%	[14]	(1)	26/17	materially
35.08%	[20]		15/5	spiritually
3.5%	[2]		0/2	you have not at all found what you were looking for
15.78%	[9]		4/5	you had an altogether different idea about life in the West
–	–		0/0	you regret leaving the USSR

12.28%/45.61% [7]/[26] 4/3 N.R.; 18/8 M.R.

67. Did you encounter antisemitism in the USSR?

85.96%	[49]		30/19	often
12.28%	[7]	(1)	1/5	rarely
–	–		0/0	not at all
1.75%	[1]		0/1	N.R.

68. If you encountered antisemitism in the USSR, it was

57.89%	[33]		21/12	in school
47.36%	[27]		16/11	at the institute (Institute of higher education.)
63.15%	[36]	(1)	22/13	getting a job
56.14%	[32]		19/13	at work
64.8%	[37]		23/14	in society at large

5.26%/73.68% [3]/[42] 1/2 N.R.; 25/17 M.R.

69. Have you encountered antisemitism in Canada?

–	–		0/0	often
33.33%	[19]		10/9	rarely
56.14%	[32]	(1)	19/12	not at all
10.52%	[6]		2/4	N.R.

70. If you have encountered antisemitism in Canada, this was

–	–		0/0	in school
–	–		0/0	at the institute
10.52%	[6]		3/3	getting a job
5.26%	[3]		2/1	at work
17.54%	[11]		6/5	in society at large

70.17%/3.5% [40]/[2] (1) 22/17 N.R.; 1/1 M.R.

71. You are

22.8%	[13]		4/9	under 30
21.05%	[12]		9/3	31-35
17.54%	[10]		3/7	36-40
24.56%	[14]	(1)	11/2	41-45
10.52%	[6]		4/2	46-50
–	–		0/0	51-55
1.75%	[1]		0/1	56-60
1.75%	[1]		0/1	over 60

72. Sex

43.85%	[25]		0/25	masculine
54.38%	[31]		31/0	feminine
1.75%	[1]	(1)		N.R.

73. The age of your children

15.78%	[9]		5/4	under 5
40.35%	[23]	(1)	13/9	6-10 years
21.05%	[12]		7/5	11-15 years
15.78%	[9]		6/3	16-20 years
14.03%	[8]		3/5	over 20

14.03%/24.56% [8]/[14] 5/3 N.R.; 9/5 M.R.

"FIST PRESS": A STUDY OF THE FINNISH-CANADIAN HANDWRITTEN NEWSPAPERS

Varpu Lindström-Best,
Multicultural History Society of Ontario

Kyösti was a coal miner. His twelve hour shift at the North Wellington mine in British Columbia had just ended and Kyösti was briskly walking toward his rooming house. After cleaning up at the wash-basin and enjoying a hearty meal serviced by a Finnish servant girl, Kyösti flopped on his bunk. Instead of sleeping, however, he pulled out a carefully folded piece of paper and in the flickering candlelight he began to write. Kyösti's article was for the local Temperance Society Aallotar's handwritten newspaper which was read aloud at their social gathering on a January evening in 1897. Kyösti wrote:

> Many cannot understand why an ordinary worker needs knowledge, is it not enough for a miner to know where to drill the hole and how much powder to put into it ... We must admit that a wise miner will not get any more money for a ton of coal, nor will his production increase ... Still, it is important not only to satisfy our material and physical needs because our souls demand nourishment as well which can only be supplied by studying and improving the mental faculties.[1]

This episode contradicts the general image of foreign workers, an image that has been perpetuated by recent historians, recording their impressions from the Anglo-Saxon pedestal. For instance, one recent publication on foreign workers states that Finns, along with many other nationalities, *probably* formed a " ... relatively undifferentiated mass of frightfully exploited, illiterate labourers, cut off from the world, and to a large extent still rooted in the village."[2]

This study of the handwritten Finnish-Canadian newspapers will look at the cultural aspirations of the immigrant workers as they were recorded by hundreds of miners, lumber workers, tailors and maids across Canada. After a brief survey of the educational background of the Finnish immigrants, the paper will examine three main purposes of the handwritten newspapers.

The first objective was to allow the immigrants a platform for written expression in their native tongue and thus a chance to exercise and improve their writing skills. The second was to communicate local information; the third, to promote particular causes such as temperance, women's emancipation, socialism and nationalism.

130

In Finland, prior to 1865, the State Lutheran Church had been largely responsible for the high literacy rate of the Finnish peasants. The church laboured diligently to instil in the people the principles of Christianity. In practice, this meant that all the members of the congregation had to learn to read the catechism in order to be confirmed. Without confirmation a Finn was ineligible to marry or to obtain a permit to leave the country. The general understanding among the Finns was that everyone would learn to read and write, if not in the two-week cramming sessions at the church, then independently under parental supervision at home.[3] In 1865, the government established, in the rural and urban districts of Finland, public schools that were independent from the church, although still based on 'Christian principles.' Subsequently, the last quarter of the nineteenth century witnessed a rapid increase in the rural public schools, which were aimed at nine-to-thirteen-year olds who had already acquired basic reading skills on their own. The Finnish immigrants to Canada before the turn of the century came mainly from rural areas where the new education plan had the greatest impact. For example, during the school year of 1875, there were 285 rural public schools with 10,000 students. Thirty years later, in 1905, there were 2,400 rural public schools with 100,000 students.[4] Education was extended to both sexes, and by 1905, out of the country's 19,000 high school students, 9,000 were girls.[5]

As the literacy rate of the Finns rose, so too, did the number of newspapers. In 1876 there were 46 newspapers; thirty years later, in 1906, there were 256. Those Finnish peasants who found the cost of the papers prohibitive formed newspaper pools, where they exchanged and shared the papers. The general custom was that the landless peasants were welcome to read the landlord's papers after he was finished with them. It was common to have a long wooden bench by the front entrance where the newspapers would await the readers. When temperance, youth, educational and labour organizations emerged in great numbers in the country after 1880, one of the first steps undertaken by each organization was to establish a reading room with a good selection of papers. Thus, the population became accustomed to reading daily newspapers. As Finland's standard of living improved, the first sign of the peasant's upward mobility was a subscription to a newspaper of his choice.

The Finnish immigrants brought with them this tradition of newspaper reading and literacy when they began to arrive in Canada in the 1880s. This was approvingly noted by Dominion Immigration Agents, who placed the Finns among the most desirable class of immigrants.[6] The *Montreal Daily Witness* reflects the dozens of articles on the subject of Finnish immigration that appeared across Canada in 1899:

> Finns are industrious and intelligent people, there not being more than two per cent of the entire population which cannot read and write.[7]

Against this background, it is easier to understand immigrants like Kyösti and their longing to read and to learn. Yet their inability to speak the host country's languages prevented them from reading the local or national newspapers. Finnish-language newspapers were ordered from the United States and Finland for the libraries and reading rooms established in Canada, but these papers did not relate to the local needs of the scattered Finnish-Canadian communities in Canada.[8]

The Finns' spontaneous response to this dilemma was to write their own newspapers with the talent and resources available. Unlike regular dailies, the handwritten paper was considered to be an educational tool in written expression. Mr. O. Roslund, the editor of a handwritten periodical published in Edmonton, Alberta in 1915, stated the purpose of the paper in the following manner:

> This handwritten newspaper or 'fist press' as we commonly call it, operates in just about every Finnish Socialist Organization local in Canada (there were 66 at this time)[9] is useful because it gives us all, men and women alike, a chance to practice and improve our writing skills, as well as our heads. Because, today it is important to have more in your heads than what the Englishman calls 'bullshit.'[10]

While the Finns were literate, they realized that their skills were very basic, often amounting to only the mastery of phonetic spelling. A Finnish tailor in Toronto who attempted to teach English to his fellow countrymen lamented in 1905 that scarcely 3 per cent of his students had any knowledge of Finnish grammar.[11]

The Finns hoped to improve their grammar and clarity of expression through practice gained by writing articles. The handwritten papers were less intimidating, because their circulation was small — often limited to friends. Although each paper had a nominal editor or two, these were not appointed because of their literary skills, but for their ability to persuade others to write. As a result, the hand-written papers are to linguists a rich source of information. Due to the phonetic spelling of the language, the authors reveal by their "accents" their province or even village of origin. With the increase in the length of residency in North America the Finns adopted new English expressions and created what is often called "Finglish." This was especially common in subject areas that the Finns had not discussed in the old country. For example, "I work as a miner's helper" translated to "Vorkin mainarin helpperinä." In a regular newspaper, such expressions, dialectal words and incorrect grammar would be edited out in the process of transforming the articles into "proper" Finnish, but in the handwritten papers the authentic style of the working-class authors has been preserved.

The second objective of the papers was to give community information, usually news that related to Finnish Canadians. The small columns and advertisements reveal the needs and hardships of the immigrants as they experienced them. The cold statistics of child mortality at the turn of the century, for example, were of real concern to the Toronto maid who wrote in her summary of 1903 local news: "Last year seven Finnish children were born and six Finnish children died, the oldest of whom was seven years old."[12]

Another example of the isolated life of the immigrants is a notice placed in an Edmonton newspaper in 1914. It reads:

> Our countryman John Walter ended his days on the tenth of this month by hanging himself about 82 miles north of here in a work camp near the Dunvegan Railroad. He had been hunting alone all winter and somehow became deranged. The deceased has been in this country for fourteen years and was thirty-five years old, a single man, originally from Vähäkryö. If anyone knows this man or has information of his relatives, please contact the following address. John Jonson, 9714 – 103 Ave., Edmonton.[13]

Newspaper advertising could often provide sociological insight into current conditions of life, e.g., advertisements by Finnish rooming houses, restaurants or ticket agents at a cost of one penny a line in Toronto. From the social angle, a very revealing advertising was the following: " . . . food and rooms available both night and day, good food and satisfactory service especially for women."[14]

Apparently, loneliness was one of the most distressing social problems as shown by the great frequency of advertisements, placed by lonely men and women looking for a companion with "serious intentions." Thus, loneliness caused by geographic isolation prompted two women from Extension, British Columbia to write:

> Hei, Hei You Finnish boys!
> Here are two happy maidens who want eternal guides to their life here in the Canadian shores. Because we are lonely as a bird in a wind-swept branch, we would like to leave this loneliness and begin a friendship with single men. We are not too fat and not too skinny but in the best meaty condition. We are not too tall and not too short, 11 feet all total and 87 years . . . so that we are not too young and not too old, but in the best sale condition to tie those love knots. Letters from all are welcome..Searching in Extension, Longing in Canada.[15]

The third reason for writing and publishing papers was to promote the cause of a given organization. The handwritten papers were invariably non-profit, group efforts rather than commercial enterprises. The oldest surviving papers are from Vancouver Island and date from 1896. Until the First World

War the papers promoted mainly the ideas of temperance, women's emancipation and socialism. From the very beginning the papers were cautiously encouraging women to participate in activities outside the home, in order that they might become better educators of their sons. By 1914 women had clarified their position in the following manner:

> Woman is like a doormat that men trample on at will. Woman must, generally speaking, submit to her husband's will and is left to his discretion, even if her intellect surpasses his. Women have been kept as breeding machines whose only function was to give birth to descendants and to satisfy the man's often licentious and selfish sexual pleasures.
>
> .... Dear women! Develop your brains, increase your knowledge of reading literature and keep abreast with the times, then you will fully understand your wretched position and can fight as equals beside men for a new future.[16]

The papers that were dedicated to the teaching of socialism and to the raising of working class consciousness were the most numerous as well as the most widely circulated. Until the thirties, the Finnish communities were dominated by the left-wing organizations whose doctrines struck a responsive chord in the struggling immigrant's mind:

> When Will the Poor Discover Their Strength? We workers are a strange lot. We make up 80% of the population yet submit to the laws made by the small ruling minority. We fill the store houses, yet our children wear rags. We dig the coal, yet we must shiver with cold. We build the palaces, yet we live in shacks. We build the railroads and steamships, yet we can't travel on them because we have no gold, even though we dig that too from the mountains . . . We workers are truly a strange lot![17]

The depression years saw a considerable shift in the composition of Finnish immigrant groups in Canada and a noticeable change in the political attitudes which divided the communities into 'red' and 'white.' A new national Finnish organization called the 'Loyal Finns in Canada' was founded. The handwritten newspapers from this era are nationalistic and conservative. In these papers are found the most colourful illustrations and an abundance of sentimental poetry. A handwritten paper from Sudbury, Ontario, in 1932 explained the change in the political climate:

> When a white Finn arrived to this continent he was immediately greeted by red vultures, he was dragged to the committees of investigation, his life was threatened and he was forced to leave his job. Unable to speak English he could not defend himself but had to submit (to the socialists) . . . We white Finns were scattered across Canada, but now that we have joined together (as Loyal Finns in Canada) we see how the Finnish Lion

awakens and the red vulture trembles with fear. Now we can breathe freely.[18]

The last handwritten papers were published during the Second World War, when Finland Aid organizations joined in the efforts to help the old country. These modern "fist press papers" were already typed.[19]

The tradition of handwritten papers has disappeared since the Second World War. Mimeographs, bulletins and a variety of Finnish-Canadian newspapers have taken their place. Those handwritten papers that have been preserved are only one example of the ingenuity of immigrants in meeting their cultural needs and in filling the void created by cultural and spatial isolation. Although the end product did not come out in English, it was, none the less, an expression of social and cultural needs, written by immigrants out to find a niche in Canadian life. Moreover, the immigrants believed that by self-improvement they were making a real contribution to their new country. Eighty years ago Kyösti concluded his article with these words:

> The future, the happiness and the strength of nations is based on its population's knowledge and skill.[20]

These were the words of a foreign immigrant worker with a rural background, but surely they were not the words of an "illiterate labourer, cut off from the world."

135

FOOTNOTES

¹*Koe*, North Wellington, B.C., January 1897. MHSO Accession 13, Finnish Canadian Historical Society Collection (FCHSC) C-2 File 14, Archives of Ontario (AO).

²Donald Avery, *'Dangerous Foreigners': European Immigrant Workers and Labour Radicalism in Canada, 1896-1932* (Toronto, 1979), 49.

³Eino Jutikkala, Kauko Pirinen, *Suomen Historia*, Weilin Göös (Helsinki, 1966), 265.

⁴Pentti Renvall, *Suomalaisen Kansanvallan Kehitys* (Porvoo, 1965), 82.

⁵Ibid., 85.

⁶Public Archives of Canada (PAC), Public Records Division, Immigration Branch Records, RG 76, volume 25-26, File 651.

⁷*Montreal Daily Witness*, March 20, 1899. Clipping in PAC, RG 76, volume 25-26, File 651.

⁸For information on Finnish newspapers in the United States see: *For the Common Good*, Työmies Society, Superior, (Wisconsin, 1977), article by P. George Hummasti "The Working Man's Daily Bread: Finnish American Working Class Newspapers 1900-1921." The first Canadian newspaper was called *Tyokansa*, published in Port Arthur, Ontario, from 1907-1915.

⁹Canadan Suomalainen Järjestö 25 Vuotta, 1911-1936, (Sudbury, Ontario, 1936), 38.

¹⁰*Moukari*, Edmonton, Alberta, April 30, 1915. MHSO Accession 13, FCHSC D-28 File 6, AO.

¹¹Varpu Lindström-Best, *The Finnish Immigrant Community of Toronto 1887-1913*, MHSO Occasional Paper O.P. 79-8 (Toronto, 1979), 46.

¹²*Toiwo*, No. 1, Toronto, January 9, 1904. PAC, Finnish Organization of Canada Collection, Finnish Society at Toronto Archives.

¹³*Moukari*, No. 3, 1914.

¹⁴Ibid.

¹⁵*Säde*, No. 1 (?), 1901, Extension, B.C. MHSO Accession 13, FCHSC C-2, File 15, AO.

¹⁶*Moukari*, No. 3, 1914.

¹⁷*Säde*, No. 6, Ladysmith, B.C., October 29, 1904.

¹⁸*Oottako Kuuilu?*, Sudbury, Ontario, June 1932. MHSO Accession 13, FSHSC D-17, File 9, AO.

¹⁹Newspapers from this period can be found in the MHSO Accession 13, FCHSC. For example see: *Ampiainen Ampiainen*, Winnipeg, Manitoba, 1932-1936 D-17 Files 6-10; *Sotaorpo*, Kirkland Lake, Ontario, 1941, D-16, Files 16-17 and *Suomen Apu*, Sudbury, Ontario, 1940, D-4, File 7, AO.

136

[20]*Koe*, North Wellington, B.C., January 1897.

All translations from Finnish are by the author.

SETTLEMENT, DEPRESSION AND ALIENATION: AN EPISODE FROM EARLY PRAIRIE HISTORY

Martin L. Kovacs,
University of Regina

A sensational news item appeared in the *Regina Leader* on an otherwise uneventful November day, in 1890 under the heading "Death Before Arrest," with the subtitle "Immigration Agent Vass Commits Suicide." The event had taken place at the Queen's Hotel, Wapella, about a week prior to the announcement. Julius Vass, before Constable Kelly could arrest him,

> blew out his own brains with a revolver. An investigation into his affairs took place last week and it transpired that moneys entrusted to him by the settlers had been misappropriated, but the amount, it was understood, was not large.[1]

The objectives of the present paper are to inquire into the circumstances surrounding Julius Vass' presence and his tragic end in the Canadian West, and to show the significance of the case for Canadian administration in general, and for the Hungarian colony of Esterhaz in particular.

The affair, at first sight, was very clear and logical. One of "those foreigners" had committed a crime and meted out to himself just punishment. However, there was much more to the matter than met the eye. Julius Vass was a type of immigrant for whom the strange world of American democracy had been unable to offer a niche because he was not a manual worker,[2] nor did he possess those qualities which could have landed him a position in the lower reaches of government or business administration. Settlers of his kind — that is, persons who received education in Vass' native country — would complete their education with a "maturity" (matriculation) certificate, testifying to their having successfully gone through courses of instruction for twelve years and shown their competence, mainly in literary skills, ancient languages, and the study of classics. The acquisition of such a certificate entitled its bearer to certain privileges, one of which was the possibility of becoming a reserve officer in the army and a member of the gentry. It also constituted the precondition of employment in the middle reaches of government administration. Although these prerogatives were regarded as privileges in the society of the native country, they proved to be a tremendous psychological obstacle in the egalitarian atmosphere of Canada and the United States, for they constituted a dividing wall between workers of Hungarian background and their so-called "élite." In many other ethno-cultural groups the élite and their countrymen

138

could work harmoniously, but this was not true of Hungarian settlements. Few of the would-be leaders of Magyar immigrants could or would forget their former privileged status and attempt not to maintain the 'three-foot distance,' as the appropriate Hungarian phrase expressed it, in social contacts with their compatriots. The peasant immigrants, on the other hand, in most cases tended to be suspicious of educated persons as a class, and would refuse to co-operate with them, even when circumstances warranted co-operation. Very likely, these were the reasons that prompted Julius Vass to join P. O. Esterhazy and some other "educated Hungarians" in their endeavour to recruit would-be settlers for an extensive Hungarian colony on the Canadian Plains.

The year 1885, looked very propitious for such an enterprise. The vast northern plains were without any sizable population yet. The Canadian government appeared almost desperate for new settlers,[3] because, at that stage, the prairie was practically "a graveyard of immigration schemes." Moreover, the political constellation seemed to threaten a war, at least for a while, between the British Empire — including Canada — and Imperial Russia over spheres of influence in Afghanistan.[4] Esterhazy's nimble mind perceived at once the potentiality of a military border not unlike the one that had existed between Hungary and the Ottoman Empire in the previous centuries, one peopled with some ten thousand Hungarian military settler, to be recruited from among immigrants in the United States. The objective, the blocking of a potential Russian invasion across the Behring Strait, however, was not regarded as realistic by the Governor-General of Canada, the Marquess of Lansdowne. But he deigned to receive in person "Count" Esterhazy, a former captain in the British army[5] and expressed the willingness to support the establishment of colonies of Hungarian farmers. Esterhazy was promptly introduced to high officials and given letters of introduction as well as a railway pass. The settling agent immediately began to carry out the first step of his colonization scheme; he set out in the company of "Mr. Eden, Land Commissioner of the Manitoba and North-Western Railway," and "his [Esterhazy's] private secretary," who was none other than Julius Vass. The *Regina Leader* reported that Count Esterhazy was "very much pleased with our Canadian institutions and with our prospects in the North-West, and expressed himself as delighted with the country." The report continues:

> He goes from here to look at the lands of Canadian Pacific Railway north of Broadview, thence to those of the M&NW Ry. Co. and we have no doubt that the magnificent prospects which he must be convinced of, and the inducements by way of land and settlement in the country generally will determine himself and his countrymen to take up their abode with us.[6]

Thus, Vass had attached himself to Esterhazy and his grandiose design to colonize a large portion of the Canadian West with Hungarian settlers. Just who was Vass? Very little is known about his past prior to 1885. The only source of information seems to be Lajos Gönczy, one of the original pioneer settlers of Esterhaz, who had ample opportunity during several years to observe Vass in the colony and to hear some details about his past from Vass himself and the other settlers. According to Gönczy, Gyula Vass had formerly been an officer in a hussar regiment in Kassa (now Kosice in Czechoslovakia) who had set out for Pennsylvania from Csetnek, Borsod County, together with Károly Fodor, a forester, and a certain Mór Eszláry. "They took up work in No. 3 Pit at the Leisering mines, but they — gentlemen not accustomed to hard toil — found it beyond their endurance and decided to take advantage of the free land scheme in Canada."[7] Since the interview took place about forty years after the event, the details mentioned may not be entirely accurate. Nevertheless, we may assume that Vass had been in some capacity in the Austro-Hungarian army and that he could have been a *földi* (coming from the same village or region) of Charles Fodor, a well-known resident of Whitewood. But Gönczy's assumption of the sameness of Eszlary and Esterhazy was just another guess. Esterhazy was born in Esztergom, quite distant from Csetnek, and he never used the name Eszláry.[8]

It is not known whether Vass played any role in the formation of the first 'Hungarian' colony, Hunsvalley (Hungarians' Valley), in Manitoba, which was "in active operation" by August 1888.[9] The success of the first colony helped to establish the credibility of Esterhazy's enterprise. Nevertheless, he was required to show the support and backing of an immigration society. Therefore, he organized the "Hungarian Immigration and Colonization Society" in the spring of 1886, and reported the fact to John Lowe, stating that

> . . . Mr. Julius Vass, our secretary . . . requested me to allow him to accompany me on my present trip to Canada and he proposes to undertake this at his own expense. I regard Mr. Vass as one deserving every possible encouragement and courtesy; he is a gentleman in the strict interpretation of the meaning of the word; his father in Hungary is quite wealthy.[10]

A month later Esterhazy reached Toronto with the first group of immigrants for what was to become the colony of Esterhaz. He had to inform John Lowe:

> . . . Mr. Vass, our secretary, wires me he cannot possibly join our Detachment, tomorrow, but that he will proceed to Toronto with his people next week; I am therefore now leaving here for Owen Sound and will embark with our Immigrants for Port Arthur tomorrow.[11]

By June 8, 1886, Esterhazy was ready to travel on to the Qu'Appelle Valley to settle his party of Hungarians north of Whitewood in Township 19, Range 2.

The next group (led by Vass), consisting of about thirty families, was expected to arrive in Winnipeg on the following day.[12] Indeed, the departure of "several Hungarian families" for Whitewood took place on the day indicated.[13] By the beginning of July, George A. Hill, the government land guide, was in a position to report the successful settling of Esterhazy's Hungarians "on a block of fertile land twenty-two miles north of Whitewood." He added: "They are an excellent class of immigrants, being industrious, temperate, frugal, and intelligent. Count Esterhazy has taken up land himself . . . "[14]

Thus, Esterhazy's second settlement was taking shape. The settlers were happy because the soil was fertile, the site was close to water and trees, and the settling agent had arranged for a loan for each settler with the support of Sir George Stephen, the President, and through the agency of the Canada North-West Land Company, as represented by its manager, W. B. Scarth. The loan was sufficient for the purchase of animals and farming equipment and also for the erection of a frame house.[15] It was the Company that purchased and distributed equipment and animals. The Company provided the material and the tradesmen for the building of the houses. In other words, the settlers just did not have any access to the loan. After a promising beginning, things started to turn for the worse. One of the terrible prairie fires swept over the area, destroying the hay stored for the winter, and some other belongings. It also made impossible the accommodation of a large group of settlers brought by Esterhazy at the beginning of October.[16] The men and their families had to be taken by Esterhazy to Medicine Hat and Lethbridge. However, the attempts of the managers of the mines to take advantage of the needs of these would-be miners,[17] combined with the effects of the most terrible winter in living memory, prompted many of the men to leave their places of employment and return to Winnipeg with bitter complaints against everyone who had anything to do with their trip to the prairie. One unpleasant consequence of the affair was that the employment of Esterhazy as settling agent was terminated by the government, despite the fact that he had produced documentary evidence of his innocence in the matter.[18] He felt that he was being sacrificed to shield others, and came to the conclusion that W. B. Scarth and the Canada North-West Land Company had much to do with his loss of employment. Consequently, he refused to settle on the homestead chosen by him or to take over the equipment, animals, and house provided by the Company from the loan referred to above. Under the circumstances, his official contact with the colony, by that time named Esterhaz, had come to an end. Yet, before his departure from there to recruit further immigrants for the already existing and the projected Hungarian colonies, Esterhazy left Julius Vass in charge of the settlement until his return.[19]

Towards the end of January, 1887, just before the time of the termination of his services by the government, the settling agent still had occasion to submit Vass' two reports to John Lowe, Secretary, Department of Agriculture, Ottawa. Esterhazy's letter is of interest for two reasons: first, because he referred to Vass as "postmaster, Esterhaz, N.W.T. and Superintendent of the Hungarian Colony," and second, because of Vass' complaint about the first conflicts among the colonists.[20]

Julius Vass was left to his own devices to see the colonists through the cruel winter of 1886-1887. He outlined the difficulties in one of his later letters:

> This colony of Hungarians was founded by Count Esterhazy in June 1886, bringing in with himself, thirty-seven settlers; after staying a few weeks, Esterhazy left and has never since been near the colony; the majority of the original settlers were utterly unfit for the life here. When Esterhaz [sic] deserted them they were without the means of living through the coming winter; by help from my private purse and in various other ways I managed to drag these poor people through this first winter, but such was their suffering . . . that out of the thirty-seven brought by Esterhaz, there are only nine at present left in the colony.[21]

In addition to the unusual severity of the winter, 1886 marked the beginning of a depression which was to worsen in the following year. The colonists who left Esterhaz did not do so in one group, nor in the same year.[22] It appears that their departures were spread over about three years. Vass found himself in a difficult position, yet he believed that he was officially acting for the government and the Canada North-West Land Company. To the Minister of Agriculture he wrote:

> I have never despaired of the colony in spite of all we have had to go through. I have, by constantly encouraging those who were here, and using my influence to induce others whom I thought would make good settlers, to come out to us. Brought this colony from a half-deserted and utterly dispirited colony to be one of the most prosperous and thriving colonies in the North-West . . . Should you wish for any further particulars or proof of the prosperity of this colony, I am at liberty to refer you to W.B. Scarth, esq., MP, L. A. Hamilton, esq., Canadian Pacific Land Commissioner, both of whom lately visited this colony, and to the Hon. E. Dewdney, MP & Minister of the Interior.[23]

Other rather startling assertions were made by Vass in the same communication: "Since I came up here in June '86 I have been constantly working in the interests of the government and this colony & this without any remuneration." Several sources agree that Vass had come from a family of reasonable means in Hungary.[24] Therefore, we may accept his claim when he writes: "Of course I have had to neglect my private interests and, had I not had

private means, it would have been impossible for me to have done as I have."
No doubt, his money had been spent: "I find now that I cannot continue to go
on as I have been doing and should the government not see their way to appoint
me as emigration agent for this colony, I shall be obliged in the future to look
only to my private interests." Apparently he was already in dire need and in an
impossible situation. He had invested his time and money in government business. It was an either/or situation.

> Do not think I am making this application for any mercenary motive. I am
> not; what I have told you is the simple truth, as I cannot afford to continue
> to neglect my private affairs any longer without some actual appointment
> from the government.[25]

It is not that Vass had not tried to draw attention to his plight previously.
In the fall of 1887 he had to state: "I have been waiting for some time to hear
from your department as to a claim for services rendered . . . I sent my a/c to
Mr. W. B. Scarth, Esq., when he was in Ottawa, who I believe submitted it to
you, and I also sent a copy to you personally." Since Vass' account was for
"services rendered in conjunction with Count Esterhazy in bringing Hungarian
immigrants to this country in the spring of 1886,"[26] it was rejected by Lowe. He
nevertheless felt justified in sending a cheque for $100 because Vass had
"rendered certain services in furthering Hungarian immigration and settlement
which call for some recognition from the Department." However, Lowe added a
most significant proviso, that the sum would be " . . . for such services from the
date of the rendering of your account [May 3, 1887] to the first of November
last."[27]

The importance of the previous sentence lies in the fact that the immigration authorities felt that they were obliged to pay Vass a considerable amount
for what they defined as the rendering of "certain services in furthering
Hungarian immigration and settlement." Since the payment covered a good
portion of the time Vass spent at Esterhaz, being in *de facto* charge of the
administration of the settlement, it seems manifest that the payment and the
statement represented an implicit admission, on the part of the government, of
a definite commitment to Vass. Indeed, Géyza de Döry had occasion, later in
the same year, to remark that Vass did not plant potatoes,[28] perhaps for lack of
time owing to communal business.

As for Vass' letter of October 9, 1888, it succeeded in drawing a
favourable response from the Minister of the Department of Agriculture. He
regarded the unspecified "work done" by Vass as "most useful," but could not
give him a position as agent "at present."[29] Nevertheless, J. Carling found
"upon consideration of representations made to him," the possibility to allow
Vass an "honorarium of $100 in consideration of services and expenses incurred

[by him] for promoting the success of Hungarian colonization." Furthermore, the payment was to be made in two fifty dollar instalments, one of which was to be paid immediately and the other during the winter. The Department was careful to point out that the arrangement did not extend beyond that season.[30] At the beginning of the following year, Rufus Stephenson, who carried out an inspection of Esterhaz on behalf of the Department of the Interior, reported, "Mr. J. Vass is doing valuable work, and his good judgement and sound advice is much relied on by the settlers in this locality."[31]

Up to mid-1888, the problem for Vass had been how to obtain some sort of allowance or periodical allocations for his services as manager of the Esterhaz colony. He was describing himself as such in his correspondence with government departments and the Canada North-West Land Company without ever being challenged on that point. However, in the summer of 1888 Vass became aware of a potentially much better opportunity for employment when voices were raised at Esterhaz as well as in Whitewood and its area about the untenable conditions that immigrants arriving from Europe had to encounter at Whitewood station. It was, from the mid-'80s onwards, the terminal and distribution-point for immigrants, but without any facilities whatever. On arrival at the station the immigrants were told by the conductor of the train to pick up their baggage and get off. From that point, in accordance with the government's strict policy of non-interference with the individual's rights and responsibilities, they were expected to look after themselves.

Perhaps owing to the magnitude of other difficulties, no serious criticism had developed before 1888 to this insensitive approach to the welfare of new immigrants. But this was also prompted by the courtesy and helpfulness of the CPR agent at Whitewood station, Assiniboia, a Mr. Hillier, who had permitted immigrants the use of the station waiting-room, "to the great inconvenience and annoyance of the travelling public." Finally, owing to continual complaints by the public, the General Superintendent of the CPR refused to tolerate the practice any longer. Since the immigrants usually came with insufficient funds or none at all, hotel-keepers would refuse to receive them and there were no vacant houses available. Therefore, A. G. Thorburn, the MLA for Whitewood district, thought it was his duty to point out to the Minister of the Interior (E. Dewdney) the necessity of the erection of an immigration shed that would offer cooking facilities and sleeping accommodation. He did not neglect to mention that the new arrivals, mainly Swedes, Bohemians, Hungarians, and Icelanders, had often to cover about twenty-five or thirty miles before reaching their actual destinations.[32] Apparently, the Member of the Legislative Assembly did not want to or could not mail his letter promptly, but handed it over to the local justice of the peace, Daniel Campbell, who did not choose to send it off until he had obtained a petition from the Esterhaz colony. The petition was signed by

144

forty-five colonists, including Julius Vass and, in addition to the Hungarians, by the Slavic settlers. They referred to the tremendous inconvenience (and often downright hardship) of having to shop for even the smallest items in far-away Whitewood, and of having to stay overnight in the town and pay excessive fees for accommodation. At that stage the only alternative was to spend the night in the open air. They also drew attention to their own sorrowful experiences as newcomers who, in the beginning, had been unable to make themselves understood and had found it extremely hard to obtain even the slightest or the most urgent information, owing to the lack of anyone in Whitewood who, on their arrival, could understand their language. In their view it was imperative to set up the position of an immigration agent at Whitewood as soon as possible.[33]

Daniel Campbell's letter summarized the contents of the two letters enclosed, and presented further arguments for the erection of an immigration shack and for the appointment of an agent. He pointed out that ninety heads of families, mostly foreigners, had arrived during the season. He brought up the fact that the real reason for the refusal by the railway authorities to allow the station's waiting-room to be used by immigrants, was that a family of Swedes, the preceding July, had had the measles and had infected some nineteen persons in Whitewood alone. Moreover, he brought up the frequent complaint of the newcomers "of the treatment they receive on arrival and [that they] become very much discouraged." Finally, he gave an account of a nearly-fatal accident suffered by a Hungarian who, loaded "with a heavy portmanteau strapped across his back," was trapped to his armpits in a snowbank. Campbell declared that, had it not been for his own timely arrival on the scene the man would surely have frozen to death. In the words of the justice of the peace:

I had to spend over two hours bringing him round; he was seriously ill for three weeks after that . . . I may also inform your honor that there is no place, so far as I am aware, to accommodate immigrants between Brandon and Qu'Appelle and one built here would supply the needs of a large area of country, from its central and postal facilities, seventeen post-offices being supplied from the Whitewood post-office.[34]

It appears that the facts and the circumstances referred to in the three statements were weighty and serious enough to cause the Minister's secretary to endorse the file in the following manner: "Please have this acknowledged and inform Mr. Campbell that Minister has laid matter before Minister of Agriculture for his favourable consideration. Then transfer file to Mr. Carling." The endorsement was preceded by the word "Rush".

No doubt, Vass was told after these developments by the Department of Agriculture to keep up communication with them. As a result, he reported to the Deputy Minister, John Lowe, Rufus Stephenson's visit to inspect the colony.

Vass mentioned that he was asked by Stephenson to supply a statement about the presence in the colony of a number of newcomers who were actually "in the act of taking up land, but whom, as they did not have their entries, Mr. Stephenson would not include in his report." Then Vass added a rather cryptic statement: "You are aware of the position in which I stand here and I would ask you to use your influence so that something definite may be decided respecting me."[35]

After these previous and seemingly futile efforts, Vass must have felt great uneasiness about the quick passage of time and decided to approach his superiors, The Canada North-West Land Company, for whom he really worked. M. R. Currie, the Moosomin agent of the Land Company, saw his way clear to putting on paper a very favourable character reference for Vass:

> It is evident from what I see that Mr. Vass is doing all in his power and doing a great deal towards the settlement of this district. I believe that some seventy homesteaders will be located by him during the coming season if his application, already forwarded to Ottawa, was favourably read. I am convinced he has worked honestly in the interests of what is now the Railway Company and do not know anywhere in Manitoba and the North-West a more suitable and more reliable man who could be employed by the Government in the interest of foreign emigration.[36]

Now it was W. B. Scarth's turn to support Currie's statement concerning Vass in unreservedly positive terms:

> I cannot too highly recommend Mr. Vass to your consideration. He is doing excellent work, and I really think you should try to arrange some small annual salary for him.

Furthermore, Scarth urged Carling to consider the matter as soon as possible and to keep him posted.[37] Sensing Vass' growing uneasiness, he sent a copy of the Department of Agriculture's reply to Scarth's note concerning Vass, and attached a brief note of his own, in which he referred to the strong support given to Vass' case.[38] A month passed, but no favourable reply was received from the Department of Agriculture. Vass turned directly to the Minister of the Interior, the most influential among his acquaintances, listing favourable comments made by Scarth and Rufus Stephenson that referred to his knowledge of language, to the prospect of increasing immigration to the Whitewood area, as well as to the fact that he had been naturalized shortly before. He concluded the letter:

> I am sure my being appointed lies in your hands, and I sincerely trust I may receive a favourable reply at as early a date as possible. Thanking you for the interest you have hitherto taken in my behalf . . .[39]

Apparently the Minister of the Interior had formed a favourable enough opinion of Vass and his case to intervene on his behalf with his colleague in charge of the portfolio of Agriculture. He had expressed his intention in the past to speak to Carling personally about the matter the last time, when Carling had been at Dewdney's office, but had forgotten to do so. He drew attention to his (Dewdney's) support for Vass: "I would do what I could for him in recommending him to your notice, altho' the remuneration might be small. He is a good man and I would be glad if you could keep him in mind at the right time."[40] At the beginning of June of the same year, Vass expressed his gratitude to Dewdney for having used his influence on his behalf, but felt that he had to emphasize the question of remuneration for the work as immigration agent at Whitewood. He expressed the hope that his pay should be enough to permit him to carry on "without any financial loss to myself, as has been my experience in the past." He cited the inconvenience that he had to endure in his own house, where, for lack of other accommodation, he had to put up new arrivals. He also referred to how often it had been necessary for him to be in Whitewood on official business despite the fact that his residence was at Esterhaz.[41]

Perhaps Vass had found the proper tone in which to address the Minister; more likely the latter had been pleased with what he saw on his visit to Esterhaz and with Vass' personality. In any case, he acted immediately on receipt of Vass' letter and wrote, confidentially, to Carling. He expressed his view, that the matter of constructing an immigration shack at Whitewood should be given high priority. Then he added a sentence which only he and the addressee could interpret properly: "I wish this not only in the interests of the country, but for personal reasons."[42]

Inevitably, the day of reckoning came. From different quarters complaints were lodged based on rumours concerning the apparent disorder in the administration of homesteads and money deriving from the sale of belongings left behind by settlers who had abandoned their land.[43] R. S. Park, Homestead Inspector, Whitewood, was given the task, on Ottawa's instructions, to keep the matter within its confines rather than handing it over to a law court. Thus, evidence under oath was taken from Julius Vass and twenty-nine other settlers of Esterhaz about alleged misappropriations, by Vass, of the colonists' funds. It may strike the modern reader as very peculiar that, in the first place, a homestead inspector should collect evidence under oath at all, in what was apparently a criminal case. Nor does it seem proper not to warn the suspect about the possible consequences of his statement and not to explain to him his right to the presence of a lawyer.

No doubt, under the existing circumstances, Park was regarded as the nearest representative of the government, irrespective of his competence. In any case, Vass' statement, dated 24 October 1890 at Esterhaz, again stressed that he was working in the interests of the colonists and of the Company. He declared emphatically, "I considered myself an agent of the Company. All accounts made by me in reference to this Colony were signed by me as agent and were always accepted by the Company aforesaid as if I were their lawful agent." Then followed the painful enumeration, item by item, of moneys received and spent without the knowledge of the Company. The grand total of the funds not accounted for — $800 — also included $140 allotted by the government to Vass for the purchase of a horse and buckboard. The amount had been spent by him on board and for the payment of unspecified debts and sundry purchases for himself.

The reason given for having spent the money was:

> he had no salary from the Company; remuneration was promised to him by Mr. Scarth but no amount was stated. The Company paid him some $250 for four years and half's service: that amount is all he received from the Company.

It was never his intention, he said, to cause a loss to anyone.[44] The statement was signed by Vass.

There is no doubt that legally Vass was guilty of misappropriating public funds. The disturbing fact was that sums paid to, but not remitted by, Vass were not regarded by the authorities as government or as Company funds. They claimed that Vass had not been a duly appointed agent. Moreover, the amounts embezzled by Vass failed to become "public by reaching the proper organs of the Government and the Company."[45]

What, then, were the consequences of the Vass case? In the first place, Vass himself meted out his own punishment, which seems to indicate both remorse and a high degree of personal difficulties. However, his suicide was doubtless a welcome and convenient solution for persons in high and responsible positions, who wanted to show their efficiency. Even if one is inclined to recall Clifford Sifton's hardly complimentary reference to the way in which the business of immigration administration was handled in the early days by the Department of Agriculture ("the office of circumlocution"), one must not forget the volume and the tremendous variety of work that John Lowe, the Secretary, Department of Agriculture, was expected to perform in the late 1880s and early 1890s. Nevertheless, many officials had come to learn, through bitter experience, the usefulness of the simple device of disclaiming responsibility — "passing the buck" — whenever necessary and possible. Had there been an open trial in the Vass case, a number of awkward questions could have been asked: Whose "oversight" was responsible for the non-payment or, rather, underpayment of the agent or village manager, or both? How was it possible for Vass to receive fees for the public and the Company if he was not an agent assigned for the purpose? Why had his defalcations not been noticed before? Why was he so well regarded by Scarth[46] and Dewdney?

Instead of speculating[47] it can be stated with certainty that a spate of trouble followed from the event as far as the newer settlers of Esterhaz were concerned. A number of them had carried out their land selections with more or less relish, after which they went and saw the "Manager" and paid the ten-dollar fee for their homesteads which, however, fairly often were still registered under the names of one-time settlers who had abandoned them, discouraged by the difficulties of the first year or two. Besides, the fees were not officially received. On top of all this, the Company regarded many abandoned homesteads as securities for the loans allowed by Sir George Stephen — that is, the Canadian Pacific Railway. Consequently, a number of complications, which may be categorized under the designation "Land Troubles," developed over the legal position of the new occupants. The disentanglement of the legal problems took close to a decade and represented a whole era in the life of the colony.

It may be assumed that the Vass case and subsequent difficulties served as an object lesson for the higher administration as to what weaknesses in the system should be eliminated, but they also called attention to the need to resolve, for the area, the complicated problems of ownership and to deal with the iniquitous position that arose because of loans owed to the Canadian Pacific Railway Company.

Since Vass had been the postmaster of Esterhaz Post Office, the position became vacant with Vass' suicide. It was taken over by a member of the nearby Czech settlement of Colin. The Hungarians applied for a new post office, and as a result, the whole Magyar community became known as Kaposvar[48] and the name "Esterhaz" was no more.[49] As to Julius Vass, he appears to have been basically a decent, but sadly alienated, person who tried to find short-cuts towards the achievement of social and economic security, and who finally had to succumb to the circumstances and to accept responsibility for his mistakes as well as those of others.[50]

FOOTNOTES

[1] *Regina Leader*, November 4, 1890.

[2] *Kanadai Magyar Ujsag* (Canadian Hungarian News; hereinafter *KMU*) May 7, 1927. See also Paul Santha, *"A Kanadai magyarság története"* (A History of Hungarians in Canada) in *A Kanadai magyar ujság képes nagy naptára 1928-ra* (The Great Pictorial Calendar of the Canadian Hungarian News for 1928) (Winnipeg, 1927; hereinafter *KMT*), 110.

[3] For Canadian initiative in Hungarian immigration and P. O. Esterhazy's related efforts in Hungary see Martin L. Kovacs, "Aspects of Hungarian Peasant Emigration from Pre-1914 Hungary," in Ivan Volgyes, ed., *The Peasantry of Eastern Europe*, 2 vols. (New York, 1979), vol. I, 119-32.

[4] "A Conflict Inevitable. England and Russia Almost Sure to Fight" read the headlines of the *New York Times*, April 24, 1885.

[5] P. O. Esterhazy to the Marquess of Lansdowne, Gov. Gen. (1883-1888), Ottawa, May 9, 1885. RG 7, G20, vol. 222, no. 359. Public Archives of Canada (hereinafter *PAC*).

[6] *Regina Leader*, June 16, 1885.

[7] *KMU*, May 7, 1927. In Gönczy's opinion, Mór Eszláry was the previous name of P. O. Esterhazy and that, in turn, had derived from Barth or Barcs. This, of course, was true to such extent that Esterhazy's original name, Packh, could sound somewhat like Barth.

[8] Paul Oscar Esterhazy (1831-1912) had been born into the Packh family and was known until 1867 as Johann Baptist Packh. For further information see Martin L. Kovacs, *Esterhazy and Early Hungarian Immigration to Canada* (Regina: Canadian Plains Research Center, 1974; hereinafter Kovacs, *Esterhazy*), 33-35.

[9] P. O. Esterhazy to John Carling, Minister of Agriculture, Ottawa, October 1, 1886. RG 17, vol. 505, F: 55534. *PAC*.

[10] Fordham, N.Y., April 25, 1886. RG 17, vol. 480, F: 52667. *PAC*.

[11] Toronto, May 28, 1886. RG 17, I-1, vol. 485, F: 53199. *PAC*.

[12] *Manitoba Daily Free Press*, June 8, 1886. Contrary to the reminiscences of pioneers still alive in the mid-1920s (Santha, *KMT*, 110), Vass was not a member of the first group of immigrants who arrived in (future) Esterhaz from Pennsylvania in June 1886.

[13] *Manitoba Daily Free Press*, June 10, 1886.

[14] Ibid., July 2, 1886. SE7, Township 19, Range 1, West 2nd M. was the homestead selected, but never taken up, by Esterhazy. Incidentally the same quarter-section had been chosen as the site for the planned village of Esterhaz (RG 17, I-1, vol. 490, F: 53751, *PAC*). The house built on it became Vass' headquarters and it also accommodated the Esterhaz Post Office with Vass as the postmaster (Report of Count P. O. Esterhazy, December 31, 1886, *Sessional Papers*, no. 12, 1887, 237-38).

[15] The total of the loan was $25,000; it also covered the purchase of farming equipment, food, tools, and cattle. *Sessional Papers*, no. 12, 1887, 238.

150

[16]P. O. Esterhazy to John Lowe, Secretary, Department of Agriculture (hereinafter: J. Lowe), Brandon, Manitoba, October 17, 1886. RG, I-1, vol. 508, F: 55881, *PAC.* Esterhazy's makeshift solution of placing the newcomers on homesteads near Regina apparently did not work.

[17]Concerning the first Hungarian miners in Lethbridge and Medicine Hat see Martin L. Kovacs, "Hungarian Communities in Early Alberta and Saskatchewan," in Howard Palmer and Donald Smith, eds., *The New Provinces: Alberta and Saskatchewan, 1905-1980* (Vancouver, 1980), 101-30.

[18]P. O. Esterhazy to J. Lowe, Fordham, New York, December 17, 1886. RG, I-1, vol. 517, F: 57040. *PAC.*

[19]Vass was sending reports to Esterhazy for a while, such as the one dated November 25, 1886, in which he stated that the building of 25 frame houses had been completed and that "these and other temporary houses afford now sufficient shelter and comfort for the winter." RG 17, I-1, vol. 525, F: 58067. *PAC.*

[20]Fordham, N.Y., January 20, 1887, RG 17, I-1, vol. 521, F: 57632. *PAC.*

[21]J. Vass to J. Carling, Minister of Agriculture, Esterhaz, October 9, 1887, RG 17, I-1, vol. 594, F: 67179. *PAC.*

[22]In retrospect, the pioneers interviewed by Santha in the 1920s tended to blame Vass for the fact that later immigrants were not given any food or other assistance by the government. Of course, the last (October 1886) group of the original immigrants had already been denied this favour. *KMT,* 114.

[23]J. Vass to J. Carling, Minister of Agriculture, Esterhaz, October 9, 1887, RG I-1, vol. 594, F: 67179. *PAC.*

[24]Thus, Louis Gönczy claims that "after the day of his [Vass'] suicide, a remittance of $12,000 arrived from the old country, sent by his father." *KMU,* May 7, 1927. It is likely that some money did arrive, but the amount was clearly exaggerated. See also *Leader Post,* June 9, 1966.

[25]Vass to J. Carling, Esterhaz, October 9, 1888.

[26]Vass to J. Lowe, Whitewood, September 16, 1887. RG 17, I-1, vol. 549, F: 61536. *PAC.*

[27]J. Lowe to Vass, Ottawa, November 17, 1887. RG 17, vol. 1592, p. 180. *PAC.*

[28]Döry had recently paid a visit to Esterhaz and spent eight days there in his capacity as manager, Hungarian Colony, "Hunsvalley," and prepared a report on the colony. He thought that Vass' omission to plant potatoes might serve as a bad example to the settlers of Esterhaz. Döry to P. O. Esterhazy, Hunsvalley, Manitoba, December 15, 1887. RG 17, I-1, vol. 568, F: 63944. *PAC.*

[29]J. Lowe to Vass, Ottawa, October 24, 1888. RG 17, vol. 1566, p. 7. *PAC.*

[30]J. Lowe to Vass, Ottawa, November 7, 1888. RG 17, vol. 1568, p. 29. *PAC.*

[31]Rufus Stephenson, *Summary of Reports, Supplement to the Annual Report of the Department of the Interior* for the *Year 1888*, (Ottawa: Queen's Printer, 1889), p. 5.

"Hungarian (Esterhazy) Colony, N.W.T."

[32]A. G. Thorburn to the Minister of the Interior, Whitewood, July 27, 1888. RG 17, I-1, vol. 613, F: 67480. *PAC.*

[33]"Forty-five settlers" to E. Dewdney, Minister of the Interior, Esterhaz, Assiniboia, NWT, September 26, 1888 (written in Hungarian). RG 17, I-1, vol. 613, F: 67480. *PAC.*

[34]Daniel Campbell to the Minister of the Interior, Whitewood, October 15, 1888. RG 17, I-1, vol. 613, F: 67480. *PAC.*

[35]Julius Vass, "Manager of the Hungarian Colony," to J. Lowe, Esterhaz, February 17, 1889. RG 17, I-1, vol. 605, F: 68491. *PAC.*

[36]M. R. Currie, agent, the Canada North-West Land Co. Ltd., Moosomin, March 29, 1889. RG 17, I-1, vol. 609, F: 68955. *PAC.*

[37]W. B. Scarth to J. Carling, Minister of Agriculture, Ottawa, April 6, 1889. RG 17, I-1, vol. 609, F: 68955. *PAC.*

[38]H. B. Small, Secretary, Department of Agriculture to W. B. Scarth, MP, House of Commons, Ottawa, April 11, 1889 and W. B. Scarth to J. Vass, Esterhaz P. O., Ottawa, April 15, 1889. RG 17, I-1, vol. 614, F: 69566. *PAC.*

[39]J. Vass to E. Dewdney, Minister of the Interior, Esterhaz, May 14, 1889. RG 17, I-1, vol. 614, F: 69566. *PAC.*

[40]The Hon. E. Dewdney to the Hon. J. Carling, Ottawa, May 25, 1889. RG 17, I-1, vol. 614, F: 69566. *PAC.*

[41]J. Vass to the Hon. E. Dewdney, Esterhaz, June 6, 1889. RG 17, I-1, vol. 623, F: 70641. *PAC.*

[42]The Hon. E. Dewdney to the Hon. John Carling, Ottawa, June 10, 1889. RG 17, I-1, vol. 623, F: 70641. *PAC.*

[43]William Cosgrave, a nearby settler, who had assisted Vass in English correspondence summarily related events in the following way: "[Vass] acted as agent and always when entering [made entries] which would come to me . . . this Agent appeared to have Govt. authority to enter on odd or even sections. The N.W.L.C. or Lord Mountstephen [formerly Sir George Stephen] advanced money to build houses, buy cattle &c. At the time entries were made mortgages were registered. Many of the people did not stay more than six months and when leaving handed back cattle, implements &c. to the agent referred to, others coming would pay part of said mortgage and in addition $12.00 for a new entry which, of course could not be done without vacating 1st Mortgage. In this way many paid and never got entry and some entries were made and no person ever appeared . . . I went over Vass' books and often told him he was getting into a bad muddle, he would always reply, 'Oh, Mr. Scarth wants to enter all at once.' I . . . replied no matter what Mr. S. wants you must keep your people right. I saw things getting worse and wrote to Ottawa. The Interior Dept. then went to work and soon after the poor fellow shot himself. This N.W.L'd Coy or L.M.S. may have lost money but it was their own fault. I know more than any living man of the money transactions . . . I should have added that Mr. Vass was a Govt. servant when doing business here as Agent viz. Immigration Agent at Whitewood." W. Cosgrave to the Minister of the Interior [Clifford Sifton]. December 24, 1896. Homestead Files, Dept. of Interior, F: 338350. Saskatchewan

Provincial Archives, Saskatoon [SPAS].

⁴⁴R. S. Park, to H. H. Smith, Dominion Land Commissioner (Winnipeg), Whitewood, October 24, 1890. RG 15, B-1a, vol. 104, F: 247925. *PAC*.

⁴⁵Vass' status actually had to be decided upon at the ministerial level: "Vass . . . did act as a Land Guide for a short time, but that was the full extent of his authority, and the record shows . . . that the Hon. Sir John Thompson, when acting as Minister of Interior in 1890, decided that this did not constitute him our agent to receive moneys, or make us liable for his acts." Memorandum: Deputy Minister of the Interior to Hon. Clifford Sifton, Minister of the Interior, January 27, 1897. Homestead Files, Department of the Interior F: 338350. SPAS.

⁴⁶Actually, the Vass case was to haunt both the government departments and W. B. Scarth, together with the Canada North-West Land Company, for several years to come. Thus, Scarth had to state his views rather forcefully in 1893: "Most of the original Hungarians turned out to have been very badly selected by Esterhazie [!] and abandoned their homesteads, leaving chattels and houses behind them. Through Mr. Vass, the then Secretary of the Hungarian colonization, we managed to get parties direct from Hungary who had been accustomed to farming, to take the places of those who had left, thus keeping up what has really turned out to be a good colony. Some of those who thus came out took the homesteads which had belonged to the original homesteaders, upon which we had erected houses. Others of them took new homesteads and the chattels that had been left by those who had gone. Had we not adopted this course, there was nothing for us but to sell these chattels at a large loss to Lord Mountstephen and, had we done this, it would have been no object to us to bring out new and good colonists to take the places of those who left. We had also to treat the matter rapidly or we could not have arranged to bring new settlers out. The result of our efforts is a well-settled colony with good farmers, and I think that the Government should endeavor to strain every point to meet our views." Scarth, Land Commissioner, CNWLC, Ltd. to the Commissioner, Dominion Lands, Winnipeg, December 27, 1893. Homestead Files, Dept. of Interior, F: 307736. SPAS.

⁴⁷It is relevant to note that Vass appeared uncommonly nervous about P. O. Esterhazy. " . . . Now I hear Esterhazy's coming up here again & I write to you to ask you to stop him; we want neither him nor his settlers. They are no good. If he comes there will be trouble again as there was before . . . I must ask you to use your influence to prevent Esterhazy interfering in any way in the affairs of the colony . . . P.S.: Please let me hear your opinion as to Esterhazy['s] movements." J. Vass to J. Lowe, Esterhaz, August 13, 1888. RG 17, I-1, vol. 588, F: 66471. *PAC*. What Vass had anticipated did come about. In a letter to Lowe, P. O. Esterhazy had the following to say: " . . . Mr. Vass, altho' called by me to explain the reason why he had opened some twenty-five to thirty letters addressed to me by Hungarian families on the other side . . . and altho' urgently asked to communicate with me the contents of such letters and the addresses of the senders, he has, with unpardonable neglect, — disregarded to answer my questions and he has failed to clear himself of the serious charges brought against him also by others of tampering with the mails entrusted to him as postmaster . . . " Esterhazy to J. Lowe, New York, November 17, 1888. RG 17, I-1, vol. 597, F: 67464. *PAC*. Could it be that Vass' great service to Scarth in repopulating Esterhaz had actually consisted in the opening of correspondence meant for P. O. Esterhazy?

⁴⁸"The post office was one of the social centres of the settlement since the weekly mail from Whitewood, usually on Fridays, was a good opportunity for social intercourse. The postmaster, though with a low salary, had great authority in this privileged position. This was

a reason for rivalry between the Hungarian and Bohemian sections of the colony, each of them making efforts to have the post office on their own territory . . . After the tragic death of Julius Vass, the Bohemians succeeded in moving the post office one-and-a-half miles west of their colony . . . " Msgr. Paul Santha, "Social Life and Customs of the Pioneer Settlers," *Local Histories — Esterhazy*, F: 316, Saskatchewan Provincial Archives, Regina.

[49]Almost the same designation, however was resurrected in 1902, when the new railway station in the vicinity was called Esterhazy and a village (later, town) of the same name grew up around it. See Kovacs, *Esterhazy* 24-27.

[50]All sorts of stress-situations may result in symptoms of alienation, some of which would be the loss of personal values and, ultimately, suicide. See. M. L. Kovacs and A. J. Cropley, *Immigrants and Society: Alienation and Assimilation* (Sydney, Australia: McGraw-Hill Book Company, 1975), passim.

ORAL HISTORY: REFLECTIONS OF THE MEMBERS OF THREE WAVES OF HUNGARIAN IMMIGRANTS IN ONTARIO

Susan M. Papp-Zubrits,
The Multicultural History Society of Ontario

There has been a significant Hungarian presence in Canada for close to a hundred years. The majority of the first Hungarian immigrants who came around the turn of the century were engaged in agriculture and lived mainly in the Hungarian settlements of Saskatchewan and to a much lesser extent, Manitoba. Some years after the First World War, this situation changed dramatically. Hungarian immigrants settled in growing numbers in regions outside the Canadian prairies and in urban areas. Today, half of Canada's Hungarian population of 132,000 lives in Ontario and four out of every five Hungarians are urban residents.[1]

This more recent Hungarian immigration occurred in three distinct waves: during the 1920s and 1930s, when some 33,000 immigrants came; after the Second World War, when approximately 10,000 Displaced Persons were admitted; and following the Hungarian Revolution of 1956, when the largest wave of 38,000 refugees arrived. Each wave was markedly different.

This paper will examine the differences and similarities between these groups, emphasizing in particular, the following topics: the immigrants' aspirations prior to emigration, the passage, introduction to Canadian way of life, rate of assimilation and apparent contributions. The examining process and the discussion of many incidents related in this paper are based on taped interviews found in the oral history collection of the Multicultural History Society of Ontario.

The traditional sources of immigration history often contain factual information drawn from statistics dealing with age and sex distributions, settlement patterns, occupational breakdowns and language retention. Oral history, however, provides the historian with the added dimension of the lives and experiences of individual immigrants; if properly handled it may become an interesting and revealing source for the better understanding of the complex processes of migration as well as cultural, social and economic adjustments. The purpose of this paper is to present the impressions, opinions and attitudes of some Ontario representatives of the three waves of Hungarian immigrants, rather than an in-depth analysis and history of the subject as a whole.

Newcomers entering Canada during the inter-war years left Hungary because of political changes and the economic collapse which followed the end of the First World War. Others emigrated from areas detached from Hungary by the Treaty of Trianon: from the southern segment of Czechoslovakia, from Transylvania in Rumania, and the regions of Bacska-Banat in Yugoslavia. By and large, these immigrants came from small towns and rural areas, and were single men between 20 and 35 years of age. Many of them were skilled tradesmen (i.e., butchers, carpenters, shoemakers, blacksmiths, and so on). Surprisingly, some of these new arrivals had never heard of Canada prior to emigration.

George Gyülvészi, who later became one of the most successful tobacco farmers in the Delhi district of southern Ontario, wanted to emigrate in 1928 to Canada or any other country that would take him, rather than live as a member of an ethnic minority in Rumania.[2] A newcomer from northern Hungary emigrated because his prospects in his native country were limited; the only employment opportunity in the district was an old leather factory, which he had only seen from the outside.[3]

Despite the fact that the majority of the Hungarian immigrants were directed to Winnipeg and that they had initially applied for farm work, a large number, after experiencing the harsh prairie winter, eventually came to southern Ontario. Paul Rapai, who was atypical of the majority in so far as he was a graduate of a Hungarian agricultural college, arrived in Canada in May 1929.[4] He was hired by an English farmer near Kipling, Saskatchewan, but on the night before the farmer came to fetch him, ten inches of snow fell on the prairies. Rapai decided to leave Saskatchewan, the next morning. His reason: "there can't possibly be good conditions for farming where ten inches of snow falls in mid-May."

By 1931, a number of Ontarian cities contained Hungarian communities in the strength of over one thousand. These were Hamilton, Toronto, Welland and Windsor. Also in Brantford, Kitchener, Oshawa, St. Catharines, Niagara Falls and Port Colborne there were groups of over a hundred residents. The Hungarians were drawn to these cities by the great variety of industrial jobs. In 1931, Hamilton had the largest Hungarian community in Ontario, since the immigrants found readily-available work in steel mills and iron foundries. Numerous Hungarians were attracted to the Welland-Port Colborne area around the time of the building of the Welland Canal. After the canal was completed, they moved over to textile mills and rubber factories. A Roman Catholic priest, Fr. László Forgách, who was in Welland during the 1930s, related the pitiful working conditions in the textile mills.[5] This Hungarian parish priest became accidentally involved through his parishioners in a strike against Dominion Textiles Limited. At one point Forgách was even offered a bribe by the company management, which he flatly refused, to convince his parishioners of the need to return to work. When the dispute was finally settled and some workers were dismissed for their part in the strike, Forgách went before management to plead for their jobs.

In Windsor, a significant number of Hungarians worked in the automobile manufacturing industry, initially as daily commuters to Detroit and later, when the automobile assembly plants were built there, in Windsor itself.[6]

The first Hungarian organizations founded in Ontario, with the exception of the churches, provided sick benefits and funeral benefits. At a time when there were no forms of social insurance, i.e., unemployment compensation or health insurance, the Hungarian immigrants established mutual benefit societies and self-help organizations to protect themselves from the uncertainties of life in a strange country. Besides, these groups also organized meetings and social events, where the immigrants, largely isolated from the host society by various barriers, could find companionship amongst their fellow countrymen. The first Hungarian self-help organizations in Ontario were the Brantford Hungarian Mutual Benefit Society and the Welland Hungarian Self-Culture Society, founded in 1913 and 1921 respectively. By the 1930s, similar societies were active in most cities in Ontario with a sizable Hungarian community.

The first Hungarian congregations organized in Ontario were of the Presbyterian faith. They were founded in 1926, in Welland and Hamilton. The Hungarian Roman Catholics were first organized in 1928 in Welland and in Toronto. There were communities where four or five Hungarian congregations were active at once, including Baptists, Lutherans and Greek Catholics. Only the larger congregations had permanent ministers, in part because of their inability to support them during the depression but mainly because there were not enough Hungarian-speaking clergymen available. The few such priests and ministers in Ontario set up missions in the surrounding communities and often spent a considerable amount of their time travelling from one congregation to another.[7]

These immigrants, not unlike most first-generation settlers in other ethnic groups, found adjustment and assimilation very difficult. Their attachment to the homeland was still very much alive through memories and ties of kinship and friendship. The need to meet and speak with people of the same social and cultural background was reflected in their settling in close proximity to fellow countrymen. One immigrant, Joseph Jager, who came to Toronto in 1928, related the way he assisted the Roman Catholic congregation in the building of the church hall.[8] Jager, a shoemaker, after working eight to ten hours in a shoe factory, would go down to the church hall, where, joined by others, he willingly participated until midnight in the building of the church. Jager did not regard this activity as being burdensome. Of course, he was in the company of people to whom he could relate and this was more than he could say for his work in the shoe factory. Moreover, the building of the church hall did not seem difficult or tiresome, as most of the volunteers brought large decanters of wine with them so that the work would proceed with greater vigour.

There were about half as many Hungarian women as there were men in Ontario during the inter-war years.[9] This led to much rivalry among the men for the limited number of eligible women available. The situation was described by an immigrant in the following manner:

> If we had a dance, the few women who came were never given a chance to rest, everyone wanted to dance at least once with them. By the end of the evening, the poor women had danced for so long that they practically had their clothes shaken off of them.[10]

Immigrant single men, once they established themselves in Canada, sent for wives or financees, or returned to Hungary to find themselves brides and bring them back to Canada.

An immigrant was considered lucky if he obtained accommodation in one of the few boarding houses run by Hungarian women. When Mrs. Mary Gabura came to this country her husband had just lost his job. Friends of her husband, upon hearing that the young woman had already arrived, collected money amongst themselves and purchased a large boarding house in Toronto. It was assumed that the Hungarian woman would willingly take on the awesome tasks involved in running a boarding house. She had in fact, very little choice. When Mary Gabura arrived, she was welcomed by her husband and seven other men and a large, run-down boarding house. She related how she cooked the meals, laundered and mended the boarders' clothes and cleaned the house in addition to raising four small children.

According to Mrs. Gabura, Hungarian men missed good home-cooked meals most of all and begged her to cook for non-boarders as well. She described the schedule for meals at the boarding house in the following manner:

> At five o'clock the men from Massey-Harris came, they ate first. Then those who worked at the tire factory came later, at ten o'clock. Every night at 11:00 p.m., I was still in the kitchen, giving dinner. After that the dishes still had to be done, and I was there again at 5:00 a.m., because I had to serve breakfast to the men who left early, to make coffee and fry eggs and then, because the Massey-Harris plant was so close, they even came home for lunch.[11]

The Hungarian community in Ontario encountered and dealt with numerous obstacles during the inter-war years. First and foremost, they were forced to contend with the depressed economic and labour conditions of the

1930s. Many Hungarian immigrants worked at transient jobs during these years. A considerable number of Hungarians were attracted to the tobacco districts of Southern Ontario, because the farming of tobacco in this area offered the possibility of a more permanent existence. They further encountered many difficulties and setbacks in establishing their community centres, organizations and religious institutions. Leftist groups, among them the Canadian Hungarian Workers' and Farmers' Clubs, grew in membership and support. The community was characterized by strong antagonisms between the left and the right.

During the Second World War, Hungarian immigration to Canada was again halted. Hungarians were listed as "enemy aliens" and, because of this, the activities of various segments of the community, in particular of leftist organizations, came under varying degrees of scrutiny and control. The Hungarians of Montreal were requested by the government to form a co-ordinating body of representatives from all the Hungarian churches and societies so that Dominion authorities could keep track of the community's activities. Many of the methods used by the various government agencies in gathering information became known mainly through taped interviews conducted with community leaders, as no written records of cases of surveillance were ever retained. For example, Hungarian ministers were approached by R.C.M.P. officials and requested to act as informants concerning alleged communist agitators.[12] In 1946, sixteen Hungarian-Canadian community leaders from across the country were invited to a special meeting in Ottawa. The participants were not told of the proposed topic of the meeting, only that it was of importance to Hungarians in Canada.

A community leader who attended the meeting and who came from the tobacco district related the details of it.[13] The assembled Hungarians were addressed by the minister of immigration who requested that each of the community leaders organize, with the help of the community, independent social and religious institutions for Hungarian-Canadians. The minister emphasized that these organizations not be affiliated with any political movement. The government spokesman justified these requests by alleging that Hungarians generally had a reputation for being communist agitators, and, while the government knew that this was not so, the Canadian public might accept it as a fact — unless proved differently.

The "Displaced Persons" who emigrated from Hungary following the Second World War were significantly different from the inter-war immigrants. A large percentage of the post-war immigrants were from the urban centres. Moreover, they were members of the middle and upper middle classes; most were well-educated and established in their careers when they left their homeland. They emigrated with their families and were older, their average ages ranging between thirty and forty.

Canada's immigration policies and requirements, however, were much the same as before the war: the Dominion sought farm labourers, construction workers and domestic servants. Between 1948 and 1952, 10,151 Hungarian Displaced Persons were admitted to Canada,[14] 1951 being a peak year, during which 4,376 Hungarians came.

From interviews conducted with Hungarian-Canadians who emigrated during the post-World-War period, a number of common factors may be identified in terms of shared backgrounds, goals and experiences. The interviews (in the collection of the Multicultural History Society of Ontario) were conducted with individuals active in the organizational life of the Hungarian community of Toronto, such as: directors, founders and presidents of various organizations, newspaper editors/publishers and religious leaders. Many of the immigrants were professionals in Hungary: lawyers, doctors, engineers, army officers, diplomats, journalists and writers. Most of them left Hungary in 1945, but the immigration process to Canada (and other countries) did not start until the end of 1948. Refugees at that time were described as "Displaced Persons." These interviewees emphasized the fact that they wanted to give the new circumstances a chance in their country of adoption and hoped to rebuild their lives and careers.

The processing of applications and the final acceptance of these post-war immigrants to Canada, would take a long time. Those who were accepted usually came under a one-year contract as farm labourers, logging camp or construction workers to be employed in rural areas of the province. After completing the year, most of the Displaced Persons relocated in urban areas; in particular, Toronto's Hungarian community was significantly enlarged by these newcomers.

Many of these new arrivals strove with great determination to rebuild their lives and attain employment of some status. Thus, a certain former general-staff officer after a start as a domestic servant (together with his wife), was employed in succession as an unskilled labourer, a display manager for Zellers, a laboratory assistant, and finally became the Director of Administration at the Metro Toronto Emergency Organization.[15]

Clashes with earlier immigrants were few, mainly because the goals and aspirations of the newcomers were markedly different. Despite some initial resentment, a mutual need for co-operation arose — the newcomers needed the support of "established" Hungarians in finding employment and accomodation; and the latter felt the need for a fresh influx of immigrants to maintain and expand community centres and churches. This, however, was often a definite role reversal, when a group of generally well-educated Hungarians from urban areas--some of them members of the former "establishment" in Hungary —

became dependent on the assistance of their fellow-countrymen, frequently former peasants with poor education. Such a role reversal was described by Joseph Jager, an inter-war immigrant.[16] He came across his former employer, a high-ranking railroad official, on whose property Jager had once worked. The ex-official was now painting truck bodies in Canada and his wife was a domestic servant. Jager took them in as boarders in his home.

The immigrants who came after the Second World War were the most politically-conscious group when compared both with earlier arrivals and the refugees of 1956. The organizations they founded aimed at the maintenance of the traditions of the old country in view of the gradual disappearance of those traditions since the war. Numerous veterans' groups, together with the Gendarmerie Museum in Toronto and the Hungarian Air Force Museum in Oshawa, were established. These institutions were unique in the world for their collections. Also, the two largest Hungarian-language newspapers in Canada, *Kanadai Magyarság (Canadian Hungarians)* and *Magyar Élet (Hungarian Life)*, were founded and are still published by Hungarians, from this wave of immigration. These newspapers reflect the non-recognition, on the part of the émigrés, of the present government in Hungary as the legal representative of the Hungarian people. One of the publishers stated his views in the following manner. "We are émigrés, we left our homeland not for economic reasons but ideological beliefs; as long as the present government is in power we will not return. And as long as we are alive and there is energy left within us, we will maintain this view."[17]

The Displaced Persons put special emphasis on transmitting their language and their heritage to the second generation through a viable Saturday school language program and the Hungarian Scouting movement. Their influence was also felt in the leadership of the Hungarian Canadian Federation, which since 1952 has been under the direction of members of the post-war wave.

Following the Hungarian Revolution in 1956, the Hungarian-born population of the province of Ontario increased by 19,541.[18] These refugees were the youngest wave and they were regarded as the group with the least awareness of future plans and goals when compared with the previous waves of immigrants. Unlike the others who were considering emigration before doing so and had definite plans for the future, these refugees had no advance warning about the outbreak of the revolution and about the way it would end. For most, the decision to leave their homeland was made only days before the event.

Each province set up special programs to accommodate the refugees. Despite their desire to settle in urban centres of eastern Canada, efforts were made to distribute the refugees across the country. One Hungarian who came to Canada in 1957, George Zaduban, related such an attempt.[19] The airplane which brought him to Canada was filled with Hungarian refugees, most of whom were under the impression that they were landing at either Montreal or Toronto. When they landed in Edmonton, Alberta, the irate passengers registered their protests with Canadian authorities. At this point, they were told that they could go wherever they pleased, but at their own expense. Of course, few of the refugees had any significant amount of money. One group was taken by bus from Edmonton to Lethbridge, where, according to Zaduban, members of the local Hungarian community picked and chose amongst them as if they were examining a shipment of cattle. The healthiest and most robust individuals were chosen first for employment. This was their first encounter with Canadian life.

Initially, many were not even sure whether they wanted temporary asylum or permanent resettlement, depending upon their expectations of future political changes in Hungary. They learned English in a relatively short time and were adjusting with greater ease than the newcomers in previous waves, but then they were on average much younger. To choose one fairly frivolous but illustrative example, Eva Kane, formerly Eva Kuchta, a Hungarian refugee, was named "Miss Ontario" in 1962, barely five years following her arrival in Canada.[20]

Many were single. Interestingly, the various Hungarian churches were flooded with requests to perform marriages for recent refugee couples. Group weddings took place — as many as twelve couples were married on one occasion at St. Elizabeth of Hungary Roman Catholic Church in Toronto. Mrs. Theresa Lazar and her future husband who arrived in 1957, were part of one of these group wedding ceremonies. One advantage was that after their wedding mass, one large joint reception could be held for all the couples at one of the local Hungarian restaurants. As a matter of interest, Mrs. Lazar recalled that by the time the reception started, a few of the couples had already had their first marital spat.[21] Indeed, many of the couples married in this group had separated within the first year. In the informant's view, most of the young people who came out in 1956 were unattached and their sudden agreement to marry stemmed from a desperate need to combat loneliness and establish social bonds.

Hungarian-Canadian communities were enhanced and enriched by the refugees of the Revolution whose most significant contribution was in the founding of important cultural organizations: theatre companies, folk-dance groups and choirs. The cultural sophistication of many of these Hungarians and their strong desire to transplant the "Old-World" culture into their adopted homeland was best expressed by Sándor Kertész, the founder of a Hungarian theatre group in Toronto.[22] Kertész, a professional actor in Hungary, had just arrived in Toronto and obtained his first job as a bread deliverer when he began organizing the theatre group. In his experiences, the urge for an actor to practise his or her profession overrides all other needs. He named several Hungarian actors, who, after not being given an opportunity to act again, either returned in a short while to Hungary or committed suicide. Despite the fact that the members of his theatre group were cab drivers, porters, delivery boys and waiters during the day, they could still find satisfaction in being stage players at night.

Conclusion

The three waves of Hungarian immigrants in Ontario reflected marked differences in backgrounds, reasons for emigration and contributions to Canadian life. The nature and the grounds of many of these differences could be discovered to a greater extent through oral testimony than by examining traditional historical sources and census figures. Besides, reminiscences provide a more integrated picture of the immigrants experiences, since their difficulties, joys, sorrows, goals, aspirations and disappointments are highly personal.

Thus, the inter-war immigrants, because of their difficulties in adapting, felt that often they had little control over the events which life in a strange country imposed upon them. Many shared a sometimes justified fear of the host society. The interviews conducted with the post-world-war émigrés conveyed the devastating psychological effects of waiting in Displaced Persons Camps. Sometimes for years, these people did not know if and when any change in their status would occur. The refugees of 1956 related the trauma and disappointments brought about by the many sudden changes that took place in their lives. Although they adjusted with relative ease, the changes were so drastic that they suffered both mentally and emotionally for long periods afterwards.

FOOTNOTES

[1]According to the Canadian Census Statistics for 1961, of the 59,427 Hungarians living in Ontario, 48,231 were classified as urban residents.

[2]Interview with George Gyülvészi conducted by Susan Papp-Zubrits (SPZ), 24 August 1979.

[3]Interview with Joseph Jager conducted by SPZ, 13 September 1978.

[4]Interview with Paul Rapai conducted by SPZ, 21 August 1979.

[5]Interview with Fr. László Forgách conducted by SPZ, 25 August 1978.

[6]Name of interviewee withheld by request — interview conducted by SPZ, 13 November 1977.

[7]Name of interviewee withheld by request — interview conducted by SPZ, 23 August 1979.

[8]Interview with Joseph Jager conducted by SPZ, 13 September 1978.

[9]According to Canadian Census Statistics of 1931, the male-female ratio of the Hungarian-born population of the Province was 6,784 to 3,690.

[10]Interview with Joseph Jager conducted by SPZ, 13 September 1978.

[11]Interview with Mrs. Mary Gabura conducted by Carmela Patrias, February 1977.

[12]Interview with Rev. Charles Steinmetz conducted by Carmela Patrias and SPZ, 28 March 1979.

[13]Interview with Paul Rapai conducted by SPZ, 21 August 1979.

[14]Report of the Royal Commission on Bilingualism and Biculturalism. *The Cultural Contribution of the Other Ethnic Groups* (Ottawa, 1970), 244-45.

[15]Interview with Miklós Korponay conducted by SPZ, 8 November 1978.

[16]Interview with Joseph Jager conducted by SPZ, 12 September 1978.

[17]Interview with István Vörösváry-Weller conducted by SPZ, 19 September 1978.

[18]Based on Ontario Census Statistics; the figure indicates an increase in the Hungarian-born population of the Province between 1950 and 1960.

[19]Interview with George Zaduban conducted by SPZ, 24 March 1979.

[20]*Világhiradó* (Illustrated World Review, Toronto), June 1962, 32.

[21]Interview with Mrs. Theresa Lazar conducted by SPZ, 9 January 1980.

[22]Interview with Sándor Kertész conducted by SPZ, 28 November 1978.

WHY 1956? RECENT CULTURAL CHANGES IN THE HUNGARIAN CANADIAN COMMUNITY

George Bisztray,
University of Toronto

A Hungarian Canadian author and refugee of 1956 described with displeasure in one of his short stories how an immigrant who arrived in Canada as a refugee of World War II reprimanded his friend, the owner of a bookstore, for selling current, high quality literature, because it was published in Hungary. The editor of a respected Toronto Hungarian weekly, also a refugee of 1956, had occasion to relate in a taped interview how he had come to found a newspaper in the early sixties because of a lack of Hungarian Canadian newspapers with whose policy he could identify. Another refugee, a poet, found the political pressure exerted by certain Hungarian Canadian organizations hardly compatible with the freedom needed for poetic expression.

These comments, all found in statements of the refugees of 1956, indicate varying degrees of dissatisfaction with the values the newcomers found — values cultivated by earlier immigrants from Hungary. From a historical perspective, one may question the fairness and depth of the judgment expressed. Yet with all their differences, these statements seem to reflect a conflict between the two post-1945 waves of Hungarian immigrants to Canada that took place less than ten years apart — those of the displaced persons [DPs] and the refugees of 1956.

It has been claimed, although until recently hardly supported by sufficient facts, that the Hungarian refugees of 1956-1957 were strikingly different from previous immigrant groups arriving from that country. Until the Second World War, well over 80 per cent of immigrants from Hungary (54,598 in 1941)[1] had been categorized occupationally as agricultural labourers. The DPs, on the other hand, encompassed a considerable number of ex-military officers and ex-civil servants of the inter-war government, as well as priests and some intellectuals. They also tended to constitute an older age group, and numbered 10,151.[2] Most of them had originally regarded their stay in Canada as temporary. After 1956, another, quite different group arrived: professionals, skilled workers, and students. Half of all the refugees were under 22 years of age, and only 30 per cent were over 45. They augmented the population of Hungarians in Canada by some 35,000;[3] 90 per cent settled down in urban areas, 47 per cent in Ontario.[4] This group arrived with the determination to stay.

In the extensive oral history collection of the Multicultural History Society of Ontario (Toronto), logs reveal personal data concerning prominent Hungarian Canadians with whom interviews were conducted and taped. Statistical samples (however limited they are – see Table below), show essential divergences between the two groups. The high rate (33 per cent) of former members of civilian administration and the officer corps in the one, and the absence of persons of such backgrounds under the other headings (#2 and 3) is unexpected, and so is the high representation of artists and professionals with advanced education in the same categories. These figures display tendencies towards notable differences in the distribution of the social elite between the waves of Hungarian immigrants.

Two projects have been undertaken recently which will shed light on many heretofore unresearched aspects of the history of Hungarian Canadians. One is a monograph on Hungarian Canadians written by Professors L. Body, N. Dreisziger, M. Kovacs and B. Kovrig, under the editorship of Professor Dreisziger.[5] The other publication is a recent special Hungarian issue edited by Susan M. Papp, of *Polyphony: The Bulletin of the Multicultural History Society of Ontario*, which focuses on the Hungarian heritage in Ontario.[6] Data contained in these two publications, especially in my own contributions to the special issue of *Polyphony*,[7] as well as my findings resulting from a research project which was done two years ago on Hungarian Canadian literature,[8] have enabled me to advance the above argument.

A quadripartite thesis may be discerned in the book edited by Professor Dreisziger. Hungarian immigrants prior to 1914 mostly worked as farmers and established their institutions, including churches and mutual benefit societies. The new arrivals of the 1920s and 1930s already contained a large segment of urban elements who tended to end up as industrial workers in the east and who were keen on "cultural clubs." The post-Second-World-War immigrants, on the other hand, were predominantly ex-civil servants and ex-army officers who would found political and social organizations. However, the refugees of the uprising of 1956, overwhelmingly young skilled workers or aspirants for higher degrees,in most cases contributed to the cultural development of their new country, often as professionals and in such fields as the arts, the media, and ethnic literature.[9]

Perhaps at this stage we may concentrate on the two major post-war waves of Hungarian immigration to Canada: the ones in 1945-52 and 1956-57 respectively.

The overwhelming majority of the former wave arrived years after the war, in the early 1950s, and although the newcomers of the latter followed with

PROFESSIONAL DISTRIBUTION OF THREE RECENT

HUNGARIAN IMMIGRANT GROUPS:*

	No. 1 1945-1956	No. 2 1956-1966	No. 3 1966-
Artists, incl. designers	2[13.3%]	5[26.3%]	5[55.5%]
Media people, journalists	1[6.6%]	4[21.0%]	1[11.0%]
Highly qualified professionals; university teachers	2[13.3%]	5[26.3%]	3[33.0%]
Civil servants	3[20.0%]	–	–
Army officers	2[13.3%]	–	–
Ministers; members of religious orders	2[13.3%]	2[10.5%]	–
Those pursuing higher studies at time of arrival or shortly thereafter	1[6.6%]	3[16.0%]	–
Those with no education or training at the time of arrival	2[13.3%]	–	–
TOTAL:	15	19	9

* Based on logs of personal interviews deposited with the Multicultural History Society of Ontario, Toronto.

as little as five years delay, there is no doubt that a qualitatively new cultural awareness dawned on Hungarian Canadians with the arrival of the post-revolution refugees. Indeed, the young and well-educated newcomers were eager to enjoy both Canadian democracy and the technical conveniences of the Western world. However, they could not forget the vibrant literary, musical, and theatre life of the old country — that is, the cultural atmosphere they could not experience in Canada. One reason for this state of affairs was the inability of previous Hungarian immigrants to bring about lasting cultural establishments. The post-1956 refugees therefore set out to recreate whatever they missed from their past. The examples of what has been achieved in this respect are drawn from Ontario, the province in which, as has been stated previously, most immigrants reside.[10]

Existing cultural organizations tried to attract the many young refugees by establishing youth extensions for them. The Helicon Society in Toronto was notably successful in this respect. Later on, the newcomers founded their own organizations. Besides self-expression in intellectual dialogues, which lecture programs and literary evenings of cultural societies provided, self-expression and enjoyment of the performing arts also became significant objectives for the post-1956 Hungarian Canadians. In Toronto, two Hungarian theatres were established after the revolution — one of these still survives. A recent attempt to transplant the style of Central European "literary stages" has been the "Podium Project," launched in 1977. The Kodaly Choir, an orchestra, a children's choir and a folk dance group were gradually formed between 1960 and 1962. Hungarian language programs appeared in the media (radio and TV) in different seasons but with increasing frequency. The Hungarian Cultural Centre of Toronto houses the János Halász Library, a unique collection of several thousand volumes of Hungarian books, many of them not available elsewhere in Canada.

An enumeration of such achievements could go on, and many details and data could be quoted. The general impression one receives from a survey of Hungarian cultural institutions and organizations in Ontario is the variety of orientations. There are few areas of Hungarian-Canadian cultural life in which individual Hungarians should not have left their mark. The same variety prevails in the Hungarian-Canadian press. Although its past reaches back several decades before the war,[11] the radically novel socio-cultural climate, the creation of the two waves of post-war immigrants, resulted in an unprecedented scale of journalistic preoccupations and aspirations. Also, it demonstrated the existence of such needs as keeping informed about occurrences in the old country and about events in the local Hungarian-Canadian community.

The Archives of the Multicultural History Society of Ontario have records of twenty-eight Hungarian-Canadian periodicals on file dating since the Second World War. Besides four organizational newsletters, there are twenty-four titles, of which one goes back to the 1920s; four were founded between 1945 and 1956; and the remaining nineteen were launched after 1956. This latter figure is an impressive one and, in addition to indicating a more prosperous era, seems to support the inference that the 1956 refugees' interest in world affairs and cultural items far exceeded in intensity and diversity that of previous post-war immigrants. At the same time, according to statistical evidence, of the four papers founded between 1945 and 1956, three (75 per cent) still appear in print, whereas of the nineteen launched after 1956, only seven (37 per cent) still carry on.[12] The dwindling number of post-1956 publications seems to prove partly the greater tendency of this group to adopt reading in English, and partly, a reduction in the attractiveness to its members of political ideology and social organizations represented as a rule by Hungarian-language newspapers. On a more optimistic note, if two still-born regional papers out of the twenty-four periodicals are excluded, approximately 50 per cent of the post-war Hungarian-Canadian papers are still published on a regular basis. There are no control data easily available about comparable ethnic publications, but the 50 per cent figure seems to demonstrate a significant level of viability on the part of the Hungarian-Canadian press.

My documentation does not cover products of the arts, including visual media, to demonstrate socio-cultural changes in the Hungarian communities of Ontario or, more ambitiously stated, Canada. One particular art, literature, comes to mind at this point, as deserving a brief discussion.

Literature can be approached from extrinsic (sociological, political, anthropological, informational) and intrinsic (formal-aesthetic) angles.[13] Taking the latter perspective, we become aware of the gradual emergence since 1956 of an artistically significant Hungarian-Canadian literature, ostensibly a direct result of the social composition of the immigrants arriving after that date. In fact, four of the five leading Canadian poets writing in Hungarian are post-1956 immigrants.[14] The same wave of newcomers also created the preconditions necessary for the further development of Hungarian-Canadian literature. Consequently, several young immigrants of the 1970s have also found it rewarding to write poetry as a means of self-expression. Although the quality of present-day Hungarian-Canadian literature is very uneven, it nevertheless exists both as an institution and as a literary phenomenon.[15]

Our task is now to synthesize this survey of recent developments in Hungarian Canadian cultural life and return to the initial question: Why 1956? In what respects did the most recent wave of immigrants create landmarks in the history of Hungarian-Canadians? No doubt, results of current research, pioneering yet overdue, recently published, or about to be, will certainly facilitate explanations of varying types. Thus one, seldom-considered reason for the weight of the 1956 influx, namely, the social and behavioural changes brought forth in Hungary and its inhabitants by the post-war regime, needs mentioning.

The refugees of 1956 had been thoroughly fed up with the number of political organizations they were forced to join in Hungary: youth organizations, labour unions, the "democratic" women's movement, Hungarian-Soviet Friendship Association, eventually the Party, and so on, and so on. Consequently, they may have grown sceptical of any political and social organization, including those of the earlier immigrants. Yet the same refugees were eager to form professional and cultural groups of their own. This paradox is hard to grasp without taking into consideration the changes in Hungarian attitudes during the post-war years, which mostly derive from the same overwhelming metamorphosis: the Hungarian society's transformation after the war into one of an unprecedented degree of mobility. Prior to that time, Hungary was a country with clearly marked and rigid social models, roles and functions. Mobility was restricted, since considerable anomalies existed in the social structure. To give a painful example: in 1935, 24.3 per cent of the arable land in the country was owned by 80 per cent of all agrarian households[16] —

which means that these households owned either no land or only a small patch. These conditions were reflected in other social phenomena as well — for instance, in the low representation of rural and working class families in higher education.

After the Second World War new social functions and roles opened up to lower-class Hungarians. Vast changes in outlook were brought about, particularly in that of the younger generations, by the radical social upheaval and the often senseless uprooting of the traditional equilibrium. Democracy and social equality promised by the new system appealed to many. Once the refugees of 1956 arrived in Canada, they certainly shared the anti-Soviet sentiments of the previous, post-war immigrants but were suspicious as to just how far the claim for national restitution, raised by earlier immigrants, extended. To withdraw small landed property from the collective farms was fine, but should it be returned to the big landowner or the Catholic church again? The abolition of the ludicrous but mandatory ideological seminars at the universities sounded appealing, but then could the children of workers and peasants as well receive higher education? The refugees did not find sufficient reassurance with the previous group, and this created both a cultural and a credibility gap, which alienated the new immigrants from the politically oriented organizations of the previous immigrants, or from the formation of similar, viable organizations of their own. Nor did the two groups come to know and understand each other sufficiently. On the one hand the new immigrants had been taught in Hungary that the post-war refugees were but fossils of the old, reactionary ruling class. On the other hand many earlier immigrants soon started associating the newcomers with communist contamination, just because these held views different from theirs.

Professor Dreisziger suggests that the communist system in Hungary was a welfare system which provided the youth as well as the previous lower stratum of the society with a number of privileges.[17] However, the greatest privilege granted to the post-war generation, it seems, was the chance of social mobility combined with the never fulfilled ideal of truly democratic social equality. The refugees found these two promises more or less fully realized in the Western world. Besides, they came to stay. Consequently, their collective ambitions were social and cultural rather than political.

Another proposition stemming from Professor Dreisziger is that the refugees of 1956, unlike immigrants driven by previous social and political necessities, agonized about their decision to leave their homeland after taking the decisive step, since the opportunity to leave Hungary came so unexpectedly.[18] The question arises whether this "agony" was not related to an existentialist self-analysis, and the attempt to cope with the loneliness of modern Western man in general. If so, it should mean that the highly educated, culturally-oriented generation of 1956 was, with all its obsessions and insecurities, at least as much in accord with the cultural and social currents of the modern world as the more politically oriented and group-conscious generation of 1945-1951. The latter tended to believe that they were fulfilling some mission, whereas the new immigrants had more individualistic aims.

For all that, it would be a mistake to exaggerate the conflict between the two post-war immigrant generations. Instead of being contrary, their aspirations and achievements were somewhat complementary. Both contributed in their own ways to the communal survival and culture of Hungarian Canadians (and hopefully) to the ultimate advantage of Canadian society as a whole. The realization that strength lies not only in shared aspirations but also in obvious differences is still a matter Hungarian Canadians have yet to accept fully. Still, this is also the case with other East-Central European ethnic communities.

172

FOOTNOTES

[1] *Eighth Census of Canada*, II, 321.

[2] *Report of the Royal Commission on Bilingualism and Biculturalism* (Ottawa 1967-70), III, 244 (The total figures for the years 1948-52 in "Appendices," Table A-1).

[3] The Department of Citizenship and Immigration reported 37,727 Hungarian refugee arrivals between 1956 and 1960; Census of Canada, 1961, reported 34,396 arrivals between 1956 and 1961. For sources of these data and possible explanations of the discrepancy, cf. the manuscript *Struggle and Hope: The Hungarian Canadian Experience*, ed. N. F. Dreisziger, Chapter 5, Notes 42 and 60.

[4] Ibid., Chapter 5, MS pp. 27-28.

[5] Ibid., scheduled publication 1982.

[6] Volume II, Nos. 2-3 (1979-80).

[7] Two articles entitled "The Hungarian Canadian Press" (pp. 54-58) and "Cultural Institutions" (pp. 70-76).

[8] The project was supported by a grant from the Secretary of State Multiculturalism Directorate. The first interview was conducted in June 1978, the last in March 1979.

[9] *Struggle and Hope*, Chapter 5, MS, pp. 28-30, 35-36, 40-43. A paper delivered at a recent conference, however, emphasizes the permanence of cultural interest among Hungarian immigrants in Ontario since 1910 as a whole by pointing out the high number of cultural institutions in operation for decades (Susan M. Papp, "The Organizational Development of the Hungarian Community in Ontario," Fifth Annual Conference of the American Hungarian Educators' Association, 1980). Although this is an important quantitative (statistical) element, one should be mindful of Professor Dreisziger's remark in *Struggle and Hope* that the standards achieved by the cultural groups established after 1956 "constituted a new departure" and represented a "semi- or even professional level" (Chapter 5, MS p. 29). That is, the post-1956 cultural organizations constituted a qualitatively new phenomenon.

[10] Between 1951 and 1961, the Hungarian-born population of Ontario increased by 19,541 (Ontario Statistics quoted in *Polyphony*, II, 2-3, p. 68).

[11] For a survey of the Hungarian-Canadian press prior to World War II, cf. Jenö Rúzsa, *A kanadai magyarság története* (Toronto, 1940), pp. 362-72.

[12] G. Bisztray, "The Hungarian Canadian Press," *Polyphony*, II, 2-3, p. 58.

[13] The widely accepted terms "extrinsic" and "intrinsic" approach and their criteria derive from R. Wellek and A. Warren's *Theory of Literature* (New York, 1949).

[14] Tamás Tüz arrived in Canada in 1956, László Kemenes Gefin and György Vitéz in 1957, György Faludy in 1967. The exception is Ferenc Fáy who immigrated in 1951.

[15] There is hardly anything written about Hungarian-Canadian literature. Certain findings of my research project of 1978-79 will be printed in the collective volume *Ethnicity and the Writer in Canada* (to be published by the Canadian Institute of Ukrainian Studies in 1981).

[16]Source of data: *Information Hungary*, ed. F. Erdei (Oxford, 1968), p. 413.

[17]*Struggle and Hope*, Chapter 5, MS pp. 25-26.

[18]Ibid., p. 26.

174

GERMAN SETTLEMENTS IN SASKATCHEWAN

Alan B. Anderson,
Department of Sociology
University of Saskatchewan

Migrant Motivation: Immigration into Western Canada *

When examining the general reasons for migration, one should distinguish between the factors pushing the migrant from his mother-country and those pulling him to a new land. Principal "push" factors include overpopulation, impoverishment, political discontent, and persecution. Significant "pull" factors are a government's recruitment of immigrants required to settle sparsely populated regions, recruitment by agencies seeking cheap labour, the influence of settlers writing home, and businesses that encourage immigration because they make money transporting settlers.

Toward the end of the nineteenth century the Canadian government mounted an intensive campaign to attract immigrants, especially since the 1891 census had shown only a slow population growth during the previous decade.[1] When Clifford Sifton became Minister of the Interior in 1896, he immediately began a program to encourage immigration. Agents were appointed in Europe, even though most countries there had strict laws against emigration. Invitations to migrants were publicized through circulars, exhibits, and advertisements; transportation companies were federally subsidized. Every sort of device was employed to attract immigrants. Moreover, the flow of Central and Eastern European migrants to the Canadian Prairies was, no doubt, soon enhanced by the imposition of American quota restrictions.

Many of the 160,000 continental settlers in Saskatchewan by 1911 came through the efforts of the North Atlantic Trading Company. The company, which had an agreement with the Canadian Government dating from 1899, was required to spend at least $15,000 a year to secure immigrants from continental Europe.[2] In turn, it received one pound sterling for every farmer who settled. This contract was renewed in 1904 for ten years, but was then cancelled only two years later due to a manipulation of finances. Apparently payments were claimed for immigrants who had come to Canada under other auspices. The hostility of European governments toward clandestine immigration propaganda

---

* This section of the paper has been revised from Anderson, A. B., "Assimilation in the Bloc Settlements of North-Central Saskatchewan: A Comparative Study of Identity Change Among Seven Ethno-Religious Groups in a Canadian Prairie Region." Ph.D. thesis in Sociology, University of Saskatchewan, 1972. – Hereinafter: "Anderson, 1972."

175

was another factor leading to the contract cancellation. Nonetheless, by 1906, the company had received immense sums from the Wilfrid Laurier government.[3]

The Sifton policy of open immigration from continental Europe was not without its critics. The provincial attitude differed markedly from the federal government's because of financial difficulties accentuated by the rush of immigrants. The continued and accelerating influx created demands for heavy expenditures on educational facilities, public works, and other provincial services. Sifton's policy also conflicted sharply with the desire to preserve an "English-speaking peoples only" region, especially in Saskatchewan. Resentment against uncontrolled immigration, particularly German and Eastern European, grew steadily. As late as 1930 at hearings conducted by the Saskatchewan Royal Commission on Immigration and Settlement, numerous briefs opposing open immigration were submitted.[4]

The Settlement Process and the Emergence of Bloc Settlements[5]

The process of settlement was a rather complicated one. It began with the Land Act of 1872, Section 33:

> Every person who is the sole head of a family and every male who has attained the age of 18 years and is a British subject or declares his intention of becoming a British subject, is entitled to apply for entry to a homestead. A quarter-section may be obtained as a homestead on payment of an entry fee of $10 and fulfillment of certain conditions of residence and cultivation. To qualify for the issuing of the patent, the settler must have resided upon his homestead for at least six months of each of three years, must have erected a habitable house thereon, and must have at least 30 acres of his holding broken, of which 20 must be cropped. A reduction may be made in the area of breaking where the land is difficult to cultivate on account of scrub or stone.

The federal government's settlement schemes were closely integrated with the railway's schemes, and these were linked with those of ethnic and religious organizations. The federal government subsidized settlement through the Colonization Department of the C.P.R. (which had offices in Britain and France). A similar C.N.R. department was not organized until 1923 (to settle immigrants on vacant lands adjacent to C.N.R. lines); as the C.N. Land Settlement Association it had main offices in Britain, the Netherlands, and the Scandinavian countries. Then there was the Canada Colonization Association, a C.P.R. subsidiary, which helped settle continental immigrants who had insufficient capital. Besides the C.C.A., the railways operated through ethnic and religious subsidiary organizations interested in establishing bloc settlements; these organizations were financially supported by the railways to the sum of $5 per each settled adult in a family or $1 per single agricultural worker.[6]

The establishment of ethnic enclaves was not unusual. Sociologists have pointed out that competition for space results in the formation of segregated ethnic islands, each of which develops a distinctive culture.[7] Members of minority groups tend to congregate in areas where they can speak their own language and follow their own customs. Often, since immigrants felt the hostility of the larger society, they segregated themselves into well-defined areas, or they wanted to be among co-ethnics with whom they could identify and sympathize. Once such colonies came into existence, moreover, other people of a given ethnic group tended to gravitate toward them.

C.A. Price has made some suggestive comments which are closely related to the establishment of the bloc settlements in the Prairies.[8] He has distinguished three main processes by which group settlements come into being. First, there are organized group settlements, such as those founded by organized bands of political or religious refugees or those founded when organized groups of labourers are employed to develop a particular area. Second, there are chain settlements, such as those which develop slowly and sometimes quite fortuitously as the result of chain migration, i.e., the process whereby one or two persons of a particular place in Europe settle in some locality abroad and then establish links with their friends and acquaintances at home. Third, there are gravitation group settlements formed when migrants who have travelled independently are drawn together by force of mutual attraction — common dialect or national language, similar cultural traditions and customs, or the same religion. Price added two qualifications: (a) that the original character of the settlement may change in time, and (b) that some settlements may be offshoots from an earlier one. In Saskatchewan the German settlements conform to all these categories. The establishment of ethno-religious bloc settlements in Saskatchewan, then, was partly due to organized colonization schemes and partly due to rather coincidental gravitation of co-ethnics.[9]

This settlement process had a profound impact on Canadian society in general and on certain Prairie regions in particular. Despite an immigration policy favouring immigrants only from "desirable" countries, by the 1920s Saskatchewan had twice as many immigrants of non-British as of British origin.[10] Moreover, the Canadian Prairies benefited from the diversion of farm labour from the United States.[11] Consequently, ethnic enclaves became a prominent feature of the Prairies, helping to turn Canadian society into a "cultural mosaic" largely lacking the strong national identity and melting-pot consciousness emerging in the U.S.A. These enclaves were also characterized by isolation from other enclaves of different ethnic origins and religious affiliations and from the larger society. Social organization became extremely

178

localized and characterized by the dialects, customs and traditions of particular areas in Europe.

While the Saskatchewan Royal Commission on Immigration and Settlement did not appraise the situation in 1930 as negatively as did many of the organizations submitting briefs, it did recognize that the development of isolated bloc settlements was not readily conducive to an integrated Canadian society:

> Through the province will be found many group settlements, representative of diverse racial stocks. While group settlement has many good features, nevertheless there are grave objections to its further development . . . Doubtless these groups do add diversity and elements of richness to the cultural life of the community; and also doubtless by this very diversity there is a greater opportunity to adapt newcomers to the new environment. This, in turn, may result in their more rapid economic progress. The warm welcome that may be expected from a racial brother, the overcoming of the nostalgia resulting from separation from the homeland, as well as other aids, are factors that appear to support group settlement. On the other hand, it is the rooted conviction of many of our people that group settlement tends to create blocks, thus preventing those intimate contacts without which it is impossible to create a sound citizenship.[12]

The Commission thus concluded "that homesteading be discontinued and that the remaining Crown Lands . . . be sold, (a) to residents of the province, (b) to other Canadians, (c) to British settlers, (d) to other immigrants."[13] Therefore the period of establishing bloc settlements in Saskatchewan extended primarily from the advent of Sifton's policy in 1896 to the Commission's report in 1930.[14]

Specific Reasons Behind German Migration to Saskatchewan

To understand the formation of German settlements in Saskatchewan requires some familiarity with Russian history, since a considerable proportion of immigrants came directly from German colonies in Russia, or directly via Russian-German settlements in the United States. Upon the conquest of Turkish-held territories north of the Black Sea from 1763 to 1774, Catherine II sought to populate new annexations with agricultural settlers loyal to her. As a result, an invitation was extended to farmers in Central Europe to establish ethnic colonies in Russia, stipulating that they would enjoy religious freedom, immunity from taxation for ten years followed by low taxation, exemption from military services, freedom from a mortgage on their land for ten years, freedom from serfdom, and permission to emigrate from Russia after paying all debts to the Crown. The first colonies (in 1784-1778) were organized on the Volga by

Germans from the largely Protestant region of Hesse. These *Volga-Deutsche* were distinguished from the *Schwarzmeer-Deutsch*, the Germans who later settled north of the Black Sea.[15]

There were several factors which caused Germans to emigrate from their colonies in Russia. Most important was the progressive deprivation of the rights and privileges granted by Catherine II.[16] Others were forced to emigrate from their colonies in Bessarabia, Dobruja, Bukovina, Galicia, and Hungary — for various reasons. Thus, in Dobruja, the imposition of military service in 1883 followed by a severe drought in 1884 added to the existing problem of land shortage.[17]

The German influx into the United States from Eastern Europe may have reached 200,000 annually during the early 1880s. Large areas of the Dakotas and Minnesota became replicas of the Russian-German colonies. Until the notion of German separatism became passé with the assimilated third and fourth generations, and with the surge of anti-German feeling from the First World War, the homes, schools, ethnic press, voluntary associations, and churches all collaborated in an attempt to preserve a German identity, to promote a segregated German life-style, and to prevent intermarriage with non-Germans. Even political separatism was persistently encouraged; in 1862 attempts were made to have German as an official language.[18]

The increasing problem of finding large tracts of good agricultural land caused many colonists in the United States to look north at the rapidly developing Canadian West. Germans, like others, were lured to Saskatchewan by the availability of good inexpensive farmland and the solicitation of Canadian immigration authorities and agencies. They were also attracted by the promise of exemption from military service, by the encouragement of prominent Germans invited to tour the West and organize large colonies (notably Count Hohenlohe-Langenburg, President of the German Colonial Association, and F. J. Lange, a founder of the Catholic Colonization Society). Also the successful precedent set by the earliest German settlers and the views of German newspapers and writers (such as A. E. Johann) were influential.[19]

Diverse German Origins, Religious Affiliations, and Settlement Patterns

Most of the Germans who settled in Saskatchewan did not immigrate directly from Germany. In 1916 only 15,328 residents of the prairie provinces gave Germany as their country of birth, whereas 101,944 indicated that German was their mother tongue.[20] According to one estimate only 12% of the ethnic German immigrants who arrived in Western Canada before 1914 were *Reichsdeutsche* (that is from Germany); the remainder were mostly *Volksdeutsche* from Eastern Europe — 44% from Russia, 18% from the

Austro-Hungarian Empire, 6% from Rumania; about 18% from the United States.[21] Among the reasons why relatively few immigrants from Germany came to Saskatchewan were ignorance of Canada, fear of the northern climate, and the German government's discouragement of emigration.

Besides the disproportionately small representation of Germany proper among the immigrants, another surprising fact stands out in connection with their settlements; they tended to settle more on the basis of religious affiliation than according to place of origin. This resulted in the mixing of people from many areas in Eastern Europe.[22]

A number of students of German settlement in Western Canada have suggested that on the whole German immigrants were poor, had limited education, and had strong familial and religious ties; they also maintain these characteristics were essential to the successful establishment of pioneer settlements in the prairies.[23] On closer inspection, however, it would seem German settlement was very complex. Generalizations made by these scholars have sometimes been unqualified and misleading. Indeed, if most German settlers in Saskatchewan were relatively poor and uneducated, they were better educated and better situated financially than most other East European immigrants. Moreover, apparently some of the German settlements in Saskatchewan were homogeneous in both religious affiliation and precise regional origin. Other settlements revealed mixed origins yet common religion, or conversely, common origin with mixed religious affiliations. Many German immigrants sought out their own bloc settlements; others did not, electing instead to settle in ethnically heterogeneous areas. Some settlements were planned; other German concentrations came into existence gradually through chain migration, yet the best approach to distinguishing them may be according to their religious affiliation.

German Catholics

Principal Catholic Colonies

Four major settlements of German Catholics developed in Saskatchewan: St. Joseph's Colony near Balgonie, immediately east of Regina, and the adjoining Kronau-Rastadt and Odessa colonies (1886-1904); St. Peter's Colony, centring on the town of Humboldt in north-central Saskatchewan (1902-12); a second St. Joseph's Colony, in the west-central region (1905-10); and a series of adjoining colonies in the areas around Leader in southwestern Saskatchewan (1907-13).

St. Joseph's Colony, Kronau-Rastadt, and Odessa (1886-1904)

St. Joseph's Colony began in 1886 when eight families, who had migrated from the Josephstal Colony in the Liebenthal group near Odessa in South Russia or what is today Ukraine, settled near Balgonie.[24] By 1892 there were thirty families there. As a result of crop failure, however, by 1895 many were leaving. The remaining families decided in June, 1898 to organize a *dorf* (a communal village clustered around a church) in Russian-German style, since they were not used to the Canadian pattern of settling on scattered homesteads.[25]

Between 1890 and 1893 at least fifty-three families migrated from the communities of Rastadt and Muenchen in the Anajewer region northwest of Nikolajev, and from Klosterdorf near Berislav on the Dnieper,[26] to found St. Peter's Roman Catholic Parish. Some of these Russian-German immigrants decided to establish *dorfs* similar to St. Joseph's; twelve families established Rastadt-Dorf ("Seven Colony"), twenty-one others, Katharinental ("Fourteen Colony"), named after the original community of Katharinental, and another eighteen families built Speyer (named after another community in the same area of South Russia) in 1898-1899. Also the villages of Davin, Rastadt, and Kronau came into existence in this context, the latter two named after communities in South Russia.[27]

This Russian-German Catholic settlement in Saskatchewan expanded rapidly southeast to Vibank, Odessa (named for the principal port-city on the Black Sea), and Kendal, as well as south toward Sedley and Francis. By 1896 there were more than two hundred German families in the region, almost all immigrants from German colonies in South Russia.[28] Although the vast majority were Catholics, a substantial Lutheran minority had developed with the expansion of the settlement.[29]

The census data of 1971 show that of the seven incorporated towns or villages within or at the periphery of the settlement, four had German majorities — Kendal, 82.4%; Vibank, 75.0%; Odessa, 62.9%, and White City, 60.0%; the others had substantial German minorities — Francis, 48.5%; Sedley, 37.7%, and Balgonie, 25.2% (Davin and Kronau are not incorporated).

St. Peter's Colony (1902)

The Colony was largely settled with groups from the United States. With the opening of Saskatchewan to settlement in the 1890s many German settlers from the closest American states began to move north. In many instances they sent invitations back to their former parishes for further immigrants to come and to found new colonies. One such request was received by a Benedictine priest in Minnesota who persuaded his superior, the abbot at St. John's Abbey in Collegeville, to establish a German Catholic colony in Saskatchewan.[30] An exploration party was sent, headed by the abbey's Reverend Bruno Doerfler and consisting of representatives from three parishes. When the decision to establish the colony was made the newly-founded *Volksverein* German-American Land Company was responsible for buying 100,000 acres of railroad lands in the district selected and for selling it to settlers desiring more than the usual one-quarter-section homestead. The priests planned to develop parishes and expand the settlement while the Catholic Settlement Society extensively advertised the venture and assisted settlers in filing their homesteads and locating them thereon. Homesteading was in accordance with the specifications of the Canadian government.[31]

With the arrival of Benedictines from Cluny Priory in Wetaug, Illinois in 1902 and from Collegeville, Minnesota, the following year, settlement began in earnest. By the end of 1903, over a thousand homesteads had been filed and eight parishes established. Within five years there were more than 6,000 German Catholics in the Colony.[32] Most were second or third generation German-Americans, whose forefathers had immigrated from the *Reich* to Minnesota, the Dakotas, Wisconsin, Iowa, Nebraska, and Kansas, although some were from Russian-German colonies and from the Banat region of Hungary (now in Yugoslavia and Rumania).[33] By 1905 the Order of St. Benedict had grown into a complex organization governing schools, associations, and whole communities. A German-language newspaper, *Der Bote*, had begun publication at Muenster. Humboldt was rapidly being converted from "a wilderness of sloughs and bluffs" into the largest town in the region (with a population of more than 2,000 by 1914). The pioneering monk Bruno Doerfler became an abbot in 1906 while a dozen more parishes were added.[34]

The colony continued to expand and its German identity to become accentuated. Several more parishes were founded.[35] The first *Katholikentag*, a conference of German-Catholics, was held at Muenster in 1908, with delegates from various Saskatchewan settlements as well as from Minnesota and Manitoba; other *Katholikentage* were held at Humboldt in 1910 and 1914.[36] Also during this period two religious orders for women arrived from Europe. In 1911 some Sisters of St. Elizabeth, a 200 year-old order at Klagenfurt, Austria, immigrated to Humboldt, where they founded the first of a series of hospitals. Two years later Ursuline nuns left their convents at Cologne and Hesseluene, Germany, to organize a convent and school at Marysburg. Later, in 1919, they moved to Bruno, where they established a large convent and Academy.[37]

In the years following the First World War the colony had its ups and downs. One significant event was the replacement of *Der Bote* with an English language publication, the *Prairie Messenger*, in 1922. *Der Bote* had been defunct since 1918 with the legislation against printing in German. Then, the important *Katholikentage* declined in popularity, although minor ones were held, such as at Bruno in 1927 and 1931 and Cudworth in 1924; the last important general one was held at Muenster in 1933. In a brief to the Royal Commission on Immigration and Settlement in 1930, the German-Canadian Association of Saskatchewan expressed its resentment of the Canadian government refusal to grant asylum to Russian-German refugees during the 1920s, and it requested, somewhat belatedly, to have Germans classed as "preferred" immigrants.[38] By 1951-52, the remnants of the *Volksverein* were merged with the Catholic Immigration Society for Western Canada.

But progress as a colony was also evident. In 1921 the settlement was declared an "abbacy nullius," equivalent to an autonomous bishopric, subject directly to the Pope's authority; in other words, its status as a Benedictine colony was assured. St. Peter's College was founded at Muenster in 1920. New parishes were established as the settlement continued to expand to its current dimensions.[39]

Relatively few settlers of St. Peter's Colony immigrated directly from Europe. Most came from Minnesota and the Dakotas, although some were first-generation settlers, i.e., they had immigrated to Saskatchewan from Europe via the United States. In the Watson area, for example, out of twenty-seven original German Catholic families eight came from Minnesota, two from the Dakotas, nine from other Midwestern states, two from Europe (Austria and Russia) after a brief stay in the United States, and six directly from Europe (Germany, Belgium, Russia, and Switzerland).[40]

Not only was the colony founded by Benedictine priests from German Catholic settlements in the U.S.A., it maintained close ties with its American counterparts. St. John's Abbey, Collegeville, Minnesota, continued to send priests to St. Peter's Colony; the first abbot at St. Peter's and his replacement in 1919 were from St. John's.[41] Other priests came from Benedictine abbeys in Illinois and Kansas, although some arrived from Innsbruck, Austria, and Muensterschwarzach, Bavaria, as well.

By 1971 the German Catholic population of St. Peter's Colony, one of the largest German bloc settlements in Saskatchewan, had some 9,500 inhabitants. It included an urban town (Humboldt), several rural towns (Cudworth and Bruno), three major incorporated villages (Lake Lenore, Middle Lake and Muenster), four minor incorporated villages (Annaheim, Englefeld, St. Gregor, and St. Benedict), some unincorporated villages (Carmel and Pilger), two hamlets (Fulda and Marysburg), and over a hundred named localities. In addition to the German Catholics of St. Peter's Colony proper, there were several thousand people of German origin in adjacent areas (due to the expansion of settlements): majorities in Allan, Lampard, Romance, and Sinnett (Catholic), Jansen and Esk (Lutheran), and Drake (Mennonite); a significant minority (at least 25%) in Watson, Young, Zelma, and Wimmer (Catholic), Leroy and

184

Dafoe (Catholic and Lutheran), and Guernsey (Mennonite); and a smaller
minority (less than 25%) in Naicam, Spalding, and Daphne (Catholic and
Lutheran).

Table I identifies the German population in each incorporated community
within and near St. Peter's Colony in 1971.[42]

**TABLE I: German Population in Incorporated Communities,
St. Peter's Colony, 1971.**

	Total Population:	German Population:	German Proportion:
Towns:			
Bruno	715	450	62.9%
Cudworth	885	270	30.5%
Humboldt	3,970	1,930	48.6%
Naicam	770	140	18.2%
Wakaw	1,015	140	13.8%
Watson	885	265	29.9%
Villages:			
Englefeld	270	170	63.0%
Lake Lenore	440	285	64.8%
Middle Lake	315	225	71.4%
Muenster	240	155	64.6%
Pilger	120	100	83.3%
St. Benedict	165	95	57.6%
St. Gregor	115	80	69.6%
Spalding	350	60	17.1%

In analyzing the success of the inhabitants of St. Peter's Colony in
maintaining their German identity, it is instructive to describe their efforts to
retain a German Catholic education.[43] In many ways the German Catholic case
paralleled the French Catholic one; but there were also significant differences.
As early as 1892 a member of the Territorial House of Commons attempted to
introduce a bill which would have required all schools to teach in the English
language. The attempt failed; but an ordinance of that year reduced the
Catholic voice in school matters by changing the composition of the Board of
Education. Instead of an equal partnership with non-Catholics, Catholics now
sat as non-voting advisory members of an Executive Council. As with the
French, German Catholics were assured in 1901 that a local school board could
arrange to employ competent teachers to give instructions in their mother-
tongue; later it was stipulated that such instruction should occur in the last
hour of the school day and be a reading, composition and grammar course.

By 1907, Prior Bruno, founder and guiding-light of St. Peter's German
Catholic Colony, had requested Premier Walter Scott to allow German as a

language of instruction at any time during the school day. Scott's government (1905-16) would not accept this proposal. Instead, the government's policy of "gradualism," whereby school inspectors encouraged country school districts to adhere gradually to regulations, was quite effective among German Catholics.

It is difficult to summarize succinctly the actual situation in St. Peter's Colony because of conflicting reports. The *Daily Phoenix* suggested there were as many as forty-five private schools with 1,200 pupils using German rather than English as the language of instruction; they were established by the church to avoid government control. Prior Bruno countered with his own facts: there were only fifteen private schools, they were all bilingual with ample teaching in English, and all students were expected to be proficient in English. Governmental school inspectors' reports appear to support Prior Bruno. There were some fifteen major separate schools founded by the Benedictines, each with 50-60 students. While these schools hoped to preserve the German language and the Catholic religion, they were bilingual and came up to government expectations; as one report states, "No case has arisen of neglect for the teaching of English." Apparently both religious and secular teachers were employed. While many schools were up-to-date, those in the western part of the colony were reported as overcrowded, ill-equipped, unventilated, and staffed by unqualified teachers. One inspector complained that public schools adhering to government regulations were "practically empty." Some were indistinguishable from the separate schools since they were oriented toward German Catholic traditions and used the German language extensively. It seems safe to conclude that under the Scott government the majority of schools in the colony, separate as well as public, were strongly oriented toward ethno-religious group control.[44]

This situation changed rapidly during the Martin administration (1917-1922). Any tolerance of German language instruction by the British-origin population tended to disappear during the First World War when Canada was at war. A revision to the School Act in 1919 brought the obliteration of German language teaching during school hours and the removal of Catholic symbolism from public schools. Except for some anomalies there was a marked re-orientation of schools in the settlement; separate schools shifted from a strong ethnic and religious identification to an almost exclusively religious one, while public schools moved away from their ethnic link.[45]

In a recent chapter on ethnic identity change in ethno-religious bloc settlements in Saskatchewan, the present author has described in detail the results of a survey conducted in St. Peter's Colony and other settlements.[46] An extensive and broad sample (N=190 families) showed that 41.1% of those interviewed noted a major loss of German identity in the colony, and another 58.9% described the loss as relatively minor. Of the first-generation respondents (i.e., the initial settlers) 73.0% favoured the preservation of the German identity, compared to only 34.6% of the second generation and 10.5% of the third or fourth. Another 13.7% preferred to speak German both at home and in the local community, 15.3% used German at home but English outside, 64.2% spoke English at home and outside (although they could speak German), while 6.8% could speak only English. The proportion of the German-origin population in Saskatchewan speaking German declined from 73% in 1941 to 58% in 1951, 41% in 1961, and 42% in 1971; only 10% however, still spoke German as their primary language at home). Among respondents in St. Peter's Colony, no cases were found of people speaking only German; 29.0% used German fairly often, and a surprising 93.2% could speak or understand some German. Broken down by generation, 45.9% of the first generation (immigrant settlers) were now speaking English primarily or exclusively, compared to 71.8% of the second and 82.7% of the third (or more).

Although an increasing proportion of these people paid less and less attention to their German ethnicity, they have none the less remained staunch Catholics: 93.7% of the respondents attended church regularly (94.6% of the first generation, 97.4% of the second, and 89.3% of the third or more). Finally, 90.0% of the married respondents had married other German Catholics; 69.5% expressed their opposition to marrying non-Catholics, whereas only 10.0% were opposed to marrying non-Germans.

St. Joseph's Colony at Kerrobert (1905–1910)

Only a couple of years after the inception of St. Peter's Colony, plans were already being made for the establishment of a larger German Catholic colony. F. J. Lange, a founder of the Catholic Colonization Society, conceived the idea of a vast German Catholic colony covering two hundred townships — about four times the size of the St. Peter's Colony. In arranging land concessions for St. Peter's Colony, Lange had heard some settlers — especially the minority who had come from South Russia — complain about the parkland type of land (partially bush-covered) comprising much of the colony; evidently these settlers preferred treeless, open prairie. During the summer of 1904, then, Lange selected the Tramping Lake area in west-central Saskatchewan as the focal-point for new settlements.[47]

The resulting St. Joseph's Colony covered a larger land area than St. Peter's Colony, but it never attained the population of the earlier colony. Lange's high expectations were not entirely fulfilled; government officials agreed to the bloc purchase of seventy-seven townships by the Catholic Colonization Society, but only fifty-five (equivalent to the extent of St. Peter's Colony) ever had German majorities. As in St. Peter's Colony, the Catholic Colonization Society collaborated with a religious order — in this case the Oblate Order from Hunfeld, Germany — in the planning, development and settling of the colony.

Although the first settlers arrived in the Tramping Lake area in early summer, 1905, the settlement there did not develop as rapidly as St. Peter's Colony. By 1911 it had 5,300 people of German origin, and had grown to an estimated 7-8,000 by 1914.[48] Most settlers were Black Sea Germans, at first arriving via the Dakotas, although later in 1908-10 they usually came directly from South Russia.[49]

Place names within the colony indicated the Russian-German origin of the settlers. Leipzig was probably named after a community established in 1815 in the Bessarabian colonies by migrants who were originally from Southwestern Germany and Alsace but who had settled for some time in Poland. Grosswerder was perhaps named after a Catholic community in the Belowesch colonies east of Chernigov, established by immigrants from Upper Hesse in 1766, or after a daughter community founded in 1831 in the Mariupol colonies near the Bergthal Mennonite colony.[50]

Table II identifies the German ethnic population in incorporated towns and villages within and near St. Joseph's Colony in 1971. In addition to these incorporated communities and rural parishes, a number of unincorporated areas had a considerable German proportion, especially Palo, Traynen, Revenue, Verulam, Reward, Hallam, Heart's Hill, Cactus Lake, Millerdale, and Druid.

The Leader Colonies (1907-1913)

As the settlement process in St. Joseph's Colony neared completion, a fourth major German Catholic colony — or rather a series of colonies — developed around the town of Leader in southwestern Saskatchewan. As early as 1889 a large Russian-German settlement of migrants from Volhynia and Galicia began to settle just across the border in Alberta; eventually the Russian-Germans would people a large expanse of territory on both sides of the border (between Leader, Maple Creek, and Medicine Hat). Beginning in 1908, they established a series of colonies and parishes on the Saskatchewan side, including Lancer Parish, Prelate Parish, Prussia Colony (centred on Leader), Mendham Parish, St. Mary's Colony, Liebenthal Colony, and Krassna-Rastadt Colony.[51]

While these adjoining colonies around Leader were predominantly Catholic, they included several pockets of strongly Protestant settlement.

Table III identifies German populations of incorporated towns and villages in this region in 1971. Unincorporated communities in the region with substantial German proportions include Blumenfeld, Lemsford, Westerham, Estuary, Krupp, Horsham, Tunstall, and Hatton.

188

TABLE II: German Population in Incorporated Communities, St. Joseph's Colony (Kerrobert), 1971

	Total Population:	German Population:	German Proportion:
Towns:			
Kerrobert	1,215	400	32.9%
Luseland	750	365	48.7%
Macklin	855	595	69.6%
Scott	215	90	41.9%
Unity	2,360	815	34.5%
Wilkie	1,685	760	45.1%
Villages:			
Coleville	440	70	15.9%
Denzil	315	210	66.6%
Dodsland	365	75	20.5%
Evesham	80	40	50.0%
Handel	80	45	56.3%
Kelfield	20	10	50.0%
Landis	265	85	32.1%
Leipzig	65	65	100.0%
Major	170	75	44.1%
Primate	85	70	82.4%
Salvador	50	20	40.0%
Springwater	110	20	18.2%
Tramping Lake	270	215	79.6%

TABLE III: German Population in Incorporated Communities, Leader Region, 1971.

	Total Population:	German Population:	German Proportion:
Towns:			
Leader	1,120	640	57.1%
Maple Creek	2,270	450	19.8%
Villages:			
Burstall	550	245	44.5%
Fox Valley	480	290	60.4%
Golden Prairie	145	75	51.7%
Lancer	205	150	73.2%
Mendham	175	145	82.9%
Portreeve	60	25	41.7%
Prelate	420	270	64.3%
Richmound	210	160	76.2%
Sceptre	230	60	26.1%

Smaller Catholic Settlements

While the four major German Catholic settlements were developing, a number of smaller Catholic concentrations came into existence. One of the earliest was in the Grayson-Killaly area immediately south of Melville; it was settled largely by *Volksdeutsche* from Bukovina, Bessarabia, Galicia, and Poland. Grayson, first settled in 1896, was initially called Nieven, but in 1903 was renamed after a C.P.R. railway construction contractor. The Mariahilf Catholic Colony outside Killaly was founded in 1900, while the Killaly Catholic parish came into being in 1910.[52]

All across the southernmost regions of Saskatchewan small German Catholic concentrations came into existence. In the southwest, German Catholics began to settle near Shaunavon in 1907 and 1908, establishing a strong parish by 1912. About one in five people in Shaunavon today is of German origin. In the south-central region, the Billimun Colony, named after a German community in Russia, was founded outside Mankota by Catholic Russian-Germans between 1910 and 1912.[53]

In all these communities, whether towns of over a thousand or tiny hamlets of a handful, Germans now constitute only a minority. The highest proportion is found at Horizon, little more than a rural locality, where half of the few remaining people are German. At Mankota (pop. 430 in 1971), 30.2% are German while Vanguard (25.8%), and Rockglen (24.8%), Mossbank (21.6%), Khedive (21.4%), Spring Valley (21.4%), and Mazenod (20.0%) retain substantial German minorities. Germans now are less significant at Pangman (18.4%), Bengough (13.6%), Assiniboia (13.3%), Ceylon (12.7%), and Avonlea (only 5.0%). Of course, community size should be considered as this relates to the distribution and concentration of German-origin population. In the southeastern region, German Catholic concentrations tended to form within predominantly Lutheran areas (discussed below). An exception was the Windthorst settlement near Kipling, named after Ludwig Windthorst, one of the organizers and leaders of the Centrist Party in Germany and an able opponent of Count Bismarck. Windthorst was settled early in this century by Russian-German immigrants (mostly Catholic but including some Lutherans), from the Vladimir-Volynskij area north of Lemberg (Lviv) and other Volhynian-Galician German communities.[54]

In the northwestern region of the Saskatchewan prairie (i.e., the southern half of the province as a whole), the St. Walburg area was first settled by people of German origin, primarily Catholics from the *Reich*, Bavaria, Austria, and Luxembourg, in 1902-12; German Lutherans did not establish a church at St. Walburg until 1926.[55] German settlement in the region developed gradually. German Catholics settled around Goodsoil, about a hundred kilometres north of St. Walburg, during the 1920s and later around the neighbouring community of Peerless, as well as further west with Mennonites around Pierceland near the

Alberta border. In 1929 immigrants arrived directly from Germany (mostly from Thueringen, but others from Holstein, Westfalen, Mecklenburg and the Baltic coast) to establish the Loon River Colony between St. Walburg and the more northerly communities.[56] Ironically, a German presence in the district was maintained, because the returning migrants were replaced by German refugees from the Sudetenland, newly annexed to Hitler's *Reich* in 1938. Today Germans constitute little more than a quarter of the population of St. Walburg (26.6% in 1971), but almost two-thirds (65.9%) of Goodsoil and a majority in the Barthel-Loon River district.

Catholic Minorities Within Lutheran Settlements

Catholic minorities living within non-Catholic settlements were not uncommon. Several strong Catholic concentrations could be noted within — and at the periphery of — the large Neu Elsass Colony (1885) in central Saskatchewan. The part of the colony situated west of Last Mountain Lake, and adjacent districts, were predominantly Catholic.[57] North of the colony, the communities of Quinton, Raymore, and Semans were largely Catholic. Catholics were mixed with Lutherans at Strasbourg (the colony's centre)[58] and Govan, Southey, Cupar, and Dysart.

In the Hohenlohe Colony (1886) Catholics from the Black Sea colonies and from Bavaria settled in the Langenburg-Churchbridge area as early as 1889, developing compact Catholic districts within the predominantly Lutheran colony.[59]

German settlement in the Lanigan area in central Saskatchewan involved Lutherans, Catholics, and several varieties of Mennonites. Most of the Catholics concentrated in the district between Lanigan and Watson, in and around the town of Leroy and in the rural localities of Sinnett, Klatt, Dietrick, and Romance (St. Oswald parish). In St. Patrick's parish they mingled with Irish Catholics; while outside the bounds of St. Peter's Colony, they could be viewed essentially as an extension of that colony.

Finally, there were several Catholic concentrations within German Lutheran settlements in southeastern Saskatchewan. A considerable German population lived in the Lampman-Estevan area. While the population was largely Lutheran and other Protestant, strong Catholic pockets developed, notably around Steelman and in the Maryland-Landau Colony. German Catholics were also found at Lampman, Estevan, Roche Percée and Oxbow. Another German Catholic colony, Marienthal, was established west of Estevan and south of Torquay on the U.S. border; some Catholics were also found nearby at Lake Alma. North-west of Weyburn, Catholics constituted a minority within the early Yellow Grass settlement (1892). The Catholic proportion increases as one heads toward Wilcox. However, there were large areas settled by German Protestants.

German Lutherans and Baptists

Principal Lutheran and Baptist Colonies

Just as German Catholics founded four major settlements in Saskatchewan, and a variety of smaller settlements, so too the Lutherans and Baptists of German descent established four principal colonies plus numerous smaller ones. While the major Catholic colonies came into being in rapid succession, the Protestant ones (excluding Mennonites and Hutterites) were all set up almost simultaneously, between 1884 and 1887. The largest Lutheran/Baptist settlements, then, were already in place by the time the first Catholic settlement began to develop. These four major Protestant colonies were: Neu Elsass (1884), Hohenlohe (1885), Edenwold (1885), and the Volga German Colony (1887).

Neu Elsass Colony (1884)

The Neu Elsass (New Alsace) Colony was the first German colony to develop in Saskatchewan. In 1884 twenty-two families took up homesteads around Strasbourg, approximately eighty kilometres north of Regina; they were led by D. W. Riedl, an enterprising German immigration agent from Winnipeg.[60] Ultimately the community may have been named after Strasbourg, the principal city of the German-speaking province of Alsace in France.[61] It is more likely, however, that both the community and colony were named after the communities of Strassburg and Elsass within the Kurtschurgan colonies northwest of Odessa, in South Russia, which had in turn been established by Alsatian migrants in 1808 and 1809. Still another possibility is that, since some of the settlers came from Russian-German colonies in the United States, the Alsatian nomenclature may have been imported from several American colonies.[62]

The original bounds of Neu Elsass Colony (about 1885) included Strasbourg, Duval, Bulyea, Earl Grey, Gibbs, Silton, Dilke, Holdfast, Penzance, and Liberty; all in the region around the central and southern portion of Last Mountain Lake. However, the German settlement expanded into surrounding areas, doubling its territory. The population remains predominantly Lutheran.[63]

Table IV provides census data on the size and proportion of German population in each community in 1971.

TABLE IV: German Population in Incorporated Communities,
New Alsace Colony, 1971.

	Total Population:	German Population:	German Proportion:
Towns:			
Strasbourg	830	285	34.3%
Cupar	560	75	13.4%
Govan	405	85	21.0%
Imperial	515	50	9.7%
Lumsden	900	165	18.3%
Nokomis	475	165	34.7%
Raymore	615	135	22.0%
Villages:			
Aylesbury	70	25	35.7%
Bethune	285	45	15.8%
Bulyea	115	25	21.7%
Chamberlain	160	95	59.4%
Craven	115	20	17.4%
Dilke	115	40	34.8%
Disley	50	5	10.0%
Duval	160	65	40.6%
Dysart	260	70	26.9%
Earl Grey	205	120	58.5%
Holdfast	460	265	57.6%
Liberty	165	50	30.3%
Lipton	375	215	57.3%
Markinch	80	60	75.0%
Penzance	50	10	20.0%
Quinton	160	55	34.4%
Semans	345	45	13.0%
Silton	55	10	18.2%
Southey	595	395	66.4%

Note: Serath, Gregherd, Stalwart, Gibbs, and Fairy Hill were not incorporated in 1971.

Hohenlohe Colony (1885)

The Hohenlohe Colony began to develop around Langenburg, close to the Manitoba border, at the same time as the Neu Elsass Colony. It was named after Count Hohenlohe-Langenburg, president of the German Colonial Association, who had toured the West and encouraged German settlement.[64] Under the guidance of D. W. Riedl (the immigration agent also instrumental in the founding of Neu Elsass Colony), German Lutherans began to settle around Langenburg in 1885, in the Landshut, Hoffenthal, Hoffnungsthal, Beresina, and Landestreu districts; they came from the *Reich* as well as from Galicia, Volhynia, and other Russian colonies.[65] While the colony retained a Lutheran majority, in 1889 Catholics from Bavaria and the Black Sea colonies arrived.

The Russian-German proportion here was further augmented with the arrival of settlers from the Bessarabian colonies in 1891. By 1896 the colony included fifty to sixty Russian-German families with approximately three hundred members.[66]

Both the town of Langenburg and the village of MacNutt retain German majorities, but the German population is outnumbered by the Icelandic in the neighbouring town of Churchbridge:

	Total Population:	German Population:	German Proportion:
Towns:			
Langenburg	1,220	640	52.5%
MacNutt	210	120	57.1%
Churchbridge	965	275	28.5%

The Volga German Colony North of Yorkton (1887)

To the north of Langenburg, the Hohenlohe Colony merges with another major Protestant German settlement. It stretches westward from the Manitoba border into the country immediately north of Yorkton. Only a few years after the Hohenlohe and Neu Elsass Colonies began to develop, Baptist immigrants from the Volga colonies in Russia[67] settled around Ebenezer.[68] A strong Volga Baptist colony spread from there to Gorlitz, Hampton, Rhein, and Springside; to the east Volga Lutherans concentrated around Rhein, Stornoway, Runnymede, and Togo (where they merged with the German Lutherans of the Hohenlohe Colony to the south).[69] In addition to these Volga Germans of Baptist or Lutheran religion, Volhynian Germans settled in Yorkton.[70]

Expansion of the vast Ukrainian settlement around Yorkton has steadily diminished the German portion of these communities; now none (at least the incorporated ones for which census data are available) retains a German majority. Table V further shows the proportion of the German population in the area around Yorkton.

Edenwald Colony (1885)

In 1885 a group of Baptist immigrants from the region of Dobruja, in Rumania, founded the colony of New Tulcea (later renamed Edenwald, then Edenwold), northeast of Regina.[71] Religious quarrels as well as difficult economic and political conditions (Dobruja became part of Rumania in 1878, bringing about the revoking of privileges, restriction of landholdings, and state control of schools) resulted in the emigration of Germans from Dobruja to North Dakota (1884) and Saskatchewan (1885).

TABLE V: German Population in Incorporated Communities,
Volga German Colony (Yorkton), 1971.

	Total Population:	German Population:	German Proportion:
City:			
Yorkton	13,440	2,215	16.5%
Villages:			
Ebenezer	120	55	45.8%
Rhein	305	145	47.5%
Springside	335	90	26.9%
Stornoway	45	10	22.2%
Togo	210	55	26.2%

Note: Runnymede, Hampton, Gorlitz are unincorporated.

Gradually the Saskatchewan colony became more heterogeneous both in terms of the origins of its German population and their religious preferences. The colony's name was changed from New Tulcea to Edenwold by German immigrants from Bukovina; other Germans arrived from German colonies in Poland, Galicia, and Russia, and from the *Reich* itself.[72] By 1889 the colony had a Lutheran majority; a strong Lutheran congregation had been formed by 1893.[73] Also Adventists concentrated in the area of Edenwold.

By 1971 exactly two-thirds of the population of Edenwold (90 out of 135) were still of German origin. The other communities in the area — Frankslake, Zehner, and Avonhurst — were unincorporated hamlets.

Other German Lutheran Concentrations

A variety of other, smaller German Lutheran settlements were scattered across Saskatchewan.[74] In the southeastern portion of the province, a concentration, mixed with other German Protestants, and some Catholics, developed around Lampman and nearby communities. The origins of these Germans were diverse. Volga Germans settled in the Arcola area.[75] None of the incorporated communities retained a German majority by 1971, however; Germans constituted a third of the population at Lampman and slighly less than a quarter (24.1%) in the small city of Estevan; there were much smaller minorities at Alameda (21.2%), Roche Percée (18.5%), Bienfait (18.3%), Oxbow (16.6%), Benson (15.8%), Stoughton (14.3%).

In southern Saskatchewan, German and Norwegian Lutherans settled together in a number of communities.[76] Today Germans make up only a small minority of the populations, a higher proportion (25%) at Torquay. Volhynian Germans, mostly Lutherans but including some Catholics, settled around Yellow Grass as early as 1896; here their descendants still make up a little more than a quarter (27.2% in 1971) of the village population.[77]

German concentrations in the south-central region were predominantly Catholic, although small concentrations of Lutherans were found in the Spring Valley-Ormiston-Crane Valley area (Pangman, Mossbank, Assiniboia, Scout Lake, and Coronach). Further west, a chiefly Lutheran settlement of Volga Germans emerged near Hodgeville while German Lutherans mixed with Mennonites at Hodgeville, Kelstern, St. Boswells, Vogel, and with both Mennonites and Adventists at Flowing Well. Lutheran settlement extended north to the Chaplin-Ernfold-Maen area, and minorities were found within the vast Mennonite settlement in the Swift Current and Vermilion Hills regions (e.g., at Waldeck, Central Butte, and Elbow). Further west, in southwestern Saskatchewan, German Lutherans settled around Gull Lake-Simmie-Illerbrun (named in 1907 after an early settler from North Dakota) and Maple Creek (21.7% German); Russian-Germans were found south of the Cypress Hills around Consul-Vidora-Robsart. North of Maple Creek, within the predominantly Catholic settlement of Leader, was a largely Lutheran community, Burstall. In 1914 a Lutheran congregation settled at Mendham and an Evangelical one followed the next year; Leader itself had Lutheran, Apostolic, and United Brethren churches in addition to its strong Catholic parish.

Just across the South Saskatchewan River, north from Leader, the Eatonia-Dankin-Glidden area was settled by a mixture of Lutherans, Catholics, Mennonites, and most recently, Hutterites of German origin. In 1971 53.8% of the Glidden residents (pop. 65) were German; in Eatonia (pop. 635), 39.4%. Within St. Joseph's German Catholic Colony, occupying most of west-central Saskatchewan, Lutherans were concentrated around Luseland, Kerrobert, and Wilkie. Further north a strong German Lutheran church was established at St. Walburg in 1937; another German Lutheran congregation was founded in this region at Meadow Lake.

In central Saskatchewan, small concentrations of German Lutherans developed within or near Mennonite settlements.[78] In Dundurn and the Strehlow rural district German Lutherans actually settled a couple of decades before the Mennonites arrived — in Dundurn under the leadership of E. J. Meilicke, from Minnesota, in Strehlow the early German-American homesteaders, Hugo Strehlow and Reinhold Tamke. Many German Lutherans settled in and near Lanigan — Leroy, Watrous, Jansen, Esk, and Dafoe. Approximately two-thirds of the village of Jansen were Germans from Russia. In the nearby hamlet of Dafoe they came from the Volga.[79]

The history of the once-large Lutheran congregation at Esk is typical of numerous communities. Founded in 1906, the first church building was constructed the following year. Recurrent population losses saw incorporation into the adjacent Lutheran congregation of Lanigan. With the shift of conference affiliation from the LCA (Lutheran Church of America) or the ALC (American Lutheran Church) in 1966, the Church was first incorporated with Leroy, then found itself affiliated with the ELCC (Evangelical Lutheran Church of Canada), and was finally closed completely in 1967. Esk was never more than a small, unincorporated village.

In the east-central region, a small but cohesive German Protestant settlement, Neudorf, developed west of the city of Melville (pop. 5,320, 31.4% German). The village (pop. 455, 71.4% German) was first settled in 1890 by Russian-German Lutherans.[80] The neighbouring community of Lemberg (pop. 445, 58.4% Germans) was presumably settled by German Lutherans from Galicia, as this is the German name for the principal city of Galicia in the western Ukraine (Lviv).[81] As noted above, a German Lutheran congregation was established in the mainly Catholic village of Killaly (pop. 135, 70.4% German) in 1926, and another at Waldron (pop. 70, 35.7% German). Both Lutherans and Mennonites settled around Duff (pop. 80, 68.8% German), while German Baptists settled at Fernwood (pop. 115, 39.1% German) and Catholics at Goodeve (pop. 200, 7.5% German).[82]

German Lutherans were also scattered throughout the region to the south across the Qu'Appelle Valley. The Whitewood area was settled by German-Swiss as well as *Reichsdeutsche* from Hannover; the small village of Oakshela, between Broadview and Grenfell, by *Volksdeutsche* from Galicia and Volhynia. Polish-Germans, specifically from the Tomaszow-Mazowiecki and Wengrow area in Poland, settled around Wapella in 1928 and built their Lutheran church in 1936. Other Germans settled around Fairlight, Kennedy, and Kipling.[83] Today Germans constitute a small minority in those communities: 10.4% at Whitewood, 18.6% at Broadview, 27.4% at Grenfell, 15.7% at Wapella, 22.2% at Fairlight, and 15.1% at Kipling. The Windthorst Colony west of Kipling was largely Catholic, but it included some Lutheran families.[84] Further West, substantial pockets of Lutheran settlement developed within the large Catholic colony between Odessa and Balgonie, as early as 1891, when Lutherans arrived from the Black Sea and Bukovinian colonies. They organized a Lutheran congregation at Vibank in 1909, later affiliated with others at Kronau and Davin, and another at Francis. Now let us have a look at the Mennonites, many of whose ancestors had come from Germany.

The Mennonites

Historical Background

By the end of the nineteenth century, the Mennonites had some 400 villages and estates in fifty settlements in Russia, covering 5,816 square miles with a population of 120,000.[85]

In 1874 Russian nationalism caught up with these colonists. Their military and taxation exemptions were revoked; their political autonomy was disrupted as colonies were incorporated into larger Russian administrative units; records and schools had to use Russian; and "unqualified" Mennonite school teachers were replaced by Russian ones. Mennonites, Hutterites and other Russian-German Protestants began emigrating to southeastern South Dakota. Other conservative Mennonites from the Chortitza Colony moved to the East Reserve in the Steinbach area of Manitoba (southeast of Winnipeg). In 1875 the conservative Mennonites of the Furstenland and Bergthal colonies moved to the West Reserve in the Morden and Winkler area southwest of Winnipeg. After 1891 the overpopulation of these Manitoba "reserves" led to the emigration of some of the Rosthern area of later Saskatchewan. In 1900 they began to move into the Swift Current region.

The Rosthern and Saskatchewan Valley Colony

The Rosthern and Saskatchewan Valley Colony, settled between 1891 and 1918, developed rapidly into a major bloc settlement similar to forerunners in South Russia. Centring on Rosthern-Hague-Osler, the initial settlement came into existence around Rosthern when immigrants of the *Rosenort Gemeinde* (later General Conference Mennonites) arrived from West Prussia, Russia, and Manitoba.[86] Furstenlanders migrated from the West Reserve in Manitoba to settle around Hague in 1895. A compact reserve consisting of as many as twenty villages was then established south of Rosthern, between Hague and Osler, by Old Colony Mennonites from Manitoba in 1895-1905.[87] The social organization in the conservative colonies in South Russia was systematically duplicated in north-central Saskatchewan — wide streets (a custom developed in Russia due to the possibility of thatched roofs catching fire), a *Schult* (village overseer), German-language schools and churches.[88]

These adjoining Mennonite settlements then expanded between 1898 and 1918 into a single vast colony 30 miles in diameter. New communities and congregations were established by Brethren from the American Midwest (particularly Minnesota, Nebraska, Kansas, and Oklahoma), by settlers direct from Russia, or by others coming via Manitoba.[89]

Most of the conservative Mennonites in the settlement arrived immediately from the West Reserve in Manitoba. They or their predecessors had come to Manitoba from the Chortitza Colony (1789) west of Alexandrovsk (Zaporozhe), and from the Bergthal Colony which had been established in the Mariupol area between 1836 and 1852. Some later arrivals included emigrants from the Molotschna Colony, established between 1803 and 1824. Waldheim, for example, was named after a community founded by Russian and Volhynian Mennonites within the Molotschna Colony.[90]

Between 1906 and 1914, the population of Rosthern grew from 918 to 1,500, Langham increased from 249 to 600. By 1914 Aberdeen had over 300 inhabitants. Hague and Warman over 200, and Dalmeny and Osler more than 100. Rosthern boasted a German language academy and several German-language churches; at least four prosperous Mennonite farmers near that town were farming 10 to 15 quarter-sections of land.[91]

The exodus of several thousand conservative Sommerfelder, Bergthaler, and Chortitza Mennonites from Saskatchewan and Manitoba to Mexico and Paraguay between 1922 and 1928 was offset by a renewed influx of brethren, as well as German Lutherans, from Russia. The Canadian Mennonite Coloniza-tion Board was organized in 1922, and the Lutheran Immigration Board the following year, to assist immigrants from Russia and those in refugee camps to escape famine and the new Communist regime. The boards were financed by annual grants from the C.P.R. amounting to $5 per adult agricultural family and $1 per single farmer. By 1930, when the Soviet government forbade further emigration, 19,891 Mennonites and 12,310 Lutherans had arrived in Canada. The total cost to the C.P.R., which advanced credits to cover their passage, came to $1,924,727. Almost 8,000 of the Mennonites, joined by small groups of Lutherans, settled in Saskatchewan (close to 3,000 in the Rosthern Colony alone). The Canadian Colonization Association (C.C.A.), the boards, and ministers co-operated in settling the immigrants on tracts of land recently placed on the market (often these tracts were part of large farms forced to divide and sell due to high overhead during a period of deflation). Commissions of 1.25% were paid by the C.C.A. to a board or by a board to the C.C.A. for finding land and subsidizing settlement.[92]

The influx of *Russlander* (Russian Mennonites arriving in the 1920s, distinguished from the *Kanadier*, who arrived earlier) was met with some opposition. In 1919 the Canadian government had passed Orders-in-Council prohibiting Mennonites as well as Hutterites and Doukhobors from settling in Canada.[93] When the Orders were repealed in 1922 by the new Liberal govern-ment, English Canadians continued their outcry against the Mennonite "flood" which "flooded to church while our boys fought," "don't conform to Canadian school laws," and brought "unsanitary habits and Asiatic diseases."[94]

Nevertheless, by 1971 the Rosthern and Saskatchewan Valley bloc settle-ment originally covering at least forty-two townships, included about 10,700 people of German and Dutch origin in or near two urban towns (Rosthern and Warman), two rural towns (Langham and Waldheim), six major incorporated villages (Aberdeen, Dalmeny, Hague, Hepburn, Laird, and Martensville), a minor incorporated village (Osler), two unincorporated villages (Neuanlage and Neuhorst), four hamlets (Blumenheim, Blumenthal, Gruenfeld, and Gruenthal), and at least 75 named localities (see Map).[95]

Table VI shows the proportion of the German/Dutch population in the Rosthern and Saskatchewan Valley bloc settlement.

The Mennonites, like other immigrants, attempted to retain their own schools in this settlement.[96] But the Old Colonists, who immigrated into Saskatchewan had attitudes destined to conflict with the public school system. In the first place, they did not consider education *per se* as an ideal; beyond the minimum high-school level education was frowned upon and considered a waste of time and money. Any enthusiasm they may have shown for education was related to a desire to control completely their schools so that their language and religion could be taught and hence maintained. These Mennonites felt that linguistic preservation and retention of religion went hand-in-hand; preservation was possible only in strict isolation, not just from the general society, but even from less conservative Mennonites.

There were eleven private schools and no public schools in the four townships comprising the heart of the Old Colony within the Rosthern settlement; each school had 35 to 60 pupils. The few teachers had limited familiarity with English and were otherwise poorly qualified. Most had five to six years of education at best, and some were even illiterate in German. Salaries were meager — usually about $30 a month plus a few loads of hay or grain. Several teachers were community patriarchs with as many as eleven children. Any deviation, however slight, from Old Colony conservatism meant immediate dismissal. German texts covered successively basic German, Old Colony catechism, Old Testament and New Testament. Classes, given under very poor conditions, covered Bible history and interpretation and, to a limited extent, arithmetic and *schoenschreiben* (writing); there was no education in Canadian history, science, or the English language. In fact very few, if any, children could speak English.[97]

In 1908, when more than twenty families were excommunicated in the Old Colony alone for allowing their children to attend public schools, a Royal Commission on Mennonite Schools began a two-year investigation. It heard numerous complaints of coercion from excommunicated and progressive Mennonites; religious leaders replied simply that their actions had been predetermined in Scripture. The Commission also heard how excommunicants were ostracized from the Old Colony community as well as from their own relatives.[98]

After 1916 the Canadian government — despite earlier assurances concerning non-interference with language or religion — was no longer willing to treat the Old Colonists differently.[99] A school ordinance of 1919 forbade any use of German during school hours. As a result, some thirty-two Mennonite schools were replaced by public schools; attendance was enforced by threatening fines of $10 a month per child not attending. Yet little headway

TABLE VI: German/Dutch Population in Incorporated Communities, Rosthern and Saskatchewan Mennonite Colony, 1971.

	Total (1971) Population:	German/Dutch Population:	German/Dutch Proportion:
Towns:			
Langham	520	305	58.7%
Martensville	955	800	83.8%
Rosthern	1,405	660	47.0%
Waldheim	585	510	87.2%
Warman	785	725	92.4%
Villages:			
Aberdeen	275	115	41.8%
Dalmeny	425	330	77.6%
Hague	440	400	90.9%
Hepburn	310	275	88.7%
Laird	240	185	77.1%
Osler	195	180	92.3%

was made by the government. In the Old Colony, despite fines of more than $700 a family, not a single child attended; the threat of excommunication and ostracism was greater than the fear of fines.[100] It was not, however, until the school consolidation process began in the late 1940s that teaching in German during the school day finally ceased and, as they had feared, the Old Colony as a close-knit community disappeared.

Another group of Mennonite traditionalists was situated in the River Park-Friedland area near Aberdeen, across the South Saskatchewan River. The three private schools in this area bore a close resemblance to the Old-Colony ones across the river. Instruction was given in German by unqualified teachers, the schoolhouses were overcrowded, unventilated and poorly equipped; few pupils were educated beyond grade four. German instruction had been available at several public schools in the area, but declined as English-speaking teachers replaced German-speaking ones and as the government insisted on qualified teachers. The Mennonites, therefore, chose to send their children to private schools, leaving public schools practically empty. Of 25 enrolled, out of a possible fifty, at River Park, only five were actually attending. Of the 54 enrolled at Friedland, out of a possible 60, again only five attended. As a result, at least one public school closed. Yet, despite the intransigence of some tradition-bound families (one reportedly skimped on clothing and food for its children to pay the fines), within a few years some private schools had closed and the Mennonites in some districts, such as Edenburg and Lilly, were accepting the public school idea.[101]

Sects which were not overly conservative, nor markedly progressive, tended to retain some German language instruction but did not conflict with school regulations. By 1917 all but a very few schools in these sectarian areas were public ones with qualified teachers proficient in English. Most schools were teaching in German for the final hour of the school day (e.g., Dalmeny, Rosthern, Hepburn, New Home, Richmond, Hoffnungsfeld, and Clear Spring). The General Conference Mennonites were the most willing to abandon the German language, as they tended to regard their Mennonite identity in religious rather than ethnic terms.[102]

As part of the same general survey of ethnic identity in Saskatchewan bloc settlements,[103] in the Mennonite sample (N = 244 families) only 6.6% noted a major loss of German/Mennonite identity, in striking contrast to the German Catholics interviewed in St. Peter's Colony, although most of the remainder (85.2%) noted a minor loss. In terms of identity preservation, 95.3% of the first (settler) generation favoured retention, compared to 81.7% of the second and 64.2% of the third or fourth. Some 1.6% of the respondents could speak only German, 52.5% were bilingual, but preferred German both at home and in the local community, 14.8% were bilingual, speaking German at home but English outside, 28.3% were bilingual but yet preferred English in and out of the home and only 2.8% could only speak English. Altogether, 68.9% used German fairly often but 97.2% were familiar with that language. Of the first generation 4.8% were speaking English primarily or exclusively, compared to 31.7% of the second, and 40.0% of the third or fourth. Some 97.6% of the first generation attended church regularly, as did 86.6% of the second and 81.7% of the third or fourth. Of the married respondents, 97.6% had married other Mennonites while 56.5% expressed opposition to marrying non-Germans and 69.3% to marrying non-Mennonites. Not unexpectedly adherence to their religion proved stronger than to their ethnicity; moreover, the ratio became more strikingly lopsided from first to second and third generations.

The Swift Current-Vermilion Hills Settlement

An even more extensive Mennonite settlement developed around Swift Current and Herbert, then spread northeastward to include the Vermilion Hills region. This vast settlement had its origins in two rather different Mennonite colonies established immediately east and south of Swift Current. First to arrive were Sommerfelder Mennonites from Manitoba, who settled in the main centre — the Gouldtown area north of Herbert in 1900. They were soon joined by General Conference Mennonites and Mennonite Brethren who settled around Herbert in 1903-1905. Within a few years at least one hundred families had settled, most coming from Russian-German Mennonite colonies in the United States.[104] Meanwhile, another Mennonite colony was developing south of Swift Current. In 1904 Old Colony Mennonites from the Manitoba reserves petitioned the Dominion Government for a reservation of six townships. Within a year at least twenty villages had been founded in this colony, named after former Old Colony villages in Manitoba and Russia (see Appendix). By 1911 there were approximately 4,600 Mennonites in these two colonies.[105] From the two nuclei, the Herbert settlement and the Old Colony settlement, respectively east and south of Swift Current, Mennonite settlement expanded rapidly throughout the whole region.[106]

Table VII shows the expansion of Mennonite settlement east and south of Swift Current.

Other Mennonite Settlements

While the Rosthern-Saskatchewan Valley and Swift Current-Vermilion Hills settlements are the only extensive Mennonite settlements in Saskatchewan, there are many smaller concentrations scattered throughout the prairie portion of the province. Most dated from the *Russlander* migration — the last substantial emigration from the Mennonite colonies in Russia — during the 1920s. The arrival of *Russlander* resulted not only in the expansion of existing Mennonite colonies but also in the foundation of new settlements as large farms were broken-up in the Dundurn-Hanley, Herschel, and other areas. Some ninety families settled marginal lands to form the Meeting Lake settlement, situated in the Thickwood Hills about 130 Km. northwest of Rosthern, in 1926-30. By 1947 in the wake of the second World War, more Mennonites immigrated to the Meeting Lake and other settlements from eastern Europe. Religious persecution, forced collectivization and exile of resisters to the Urals, closure of minority institutions, famine, mass purges, and hostility toward German minorities were among the reasons for migration from Europe in this instance. Some refugees settled in the longstanding Mennonite colonies in Waterloo County and the Niagara Peninsula, Ontario. Others sailed to Paraquay, only to be faced with harsh climatic and economic conditions; this circumstance was to spark off a voluminous Mennonite migration to the Canadian Prairies from Latin America.

By 1971 the Meeting Lake and Thickwood Hills bloc settlement included about 1,500 people of German and Dutch origin in and near minor incorporated villages (Medstead and Rabbit Lake), an unincorporated village (Mayfair), a hamlet (Glenbush), and at least 20 named localities. Mennonites and other Germans formed about a third (34.3%) of the population of Medstead and more than a quarter (26.0%) at Rabbit Lake, while they were predominant in the smaller communities.[107]

In the west-central region an early congregation was established by Mennonite Brethren in Christ at Alsask, on the Alberta border, in 1910. Further north along the border other Mennonites settled around Evesham and Provost (Alberta). During the 1920s, *Russlander* Mennonites, affiliated with

TABLE VII: German/Dutch Population in Incorporated Communities, Swift Current Mennonite Settlement, 1971.

	Total (1971) Population:	German/Dutch Population:	German/Dutch Proportion:
City:			
Swift Current	15,575	4,760	30.6%
Towns:			
Central Butte	530	80	15.1%
Herbert	1,075	700	65.2%
Morse	475	240	50.5%
Villages:			
Beechy	330	50	15.2%
Chaplin	445	100	22.2%
Ernfold	75	15	20.0%
Eyebrow	215	60	27.9%
Hodgeville	400	195	48.8%
Lawson	80	20	25.0%
Lucky Lake	360	80	22.2%
Rush Lake	180	75	41.7%
Shamrock	105	15	14.3%
Stewart Valley	135	45	33.3%
Tugaske	185	25	13.5%
Waldeck	240	130	54.2%
Webb	105	35	33.3%
Woodrow	70	25	35.7%

the General Conference, settled in the Herschel-Fiske area (their church in the latter community dates from 1925), as well as around Springwater, Harris, Ardath, Superb, and Glidden. More recently a Mennonite Brethren concentration developed in the Lashburn-Waseca-Maidstone area.

Mennonites from a variety of different backgrounds settled in compact pockets in central Saskatchewan from an early date. Some Old Order Mennonite families from Lancaster County, Pennsylvania ("Pennsylvania Dutch Country") joined their kinfolk from Waterloo County, Ontario, in establishing a small congregation of about fifty members in 1905. Nearby, General Conference Mennonites from Kansas and Oklahoma formed the Nordstern (North Star) congregation at Drake in 1906-13.[108] Other Mennonite settlements were established in east-central, northeast, south-central, and southeastern Saskatchewan.[109]

The Hutterites
Historical Background

Not unlike the Mennonites, the Hutterites also trace their origins to the Swiss Anabaptist movements of the sixteenth century; both groups immigrated, directly or indirectly, to the Canadian Prairies from German colonies in South Russia, as had most of the German Catholics. But in the intervening period of more than two centuries, their histories were quite distinct. While the Mennonite group was forming in the Netherlands, another communal Anabaptist group was developing in the Tyrol (Austria), as well as in southern Germany and Moravia (now central Czechoslovakia). In 1528 the first *Bruderhof* (communal village or colony) was established in Moravia. Five years later they were joined by a Tyrolean preacher, Jacob Hutter, from whom the sect acquired its name. Despite repeated persecution (Hutter was burned at the stake in 1536), by the end of the sixteenth century there were some 70,000 Hutterites and over ninety *Bruderhöfe*. By 1622, reduced in numbers by the Austro-Turkish and Thirty Years' Wars, they had been driven from Moravia; some 20,000 emigrated to northern Hungary (now the Slovak segment of Czechoslovakia), Hungary proper, and Transylvania (south-eastern Hungary, now in Rumania), where they established more than thirty new colonies. Persecution continued, however, particularly from Jesuits seeking to convert them in northern Hungary (now Slovakia); their number was further reduced. A small group briefly re-established at Kreutz, Transylvania, between 1763 and 1770, caught in the midst of the Russo-Turkish Wars, trekked to Russia, to found the Vishenka Colony (about 200 miles northeast of Kiev). In 1802 they settled nearby Radichev, and in 1842 they joined the Mennonites in the Molotschna area.

Their rather unsettled existence in Europe was terminated altogether in 1874 when all remaining Hutterites, numbering nearly 800, moved *en masse* to South Dakota, along with Mennonites and other Russian-German Protestant groups escaping the repeal of their military exemption.[110]

The Move Into Saskatchewan

Prior to 1956 there were no Hutterite colonies in Saskatchewan. Out of at least thirty-two established by 1980, all are in the western half of the province, and are equally divided between the *Dariusleut* and *Lehrerleut*. They are most heavily concentrated in the southwestern region. Here the *Dariusleut* have formed ten and the *Lehrerleut* eight colonies.[111] With the proliferation of Hutterite colonies in Saskatchewan since the mid-1950s, one might think that there has been a reversion to the Old Colony style of education. But this was not so. While closely resembling the Old Colony Mennonites in many ways, the Hutterites have long had a unique system of education conforming both to their traditions and to the school regulations of the general society. Each Hutterite colony has two schools in the same building: a German one emphasizing Hutterite beliefs, norms, life-style, and discipline, and an English one emphasizing facts about the outside world. In order to check the possible erosion of Hutterite values by the teacher of the English school (supplied by the public school board), the school is preceded each day by its German counterpart. It may be visited by colony elders when in session, its decor must be simple, its teacher may be "advised" by the colony pastor, and its texts may be censored to conform to Hutterite expectations. Usually, though, its influence is sufficiently controlled through its pupils' awareness of its preoccupation with worldly matters and of its consequent "moral" weakness. However, one has to note that the Hutterites are quite up-to-date in farming technology, even if it is rare for Hutterites to have more than the minimum education required by school regulations.[112]

The Jews

Recurrent pogroms in Eastern Europe, particularly during the 1880s, drove numerous Jews to North America. Although they came from a diversity of regions — Lithuania, Byelorussia, Poland, Volhynia, Ukraine, Bessarabia — they all spoke Yiddish (essentially a German dialect) and faced increasing persecution within the Russian Empire. Those who immigrated from Galicia and Bukovina had been under Austrian control.

Assisted by the Jewish Colonization Association, and by benefactors such as Hermann Landau, a prominent Anglo-Jewish financier who was a C.P.R. representative in London, several hundred Jewish familes came to Saskatchewan. Although a few families had arrived near Moosomin by 1882, at Oxbow between 1884 and 1887, and at Estevan by 1885, the first substantial Jewish colony developed near Wapella.[113]

An equivalent number of families settled in the Hirsch Colony, some twenty-five kilometres east of Estevan, beginning in 1892. In 1901 Rumanian Jews settled in the Herzl Colony near Lipton as well as at Yorkton and Theodore. Jews settled in Melfort in 1904-11, and nearby the Edenbridge Colony became a sizeable Jewish community, settled by Lithuanian Jews. In 1906 and 1920 the Sonnenfeld and Hoffer Colonies developed near Oungre, close to the American border. Small numbers of Jews also settled at widely scattered locations (including Maxwellton, Limerick, Kamsack, White Bear, Watrous, and Alsask).

Over the years drought, intermarriage, assimilation, rural decline and urbanization have reduced the Jewish agricultural colonies to very few, if any, remaining families. Many of the former Jewish farmers moved to urban areas — particularly the two major cities of the province.

Conclusion

The German settlement of Saskatchewan has been impressive. Tens of thousands of German-origin immigrants, representing a variety of religious affiliations, came to this province from diverse countries. Some of their numerous settlements in the Saskatchewan prairie, covered vast areas. Today their descendants, modestly counted in the census only through the male lineage, number more than two hundred thousand still resident in the province. At least one out of every five people in Saskatchewan can claim a German surname.

In retrospect, the reasons for people of German origin to migrate to Saskatchewan were varied: many regarded themselves as refugees (Mennonites, Hutterites), while others were opportunists anxious to obtain large tracts of good farmland at minimal cost (e.g., German-American settlers).

Their origins and routes to Saskatchewan also varied: some (in fact, only a small minority) came directly from Germany; many more arrived from former German colonies in Russia and other Eastern European countries; while an amalgam of recent Russian-German immigrants as well as longer-resident German-Americans moved north into Saskatchewan often from German settlements in the United States.

German settlers in Saskatchewan represented a diversity of religious groupings: not simply Catholics and Lutherans (as in Germany itself) but also a number of groups less evident or nonexistent in Germany, while more prominent in Eastern Europe — Mennonites, Hutterites, Baptists, Adventists, Jews.

The Germans of Saskatchewan did not speak a common German tongue, but *hochdeutsch* and *plattdeutsch*; Swabian, Bavarian, Württemberger and other regional dialects; as well as hybrid Germanic languages — Alsatian, Yiddish, Russo-Mennonite dialects. Perhaps some who arrived, such as some German-Americans, had already lost their traditional German mother tongue, preferring to speak English as a lingua-franca.

The settlements established by these various German groups ranged from small ones with populations of only a few hundreds to vast colonies containing over ten thousand residents. The cultural viability of an ethnic community may well depend in large measure on its extent and the size of its population. Moreover, some settlements resulted from careful planning; others were more spontaneous.

Clearly, the ability or desire of these German-origin settlers in Saskatchewan, and more so their descendants, has varied in respect of the presentation of a unique German identity. This paper has provided detailed data on the German Catholics of St. Peter's Colony and the Mennonites of the Rosthern settlement. The comparing of these two settlements representing different ethnoreligious origin shows significant differences, with the German Catholics being far less "German" in most respects than the Mennonites studied. Yet in both groups we noted a definite trend toward cultural, linguistic, and marital assimilation. The smallest group discussed in this paper, the Jews, has already virtually disappeared from rural Saskatchewan.

The final questions must be whether the large number of people of German ethnic origin in Saskatchewan will take more of an interest in the vital role their predecessors played in the settling and development of this province; whether they will be encouraged and able to arrest loss of their German identity, and whether they will retain an awareness of the fascinating and intricate historical background connected with the foundation of the many German settlements in Saskatchewan. Indeed, perhaps the most dynamic force in promoting an interest in German-Canadian identity and history of settlement in Saskatchewan comes not so much from the descendants of original settlers in rural colonies as from more recent immigrants in the cities, who have established — and in some cases re-established — active German clubs and institutions.

FOOTNOTES

[1]R. England, *The Central European Immigrant to Canada* (Toronto, 1929), 14-20. Immigration may be seen primarily as an individual undertaking or collective drift rather than the organized movement of an integrated group, even if governments do control, regulate, direct, and encourage or discourage the process. Cf. Berry, *Race and Ethnic Relations* (Boston, 1958), 94.

[2]Immigrants came mainly from the Low Countries (the Netherlands and Belgium), the predominantly German countries (Germany, Luxembourg, and Switzerland), Scandinavia (Denmark, Norway, Sweden, and Finland), as well as Central and Eastern Europe (Austria-Hungary and Russia).

[3]Saskatchewan Royal Commission on Immigration and Settlement, Report (Regina, 1930), 42-3. – Hereinafter: SRCIS.

[4]Briefs were presented by the Saskatchewan section of the United Farmers of Canada, the Saskatchewan Command of the Canadian Legion, the Saskatoon Labour Trades Council, the Regina Assembly of the Native Sons of Canada, the Ku Klux Klan, and the Provincial Grand Lodge of the Orange Order in Saskatchewan.

[5]Revised from Anderson, 1972.

[6]SRCIS, 176-188; England, 22-38.

[7]T. Shibutani and K. M. Kwan, *Ethnic Stratification: A Comparative Approach* (New York, 1965).

[8]C. A. Price, "Immigration and Group Settlement," in W. D. Borrie, ed., *The Cultural Integration of Immigrants* (Paris, 1959), 270-72.

[9]C. A. Dawson and E. R. Younge, *Pioneering in the Prairie Provinces: The Social Side of the Settlement Process* (Toronto: Macmillan, 1940), 12-16 and C. A. Dawson, *Group Settlement: Ethnic Communities in Western Canada* (Toronto, 1936), 378-380.

[10]SRCIS, 193. Vast areas of the province were incorporated into ethnic bloc settlements; some included over thirty towns and villages.

[11]O. Handlin, *Race and Nationality in American Life* (Garden City, New York, 1957), 90.

[12]SRCIS, 197-98.

[13]SRCIS, 15.

[14]It must be stated that certain areas had been settled prior to that period and some of the original bloc settlements have expanded considerably since 1930, and that the vast majority of settlements were formed during a more restricted period, the first decade of this century.

[15]In the Black Sea region colonies were also founded by Swedish and German Lutherans from the Baltic coast (1787-1804), and by German Catholics and Lutherans from predominantly Protestant Prussia, as well as from mixed Catholic-Protestant Alsace-Lorraine, Rhineland, Baden-Württemberg, Switzerland, Silesia, Bohemia, Posen and central Poland (1789-1855); Mennonites from East and West Prussia (1790-1854); Hutterites of Austrian

and Moravian origin (1843); Jews (1809-50); as well as Bulgarians (1801-1904). Cf. P. C. Keller (Rev.), *The German Colonies in South Russia, 1804-1904* (Die Deutschen Kolonien in Suedrussland) (Odessa, 1905), and A. Giesinger, *From Catherine to Krushchev: The Story of Russia's Germans* (Battleford, Saskatchewan, 1974).

[16]Particularly the *ukase* of June 4, 1871, which subjected Russian-Germans to military service, removed their right to extensive political autonomy, and increased the pressure toward Russification in community schools. See K. Tischler, *The German Canadians in Saskatchewan with Particular Reference to the Language Problem, 1900-1930, M.A. Thesis in History, University of Saskatchewan, Saskatoon, 1978 3-4;* J. S. Height, *Paradise on the Steppe* (Tuebingen, 1972) and Giesinger, 1974.

[17]See H. Lehmann, *Das Deutschtum in Westkanada* (Berlin, 1939) and Tischler.

[18]See G. L. Maron, *The Germans in Canada* (Winnipeg, 1911), 6-7; M. M. Gordon, *Assimilation in American Life* (New York, 1964), 132-35; N. Glazer, "Ethnic Groups in America: From National Culture to Ideology," in M. Kurokowa, ed., *Minority Responses* (New York, 1970), 76-80; A. M. and C. B. Rose, *America Divided: Minority Group Relations in the United States* (New York, 1948), 207; Dawson, 275-79.

[19]See Tischler, 2-5. A. S. Morton and C. Martin, *History of Prairie Settlement and "Dominion Lands" Policy* (Toronto, 1938), 110-19, 128-31; A. E. Johann, *Mit zwanzig Dollar in den Wilden Westen* (Berlin, 1928).

[20]Tischler, 2.

[21]Lehmann, 93.

[22]Tischler, 2; K. Karger, *14 Jahre unter Englaendern: Ein Auswandererschicksal in Kanada* (Breslau, 1926), vol. 1, 2; Lehmann, 85; J. W. Dafoe, *Clifford Sifton in Relation to His Times* (Toronto, 1931), 320; Giesinger, 364.

[23]For example, Tischler, 6; Lehmann, 107.

[24]The settlers of St. Joseph's Colony descended from the colonists of Josephstal Colony in South Russia. These in turn had come from Alsace and southwestern Germany in 1904.

[25]See A. Becker, "St. Joseph's Colony, Balgonie," *Saskatchewan History*, 20 (1967) 1; A. Zimmermann, *Zum fuenfzehnjaehrigen Jubilaeum; Die Roemisch-katholische Pfarrei St. Joseph bei Balgonie, Saskatchewan* (n.p., 1936); Lehmann, *passim* and Giesinger, 360-61.

[26]These settlers had their ancestors in the Palatinate, Baden, Alsace as well as in Austria, Swabia and southwestern Germany (see Giesinger, 361 and *passim*).

[27]H. Metzger, *Geschichtlicher Abriss ueber die St. Peter's-Pfarrei und Anlegung der Kolonien Rastadt, Katharinenthal und Speyer* (Regina, 1930); Lehmann, *passim*; and Giesinger, 261 and *passim*.

[28]Giesinger, 361.

[29]It is interesting to note that during the 1930s the strongly nationalistic, even pro-National Socialist, *Deutscher Bund* organization was active in this settlement, with an *Ortsgruppe* (a major local *bund* chapter, having at least fifteen members) at Vibank and a *Stutzpunkt* (a minor chapter, with at least five members) at Kronau — J. F. Wagner, "'*Heim ins Reich*': The Story of the Loon River's Nazis," *Saskatchewan History*, 19 (1976), 41-49.

[30]This abbey was in the heart of a German Catholic colony in Stearns Country (which included numerous rural communities centred on the city of St. Cloud and the small communities of St. Augusta, Luxembourg, St. Nicholas, St. Joseph, Collegeville, St. Martin, Freeport, New Munich, Greenwald, Meier Grove, Melrose, St. Rosa, St. Anthony, St. Francis, St. Anna, St. Wendel, and St. Stephen).

[31]In 1902 this company, in conjunction with priests of the Order of St. Benedict and the Catholic Settlement Society of St. Paul, Minnesota, obtained colonization rights to a vast areas in north-central Saskatchewan — a territory of fifty townships covering 1800 square miles – P. Windschiegl, (Rev.), *Fifty Golden Years* (Muenster, 1953); Dawson, *passim*.

[32]St. Peter's Monastery and parish at Muenster (six miles east of Humboldt), St. Boniface (Leofeld), St. Benedict (southwest of the present village of St. Benedict), Englefeld, Annaheim, Bruno, St. Joseph (Old Fulda), and Marysburg (see Windschiegl and Tischler).

[33]Giesinger, 365.

[34]Anderson, 1972. — Lake Lenore and St. John Baptist (Willmont, named after Willmont, Minnesota) in 1904; Humboldt, Watson, St. Martin (east of Annaheim), St. Scholastica (south of Humboldt), and St. Patrick's (west of Leroy) in 1905; St. Oswald (near Romance) and Immaculate Conception (southwest of Humboldt) in 1906; Dana, St. Gregor, and St. Bernard (Old Pilger) in 1907.

[35]St. Leo in the St. Meinrad district (northeast of Cudworth), St. Gertrude (south of Muenster), and Carmel in 1908; Peterson in 1909 (although the church was not erected until 1924) and Cudworth in 1912. By 1914 Cudworth had a population of over 300 (Anderson, 1972).

[36]In 1909 the *Volksverein*, a German Catholic voluntary association, was formed in Winnipeg; it was to play an active role in St. Peter's Colony for many years.

[37]See Windschiegl.

[38]SRCIS.

[39]Naicam and Holy Family Mission were founded in 1925; St. Benedict in 1930; modern Pilger in the early 1930s; St. James (east of Lake Lenore) in 1933; Middle Lake in 1936 (where a *Deutscher Bund Stutzpunkt* was organized); and St. Gertrude was re-established in 1946).

[40]Anderson, 1972.

[41]The second abbot, in fact, had been subprior of St. John's. He was blessed as abbot by the bishop of Bismark, North Dakota, in the heart of the vast Russian-German area in central and south-central North Dakota from which many immigrants had come to St. Peter's Colony. Also situated in this area was St. Mary's Assumption Abbey at Richardton, which maintained a close connection with both St. John's and St. Peter's.

[42]Note: Unincorporated communities in the colony include — amongst others — Carmel, Peterson, Totzke, Dana, Muskikee Springs, Bremen, Leofeld, Leofnard, Ens, Willmont, Fulda, Marysburg, Moseley, Daylesford, Annaheim, Daphne, Romance, Burr and Wimmer.

[43]Anderson, 1972; by the same author, "Ethnic Identity in Saskatchewan in Bloc Settlements: A Sociological Appraisal," in Howard Palmer, ed., *The Settlement of the West*

(Calgary, 1977), and "Ethnicity and Language in Saskatchewan Schools," paper presented in a Symposium on Ethnicity on the Great Plains, University of Nebraska-Lincoln, April 6-7, 1978 — hereinafter, Anderson, 1977 and 1978 respectively.

[44]Anderson, 1978.

[45]Anderson, 1978.

[46]Anderson, 1977.

[47]P. Schulte, *Bilder and Blaetter zum Silbernen Jubilaeum der St. Joseph's Kolonie* (Regina, 1930) and Tischler, 10.

[48]Schulte, 33; Lehmann, 183; and Giesinger, 366.

[49]Giesinger, 355.

[50]Among the first parishes established in St. Joseph's Colony were Tramping Lake (1905), St. Franziskus, Leipzig, Handel, Karmelheim, Broadacres, Kerrobert, Denzil, Grosswerder, St. Peter, St. Donatus, Primate, Macklin, St. Johannes, and Rosenkranz (see map). Although most German settlers in St. Joseph's Colony were Catholics, several hundred Lutherans were concentrated in the Luseland-Kerrobert and Wilkie areas. During the 1930s *Deutscher Bund Stutzpunkte* were organized at Wilkie, Macklin, and Biggar. But the *Volksdeutsche* of St. Joseph's Colony showed relatively little interest in this nationalistic organization.

[51]Mendham Parish, settled 1909-13 but not officially established until 1913, served the rural districts of Liebenthal, Blumenfeld, Rosenthal, and Josephstal. Liebenthal was named after Liebenthal, Kansas, from which some of its settlers had migrated; this Russian-German colony in the United States in turn had been established by migrants from the Liebenthal group of Catholic colonies immediately west of Odessa, founded in 1804-6 largely by migrants from Alsace and southwestern German regions. Germans from a wide variety of regions had settled in central Poland in 1795-1806, then moved to establish colonies in the southern Bessarabian region south-west of the Liebenthal colonies after 1814. In particular these Bessarabian colonists were the forefathers of the founders of the Krassna-Rastadt and St. Mary's Colonies in Saskatchewan; a Krassna Colony had been founded near Akkerman (Belgorod Dnestrovskij) in Bessarabia in 1815. *Deutscher Bund* chapters included an *Ortsgruppe* at Leader and *Stutzpunkte* at Burstall and Prelate.

[52]Grayson and Goodeve (northwest of Melville) also had Catholic churches. In spite of its relatively small size, Grayson boasted a *Deutscher Bund Ortsgruppe* during the 1930s. In 1971 two-thirds of its population was of German extraction, compared to 70.4% in Killaly. Another small Catholic colony emerged around the town of Allan between 1903 and 1909 at the same time St. Peter's Colony was developing little more than 50 Km away. A *Deutscher Bund Stutzpunkt* was organized in the nearby community of Young. In 1971 exactly half of the population of Allan was German, as was 29.3% of Young.

[53]Other German Catholic communities in this region included one in the Vanguard-Esme area (settled 1908 to 1913, parish 1913), Bateman-Coppen, Rockglen-Pickthal-Assiniboia in the Wood Mountain area, Verwood-Horizon-Viceroy-Bengough, Mazenod-Vantage-Mossbank, Ceylon-Pangman-Khedive, and Claybank-Spring Valley-Avonlea-Bayard. Many of these Germans came from the midwestern United States, particularly from German-American settlements, founded by immigrants from the original German colonies in Russia.

Spring Valley was first settled in 1913 by the large Reimann family, who moved from Browns Valley, Minnesota. Among the first settlers at Horizon were the Kisslerings and Hestermans. Many of the first settlers came in 1907 by the old wagon trail from Winnipeg to Wood Mountain. A *Deutscher Bund Ortsgruppe* was founded at Claybank, while *Stutzpunkte* were established at Mossbank, Avonlea, and Bayard.

[54]These particular German colonies in Russia had been established ca. 1783-1875; heavy German emigration from Volhynia and Galicia occurred between 1890 and 1914 (Giesinger 1974, 128-32).

[55]It is interesting to note that the community may have been named either for an English nun who died in 779 and who was canonized for her untiring work with the German people, or for Mrs. Walburga Musch, a pioneer settler who was a much-respected community and church worker (Russell 1973).

[56]These immigrants, as well as the Germans around Goodsoil, apparently were ardent nationalists. In fact, Goodsoil boasted the strongest *Deutscher Bund* chapter in the entire province (an *Ortsgruppe* with forty members), and strong *Ortsgruppen* were also organized at Loon River, St. Walburg, and Paradise Hill, as well as a *Stutzpunkt* at Blue Bell near Pierceland. In view of their strong pro-National-Socialist sentiments, the Loon River Germans decided in 1939 to return "heim ins Reich" – home to the *Reich* (see Wagner).

[57]These areas included the territory extending from Lumsden northward through Dilke, Chamberlain, Holdfast, Penzance, Liberty, Stalwart, to Imperial. The Liberty district, one might note in passing, was originally called Wolffton (or Wolff Valley School District); one version suggests that it was renamed by a settler from Liberty, New York, although most of the early settlers were Catholics from Oklahoma, Missouri, and Kansas, with some from Michigan, North Dakota, and Illinois.

[58]Nevertheless a Catholic parish was not organized here until 1943.

[59]Giesinger, 361-62.

[60]Tischler, 16.

[61]Elsass was in Germany between the Franco-Prussian War, 1870-71, and the First World War, 1914-18, i.e., the period when Neu Elsass Colony was founded in Saskatchewan.

[62]Colonies in America were founded by immigrants ultimately of Alsatian origin, e.g., in Kansas, South Dakota, and North Dakota (Giesinger, 345, 356-58).

[63]Strasbourg, Markinch, the Fairy Hill district, Duval, Govan, Earl Grey, Cupar, and Lipton are all Lutheran. Baptists concentrated around Serath, Gregherd, Southey, Earl Grey (where a Baptist congregation was founded by Swedes, not Germans in 1906), Nokomis, and Strasbourg. As noted above, certain communities in the region were strongly Catholic; these included the communities located in the portion of the settlement west of Last Mountain Lake. In Strasbourg itself, a Lutheran church was built in 1907, followed by a Baptist one in 1927, Catholic in 1943, and Adventist in 1953.

As regards political attitudes the *Deutscher Bund* received little support in the settlement during the Thirties; *Stutzpunkte were organized at Quinton and Disley (the latter community never grew larger than a hamlet).*

[64]*Sessional Papers*, 1885, col. 18, p. 160.

[65]Giesinger, 361-62; Tischler, 16; G. Johnson, "Swabian Folk Ways," *Saskatchewan History*, 13 (1960), 2, 73-75; N. J. Threiner, *A History of Emmanuel Evangelical Lutheran Church*, Landestreu, Saskatchewan, 1895-1970 (n.p., 1970).

[66]Giesinger, 362. A unique self-help organization which came into being in this colony in the early pioneering years was the Germania Mutual Fire Insurance Company of Langenburg, first advocated in 1909 by Georg Haas, a prominent farmer in the Hoffenthal district, who had migrated from Menno, South Dakota; G. Johnson, "The Germania Mutual Fire Insurance of Langenburg," *Saskatchewan History*, 14 (1961), 1, 27-29.

[67]The Russian colonies from which the later Ebenezer Baptists emigrated had been founded in 1764-1848 near Saratov, mostly by Protestant and Catholic migrants from Hesse; "daughter" colonies were established in 1772-1802, 1848-64, 1849-63, and 1952-53.

[68]Giesinger, 361, 364.

[69]*Deutscher Bund Stutzpunkte* were organized at Togo and Runnymede during the 1930s. Giesinger, 364.

[70]Giesinger, 364.

[71]Migrants from the German colonies near Odessa and in Bessarabia had resettled in Dobruja during the 1840s-50s, founding four colonies near Tulcea: Malcoci, a Catholic colony, in 1843, followed by the three Protestant colonies of Atmagea (in 1848), Kataloi and Cincurova (in 1857). During the 1860s Baptist missionaries from the Danzig congregation in Russia were responsible for creating a Baptist majority in Kataloi and a significant Baptist proportion in the other two Protestant colonies (Giesinger, 360).

[72]Giesinger, 360; Tischler, 16.

[73]Tischler, 16.

[74]E. Althausen, *Zersplitterung oder Verbindung?* (Berlin, 1921); A. Fricke, *Geschichtlicher Ueberblick des Zwanzigjaehrigen Bestehens des Canada Districts der Evangelisch-Lutherischen Synode von Ohio und anderen Staaten* (Regina, 1921); C. Kleiner; *Festschrift zur Feier des Goldenen Jubilaeums der Evangelisch-Lutherischen Synode von Manitoba und anderen Provinzen, 1897-1947* (n.p., 1947); P. E. Wiegner, *The Origin and Development of the Manitoba-Saskatchewan District of the Lutheran Church, Missouri Synod* (n.p., 1957).

[75]*Deutscher Bund Ortsgruppen* were established at Stoughton and Oxbow – Giesinger, 364.

[76]Some such Lutheran settlements are Torquay, Oungre, Tribune, Bromhead, Minton (1912), Lake Alma, Gladmar, and Regway, to the west of Estevan; at Midale, between Estevan and Weyburn; and at Ibsen and Lang near Yellow Grass, northwest of Weyburn.

[77]Giesinger, 364.

[78]Examples of such small concentrations of German Lutherans were at Spiritwood, Meeting Lake, Belbutte, Radisson, Rosthern, Laird, Hague (where Volhynian migrants settled), near Aberdeen, and Carrot River. (Giesinger, 364).

[79]Giesinger, 364.

[80]Neudorf (simply meaning "new village or town") may have been named after a community in the Prischib colonies, west of the Mennonite Molotschna Colony. This in turn had been established in 1805 by migrants from southwestern Germany who had settled for some time in Poland. On the other hand, it may have been named after a community in the Gluckstal colonies on the Dniester, founded in 1809 by Wurttembergers and some Alsatians.

[81]As in most Galician, Black Sea, and Bessarabian German colonies and their offshoots in Saskatchewan, in Lemberg, the Germans spoke a Swabian dialect, because their forefathers had migrated to the Russian colonies from Swabia and other southwest German regions (Johnson, 73-75).

[82]During the Thirties a *Deutscher Bund Ortsgruppe* operated at Melville, while *Stutzpunkte* were organized at Lemberg and Goodeve.

[83]*Deutscher Bund Ortsgruppen* were organized at Whitewood and Broadview, *Stutzpunkte* at Oakshela and Wapella.

[84]For example, Wilhelm Pusch (1878-1926) had emigrated from Vladimir-Volynskij in Volhynia in 1909 to settle here at Windthorst; there, he married Pauline Hirsekorn (1878-1952), born in Marindorf; and their children intermarried with other settlers in the colony — Dresslers, Zaisers, Schmieders.

[85]F. H. Epp, *Mennonite Exodus* (Altona, Manitoba, 1962); and *Mennonites in Canada 1786-1920: The History of a Separate People* (Toronto, 1974).

[86]Epp, *Mennonites in Canada*.

[87]Driedger, *A Sect in Modern Society*, and *Mennonite Change*. The so-called "Old Colony" Mennonites from the Manitoba reserves established numerous *Strassendoerfer* in the Hague and Osler areas: Neuanlage (1895); Neuhorst, Rhineland, Blumenthal, and Chortitz (1898); Osterwick, Gruenfeldt, and Gruenthal (1899); Blumenheim (1900); Hochstadt and Kronsthal (1902); and Rosenfeldt (1905).

[88]Driedger, *A Sect in Modern Society*.

[89]Specifically, these groups included Krimmer Mennonite Brethren from Kansas and Nebraska in 1899-1901; Sommerfelder or Bergthaler Mennonites from Manitoba in 1902; General Conference Mennonites largely from the Midwest (Kansas, Oklahoma, Minnesota) but also directly from Russia or via Manitoba, in 1910-12; and Bruderthaler or Evangelical Mennonite Brethren from Minnesota in 1912. Epp, *Mennonites in Canada* and A. B. Anderson and L. Driedger, "The Mennonite Family: Culture and Kin in Rural Saskatchewan" in K. Ishwaran, ed., *Canadian Families: Ethnic Variations* (Toronto, 1980).

[90]Giesinger, 362.

[91]Anderson, 1972, 72.

[92]Anderson, 1972, 72.

[93]Epp, 1962, 94-95.

[94]Cited in Anderson, 1972, 73.

[95]Ibid.

[96]Anderson, 1972, 1978.

[97]Driedger, 1955, 68-73 and 89-90.

[98]Cited in Anderson, 1972.

[99]Ibid.

[100]In 1921 sixty people were charged $1,000 apiece, another 1,500 were collectively fined $13,034, and one was sent to prison on a thirty-year sentence. The problem eased with the emigration of some 2,000 Old Colonists between 1922 and 1927. By 1930 the fines had been lowered to a dollar a month and Mennonites were permitted an hour and a half instruction in German after 3:30 p.m. Ibid. and Driedger, 1955.

[101]Anderson, 1972, 1978.

[102]Ibid. It is interesting to note that despite the traditional Mennonite pacifist stance, even in this settlement a *Deutscher Bund Ortsgruppe* was organized during the 1930s at Waldheim.

[103]Anderson, 1972, 1978.

[104]Epp, 1974, 317-18; Lehmann, 171.

[105]Lehmann, 172.

[106]General Conference Mennonites established churches within the Old Colony area at Wymark, Schoenfeld, Rheinland, and McMahon, while Mennonite Brethren built a church at McMahon and the Evangelical Mennonite Mission Conference at Wymark and Blumenhof. To the southeast, Mennonite Brethren established churches at Kelstern (1907), Flowing Well (Gnadenau congregation, 1907), and Woodrow (1909-12) while General Conference Mennonites built at Neville. To the northeast, Mennonite Brethren congregations included Brüderfeld (1901), Main Centre (1904), Herbert (1905), Greenfarm (1912), Turnhill (1913), Beechy (Friedensheim congregation, 1927), and Lucky Lake (1943); General Conference Mennonites were found around Herbert (1904), Morse, Gouldtown (1926), Glen Kerr, Eyebrow (1954), Tugaske, Central Butte, Lawson, Gilroy, and Elbow. To the west, Mennonite Brethren settled around Fox Valley (1914), General Conference Mennonites at Gull Lake, and other Mennonite concentrations developed around Cabri, Beverley, Webb, Carmichael, and Eastend.

[107]The Mennonite Brethren church at Glenbush dates from 1928 and the General Conference one from 1934; other General Conference congregations were established at Rabbit Lake and Mayfair. South of this settlement, some families settled in the Lorenzo, Fielding, and Speers areas. At an early date a concentration had developed closer to the main Rosthern settlement, in neighbouring rural districts north of the village of Borden. Mennonite Brethren had settled at Hoffnungsfeld as early as 1904, General Conference Mennonites at Great Deer in 1912, as well as in the Clear Spring and Concordia districts. Other General Conference Mennonite congregations which were established in the northwestern region included Meadow Lake, Pierceland, Compass, Daisy Meadow, and Dorintosh. A Mennonite Brethren church was also established at Meadow Lake (1935). *Rosenort Gemeinde* settled at Capasin, in heavy bush country. *Russlander* also settled in the Fairholme area west of Medstead.

[108]Epp, 1974, 318. As Mennonite settlement spread, other General Conference churches were established at Watrous (1930) and Lampard, a Mennonite Brethren church at Watrous, and Mennonites also settled around Colonsay, Nokomis, and Lanigan. The Nordheim congregation, affiliated with the General Conference, was founded west of Hanley in 1925 by *Russlander*.

[109]In the east-central region, a congregation at Wynyard was established by the Evangelical Mennonite Mission Conference, one at Foam Lake by the Mennonite Brethren; Mennonites also settled around Wishart and Sheho. To the northeast, a Sommerfelder Mennonite reserve was founded in the Carrot River area as early as 1908; later General Conference congregations served Carrot River, Lost River, and Petaigan, with a Mennonite Brethren one at Carrot River as well. Similarly, an isolated Old Colony Mennonite settlement in the Swan Plain area, a marginal, heavily-treed area near the Manitoba border, was later served by a General Conference mission. In south-central and southeastern Saskatchewan, Mennonites settled in the Truax-Dummer-Parry-Brooking area, as well as around Carnduff and Fleming.

[110]The *Schmiedeleut, Dariusleut*, and *Lehrerleut* sects, each immigrating at slightly different times, founded three initial colonies between 1874 and 1877. But about half of the Hutterites decided to homestead individually rather than communally, thus become "*Prairieleut*" affiliated with the Mennonites who settled in the same area. Some of the *Schmiedeleut* began to migrate from their South Dakota colonies into Manitoba as early as 1899; the First World War hastened the exodus of all the *Dariusleut* and *Lehrerleut* from the United States to Alberta (although some later settled in Montana).

[111]The ten *Dariusleut* colonies in southwestern Saskatchewan are: Spring Creek (1958), Maple Creek (1958), Box Elder (1960), and New Wolf (1963), all in the immediate vicinity of Maple Creek; Estuary (1958); West Bench (1960) near Eastend; Simmie (1962); Hodgeville (1969); Ponteix (1970); and Vanguard (1979). The *Lehrerleut*'s eight colonies in the same region are: Bench (1956), near Shaunavon; Tompkins (1956); Waldeck (1962); Main Centre (1962); Cypress (1963) in the Cypress Hills; Sand Lake (1964) near Masefield; Fox Valley (1966); and Abbey (1970). In west-central Saskatchewan, there are three *Dariusleut* colonies: Hillsvale (1960) near Baldwinton, Ft. Pitt (1968), and Scott (1970); and four *Lehrerleut* colonies: Smiley (1966), Miami (1968) near Glidden, Sanctuary (1969) near Kyle, and Rosetown (1969). In the central and south-central regions, the *Dariusleut* have established four colonies: Leask (1957), Riverview (1966) near Aberdeen, Arm River (1968) near Lumsden, and Hillcrest (ca. 1970) near Dundurn; the *Lehrerleut*, three: Huron (1968) near Brownlee, Clear Springs (1969) near Kenaston, and Baildon outside Moose Jaw.

[112]J. A. Hostetler, *Hutterite Society* (Baltimore, 1974).

[113]C. E. Leonoff, *Wapella Farm Settlement: A Pictorial History* (Winnipeg, 1970), 3-5. The first settler here was John Heppner, a Russian Jew, in 1886. The following year Abraham Klenman migrated from Bessarabia; by 1907 he had been instrumental in attracting some fifty Jewish families to the district. Most came directly from Bessarabia and South Russia, some from Lithuania, Galicia, and Rumania, a few after first attempting farming in North Dakota.

Appendix

SASKATCHEWAN

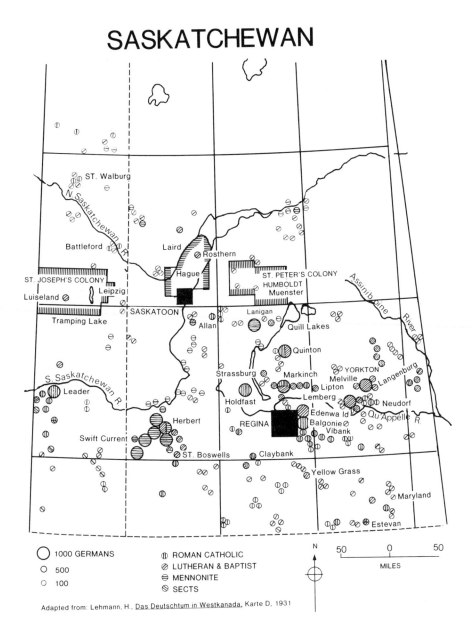

⭕ 1000 GERMANS	⬭ ROMAN CATHOLIC	
◯ 500	⬭ LUTHERAN & BAPTIST	
○ 100	⊖ MENNONITE	
	⊘ SECTS	

N — MILES — 50 0 50

Adapted from: Lehmann, H., Das Deutschtum in Westkanada, Karte D, 1931

218

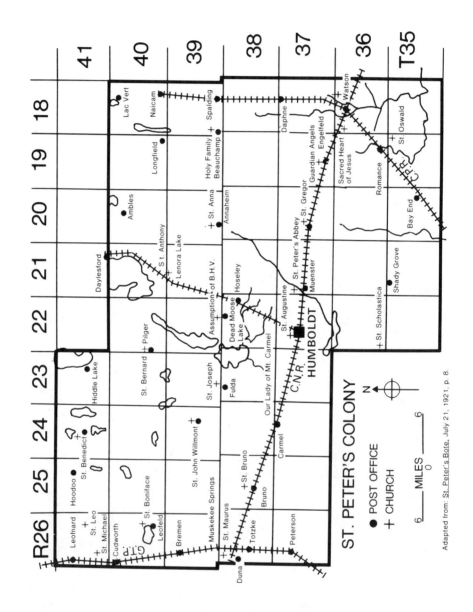

ST. PETER'S COLONY

● POST OFFICE
+ CHURCH

6 ——— MILES ——— 6
0

N

Adapted from: St. Peter's Bote, July 21, 1921, p. 8.

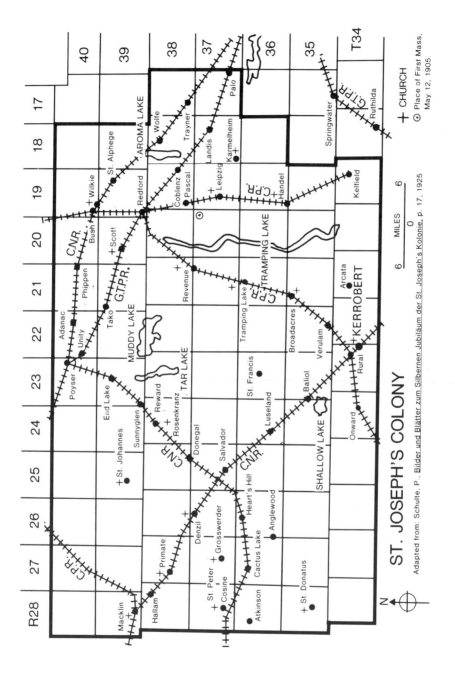

ST. JOSEPH'S COLONY

Adapted from: Schulte, P., Bilder und Blätter zum Silbernen Jubiläum der St. Joseph's Kolonie, p. 17, 1925

+ CHURCH

⊙ Place of First Mass,
   May 12, 1905.

MILES

6   0   6

HAGUE-OSLER COLONY

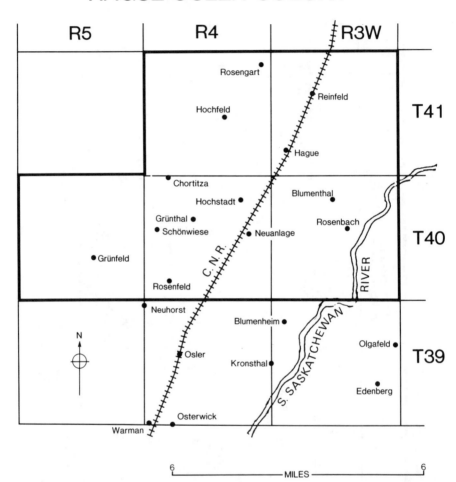

R5 | R4 | R3W

T41

Rosengart
Reinfeld
Hochfeld
Hague

Chortitza
Hochstadt
Blumenthal
Grünthal
Schönwiese
Neuanlage
Rosenbach

Grünfeld

C.N.R.

RIVER

T40

Rosenfeld

Neuhorst

N

Blumenheim

Osler
Kronsthal

S. SASKATCHEWAN

Olgafeld

T39

Edenberg

Osterwick
Warman

6 ———————— MILES ———————— 6

SWIFT CURRENT COLONY

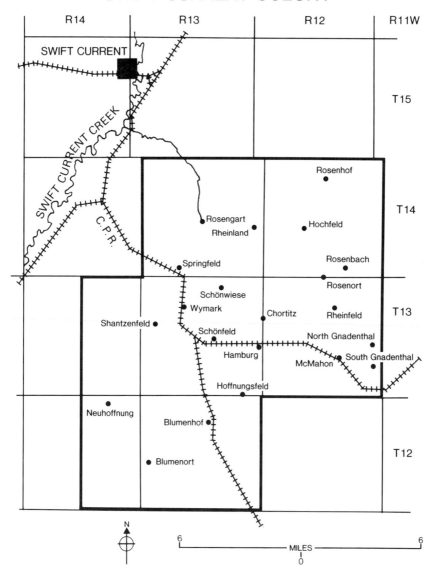

R14   R13   R12   R11W

SWIFT CURRENT

SWIFT CURRENT CREEK

C.P.R.

T15

T14

T13

T12

Rosenhof

Rosengart
Rheinland

Hochfeld

Springfeld

Rosenbach

Rosenort

Schönwiese

Wymark

Chortitz

Rheinfeld

Shantzenfeld

Schönfeld

North Gnadenthal

Hamburg

South Gnadenthal

McMahon

Hoffnungsfeld

Neuhoffnung

Blumenhof

Blumenort

N

6

MILES

0

6

GERMANS FROM RUSSIA IN ALBERTA:
AN INTRODUCTION

Tova Yedlin,
University of Alberta

The main aim of this paper is to discuss a population movement of Germans from Russia, which was, in a sense, unique, a result of a double and, in some cases, even triple migration. This objective, however, is limited to the extent that the study does not include the Mennonite and the Hutterite communities that have a large percentage of Germans among their members.

The Germans from Russia were separated from Germany both spatially and culturally for a period of two centuries. Although granted extensive privileges by the tsars, which helped the preservation of their traditional culture, they were, not unexpectedly, in one way or another influenced by the prevailing Slavic environment. There is then little doubt that the Slavic influence left behind significant and lasting traces on the culture, character and way of thinking of the *nemetskie kolonisty* as they were officially designated by the tsarist authorities.

The story of the Germans from Russia began in the eighteenth century when close to 100,000 colonists were invited to Russia and settled in three main areas: the Volga, the Black Sea region, and, following the partitions of Poland, 1772-1795, the Volhynia *guberniia*. By 1870 their numbers had grown to 450,000. They were, in the main, farmers and were given the right to keep their language, religion and traditions, all of which were outlined in Catherine's Manifesto of July, 1763.

By the second half of the nineteenth century, however, essential changes in the political, economic and cultural life of the Russian state had come to affect the status of the *nemetskie kolonisty*, which resulted in a large scale immigration to the Americas in the last decades of the century. Many arrived in Canada, settling in the Prairie Provinces. Alberta, in particular, attracted a large number of these settlers so that a sizable percentage of the province's total population are Germans from Russia and/or their descendants.

The immigration of Germans to Russia that began in the eighteenth century was part of a wider movement that brought them to a number of countries including the American colonies, Denmark, Spain, the Austrian Empire, and Prussia.[1] The reasons for the widespread dispersal were many. The wars of the late seventeenth century and the campaigns of Louis XIV in the first decade of the eighteenth century devastated large areas of the German

223

west and south, especially the principalities of the Rhineland. In the Palatinate, Baden and Württemberg, the population was heavily reduced in size, the economy dislocated, and there was political and religious chaos. Religious sects that had emerged during the Reformation were severely persecuted, a factor which led many to seek refuge in countries that would guarantee freedom of religious beliefs. The situation of the Germans in the south and in the west then was conducive to immigration, and coincided with the trend of several other European states (especially Austria, Hungary, Prussia, and Russia) to seek new settlers. The movement to leave their native lands began before the large-scale immigration to Russia.[2]

Catherine the Great of Russia (1762-1796) embarked on an extensive policy of colonization, and is generally given credit for bringing many colonists into the Russian Empire. Her Manifesto of July 22, 1763, laid the foundation for large-scale colonization.[3] It was published in a number of west-European languages, and included generous provisions for settlement anywhere in the Empire. It provided an allowance to cover transportation costs, guarantees of religious freedom, including the right to build churches, subsidies for new industries, and freedom from military and civil services. Immunity from taxation was granted for twenty years, after which time settlers were subject to the same taxation as other citizens of the Empire.[4]

The lands opened for colonization included vast regions in the province of Tobolsk in northwestern Siberia, areas in the Astrakhan *guberniia*, territories along the Volga River above and below Saratov, and lands in Orenburg and Belgorod. Two years after the issuance of the Manifesto, however, the government decided to confine the settlements to the Volga area, in spite of the original promise of a free choice. The motives for the changes were not clear, but certainly the concern about the settlers' commitment to stay was a factor in disallowing colonies close to the western frontiers. Another cause was the fear of "undesirable" influence on the native population of western political ideas that the newcomers could possibly spread among them.

As with all governments trying to recruit immigrants, the tsarist authorities carried out a vigorous advertising campaign. Thus, in 1765 a proclamation appeared in the city of Düsseldorf which read as follows:

Her Royal Majesty, the present Most Liberal Reigning Empress of all Russia ... deigns hereby to make known to each and every person of either sex; to artisans, manufacturers and to tradesmen; to agriculturists, vine-dressers, etc., that, out of a natural kind disposition to alleviate poverty, she has been moved to set aside many millions of rubles as an advance payment for a ten years' tax-free period to such free people as may desire to settle down in Her Majesty's land; ...[5]

The overwhelming majority of settlers came from the German states and free-cities. Contrary to expectations, Catherine II, a German herself, was interested in inviting not only her compatriots, but in establishing "all Europe in miniature in foreign colonies on the Russian soil, regardless of nationality and religion; Frenchmen and Greeks, Rumanians and Germans, Slavs and Swedes."[6]

An interesting detail of the advertising campaign was the failure to mention the freedom from military service, one of the Manifesto's provisions. The omission became quite important when Alexander II introduced universal military service in the 1870s, which included also the Germans.

In spite of an active anti-immigration movement by many German states, the Russian government was successful in its work of recruitment, and in 1767 a large number of colonies were established in the Volga region.[7] Citizens of Hesse were especially receptive to the Russian invitations. In fact, the authorities there considered a ban on the right to emigrate. The first united action against emigration of their citizens was taken by the Princes of the Lower Rhine in the principality of the Palatinate. In Coblenz for instance, confiscation of property was threatened. In the Bavarian provinces the assembly of the emigrants was made difficult.[8] But when the Russian government interrupted the campaign, it was not because of the pressure exerted by the German princes, but it was because of internal developments in the Russian Empire, in particular the Pugachev Rebellion (1771-74), the war with Turkey (1768-74), and the partitions of Poland (1772-95). The results of Catherine's efforts were impressive. Within ten years of her Manifesto, over 23,500 colonists settled in the Lower Volga area, near Saratov. The majority of the arrivals were German Protestants from Hesse and the Rhineland.[9]

Alexander I, the grandson of Catherine II, continued to implement the idea of colonization, with the aim to settle the areas of the Crimea and Bessarabia. In 1804 he issued a second Manifesto. Although it resembled the 1763 document, the provisions were more stringent. Taxation and other exemptions were reduced to ten years; the land allotment was specified as a maximum of 216 acres (80 dessiatines); only experienced farmers would be admitted; and there was a limit on the number of families allowed to settle each year.[10]

During Alexander's reign nearly two hundred German colonies were established in the provinces of Bessarabia, Kherson, Ekaterinoslav and the Crimea. The inhabitants came mainly from south and southwest Germany, the states of Baden, Alsace, Württemberg, the Palatinate and Hesse. Most were Protestant, although there were Catholics and Mennonites — the latter were distinguished from the rest as a distinct religious sect. The settlers were designated *nemetskie kolonisty* and thus distinguished from the Baltic Germans who came under the tsarist government through annexation, not colonization.

The settlement process begun by Catherine II and continued by Alexander I proved costly. Catherine invested five million rubles in establishing the colonies in the Volga region. The expectations that the colonists would repay the monies did not materialize. In 1819, ostensibly therefore, Alexander I issued a decree forbidding further immigration into Russia. Any future colonization was to be carried out only by special permission of the Crown.[11]

The expansion of colonies in the second half of the nineteenth century was due to the growth of the colonies that were established earlier. In the decade from 1853 to 1863 more than one hundred branches were founded in Southern Russia, Siberia, and around the cities of Samara and Saratov.

In the second half of the nineteenth century those Germans who moved to Russia came under a different kind of arrangement. They either bought land on their own and established farming settlements, or settled on estates as hired help. Others came to the cities to engage in trade. Still others arrived as temporary workers, artisans and laborers who usually returned home after a season of work. But the growth of the German immigrant community was generally the result of natural increase rather than a continuing influx of newcomers. The Germans on the Volga, for example, increased by sixteen times in the period of one hundred and forty years.[12]

The Volga Germans adopted the system of communal land-tenure of the Russian *obshchina*. Settled in compact colonies and isolated from the surrounding population, they were able to preserve their dialects, customs and traditions.[13] The Black Sea Germans, on the other hand, adopted a system of entailed estates, bought additional land and had closer contacts with the native population. Yet, given the freedoms guaranteed by the Manifesto of 1763, they were able to continue their cultural and religious life without much interference by the Russian authorities.

For over a hundred years the German settlers in the Russian Empire enjoyed preferential treatment, enabling them to prosper both economically and culturally.[14] The situation changed in the period of the Great Reforms inaugurated by Alexander II (1855-1881). Many of the privileges were taken away. The local governments, the so-called *zemstva* were entrusted with the responsibility to construct and administrate schools; the German colonies were to be controlled by Russian authorities at the district or provincial level. Also, in 1874, compulsory military service was introduced, and it was this that most motivated many Germans to leave their adopted country.

Further deterioration of the special status of the Germans occurred in the last decades of the nineteenth century when tsar Alexander III embarked on a policy of forced Russification. The Germans, because of their cultural and physical isolation, were particularly vulnerable. In 1897, Russian language instruction became mandatory, and German schools came under governmental jurisdiction.

These developments prompted many *nemetskie kolonisty* to seek a new homeland, a quest which led to the Americas, especially Canada. The government of Sir Wilfrid Laurier was particularly anxious to bring immigrants who would be willing to settle in the West. Many came directly from Russia, others arrived via the United States.

The Germans from Russia started arriving in Alberta in the last decade of the nineteenth century. The task of bringing European farmers to Canada was entrusted to recruiting agents and shipping companies such as the North Atlantic Trading Company. Among the first to petition the tsarist government for permission to emigrate were the Mennonites. They were as a group better organized than the German Catholics and Lutherans and, therefore, were more successful in obtaining authorization to leave Russia. The news that conscription was to become compulsory in 1874, and the deterioration of the economy, were to release another wave of emigration. Thus, even before the introduction of Clifford Sifton's polices, other German groups had begun to come from the Russian Empire.

The immigration movement of German Catholics, Lutherans, Baptists and Moravians was unlike that of the Mennonites, for it was a gradual process with immigrants arriving, as a rule, in small groups of five to ten families.

The German Catholics, though small in number, were markedly active. They settled at Pincher Creek in 1896, and at Spring Lake, where a community was established in 1902. The Black Sea German Catholics built settlements near Grassy Lake in 1908, and at Schuler, north-east of Medicine Hat, in 1910. Another group settled by Beiseker, north of Calgary. The Rosenheim colony near Provost was founded by Volga Germans who named the place after their former village in Russia. In the Peace River area German Catholics founded Friedensthal near Fairview and Battle River.

Among the Germans from Russia that came to Alberta, the Lutherans were more numerous and better organized. In 1889 they established a settlement near Dunmore, in southern Alberta. Two years later, the colonies of Hoftmangsau and Rosenthal (better known as Stony Plain) were founded as well as Friedensthal in Rabbit Hill, west of Nisku. The Stony Plain community grew rapidly so that by 1894, it had its own church and spiritual leader.[15] North of Nisku, the Volhynian Germans started building Lutherort in 1892. The two colonies, Friedensthal and Lutherort, merged in 1897, to form the Lutheran community of Ellerslie.[16] In the area around Wetaskiwin, Lutherans founded the settlements of New Norway, Bashaw and Stettler in 1892.

Another group that arrived in Alberta in the 1890s was the Moravian Brethren or Herrnhuter; they came from Volhynia in 1894, founding the colonies of Brüderheim, Brüderfeld and New Sarepta (named after their old home village on the Volga). They also settled in the Rabbit Hill area of Heimthal. In 1896 they built the Heimthal Moravian Church.[17]

From 1895 to 1905 the number of Germans from Russia who settled in the districts south of Edmonton increased, particularly in the Edmonton-Wetaskiwin-Camrose triangle. By 1931 there were nearly 7,000 settlers of German-Russian origin.[18] North of Edmonton the Volga Germans from Norka founded Duffield in 1897. Volga Germans also settled in the Riverside area of Calgary in 1893. By 1904 they had their own Lutheran congregation and soon began publishing a newspaper, *Der Deutsch Kanadier* ["The German Canadian"]. Although a German community was to be found in the district of Strathcona very early in the history of the city of Edmonton, these were mostly the "Reich Germans" immigrants who came directly from Germany.

Religion played a very important role in the life of the new communities. The Germans from Russia, in particular the Baptists[19] and the Moravians, usually brought their own spiritual leaders. Very often these men were the organizers as well during the period of migration. The Lutherans depended to a greater extent on leadership provided by the German-Lutheran synods in the United States, while the Catholics had priests from the German-American Benedictine order or the Oblate Fathers. Smaller communities depended on itinerant pastors.

One of the important duties of the religious leaders was to furnish instruction in the German language and in religion, a task which was carried out through the establishment of Saturday-afternoon or Sunday schools. This they did, convinced that in the absence of spiritual leadership and education in the native language, assimilation was progressing much faster. Although the immigration of Germans from Russia continued until the outbreak of the First World War, very few new colonies emerged in the years immediately preceding 1914.

The war and the revolution interrupted, at first, the emigration of Germans from Russia. But later the ravages of this tremendous upheaval and the establishment of the Soviet regime contributed strongly to renewed efforts on the part of the German community to leave. Newcomers to Alberta from the USSR usually followed local advice and joined the existing settlements.

Some Mennonite groups were successful in obtaining permission to emigrate to Canada. The Lutherans and the Catholics, weaker in both leadership and organization, lagged behind.[20] The difficulties were compounded by Canada's new immigration policies, conditioned by lowered economic activity and the status of the Soviet state as one of the "non-preferred" countries. Only when German settlers in Canada exerted pressure upon the government did experienced farmers become eligible to immigrate. In spite of

Soviet obstructionism, and after an agreement was reached with the authorities of the Weimar Republic, many immigrants reached Alberta via Germany. Their travel was financially assisted by the German government and by religious organizations in both Canada and the U.S.A.[21]

Attempts on the part of the Germans to leave the Soviet Union did not cease even when, after 1930, the government forbade all emigration. Some of these efforts illustrated the desperate mood of those wanting to leave. An escape route through Manchuria was tried, and in 1931 there were 1,100 refugees in Harbin.[22] The total number of Germans from Russia, who came to Canada in the inter-war period did not exceed 10,000, half of whom settled in the Prairie provinces in the years 1926 to 1929. The number of those who settled in Alberta is not easy to determine. Since these refugees could not set up communities of their own, it is difficult — if not impossible — to establish their number in Alberta.

The third wave of immigration of Germans from Russia came after the Second World War. In particular, Germany's war against the USSR, which had begun in June 1941, brought some significant changes in the situation of the Germans in the Soviet Union. The Volga German Autonomous Republic, founded in 1924, was liquidated in October, 1941, and its population dispersed in Siberia and Central Asia. In the western parts of the Soviet Union, the rapid advance of Nazi troops left some 300,000 Russian Germans behind Hitler's lines. As Germans they received preferential treatment. However, when the Nazi armies began to retreat after 1943, some 100,000 were forced to leave with the *Wehrmacht* and arrived in West Germany via Poland.

When the restrictions against the immigration of Germans were lifted in Canada, nearly 100,000 entered the country. One-quarter were from Russia.[23] Again, Alberta's share of these Germans is difficult to determine. The only exact count of Alberta's German population was taken in the 1971 census. According to the data, Germans numbering approximately 230,000 accounted for about 13% of the total population. In Heinz Lehmann's earlier estimate, Germans from Russia, who settled in the Prairie provinces by 1939, made up 44% of the total German immigration.[24] The Germans from Russia who came after the Second World War settled primarily in urban centers, or joined relatives and friends in the established settlements.

As to the economic, cultural and social aspects of the life in Alberta of former German colonists from Russia, interviews reveal that the beginnings of settlement were hard. Particularly in the first and second waves of immigration, most new arrivals — seasoned farmers — tended to settle on the land. Arriving with very limited material resources, they had difficulties adapting to new ways of life and overcoming language barriers. Yet they succeeded in their adjustment, because they settled in their own communities, and had their religion as a stabilizing force.

Their cultural life revolved in a large measure around religious institutions. Consequently, because they were church-centered, the primary historical sources of the group, such as publications, memoirs of spiritual leaders of the communities, local histories, biographies of individual settlers, say little of the background and past history of a given community. The Germans from Russia did not generally establish any clubs or organizations. The founding of these was left to the Reich Germans. In addition, the two World Wars contributed greatly to the withdrawal of the communities from public life because of hostile attitudes. This withdrawal could be seen in the cessation of the activities of clubs and societies and in the interruption of cultural activities. The tendency was further emphasized by restrictions on the public use of the German language. The restrictions, however, did not affect the Germans who came from Russia, for they were used to an isolated existence and could always find refuge in their religious communities. The Germans from Russia did not take a very active part in the political life of the Province. Their passivity can be understood only in the context of educational standards, language barriers, and political naïvety about the democratic process.

According to Giesinger, 300,000 Germans from Russia came to the Americas since the 1870s. The number of their descendants is close to a million and a half, of which 350,000 are in Canada.[25] The percentage of Alberta's German population (about 230,000) constituted by arrivals from Russia, and their descendants, cannot be determined at this time. The problem requires further study, as does that of the influence of the Slavic culture and environment to which they were exposed during the century and a half spent in Russia and, in many cases, the Soviet Union.

FOOTNOTES

[1] Hattie Plum Williams, *The Czar's Germans: with Particular Reference to the Volga Germans* (Lincoln, Nebraska, 1975), 24.

[2] The early beginning of German religious immigration is shown by the presence in the American colonies of nearly 225,000 German speakers at the time of the War of Independence, see Albert Bernhardt Faust, *The German Element in the United States, with Special Reference to its Political, Moral, Social and Educational Influence* (Boston, 1927), vol. I, 285.

[3] It was Tsarina Elizabeth Petrovna (1741-1762) who invited the first French Protestants to settle the vast regions of Russia. Williams, 33.

[4] Ibid., 35-42. See also Sydney Heitman, ed., *Germans from Russia in Colorado* (Ann Arbor, Michigan, 1978), 6-23.

[5] Williams, 69.

[6] Grigorii Pisarevskii, *Iz istorii inostrannoi kolonizatsii v Rossii* (From the History of Foreign Colonists in Russia) *v XVIII veke* (Moscow, 1909), 74.

[7] Williams, 98-99.

[8] Ibid., 12, 57.

[9] Pisarevskii, 169.

[10] Heitman, 13-17.

[11] Williams, 94. See also Aleksandr Augustovich Klaus, *Unsere Kolonien: Studien und Materialen zur Geschichte und Statistik der Auslandischen Kolonization in Russland* (Odessa, 1887) for detailed statistical data regarding colonization in Russia.

[12] Williams, 95.

[13] James Long, *The German-Russians: A Bibliography* (Santa Barbara, 1978), 4.

[14] Ibid.

[15] Heinz Lehmann, *Das Deutschtum in West Kanada* (Berlin, 1939), 229.

[16] Ibid.

[17] In 1946 and in 1971 respectively the community celebrated the fiftieth and seventy-fifth anniversaries of the founding of the church. In commemoration of these celebrations two publications appeared which contained the history of the Moravian Church and that of the Heimthal community. See Clement Hoyler, *Heimtal in the Making: Reminiscences of the Beginnings of a Moravian Congregation in Alberta*, 1896 [n.p., 1906], and *Heimthal Moravian Church, South Edmonton, Alberta: Historical and Present Day Reflections for the 75th Anniversary Celebrations* (n.p., 1971). The Moravian Church had its beginnings in Bohemia and was founded by followers of John Hus in 1457, as an episcopalian church. Persecuted by the authorities, the Bohemian Brethren moved to Poland where they joined the Calvinists at the Synod of Kozminek (1555). From Poland they emigrated to the province of Volhynia, by then within the border of the Russian Empire. Although small in numbers, the group remained closely knit in Alberta and left its imprint upon the history of the Province.

[18]Lehmann, 230.

[19]The Baptists came from Volhynia and settled in the district of Leduc as well as in other parts of Alberta, often joining established Lutheran settlements.

[20]Ibid., 114.

[21]The majority of immigrants were Mennonites (3,885), but there were 1,250 Lutherans, 468 Catholics, and 7 Adventists. See Adam Giesinger, *From Catherine to Krushchev: The Story of Russia's Germans* (Winnipeg, 1974), 369.

[22]Ibid.

[23]Ibid., 371.

[24]Lehmann, 91.

[25]Giesinger, 37.

REALITIES: THE COMMUNITY

REMARKS

Julius Buski, Chairman,
Alberta Cultural Heritage Council

Listening to these discussions brings to mind many of the same concerns we have discussed at meetings of our council. I can only underscore that the matters voiced cut across ethnic barriers — there is a great deal in common among them. Looking around our meeting room this morning, I notice the absence of members from all levels of government. It is unfortunate their busy schedules often do not permit them to attend gatherings as important as this one today, and they must rely on the second-hand information passed along to them by senior civil servants. This is not to disparage the fine work and dedication of the civil servants, but it does highlight a problem we face in having our concerns heard directly.

Since many of you are from out of province, I would like to take a few minutes of your time to outline the operation of our council, which is, I believe, an outstanding example of a government advisory body in the area of ethnoculturalism.

The Alberta Cultural Heritage Council came into existence as a result of recommendations made at the Alberta Cultural Heritage Conference, convened by the Government of Alberta June 16-18, 1972. Our council, in terms of the Cultural Development Act, serves as an advisory body to the Minister Responsible for Culture, the Hon. Mary LeMessurier. Council members are chosen by their ethno-cultural group in the province, with each ethno-cultural group being entitled to at least one representative on Council, and with larger groups having additional representation on the basis of their size. In addition, the council members include government appointees, who are named by the Minister in recognition of the expertise and service they can provide the Council. At present our council consists of 48 elected members, representing 41 ethno-cultural groups, and 33 government appointees.

The objects of our council, as outlined in our By-Laws, are:

1. to make recommendations and provide information and advice to the Government regarding ethno-cultural development in Alberta;
2. to give Albertans, as a people, increasing awareness of their cultures and identities;
3. to develop an appreciation of our evolving identity, through understanding of our individual ethno-cultural backgrounds and sharing of our cultural diversity and richness;

4. to preserve the cultural wealth of our past: the languages, arts, music and rites of our Native people and the contributions of our immigrant settlers.

The council is primarily an advisory body, dealing with policy recommendations. We are not a source of financing, nor are we active in programming. We do, however, provide ethnic groups with an avenue for making input into policies related to our objectives. I would urge those of you from ethno-cultural groups in Alberta to make yourselves aware of who your representative is and maintain contact with that person, so that we can have your participation in our deliberations. The council is most interested both in hearing your problems and concerns and in striving to find solutions we can recommend to the Government.

In passing, I would also like to make you aware of The Alberta Cultural Heritage Foundation, which I also have the honour of chairing. The Foundation is a funding body for projects that relate closely to the objectives I have already mentioned. Governed by a 14-member Board of Directors, we approve project grants of varying amounts for applicants who make submissions to us, and who have projects we consider worthy of support. These can be large or small, and all will be considered on the basis of their own merit. Anyone interested in further details should write the Foundation at #202, 9920 – 106 St., Edmonton.

BROADCASTING IN THIRD LANGUAGES

Roger Charest,
Canadian Broadcasting Corporation,
Edmonton, Alberta

There is a serious gap in Alberta's communication service. The problem is the lack of ethnocultural or third-language programming for the 200-odd thousand people in Edmonton whose mother tongue is neither French nor English. The people who speak a third language tend to grow invisible in the eyes of broadcasters, both because of the expediency involved in serving the majority and the financial return of attracting large audiences. In Edmonton the total time devoted to third-language broadcasts is a mere ten hours per week. It is also interesting to note that the number of hours given over to third-language broadcasting on radio in Edmonton has decreased in the last five years. Alberta, and particularly Edmonton, leads the country in number of cultural organizations and groups. The provincial government has shown the other parts of the country how it encourages cultural heritage.

Yet radio broadcasting is still a decade behind in terms of social needs within the community. During the past ten years a great deal of emphasis has been placed on cultural heritage. Has radio been a part of this new cultural awareness? Does radio educate Edmontonians about the East European community? Perhaps of interest to CEESAC members is the social function performed by third-language broadcasting. What is fulfilled through broadcasting in a minority language? What are the direct and indirect, or the manifest and latent purposes of such broadcasting? What current and possibly future links are there between this type of broadcasting and the other more general aspects of language and culture retention?

The Canadian systems of communication have been undergoing a period of tremendous change. New systems — especially those involving coaxial cable — are emerging, presenting challenges to old conceptual frameworks. Fixed ideas concerning the distinction between "mass communication" and other forms of communication are breaking down under the pressure of new technological developments and social movements. Third-language broadcasting is inescapably wedded to these changes and is of interest in that context as well. A close understanding of this area of broadcasting might provide clues to future developments in the communications system as a whole. Change is evident in the considerable overall increase that has occurred in third-language broadcasting over the last twenty years — and especially in the last ten. Hours per week of third-language programming in Canadian radio were as follows:

238

1952 —   62 hours
1958 —   144 hours
1966 —   215 hours
1973 —   526 hours
1980 — 1200 hours

Although Alberta is a leader in Canada as regards the spirit of multiculturalism in a pluralistic society, she is far behind in the area of multicultural broadcasting. On both AM and FM radio stations, the increase in third-language broadcasting can be partly attributed to the arrival on the Canadian broadcasting scene of "multilingual" radio stations. Five licences have been issued for privately-owned multilingual radio stations, all of them since 1962. It is perhaps an important note that there exists no legal or official category for multilingual stations. By law, stations are licensed as English, French, or bilingual English-French outlets. The term "multilingual station" is, however, commonly used in the broadcasting industry and is used by the five stations licensed to broadcast in third languages.

The large increase in third-language broadcasts would have taken place even without the arrival of the multilingual stations. This pattern of increase in third-language radio programming is interesting in itself, but it is also remarkable in that it challenges some of the assumptions held by scholars and market researchers alike, about general trends in radio broadcasting. The major thrust of commercial radio's response to television in the 1950s and 1960s was to reduce the amount of air time given to coherent program blocks and to adopt programming formats wherein the objective was to win audience loyalty to a particular station, rather than to a particular program. In brief, the idea was to convert the entire output of the station to a single program. Emphasis was then naturally placed on maintaining unbroken sound throughout the broadcast day. Such an environment is not favourable for the development of specialized programming, which is what most third-language programming necessarily is. Such programming breaks the continuity of the station's broadcast output. The increase in third-language programming is, therefore, something of a contradiction — or even, perhaps, a new trend — in Canadian broadcasting. It may be premature to read too much into this observation, but there might nevertheless be a clue here to some future trends in Canadian broadcasting as a whole.

Central to understanding any type of broadcasting anywhere is an appreciation of its content. Much casual misinformation exists about broadcast content; many of the informal generalizations made concerning broadcasting are based on intuitions and impressions. Sometimes, but not always, the intuitions and impressions are borne out by closer and more systematic examination. A scheme of content analysis in many different languages, in the context of the same project, offers its own special difficulties. It requires that its monitors at least be familiar with, on the one hand, the language and culture of the group for which the broadcast is intended and, on the other, the purposes and guiding principles of the content analysis project as a whole. In general, content analysis has shown itself to be a useful technique for understanding the relationship between broadcasting, and language and culture retention. What is most important to remember is that those things which are true of radio in general, are also true of third-language radio.

By far the largest single category of content in the broadcasts is recorded music. The ratio is about 70 per cent music to 30 per cent spoken word. Multilingual broadcasting cannot be regarded as a tool for persuading the public to learn another language, but clearly it can motivate those already speaking one to maintain it in the home. Children and students are also highly motivated to speak their mother tongues if they can see or hear every day that the languages are being spoken in Edmonton, that theirs are *living* languages which can bring them much closer to their cultures. The public in general has a window on the world which enables it to learn about other cultures and appreciate the music that helps form those cultures.

Most radio broadcasting in Canada is conducted in such a way that it provides a sort of music and talk background for other activities. In other words, radio listening is commonly a *secondary* activity. However, much third-language radio programming is clearly not of this type. Since much of it is broadcast at specific, scheduled times at different points on the radio spectrum, it must be assumed that audiences are specifically seeking it out, making a specific effort to tune in. Listening to third-language radio broadcasts is therefore quite often a primary activity, rather than simply a background sound. These facts may be linked to the role of broadcasting in the preservation of minority cultures.

The contributions of third-language broadcasting to this process are both direct and indirect. Directly, third-language broadcasting contributes to the listener in his use of the language. Indirectly, such broadcasts contribute by providing a sort of vehicle to promote and facilitate the personal interaction between speakers of a particular language. It does this through its emphasis on community service items, through advertising of specialized, culturally related, goods and services, and generally by acting as a focus for the internal activities of a particular linguistic sub-community. In the case of some third-language broadcasts, that the broadcast consists of music relating mostly to a specific culture and that the spoken word continuity portions are in a third language, seem at times secondary to other elements of the program, such as providing information about meetings of clubs and organizations, church activities, availability of traditional goods, services, cultural artifacts, etc.

Third-language programs, and multilingual radio in general, promote the interactional salience of minority cultural communities. This indirect contribution to minority languages and cultures is at least as important as any direct contribution. Scholars of communications have for many years seen the development of the mass media as leading in one direction only, with a shrinking variety of media messages emanating for ever fewer sources being directed at ever larger audiences. This was thought to culminate in a mass society in which tastes, lifestyles, and personal opinions would inevitably be homogenized, and in which cultural differences would be broken down. It is becoming increasingly clear that this was a simplistic theory, an extrapolation of what were probably short-run trends in the first half of the present century.

Scholars are now talking about a new age of media development in which the media become more specialized, audiences more fragmented and discriminating, and personal tastes and lifestyles more diverse. Nowhere is this trend more apparent than in the decline of mass circulation magazines and the consequent upswing in circulations of more specialized publications.

The same trends are now unfolding in broadcasting, which seem to be becoming "narrowcasting". We are all hoping that Edmonton will soon boast a new multilingual radio station, broadcasting in 23 languages. The station (CKER) has for two years been working in co-operation with a twelve-member advisory council made up of representatives from the various cultural and linguistic communities of Edmonton, to ensure fair representation in programming time and content and the maintenance of a reasonable standard of language proficiency in the daily broadcasts of third languages.

If assimilation refers to absorption into a system, and if this absorption causes a person to lose his identity, no part of assimilation is welcome. But if assimilation means becoming a part of the Canadian "mosaic" while maintaining the identity of one's cultural heritage, then it may be endorsed. CKER will foster the development and preservation of diverse cultures within the community by offering programs specializing in languages spoken in Alberta.

Radio "narrowcasting" is, in this sense, much more a herald of the future than an echo of the past.

THE UKRAINIAN COMMUNITY OF ALBERTA: AN ADDRESS

Laurence Decore,
Ukrainian Professional and Business Club,
Edmonton

The purpose of my talk is to discuss the aims, roots and realities of the Ukrainian Community of Alberta. Perhaps, I can do it through my personal experience — the impressions Laurence Decore gained when he joined the Ukrainian Professional and Business Club of Edmonton in 1964.

But first, I should introduce myself by revealing some of my background. The place of my birth was Vegreville. At the start of my schooling, it was not uncommon for children to talk in the Ukrainian language while they played, as most people around them were Ukrainians. However the "temper of the times" did not favour the use of Ukrainian in the schools. There were some instances, I can remember, when some of the teachers would become very angry if they heard Ukrainian in the school or in the school yard.

Unfortunately, because of those times, I could not develop the kind of knowledge of, and facility in, the Ukrainian language I wish I had today. Years later, the awareness of this sparked me to an activity that was to have profound consequences on my life.'

When I joined the Professional and Business Club, I realized I felt a certain comfort with others like myself. I found that there were many others who had never obtained or who had lost fluency in their native language. In a striking way, the discussion of our professional and business problems while eating pyrohy seemed all right and proper.

It was in those days that Canada was gradually entering a period of turmoil. Francophones would make forceful demands for the preservation of their culture and language. Then, the so called "other ethnic groups" began to give cause for tremors in this country. Manoly Lupul was one of the first in our community to identify our problems and the first to challenge our Club and myself to do something about it. "If we do not," he said, "then the preservation of our culture and language is doomed."

Happily, the Club undertook a project that mushroomed into tremendous activity with fruitful results. We became convinced that, unless something positive was done about education in *both* languages, our ancestral culture, our ability to read a Ukrainian book and tell people about our dances, our *pysanky*, the food we eat, about the experiences of our parents and grandparents, would

241

242

be lost forever.

We believed that we had to turn to the government for help. We explained to the officials: "We are Canadians of Ukrainian origin. We're here and we have the right to be here — these are some of the things we want as Canadians."

Now the realities of achieving certain results are rather interesting. I would like to tell you about a few of them. The members of the Club set up an ad hoc committee on multiculturalism. We met every Monday for over six months at the Prince of Wales Armouries, and we wrote briefs about cultural preservation. We referred to the inequities of the Alberta School Act, to the government's duty to recognize all cultures, and to funding. One of our briefs was delivered to Harry Strom, the Social Credit Premier of the Province. It just so happened that an election was looming on the horizon and, therefore, he was very receptive. We were able to convince the Socreds that they should amend the School Act to allow the teaching of languages without penalty. Just when we got the Socred Premier educated and committed, the government fell and a new Premier took over — Peter Lougheed. We were floored. "Oh, God," we said, "this is the end."

Luckily, in our community political activity was refined to the point where some of us were Liberals, some Conservatives, and some Social Crediters. We mustered all these resource people, selected a representative committee to exert pressure, and succeeded in extracting a commitment from Lougheed. To our amazement and pleasure, we discovered that the Tories were more receptive than we could have ever imagined. Mr. Lougheed appointed a Minister who became, I think, the most positive factor we had going for us in Alberta. But, as is usually the case, it took long and hard work on our part to sell the idea of preserving our culture and our language.

We also submitted a brief to the Joint House of Commons and Senate Committee on Multiculturalism and, to our great amazement, in a speech to the Ukrainian Congress in Winnipeg in 1972, Prime Minister Trudeau quoted a paragraph from our brief. That was the legitimization that we had sought.

Soon we realized that, because we could not take a plane to the Ukraine and get teachers and teaching aids, we had to do something here to protect our language by development both at the grassroots and at the "ivory-tower level." In other words, we had to have primary language instruction for our children in the school system and have a true and comprehensive language program at a University. In the latter instance, we embarked on a project, the aim of which was to have a chair of Ukrainian Studies established at the University of Alberta. I remember well the first meeting with the President of the University. We made our pitch and his reply was that there was no room and no money. He suggested that we approach the University of Calgary. I said, "Well, most of the Ukrainians live in northeastern Alberta; they don't live around Calgary." Unimpressed, the President insisted that they had no room and no money. But you can move mountains when you get angry and when you have some knowledge how the system works.

Once again, we approached the government to convince it that the setting up of a Chair of Ukrainian Studies was a good and worthy objective and to extract from it a commitment for the provision of funds to the University for the support of the project. This was accomplished. The first major step had been undertaken.

At about the same time, we submitted briefs to the Provincial Government requesting its involvement in a bilingual program. In this we were also successful. To our great satisfaction, our children are now enrolled in a bilingual program. My daughter is in Grade Five. She is as fluent in Ukrainian as she is in English. I am sorry to say that I am not. I am extremely proud of what she has accomplished. My little boy is also enrolled in the program. What eluded me has now become possible for my children.

The next objective which we were to realize was the establishment of the Institute of Ukrainian Studies. Problems were encountered with this goal as well. When we approached the government, its representatives were rather reluctant to make a commitment. One of their comments was that, at that time, they would be interested only if they had the co-operation from the other two Prairie Provinces.

We continued our pressure; soon Saskatchewan and Manitoba indicated that they were not interested in an institute of that kind. Undeterred, we again employed our resource people and drew on our political skills. Not long afterwards, the Institute did come into being. We had set up all the bases.

Now we are in a period of stabilization of our relations with the government, the Alberta Cultural Heritage Council and the Canadian Consultative Council on Multiculturalism.

But it seems to me that there is still one more objective to be attained. Although we have achieved a great deal in the last 8-10 years, we must further involve the federal government. We ought to have a more representative consultative group. Perhaps, all representatives should be elected by their respective communities.

We need help in the area of textbooks for our children, and funding of scholarships for Ph.D. and Master's programs at the university level. We need, and this is a strange thing to say, help with our own organization — our umbrella organization in the Ukrainian community. I noted, with great interest, that the federal government, in July, established a joint commission with the Franco-Canadian Association outside of the Province of Quebec. There is a government-funded secretariat as part of that Joint Commission and they meet three times a year. Francophones outside of Quebec have established a direct connection with the federal cabinet. Our community does not have that kind of access or ability to communicate with government.

I find it rather absurd to have to plead for an audience with the Prime Minister or the Minister of Multiculturalism. Of course, it was appropriate that this kind of commission be established for the Francophones. I welcome it. It is a great thing for them, but it should also be a great thing for other ethnic groups. All cultural groups must have equality in Canada. That is our next goal.

ROOTS, ASPIRATIONS, PROGRESS AND REALITIES

Leslie Duska, Past President
Szechenyi Society,
Hungarian Community

As a young officer of the Hungarian Army, it never occurred to me that after a few years I would be a landed immigrant in a distant country.

In order to tell you as much as possible in ten minutes, I would like to present eight snapshots as background to a Hungarian with a family of four little children arriving in this "remote" land, and what kind of impressions I got before coming to this memorable conference at the University of Alberta.

Easter time of 1941 represents the first "snapshot." German armies entered Hungary and proceeded to attack Yugoslavia. To show his opposition to this campaign, the Hungarian prime minister, Paul Teleki, committed suicide.

While German armies completed their campaign within two weeks to subdue Yugoslavia, the Hungarian ambassador General Joseph Vasváry, my former C.O., succeeded in smuggling out of Belgrade members of the French embassy, including the family-members of Général Béthouard.

In the second "snapshot," right after the war I found myself as a "private" under the High Commissioner of the French Zone of Austria, Général Béthouard. In 1947 I was transferred from Austria to the North French Zone of Rhineland-Pfalz (Rhéno-Palatin).

Another scene is shown in the third "snapshot." Monsieur Weitzel, an engineer and captain in the French Military Government in Koblenz, was responsible for the shipyards and salvage operations along the Rhine River. I was his secretary and interpreter (French-Hungarian-German) and prepared the daily progress-reports. Monsieur Weitzel liked me to call him Mon Capitaine instead of Monsieur Weitzel. In turn, he called me Mon Capitaine instead of Monsieur Duska. Well, I learned something which I never thought of before. Just because Monsieur Weitzel was born in Alsace, and despite his mother tongue being German, he was a 100% French citizen. Similarly, Général König, the Military commander of the French Zone in West Berlin, did not need to change his name or mother tongue to remain a high ranking loyal French leader.

The fourth "snapshot" is of a train in Switzerland with the passengers engaged in friendly chit-chat. One with native French talks to his neighbour in Schwytzerdütsch, and another with native German talks to his neighbour in his native Italian. Who would deny that, despite the four official languages, they all are good and proud Swiss citizens?

Calgary in 1951 is presented in the fifth "snapshot." A small Hungarian delegation of three men was received by the Roman Catholic bishop of Southern Alberta, Francis Carroll. We asked for permission to build a Hungarian church, and to invite a Hungarian priest. Bishop Carroll was not in favour of our request. But after a few minutes, the words of the Gospel rescued the almost hopeless situation. Is it not true, I ventured to ask, that on the first Pentecost "tongues of fire" descended on the head of each apostle, and they began to speak foreign languages, so that devout men from every nation under heaven could hear the apostles speaking their own languages? The permission was granted.

The sixth "snapshot" is of a great president of the United States, Abraham Lincoln, 115 years ago saying the following words: "Never consider a newcomer to become a loyal citizen, unless he retains his love for his motherland!"

The subject of the seventh snapshot" is the office of Premier Manning of Alberta in 1966. A Hungarian delegation is in the process of requesting Hungarian language instruction in accordance with the Alberta School Act (Part XII, Chapter 297, para. 387). The following years represented the *labour pains*: school board meetings (May 1967, December 1969), public hearings (May 1968, November 1968), and a discouraging stand on the part of the Department of Education. Scores of letters were written to and by the school boards, and the Curriculum Branch, Department of Education. Quoting from my April 29, 1968 reply:

> ... 5) The letter of Mr. J ... rejects a legal request for the reason, that others (Jewish, Polish, etc.) might also ask for the same right. Denying a legal request based on the School Act to any group of people in this form is a discrimination, in the 'Human Rights Year 1968.'

Finally, the Hungarian language course was granted, but in a restrictive, discouraging manner as shown in a quotation (p. 2, the *Albertan*, November 21, 1968):

> ... However, the board set conditions on its approval. Students taking courses must be residents of the school district, the number of pupils in any class must be ten or more for two consecutive years and there must be evidence of course follow-up.

Still, *Alberta was the first place* where the Hungarian language instruction got off the ground.

Real help and goodwill were demonstrated by the Lougheed government.

The eighth "snapshot" is of myself in 1974 in Ottawa, at the First Canadian Conference on Multiculturalism, submitting a recommendation: "The Government of Canada (should) match the financial contributions of ethnocultural groups in the establishment and development of university chairs for preservation and teaching of their language and culture."

The next three years revealed another series of *labour pains* preliminary to the federal goverment's making good on the recommended matching grant. In this way — finally — the first university chair of Hungarian Studies was established at the University of Toronto in 1978, to teach Hungarian language and literature at the post-secondary level. Some 135,000 Hungarian Canadians are grateful for the reaching of this modest goal, grateful to those Canadian leaders who helped to make it a reality.

We hope a helping hand will be extended in the future as well for teacher training and the development of curriculum materials, which are absolute necessities for the preservation of our language and cultural heritage.

Hungarian Studies at the University of Toronto

A follow-up by the *Hungarian Chair* to the presentation of Leslie Duska.

The history and scope of the Endowment Chair so far has been as follows.

In 1973, the Széchenyi Society, a respected, national cultural society of Hungarian Canadians, initiated a fund-raising campaign to establish a Chair of Hungarian studies in Canada. The first sentence of its campaign brochure defines the purposes of the chair as follows:

To make available and maintain in Canada, for the benefit of all Canadians, those gems of Hungarian culture (literature, language, music, art, history) to which Canada is heir through those thousands of Hungarian people who have chosen to make Canada their home.

Since the Hungarian-Canadian community could not have raised the full amount needed for the Chair within a reasonable period of time, they appealed to the federal government for additional funds. In December 1977, the government matched the already collected $300,000 with an equal amount, thereby making it possible to establish a Chair of Hungarian Studies at the University of Toronto. Instruction started in the fall of 1978 with 17 students enrolled in three credit courses. In 1978-80, 31 students were taking courses in Hungarian.

So far, the courses offered by the Chair have been focused on language, literature and cultural history. Language is taught on two levels: beginners and advanced. Further studies in language and style can be pursued within the framework of literary courses. The language of instruction of advanced literary courses (such as the one on the modern Hungarian novel) is Hungarian. For English-speaking students, who do not plan to study Hungarian language and literature, but would like to familiarize themselves with Hungarian culture and its contribution to Canada's multicultural society, an integrated course on Hungarian cultural history is offered in English every year.

The expansion of the program of Hungarian studies is one of the most urgent tasks of the Chair. Assuming that further grant funds can be secured, we hope to introduce new courses by involving specialists at the U. of T. in Hungarian economic and political history, library science and other disciplines. At present, Hungarian studies can be pursued at the undergraduate level without specialization. If course offerings increase in number and become more varied in content, it will be possible to develop a program of Hungarian Studies both as major and minor areas of study.

The basic tool for teaching and research is a well-equipped library, audio-visual materials and map collections. Consequently, expanding the University's Hungarian collection and the reference library of the Hungarian Chair is of utmost importance.

As the Hungarian Chair is an integral part of a Canadian university with extensive international contacts, participation in international education and scholarly activities is another priority. The Hungarian Chair will endeavour to maintain contact with other institutions around the world that are concerned with Hungarian culture. Thus, the American Hungarian Educators' Association, a widely-based North American association devoted to Hungarian studies, held its fifth annual conference at the University of Toronto, May 15-17, 1980. The only scholarly English-language periodical of Hungarian studies published in Canada (the *Canadian-American Review of Hungarian Studies*), published twice a year, appears now with the active support of the Chair and is distributed by the U. of T. Press.

The Hungarian-Canadian community which initiated the Chair continues to support its activities. For example, the Hungarian Cultural Centre, through its monthly publication, *Krónika*, has provided the Chair space to address the Hungarian-Canadian community on cultural matters. The Canada-wide cultural organization, Rákóczi Foundation, has annually awarded a scholarship of $1,000 to the best students in the Hungarian courses. The Széchenyi Society, organizer of the fund-raising campaign, is now making efforts to provide further funds for the expansion of the activity of the Hungarian Chair.

The first and present incumbent of the Hungarian Chair is George Bisztray, Associate Professor.

AIMS, ASPIRATIONS, REALITIES OF THE POLISH-CANADIAN COMMUNITY

Wladyslaw Gertler, President,
Canadian Polish Congress, Toronto

Preamble: Roots and History

Historians of Polish settlement in Canada trace its beginnings back some 200 years, but mass immigration of Poles started later, in the 19th century. The formation of Polish organizations began in the 1850s, almost all of them centred around parishes and Polish priests. With increased immigration, the feeling of the need for co-operation and understanding among people of Polish descent was born, but the realization of this aspiration had to wait almost another hundred years. In 1931 at Toronto, Ontario, representatives of Polish organizations in Canada met and established the first umbrella organization. It was named the "Federation of Polish Societies in Canada," and its headquarters was in Winnipeg, Manitoba, then the centre of Polish settlement. The outbreak of the Second World War, and the situation in which Poland found itself, convinced Canadians of Polish descent and their leaders of the need to reorganize their Federation. In September 1944, delegates from most of the Canadian Polish organizations met in Toronto to discuss this problem and established a new central umbrella organization, the Canadian Polish Congress, Inc., which took over the Charter of the Federation of Polish Societies in Canada. From that moment the latter ceased to exist. The main aims of the Congress were: representation of Polish Canadians before the Canadian authorities; preservation of the culture of their ancestors; contributing to the future well-being of Canada and helping their mother country defend her true interests. The headquarters of the Canadian Polish Congress was transferred to Ontario, where more than half of the Polish Canadian population lives today.

The Canadian Polish Congress, Inc. unites 165 various organizations with members of Polish descent from British Columbia to Quebec inclusively and represents the thoughts and aspirations of most Polish Canadians. The Congress has 11 branches in Canada and national headquarters in Toronto.

Aspirations, Realities, and Aims

The aspirations, realities, and aims of the Polish ethnic group in Canada are many, and it would be difficult in such a short essay as this one to discuss them all. However, the following ones are probably the most important:

The Canadian Constitution

The structure of the Canadian population today and that of 113 years ago at the time when the British North America Act became law, is entirely different. Today, no ethnic group, French and British included, represents an absolute majority. A rough breakdown of the Canadian population shows that 41 per cent are British, 30 per cent are French and 29 per cent are of other extractions. It would be only just and proper to include in the Canadian Constitution (which should be patriated without delay) a paragraph depicting the diverse ethnic character of Canada and the many cultures that contribute to forming Canada's culture, and stressing the right of every ethnic group to cultivate and preserve its own culture, including its mother-tongue — the recognized key to cultural preservation. Such an addition to the Canadian Constitution will not only reflect the true situation, but will also help consolidate all Canadians and introduce understanding and co-operation among them.

Multicultural development

a)   The policy of Multiculturalism, through the advice of the Canadian Consultative Council on Multiculturalism, represents the views of all Canadian ethnic groups (French and British included) and, through the Minister of State for Multiculturalism, should be instrumental in influencing provincial governments to allow and subsidize "third" language education within the regular school curriculum. Some provinces already follow this system, but some provide this education after hours. Third language courses could be accepted as full credits for University admission. Where feasible, ethno-cultural centres could be created with the aim of training teachers in third-language instruction and providing multicultural study programs. Such centres would both be instrumental in and — at least in part — financially responsible for the development of teaching aids and curricula in the area of multiculturalism.

b)   Ethno-cultural groups could enjoy full support from federal and provincial governments to retain and develop their ethnic cultures and mother tongues.

c)   In our opinion there might be an Inter-Ethnic Research Institute created on the federal level and funded by the Department of Multiculturalism. The tasks and aims of this institution would be to engage in the study of all aspects of ethnicity in Canada.

Ethnic Groups and public boards and commissions

The membership on federal (and for that matter, provincial) boards and commissions should reflect a mosaic-like composition of society. This is based on the fact that the diversity of the origins and traditions of one-third of

Canadians has singularly endowed them with various qualities and perspectives which will allow them to make specific and valuable contributions to various decisions in which they may participate. Canada would be richer and stronger, at least internally, by being able to take advantage of the unique values and knowledge of *all* her people.

Canadians of origin other than English or French, who have proper qualifications (obtained through training and experience) can also contribute to the well-being of the country in economic and resource development. A scrutiny of present-day federal and provincial boards and commissions reveals scarcely any members belonging in the so-called "third group" of Canadians. Many promises from authorities to correct this sad state of affairs still remain unfulfilled.

Contributions of ethno-cultural communities and the school curricula

Representatives of the many cultures, races and traditions of which the Canadian people consists should be given ample opportunity to become acquainted with one another's cultures, to get to know their values and contributions to the mainstream of Canadian culture. This can only be achieved when all school curricula and materials prepared with federal and provincial assistance will reflect past and present achievements in various fields by Canadians of non-British, non-French background and their respective contributions. Understanding, knowlege and co-operation among Canadians of all descents and walks of life should begin in school.

Stereotyping (i.e., the "song and dance approach") should be avoided. Instead, the *real* contributions of ethnic groups in economic, scientific, cultural and other areas should be primarily stressed when speaking or writing about Canadian ethnic groups.

Forum for exchange of views

There is a need to provide a forum for the exchange of views among Canada's ethno-cultural communities in order to enhance understanding and co-operation. At present each group exists in "splendid isolation." We should strive to work closer with one another and to exchange our thoughts and views and explain our cultural heritage. Such a forum could be built up among these groups, with some government initiative and assistance if necessary.

The previous five categories seem to depict the most important aims and aspirations of the Polish groups in Canada in the context of Canada's home affairs. However, of importance to us are two other points which may be regarded in a different light by Canadians of other than Polish descent.

Human Rights, value and compliance

In today's world, where two political blocs oppose each other, each country must declare, according to the sentiments and views of its people, which position it takes on human rights. Canadians of Polish descent are primarily concerned with this issue and its application. The Helsinki Final Act, the resolutions of the Belgrade Conference of 1977 and the Madrid Conference — if they are not to remain as mere pieces of paper, but as aids in the fostering of Human Rights and Justice — must be strictly adhered to by all the signatory nations. Each of these peoples should not only introduce and obey these principles in its own sphere, but also monitor compliance with them by other signatories.

Our group continually advises the Canadian government about drastic violations of those rights by other countries and tries to induce our government to take a strong and clear position on this issue in international discussions.

This issue is of considerable importance to our group, of which many members were victims of persecution for their political beliefs before coming to Canada. It is our strong conviction that freedom and the integrity of sovereign nations can survive only if basic Human Rights are not only recognized but fully adhered to by all governments.

"Refugee" and the new Immigration Act

Polish Canadians, coming from a country where basic human rights are not adhered to, or are obeyed only when it suits the self-serving interests of the government party to do so, are deeply concerned with laws and regulations that deal with the free movement of people in general, and with a person's chances to emigrate to the country of his choice. We would also be strongly interested in all Canadian regulations which might help or prevent people from our homeland to find in Canada a haven from persecution. Several times our Canadian Polish Congress has called the attention of the Federal Ministers of Immigration to the fact that justice and the very principle of helping a human being who is in need of protection and assistance, demand a new approach to the concept and definition of "who is a refugee" for the purpose of Canadian immigration laws. Canada's Immigration Act has adopted the definition of "refugee" from the United Nations Refugee Convention and Protocol.

This seems right, but in reality, it is not satisfactory and does not take into account many categories of people who are seeking relief from intolerable social and political conditions in various areas of the world. The definition also fails to take into consideration the differing conditions and treatment of people by different political systems. The above definition does not serve its purpose, i.e., "to protect and assist innocent victims of persecution and oppression." In most cases the application of the above definition requires a special extended interpretation. Most especially the condition, "well-founded fear of persecution," contained in the definition of "refugee," is almost impossible for any person to meet. This impasse may lead to much arbitrariness by officials who make decisions. In most cases, the officials have no knowledge or understanding of the real conditions prevalent in the country from which a refugee comes. It is our strong conviction that Canada, whose population forms a mosaic of so many different peoples, needs her own definition of "refugee," that will reflect a deeply grounded sense of justice and a moral duty to help others in their hour of distress.

Conclusion

As mentioned above, there are many more points and facts to ponder, and in the everyday life of our group we continually do so. We believe it was sufficient to show in this paper only the most important and characteristic of our aims and aspirations. The consideration of these should enable all interested parties to get acquainted with the feelings and thoughts of our group.

254

NOTES OF AN ADDRESS TO CEESAC

Demetrius Manolakos, Edmonton
Past President, Greek Community, Montreal

I have noticed the organizers of the Conference have relieved this morning's dialogue from the obligation of discussing our "roots". And so, we can limit ourselves to the aims, aspirations, progress and realities of those communities with which we are identified. Our advancement is evident in what we have done — we no longer are embarrassed to speak the language of our fathers — we have set up language programs, maintained our schools and established ourselves in most Canadian universities.

Others have spoken and will speak on "aims" and "aspirations," and I feel almost every ethno-cultural group in Canada can identify with whatever has already been said or will be said on this score during the Conference.

I wish to concern myself with "realities," or should I say "reality" in the singular, because I feel that it too is common to all groups. Time does not permit me to be more explicit in developing this aspect or interpretation of the reality, and so, sacrificing the narrative, I will restrict myself to a series of statements about which I solicit your reflections and conclusions.

Since the turn of the century, and in spite of the efforts of government policies to the contrary, our Greek community is the only one which has seen itself grow from less than 2,000 persons in the year 1900 to 1% of the population in 1980.

In Quebec, we are more than an official minority and, although neglected in the past, we are now much sought after. Yet, we struggle futilely for rights, although this should never have been the case in the first place if one considers the treatment ethnic groups enjoy in other provinces.

The timidity of our community may perhaps be attributed to the humility that evolved naturally from the gratitude some have felt or were brought to feel, for the opportunity we and our forefathers were given in being permitted to come here. Our people came here when others would not come and, more often than not, to do work others would not do. Yet this work, industry, sacrifice, and determination to succeed proved to be the very foundation of this great nation.

The contributions of our community have seldom been the objects of credit or acclaim other than a passing acknowledgement for our hard work and perseverance. Canadian historians have minimized and continue to minimize our contributions and place in the history and development of this country.

255

On the other hand, our intellectuals, our scientists, our athletes, our inventors, our industrialists, our artists, our performers and our politicians are always identified as "Canadians" — but the rest of us remain mere "ethnics."

Whenever one of our communities endeavours to project itself or its influence, the so-called majority, as represented by government, quickly focuses on dissension within that community and, if it does not exist, will create it!

The most common response to any community from any level of government is: "You are divided — get together and we'll see!" Recent electoral results indicate the shortcomings of the system of representation, yet recommendations to date seldom include representation by community. We are not getting our share of appointments to government posts, crown corporations, the Senate, foreign service, diplomatic corps, agencies, boards, etc., but only receive token nominations to secondary bodies, often known only to the community and tantamount to minor political rewards. If we are good enough for ourselves and our own, we should be good enough for our country that we all love. Continued obstacles and difficulties, under any pretence whatsoever, discourage the community and constitute the only reality which, if not checked, will be destructive, so there will be no need or place left for aims and aspirations.

If my statements appear bold, I have made them so in the hope of provoking answers, responses and opinions from anyone who can provide different interpretations or successfully dispute them. I would especially welcome views from government representatives who may be present and whose answers could until now almost always be predicted in advance.

It is evident we have all grown tired of donning our ethnic costumes, doing our ethnic dances or painting our ethnic easter eggs to amuse anyone who would watch us — yes, we want to share our cultures and tradition, but we also demand what we are entitled to as Canadians.

THOUGHTS ON THE NATIVE PEOPLE

J. P. O'Callaghan,
Publisher, Edmonton Journal

Although it has been 40,000 years since the first Eskimos presumably walked across the ice bridge over the Behring Strait in search of a warmer climate and ended up in the Canadian Arctic, we have still not learned how to bring northern native people fully into the mainstream of modern Canadian life. We now call them Inuit instead of Eskimo, but rarely do we call them Canadians. It is appropriate, bearing in mind the place of my birth and the fact that we are two days away from St. Patrick's Day, to recall that the first European to hit the shores of what is now Canada was probably an Irishman, Brendan the Navigator. When you appreciate that the French and the English never set foot in Canada until 400 or 500 years ago, it is a little galling for the Inuit and the Indians and the descendants of Brendan the Navigator to hear the term "founding races" used to describe those johnny-come-lately French and English.

In parentheses, I ought to issue a hasty disclaimer at this point. When I refer to the descendants of Brendan the Navigator, I am speaking in somewhat general ethnic terms rather than specific relationships of the flesh, for Brendan was a worthy monk sworn to celibacy and even the loneliness of a long voyage across the storm-tossed Atlantic in his frail craft would not be of sufficient magnitude to tempt him from the path of righteousness. I do not know that, of course, but I either assume it in a hurry or risk the wrath of being drummed out of the church. What I do know is that droves of Brendan's countrymen followed him across the Atlantic, driven by chronic famine, the search for freedom from religious persecution and oppression, and the hunger for peace of mind.

When the Irish came to the United States in their thousands they took the menial jobs. They were referred to as the "white negroes" of America. As the generations passed, they moved upwards in that most mobile of societies. They took over the police forces of Boston and New York and Philadelphia. The Kellys and the Kennedys became the power brokers of politics and the Irish ceased to be the butt of ethnic jokes. Then it was the turn of the Italians, until the Italians started pushing into the territory of the elevated Irish. Then it was the Poles, and so on.

In Canada, each of the many immigrant peoples who have found sanctuary and a new life have found it difficult initially to be accepted as full-fledged Canadians. Their names, their accents, their colour, perhaps, betray them. One of the saving graces for the majority of Canadian immigration waves was the decision by Newfoundland to join Confederation. As John Crosbie demonstrated so eloquently during the 1980 election campaign, the so-called Newfie joke was turned on the tormentor. The wheel comes full circle as the Newfies start telling ethnic jokes about the Ontario WASPs. One could see the twinkle behind John Crosbie's glasses when he accentuated his Newfoundland origins.

The question of ethnicity, of pride and origin, is one that should be obscured in Canada, because we have chosen the mosaic, rather than the American melting pot, as our pattern of nationhood. But that mosaic is not always as static as it should be. If the two so-called founding races — to neither of which I belong — have lived side by side with only a small measure of tolerance throughout the four or five centuries in which they have dominated life on this half-continent, what role can other Canadians play in preventing the nation from splintering asunder? Those of us who were not born in Canada had made the deliberate choice to be Canadians and, having made that choice, must be Canadians in every sterling sense. Those of us who were born Irish can never understand the fierce attachment to the country we left behind on the part of those who have never set foot on the shore of Bantry Bay or seen the rubble where Nelson's statue used to stand on O'Connell Street in Dublin. Two days from now I will run for cover to escape these militant Irishmen who have never visited the country in which I was born. By choosing to become Canadian, rather than being Canadian by the accident or good fortune of birth, those of us who are not of the two founding races are better able to take recognition of the contribution made by all the others who have flowed into this country after the English and the French.

When the Ukrainians arrived to pioneer the West, to duplicate the Ukrainian grainfields in the inhospitable plains at the turn of the century, they were not burdening themselves with past history. Their history, so far as Canada was concerned, started the day they set foot on Canadian soil. They brought with them their language, their culture, their moral values, their way of life. They have maintained all those values, in some measure or other, to this day. They are truly Canadians, but they are Canadians conscious of their ancestry and anxious to preserve another heritage while acquiring and building a new one. The two views are compatible, as long as the old does not take precedence over the new. When some years ago, The Edmonton Journal ran a series called Roots, outlining the ethnic mix that had gone into the development of the city of Edmonton, it was quite significant to discover that at least one in every eight Edmontonians has a Ukrainian background. Close to 60,000 people can trace their origins back to the trickle of Ukrainian settlement that began in 1897. That trickle became a warm flood of pioneering humanity, a sturdy breed that conquered the harsh climate and the heartbreaking Prairie. All of which is intended as an indication that Canada owes nothing in particular to any one race, but owes everything to the collection of races and peoples who came together to fashion this nation. We were all foreigners once; we are all Canadians now.

Leaving aside, as history regrettably always seems to do, the original native people of Canada, the other ethnic roots that have been put down in this country in recent centuries have generally been European in origin. To some extent, that may be changing. What we may be seeing in future is the sort of society that is created by the intermingling of many races, many colours, many religions, all of them contributing to a much-changed way of life. That change may not always be for the better, but if society has learned anything, surely it must be that none of us can go back. In Edmonton alone, we once traced 27 different ethnic origins for the present-day population. Some claim it could be as high as 60. You are not going to solve any racial, ethnic and religious problems that Edmonton might have by forcing all 27 or 60 of Edmonton's ethnic groups back to wherever they emanated from.

If you think Edmonton is a cosmopolitan city, then take a look at Toronto. The 1871 census showed that the proportion of British-origin Torontonians was 96 per cent.

Today, according to a recent estimate by the *Toronto Star*, about 70 per cent of Metropolitan Toronto's 2.3 million people can trace their roots back to a country other than Britain. These 1.6 million people without British roots came from 70 countries, speak 56 languages and practise 25 religions. One of the smallest pockets consists of 3,000 Swiss. The 425,000 Italians, on the other hand, outnumber the total population of nearby Hamilton.

When Great Britain gave citizenship to all subjects of her former empire, she probably never anticipated that a world war and the speeded-up aftermath of a search for identity by many native peoples would lead to an immigration dash to her shores that for sheer concentration of numbers must have come close to anything experienced by the United States in the heyday of her settlement by those of European origin. Margaret Thatcher, before becoming prime minister, was promoting an end to a certain type of immigration, the one which played solely on the white Britons' fear of being swamped by West Indians. But is our record any better?

Back in September, 1906, *Saturday Night Magazine* had this to say:

This is a white man's country, and white men will keep it so. The slant-eyed Asiatic, with his yellow skin, his unmanly humility, his cheap wants, would destroy the whole equilibrium of industry. He would slave like a Nubian, scheme like a Yankee, hoard like the proverbial Jew.

Have Toronto the Good and Canada changed all that much in the intervening 73 years? Do we not still discreetly put quotas on those coming to our shores? When we took Asians, being expelled from Uganda by that over-stuffed madman, Idi Amin, did we not ensure that those who came were more likely to be from the professional classes than from the ranks of those who might just swell our over-burdened labor forces? When we appeared to be showing compassion for the unfortunate boat people of Asia, that generosity of nationhood was appallingly snuffed out by insufferable, insensitive protectors of what is purely and simply a white man's way of life. These bigots played on the fears of those who point to the ghettos of Detroit and Atlanta as something to be avoided in Canada. If they had their way, no doubt all those with black faces would be sent back to the jungles of Africa whence their ancestors had come. Or they would tell you Toronto would become a vital and viable city once again if all Portuguese or Italians were deported. Give them time and, no doubt, they will be advocating that the Inuit should make a forced march back across the Behring Sea.

Are we, in fact, Canadians, or are we just transplanted Irish, English, Scots, Germans, Ukrainians, West Indians, Americans or whatever, pining for countries we have long forsaken? Indeed, how stubbornly should we cling to our pasts? In every generation or so, we acquire some new ethnic group to add to our mosaic — Italians, Pakistanis, Uganda Asians, West Indians, Chileans and now Vietnamese and Cambodians have followed the earlier waves of British, Scots, Irish, Hungarians, Germans, Swedes, Danes, Finns, Norwegians, Ukrainians, Dutch, Greeks, Portuguese, Poles, Yugoslavs, Macedonians, Japanese, Chinese, Spanish, Koreans, Lebanese, Syrians and Filipinos. But the colourful pattern of the mosaic seems to glare harder on the eye. Some of the newcomers have a tendency to end up with their own nationalist enclaves, preserving their old ways, their old habits, their old associations. We seem to lack the chameleon instinct. How many generations does it take before the mosaic merges into a harmony of pattern, with the racial and nationalistic colours still distinct but intermingled in such a way that nobody can tell the players without a program? How many generations will pass this way, the memories of their journey blowing off into limbo, before we accept that this country belongs to all Canadians and that there are no special-status Canadians? How do we put tolerance into race and creed, without forcing newcomers, whether they come from Asia or Europe or Africa or South America, to homogenize their cultures? We have done it before, of course.

Providing a sanctuary is not a new idea in Canada, although there were mixed feelings about the decision of perhaps as many as 100,000 young Americans to come to Canada rather than to spill their blood for jingoistic reasons in the jungles of South-East Asia. That war is over. There was an amnesty of sorts that allowed some of that exiled army to go home, but a large proportion stayed here to add their contribution in decades to come to the strain that is crossbred and mixed and truly Canadian.

We absorbed these newcomers, just as we absorbed the misfortunate and the downtrodden who had made their way by the Underground Railway to escape the misery and slavery of the cotton fields of the southern United States. We took in the Mennonites and the Doukhobors when they were in need of freedom to practise their religion and to live their way of life without interference. It is an honourable tradition in this country to find space in its vast expanse for those who yearn for freedom of expression and religion. It is a haven for those who are at odds with a previous way of life and who seek peace, contentment, and the ability to make a life style with which others will not interfere.

It is a tradition that we cannot and will not abandon, despite the "knee-jerk" reaction of some of those now ensconced here who want to deny others the same sort of tranquility that they themselves were once granted. The reason why any of us is here in the first place owes more to the age-old search for a place to call home than it does to change. Some of us may be Canadians because our fathers or grandfathers or several generations removed made the conscious choice to come here. To that extent, we are fortunate.

I, for one, I suppose, could have found myself in Van Diemen's Land, descendant of a long line of misbegotten malcontents doomed to exile by Bloody Judge Jeffreys in times past. But I did not. I am here, a free man in a free country and at a loss only at finding myself as a member of this panel trying to find some way to come to grips with a subject that both troubles and perplexes me more for what it implies than for what it says. In the first place, I have to refer to a paragraph in the letter of invitation that says somewhat ominously: "We are looking forward to your address. It is always stimulating and challenging to hear the other side of the story." Until I read that, I had not realized I was on the other side, though that is not an unusual location for me to be on, although I prefer to believe it is the rest of mankind that is on the other side to me. Am I the only one in step?

To address myself to the question of whether or not minority groups feel there has not been fair reporting of ethnics in the press, let me repeat a story that John Brown, *The Journal's* ombudsman, told me. He said that in one spell of a couple of weeks *The Journal* had somehow managed to offend at least one Ukrainian, Briton, Italian, Chinese, Fijian, Ukrainian Catholic, Roman Catholic, Protestant and Jew. As John reported it: The Ukrainian objected to our putting the Ukraine in Russia. The Briton did not like being called a Brit in a headline. The Italian was upset by a satirical piece written by Charles Lynch, which said "the ruddy Italians" were destroying the Canadian cheddar cheese market. The Chinese and Fijian rightly took exception to court reports which mentioned race. The Ukrainian Catholic said we had wrongly described a member of his church as being a Roman Catholic. The Roman Catholic said the author of a series on the Pope was not a Catholic. The Protestant said there was too much on the Pope. Finally, a lady who told John Brown she was Jewish, said her Catholic friends would be offended by a headline which talked about the papal horse-race contenders.

Is this a case of general carelessness or insensitivity by *The Journal* or were some or all of these people over-reacting in relation to their origins? Can any of us be free of guilt, knowing that we all make judgments and assessments of others based on what we believe to be their race, colour, religion, origin or sometimes — when you are dealing with new-found power and wealth — even geographic location, if you are thinking in Ontario and Alberta terms? We fill our jails with Indians because we have failed to include them in the integration process. We have taken away their traditional way of life and refused to offer them instead a white man's culture that would, in any case, be alien to their ancestry, their upbringing, their history and their ability to assume a status that is carefully and assiduously denied them. And they, bear in mind, were here before the rest of us. Are we to repeat the mistake with the Vietnamese and all those who will follow? Are we going to refuse to let them be part of our society, to be truly Canadians?

I have been asked whether *The Journal* has a policy on reporting of minority groups. I am not sure what this is supposed to mean. In Edmonton, what is a minority group? Certainly not the Ukrainians, who number one out of every eight of us. Certainly not the Germans, who are almost as numerous. Certainly not the British, who top both the Germans and Ukrainians in number. By those standards, the Irish are a true minority, but we are always the odd man out. The French, one of our two founding races, are a true minority in Edmonton. The Fijians are a minority. The Metis are a minority. The Indians are a minority. The Vietnamese are the new minority. The Chinese are a minority. The Pakistanis are a minority. The blacks are a minority. We have no special policy on any of them. If they make news, we report it. Colour, race, religion and origin do not influence the standards by which news is judged. In a country fractured by geography and the desolation of distance, there is no such thing as a national press. Each newspaper is therefore the centre of its own universe, and that means we have to operate as though we live in the community we serve, because we do live there, and our readers live there, and we have to share our experiences with one another.

Our main function is to mirror our own community. We also exist to serve the needs of the community, to be the authoritative voice of the community. If our community includes minority elements, whether they be East

Europeans or East Indians, then as part of the process of reporting the community to the community we report on the newsworthy happenings within those minority groups. But we do not accord them special status. We do not identify them as being in need of special coverage that would not be accorded to larger ethnic groupings. So far as we are concerned, if they are Edmontonians we discuss and dissect their lives in print as Edmontonians. We do not do it because they are ethnically or racially in a minority, but simply because they are members of the community we serve. If any ethnic grouping feels it is in need of special reporting or coverage simply because of its origin, then that becomes the function for specialty publications. If you want to read a column in your own language because you have never mastered the language of your new country, then one supposes that the demand of numbers of like-minded citizens will lead to the establishment of some sort of publication to cater to that special interest, that special taste, that special language or culture requirement.

A daily newspaper is not a specialty publication. It is a smorgasbord that caters to many tastes, rather than an exclusive menu for special tastes. The man whose interests lie solely in reading about yachting will buy a magazine devoted to the subject. He does not expect his daily paper to do more than take a cursory look at what is to him a totally absorbing personal interest. A man who wants to see pictures of naked girls does not subscribe to a community newspaper for that purpose. He buys *Playboy* or whatever is the current vogue in that pop art. The newspaper lives or dies solely by its relationship with its community. If that community has an overwhelming grouping of any race, colour or creed whose interests tend to be similar, then the newspaper will reflect those interests in proportion to the total population it serves.

The newspaper cannot, and should not, serve special interests in a special way. It must be an organ of information and opinion without ever becoming an echoing chamber for propagandists. It reports life as it exists. In a complex society, it is impossible for the public to be present at everything in the public's interest. The newspaper is the public's surrogate. A newspaper has to lead its community, to examine everything, and to accept nothing without question.

A newspaper should be the champion and observer and critic of the community it serves. It must be a part of the vanguard of progress, interested in social justice and fair-mindedness. A newspaper is answerable to no one but its readers. It is a measure of a newspaper's quality if it is so tied to the community it serves that its readers feel they are a part of it. Our interests with our readers are mutual and indivisible. We record history on the run. We try to put our community in perspective as we gallop down the years. In recording that history we have to do more than recognize the presence of different languages and cultures and races and religions. We have to find the common factor that links them. We have to accept that if Canada is to become a truly united nation, there must be a connection between the various people and regions of this country that stems more from just trade and natural resources. We have to make people aware of regional realities and changing philosophies. We have to make them tolerant of differences existing between the groupings of all these minorities that come together to form one nation, one people.

I have been asked whether the mass media can help to educate the public about East Europeans in general. How do you educate a public to understand the history of its times?

Surely, after 83 years of colonization of the barren west by Ukrainians and by other Europeans who followed in the creaking echoes of their ox-carts, nobody has to be educated to the awareness of the place these settlers have commanded in the history of Alberta or of the West. It is recorded in their blood and sweat and tears. Certainly, it is in these parts. The pioneers of yesterday are the entrepreneurs and the benefactors of the society they have built. It is theirs to improve upon and to benefit from because they have invested their lives in its future. Perhaps Edmonton and Northern Alberta are somewhat different from most other Canadian cities and regions. No one ethnic strain dominates our mix of culture and heritage. Perhaps that is the key to the whole question of turning a collectivity of minorities into a city or nation of one people.

Recently, I received a letter from a woman in Ottawa which began: "Pierre Trudeau and myself are planning to be married." She went on to say that since arriving in Ottawa her mail has been intercepted and her phone calls tampered with, so she has not yet been able to reach Mr. Trudeau to break the news to him that she has already given exclusively to me. The same woman also told me that United Nations Secretary-General Kurt Waldheim, Governor-General Ed Schreyer and the Pope are all communists. I ask you! The Pope a communist? Sounds like a Polish joke.

Another letter-writer wanted to investigate *The Journal* because I had obviously taken bribes from the Tories to write a scurrilous piece about Mr. Trudeau. Obviously, the amount proffered by the Tories could not have been sufficient, because still another letter-writer told me my days were numbered because of what he believed was an insulting headline about Joe Clark. When I waded through the profanity in that letter, the conclusion I inevitably came to was that I was being told as politely as that particular anonymous letter-writer could manage that we have just lost another reader.

All of which is a roundabout way of saying that any newspaper — not just *The Journal* — is so close to its community that the nerve ends start to twitch on any given day when something is said or reported that gives offence to somebody within the community. Nobody is more aware of the shifting sands of public opinion than a newspaper. And nobody has a more exacting role to play in society than a newspaper that accepts the responsibility of holding the mirror up to the community it serves. We do not accept that responsibility lightly and I do not feel we have to apologize to any minority group for the manner in which we examine its way of life. Our reporting, to the best of our ability, will be as fair and as responsible as sensitive and feeling correspondents can make it. The newspaper and its community are inseparable just as long as the newspaper understands the expectations of its readers and attempts to match them. In setting out our wares for the public to examine and to select from on a daily basis in order to satisfy its appetite for information, news and entertainment, the newspaper must always be conscious of the ethnic interests of its readers, but not to the detriment of the total interests of its audience. I believe that *The Journal* is aware of its responsibilities in this direction and will always try to honour its obligation to serve those who subscribe to it.

Minorities, whether ethnic, religious or cultural, have their different approaches to the needs of coverage, but those approaches must be in proportion to the whole and not excessive in demand. In an age when we attempt to redress imbalances in society by diving into the pool of tokenism, I believe a newspaper must resist the temptation to tread water in order to appeal to limited interests. There is a need for variety and diversity in any newspaper, but there is also the overriding requirement of stability and purpose, and that requirement is not reached by putting too much caviar and too little beef on your smorgasbord table. The meal must do more than tempt the palate; it must provide sustenance and satisfaction as well. I hope those who glance over our table are prepared to concede us the privilege of accepting that we at least try to achieve that balance.

HERITAGE LANGUAGE PROGRAMS IN ALBERTA

Fiona Pelech, President
Northern Branch of the AELTA

There is no better way to mark Alberta's 75th anniversary than to review and report on the changes in status of our heritage languages — from the time when only one language was considered Canadian and those who spoke anything else were "foreigners;" from the time when parents were obliged to conceal their ethnicity to advance in society and life around them; from the time when only a few parents were able to teach their children their mother-tongue, to the time when Albertans can be proud of their roots and can speak or learn to speak as many different languages as they wish. Seventy-five years have produced many changes. We have matured, we have become more tolerant and understanding, we have become greater as a country.

To deal with all heritage languages would be an impossibility, and so to draw a line somewhere, I have chosen to limit myself by omitting the two official languages, English and French, (except for the French Saturday schools). The rest of the languages I shall try to cover briefly from kindergarten through adult education depending on the information available. No doubt, one may discover omissions, duplications perhaps, or errors in enrolments due to semesters, or careless records, but this is a beginning and more accurate reports in the future would be welcomed.

A quick review of regulations at the federal and provincial levels of government shows that in 1969 the *Report of the Royal Commission on Bilingualism and Biculturalism (Book IV)* recommended support to cultural groups other than those of British and French extraction, but this report emphasized "culture" and excluded languages. However, as time went on, because of certain political pressures as well as the realization culture could not exist without a language, our governments started to re-assess their outlook on the preservation and the development of culture. Our present-day emphasis on language is a relatively recent phenomenon.

In Alberta, some non-official languages were taught as second languages at the high-school level, but the passing of *Section 150 of the Alberta School Act in 1970* enabled these languages to be used as languages of instruction (see Appendix I).

During the 70s, however, languages had fallen out of fashion as require-ments at the university level, and so enrolments throughout all our school systems were low. Classes were offered only where sufficient registrations warranted them, and where the school boards were willing to provide such instruction. The following table shows comparative language enrolments in Alberta High Schools for the years 1977 to 1979.

Subject	1977-78	1978-79	Subject	1977-78	1978-79
Cree 15	22	27	Latin 10	89	161
Cree 25	7	3	Latin 20	24	30
Cree 35	7	–	Latin 30	14	13
German 10	1,509	1,423	Polish 15	10	14
German 20	790	810	Polish 25	11	4
German 30	509	513	Polish 35	3	8
German 31	12	9	Russian 15	6	–
Hungarian 15	16	11	Russian 25	5	–
Hungarian 25	2	5	Russian 35	3	–
Hungarian 35	4	5	Spanish 14	13	46
Italian 15	97	95			
Italian 25	38	59	Ukrainian 10	323	347
Italian 35	30	25	Ukrainian 20	218	213
			Ukrainian 30	119	157
			Ukrainian 31	8	11

Some time elapsed for the idea of "language of instruction" to get entrenched into the minds of prominent community workers. Then, as in pioneering times when Alberta played an important part in opening up the west, so today, Alberta is forging ahead in piloting many language programs.

The first bilingual class using Ukrainian as a language of instruction opened in January of 1974. Other classes followed with enrolment as given in the tables below.

More bilingual classes are possible with greater collective efforts on the part of the government and the public. Some major problems to be overcome are that

1. Many parents are not aware of the possibilities of heritage languages being taught. Public education is necessary through the media.
2. Some parents just do not care — they give birth to the child but let the community bring it up.
3. Someone has to start the ball rolling — a group of active dedicated people.
4. Children for a particular language class are usually widely scattered,

BILINGUAL
1979-80 ENROLMENTS

Edmonton Public

	K	1	2	3	4	5	6	T
Hebrew								
Talmud Torah		30	34	17	25	21	20	147
Ukrainian								
Holyrood	10	9	13	10	8	2	8	60
Rio Terrace			5	6	7		10	28
Rundle	12	11	14	19	13	23	15	107
Northmount		11	10	6	9			36
Delwood	18	16	23	23	18	9	11	118
German								
Forest Heights		11						11
Rideau Park		23						23

Edmonton Separate

	K	1	2	3	4	5	6	T
Ukrainian								
St. Bernadette		14	12	5				31
St. Martin		33	24	27	25	19	18	146
St. Matthew		27	36	31	26	14	25	149

Calgary Public

	K	1	2	3	4	5	6	T
Yiddish/Hebrew								
I. L. Peretz		10	15	16	11	14	8	74
Calgary Hebrew		43	38	38	37	34	41	231

so that transportation is a major problem.

5. Some parents are faced with paying fees that are quite high, on top of educational taxation. Added to transportation costs, this becomes a sizable amount each month. Thus, certain income groups are eliminated.

6. Accommodation is not always provided in a suitable area. The same classroom used by several teachers raises definite problems.

7. Qualified teachers are not as easily obtainable as they are for regular courses. They have to be specialized, but training centres are scarce.

8. Audio-visual materials are often lacking and have to be assembled from scratch, usually by an already overworked teacher.

9. Study programs need to be developed by qualified personnel.

10. Books, workbooks. and so on, are not always readily available.

The *Alberta Cultural Heritage Conference* held in Edmonton June 16-18, 1972, did much to promote culture, with emphasis on the language. In his closing speech at the conference on Sunday, June 18, the Hon. Horst A. Schmid said:

> Culture is many things — Language, Music, Dance, Drama . . . The man who tries to disassociate himself from his past is an unknown to himself . . . and in many ways, he rebels against the unknown. He lacks a sense of belonging — a sense of continuity with his own people. Yet he who will not recognize that culture is also a changing living thing is likewise at war with himself and with society. He is chained to the past and forever at odds with the present, a source of great unhappiness to himself, a stumbling block to his children and his neighbors.

This first conference was a great success, having been organized into working committees dealing with the many areas affecting culture. As a final outcome of this gathering, a set of recommendations was prepared for the Minister to consider and present to the government.

As usual, the Hon. Minister acted quickly and within a few months Position Paper #7 was passed, effective November 1972 (see Appendix 2). Three resolutions stand out:

1. The establishment of a Cultural Heritage Council representative of all ethno-cultural groups in Alberta.
2. The publication of a Cultural Heritage periodical.
3. The establishment of an office to co-ordinate the development of ethno-cultural programs in Alberta.

The *Cultural Heritage Council* meets at least four times a year in different parts of the province to work with the people of that area. Various committees within the Council meet more often to deal with their specific problems. On February 8-10, 1980 the Council met in Edmonton to hear the recommendations of the Language and Educational Committees. Problems from the various schools were brought forth, discussed, and will eventually reach the Ministers in the form of recommendations to our government. The wheels of government are usually slow, but it is the people behind the wheels who get things going, and Alberta is forging ahead.

In 1974 the *Alberta Heritage Day Act* proclaimed the first Monday in August each year as a special day to recognize and celebrate the cultural heritage of Alberta. Because of the success of these celebrations, Edmonton extended its festivities to two days last year. One visitor to this event exclaimed, "There are so many interesting people here, such a richness of various cultures. Most people don't have access to that." It is important to remember that our language schools, supported by various organizations and grants from Alberta Culture, play an important part in these Heritage Day festivities. They are the ones that add colour, action, laughter, music and youthfulness to the pageantry. They are the ones that have to possess facilities for many languages. Their students no longer live in small communities and travel on foot. They are part of a multicultural, multilingual environment. We cannot deny our youth the right to learn second or third languages.

Another welcome government move in support of languages was the first *Ethno-Cultural Language Teachers' Seminar* that was sponsored by the Cultural Heritage Branch of Alberta Culture on March 11-13, 1977. Involved were 65 language schools enrolling more than 4,000 students, with thirteen different languages: Arabic, Chinese, Croatian, French, German, Greek, Hebrew, Hungarian, Hindi, Italian, Polish, Portuguese, and Ukrainian.

Many of these schools had done highly commendable work for more than 50 years, often in difficult situations and with very limited resources. Even teachers without training had given valuable service because of their competence in the language and devotion to their ethnic values. The Alberta Cultural Heritage Branch decided to give these teachers of Saturday and evening classes the recognition they rightly deserved. The Department of Education felt that by encouraging the teachers to attend the seminar, they could get the teachers to share experiences and problems so they would not feel alone in their work.

The seminar program included panel presentations, group discussions, question periods and the formulation of recommendations. Panels were conducted by specialists in language teaching, by parents and teachers involved in the language schools, by staff from Alberta Culture, and the Departments of Education and Advanced Education and Manpower. Resource persons from various language schools as well as representatives from the Edmonton Public and Separate School systems and the Federal Department also participated. The main areas of concern were:

1. Motivation — attracting and keeping students in regular attendance, obtaining effective parental co-operation, etc.
2. Teacher training — methods, self-improvement, etc.
3. Resources — funds, facilities, equipment, supplementary materials.

As a result of this seminar, an *Alberta Ethnic Language Teachers' Association* was incorporated on August 10, 1978 with the North and South Branches working in their own areas.

Though these ethno-cultural schools have been in operation for years, government authorities have given them support and recognition only since 1974. To date, these schools seem to go under several names: Saturday Schools, Heritage Language Schools, Language Support Program Schools, or Private Schools that fall under Category 3 of the Alberta Private Schools regulations effective March 22, 1978. Whatever the name, they have performed well in the past, and one hopes they will do even better in the future. (Appendix 3 presents more specific information regarding these schools.)

Further Education (see Appendix 4) classes were created by adults who felt a need to learn not only their own cultures but also that of others. Somewhere in their earlier education they missed that which is important to them now as mature Canadians. Is it that our school system is not doing enough? We have the kindergarten, elementary and high schools, accredited ethno-cultural private schools (see Appendix 5), further education, and colleges all trying to do their jobs. Perhaps there is not enough incentive for enrolment. Have our universities throughout the province eased up on language requirements for entrance, with the result that the general public places a very low priority on language study compared with other subjects?

Languages do not constitute a barrier or a threat, but are an asset, a source of cultural enrichment and a bridge to better business and cultural relations within our country and abroad. The need is increasing for Canadians to have second-language skills in order to function as effective members of the international community, whether in matters of trade and commerce, diplomacy and culture or, indeed, increasingly in humanitarian enterprises. The university, therefore, is in a unique position to take the broader view and show leadership by providing an incentive for language learning.

But this is easier said than done! Our universities cannot instantaneously impose a language requirement upon their students without some understanding of the public school systems — the "feeder" schools, as it were. And so action was started in 1979 when the Canadian Senate's Executive Committee created its Ad Hoc Committee on Second Languages, which reported on its findings. The situation was considered serious enough to create a Task Force to look into the matter further and provide recommendations for all educational bodies concerned.

Canada is not alone in this serious situation. The following quotation from the *Information Bulletin* of the Information Centre for Teachers of German at the Goethe Institute, Toronto, stated on page 1 of the most recent issue:

> The commission created by President Carter to study the situation of foreign languages in the U.S.A. has now submitted its report. According to this report only 15% of all high school students learn a foreign language (1965: 24%). Only one in twenty high school students who chose a foreign language, studies this language for more than two years. Only one in twelve colleges has a language requirement for admission (1964: 3 in 12; 1915: 85%). The report calls this situation 'scandalous.' It makes 130 recommendations for improvements of the situation; the first one is the

reintroduction of language requirements. The American commission comes to the conclusion: 'Language learning can no longer be thought of as a frill, when one in eight jobs in industry and one in five in farming depend on foreign trade.'

In the United States, at least 100 languages are spoken, in addition to English; in the Soviet Union, despite state control and the predominance of Russian, some 70 languages have had to be recognized as vehicles for teaching; in India, there are 15 national official languages and more than 50 languages in all; in Guatemala, some 20 languages; Brazil has 250 spoken languages; Nigeria has 513; and Canada claims 2 official languages with only tokenism for other languages.

Plurilingualism can enhance the quality of one's life. Knowing one's native language in addition to the daily working language, and being in full possession of one's own culture and identity as one of a people, tends to make one open-minded to universal perspectives. As well, knowing three or four languages multiplies one's area of understanding even more.

In that case, perhaps the authorities would:

1. Invite the media to emphasize the need for more language learning because of the global environment we live in today.
2. Have universities make languages a requirement in most, if not all, faculties.
3. Ask for more co-ordination between education agencies so that there is continuity and no discrimination in language learning.
4. Encourage the learning of the mother tongue first, since such learning comes naturally (A parrot squawks before it talks!).
5. Ask universities to provide more staff to train prospective teachers in "methods of teaching a language." Today's graduates concentrate on other courses at university, while languages are only a frill. It is when they start teaching that the problems surface and they cry for more help. After almost no publicity, the Alberta Ethnic Language Teachers' Association (Northern Branch) registered 34 teachers on the first night (February 20, 1980) of their workshop on methods.
6. Provide immersion classes during breaks for teachers who cannot attend method classes during week-days.
7. Provide scholarships for additional teacher training in languages.
8. Organize two-week immersion classes for a particular language for students too widely scattered to be transported daily.
9. Continue exchanges to broaden cultural perspectives.
10. Help provide classrooms in which the atmosphere would be comparable to that of other classrooms. Bare walls, lack of audio-visual aids, and the moving of materials in and then out at the end of a

lesson are not conducive to language learning.

11. Arrange for experienced personnel to travel the province assisting in the organization of language classes.

12. Improve the public's awareness of language learning and get them to reflect on their sense of values — materialism vs. education.

13. Assist in curriculum development and help standardize programs.

14. Provide more ethno-cultural TV programs in various languages to broaden our cultural outlooks.

15. Expect federal subsidy of transportation costs.

16. Arrange inter-provincial meetings for the development of better co-operation in working out programs.

17. Equalize government financial support for all languages and allow individuals to choose languages of instruction.

18. Expect our governments to place more emphasis on cultural studies of our people for better understanding.

19. Support the recommendations of the Language and Education Committees of the Senate and the Alberta Cultural Heritage Council.

20. Expect other government bodies to develop policies in keeping with those practised by Alberta Culture.

21. Entrench in the constitution the rights of Canadians of other than British or French heritage. There should be equal opportunities and support provided for all citizens to preserve and develop their cultures.

Language learning is a life-long process. Familiarity with several languages results in familiarity with the interesting and fascinating cultures of people in one's community. There is no monotony for a plurilinguist in a multicultural society!

APPENDIX 1

The School Act, 1970 — Other Languages as the Language of Instruction

Section 12

(1) In addition to his other powers specified in this Act the Minister may make regulations

(b1) Governing the use of any other language other than English or French as the language of instruction.

(2) The Minister may

(a) prescribe

(i) Courses of study or pupil programs or both, and

(ii) instructional materials, and

(b) approve any course of study or pupil program submitted to him by a board, but instruction in the course of study or pupil program shall not commence without the prior approval of the Minister in writing.

Section 150

(1) a board may authorize

(b) that any other language be used as a language of instruction in addition to the English language, in all or any of its schools.

Regulations for Instruction in a Language Other Than English or French:

The School Act pursuant to Section 12, sub-section (1), clause (b1), 1979

1. (1) A board shall not commence a program that offers instruction in any language other than English or French in a school unless it:

a. passes and delivers to the Minister a resolution authorizing the use of any language other than English or French as a language of instruction, and

b. makes provision satisfactory to the Minister for the use of English as the language of instruction for all pupils who would normally attend the school and whose parents desire such instruction.

2. The courses of study and instructional materials for the program shall be those prescribed or approved by the Minister pursuant to section 12 (2) of the School Act.

2(1) A Board shall ensure that English is used as the language of instruction for not less than 50% per day for each pupil.

APPENDIX 2

New Directions Position Paper on Alberta's Cultural Heritage

Alberta's people are representative of many divergent cultural backgrounds, and this fact is recognized by the Government of Alberta. The Government recognizes also that "every people has a characteristic culture of its own; and, ultimately, many cultures, evolving together, produce a distinct and new culture."

The Government believes that Alberta should now carefully assess the riches of the cultural wealth of its peoples, and give direction to the full utilization of this human heritage.

Because our heritage is real, because it is the sum and substance of our social expression, reaching into the distant past, influencing our lives today, pre-shaping the lives of the children of tomorrow, the Government convened a Cultural Heritage Conference in June of 1972. Representatives of over fifty ethno-cultural groups attended and their concerns, hopes and aspirations were brought forward and discussed.

Some people live under the impression that diversity of language and cultural expressions divide and weaken. The declared intent of our cultural heritage policy is that our diversity of cultural riches shall be a binding tie of unity and an increasing source of pride to our people.

The more specific objectives to which our Cultural Heritage policy is to be directed:

(1)   To give Albertans increasing pride and identity as a people.

(2)   To unite us in singular strength through understanding of our individual ethno-backgrounds; the sharing of our cultural diversity and richness, and appreciation of our evolving identity.

(3)   To preserve the cultural wealth of our past: the rites, arts, music, etc. of our native peoples; the old-world contributions of our immigrant settlers; the songs, dances, social ways that each ethno-group brought by way of cultural dowry to this new land and which, in many cases, is becoming a common cultural mosaic, uniquely our own.

(4)   To stimulate the living arts — painting, dancing, music, handicrafts, the human drama — precisely because of our diversity of heritage background, and thus help Alberta's writers, musicians, dramatists, dancers, etc. to national and international acceptance, appreciation and recognition.

At the previously mentioned Cultural Heritage Conference held in June, delegates passed many resolutions that would, with their implementation, affect many departments of Government. Among those high on the priority list of the delegates to the Cultural Heritage Conference were the following:

(1)   The establishment of a Cultural Heritage Council representative of all ethno-cultural groups in Alberta. This Council would consider and recommend programs for the development and preservation of our Cultural Heritage in Alberta.

(2)   The publication of a Cultural Heritage periodical to provide a medium for the exchange of information among the various ethno-cultural communities in Alberta and the government. It is proposed that, initially, this publication would be a bi-

monthly magazine, drawing the attention of Albertans generally to the color, drama, and richness of the cultural past, and providing a vehicle of communication among the various cultural groups of the province.

(3)   The establishment of an office within the Department of Culture, Youth and Recreation to co-ordinate the development of ethno-cultural programs in Alberta.

The Government of Alberta has accepted these priority resolutions and declares them to be in effect as of this date.

It should be emphasized that this declaration of the government's position in regard to its cultural heritage is in keeping with the human freedom of its peoples, a fluid and free policy — a springboard for natural development of the cultural richness of our people.

The overall aim of this new cultural heritage policy is to preserve that part of our cultural past worthy of preserving, enrich our cultural present, and enhance Alberta's cultural tomorrow. November, 1972.

APPENDIX 3

The *Language Support Program*, commonly referred to as "Saturday Schools," is administered by Alberta Culture. Its aim is to assist language programs in the ethno-cultural language schools of Alberta. Ethno-cultural language schools are defined as those schools operated for, and administered by, ethno-cultural organizations with instructional classes held outside the public or separate school system. Grants are based on the number of students enrolled in a particular language school. In 1976 the grant amounted to $15.00 per student; for the 1978-79 fiscal year the amount was $20.00 per student.

To be eligible for a grant, language schools must offer a minimum of 50 instructional hours per school year and students must attend at least 60% of the total classes. Organizations are eligible for only one grant per year under the Language Support Policy. There are no age restrictions for this program and language courses have been offered from the kindergarten to the adult level; however, the majority of students enrolled in such programs appear to be elementary school children.

This program has grown quite considerably since its inception. In 1974, the first year of the program, there were 13 language schools in operation throughout the province with a total enrolment of 1,158 students. During the 1978-79 school year 4,453 students were enrolled in 71 Saturday Schools.

LANGUAGE SUPPORT PROGRAM SUMMARY

Year	Grant Per Student	Language Schools in Operation	Students Enrolled	Total Grant Awarded
1974-75	$15.00	13	1,158	$17,370.00
1975-76	$16.50	43	2,750	$45,375.00
1976-77	$16.50	65	4,321	$71,122.50
1977-78	$18.00	75	4,173	$75,114.00
1978-79	$20.00	71	4,453	$89,060.00
1979-80	$22.00	79	4,651	$102,322.00

In 1980, the following schools were registered with the Alberta Cultural Heritage Branch, offering instruction to 4,651 students:

LANGUAGE SUPPORT PROGRAM
1979/80

School	*Students*
Calgary	
Arabic Islamic Cultural School	199
Canadian Christian Association of the Middle East	—
Bengali Language School	28
Calgary Chinese School (Mandarin)	105
Calgary Chinese Public School (Cantonese)	128
Calgary Croatian Catholic School	44
German Canadian Club Language School	137

Gurdwara Shriguru Singh Sabha – Punjabi (India)	26
Dante's School of Italian Language	177
Metro Edmonton Japanese Community School	54
Polish, Henryk Sienkiewicz's School	152
Portuguese Language Program	167
Holy Cross Ukrainian School	24
St. Andrew's Cultural Program – Ukr.	63
St. Basil's Sadochok (Kindergarten) – Ukr.	56
St. Elia's Ukrainian School	10
St. John's Ukrainian School & Day Care Centre	39
St. Michael's Ukrainian Language School	24
St. Nicholas Parish Cultural Classes – Ukr.	13
Ivan Franko School of Ukr. Studies	59
Ukrainian School of St. George's Parish	48
Ukrainian Language Arts Society of St. Basil's	65
St. Josaphat's Cathedral Ukrainian School	18
Ukrainian Youth Association Language School	11

Additional
Edmonton Talmud Torah – Hebrew	208

Northern Alberta
Lac La Biche Muslim Assoc. Language School, Arabic	72
"Le Coin Des Lutins" – Bonnyville – French	23
Pineview Cultural Heritage Society – Ft. Sask. French	19
Grassland Ukrainian Language Association – Grassland	77
Holy Trinity Ukrainian Language School – Vegreville	25
New Kiew School – Ukrainian (Vegreville)	18
Peace River Ukrainian Language School	10
Troyanda – Ukrainian (Grande Prairie)	18
Ukrainian Orthodox Language School – Vegreville	29

LANGUAGES OFFERED BY ETHNO-CULTURAL LANGUAGE SCHOOLS
(Comparative figures for 1977-78 and 1978-79)

Language	No. of Schools in 1977-78	No. of Schools in 1978-79	% of Total No. in 1977-78	% of Total No. 1978-79
Ukrainian	21	22	28.0	31.1
German	11	10	14.7	14.2
French	6	5	8.0	7.1
Arabic	3	4	4.0	5.7
Chinese	4	4	5.3	5.7
Hebrew	4	3	5.3	4.2
Hungarian	3	3	4.0	4.2
Italian	4	3	5.3	4.2
Japanese	2	3	2.7	4.2
Croatian	2	2	2.7	2.8
Greek	2	2	2.7	2.8
Polish	4	2	5.3	2.8
Swedish	2	2	2.7	2.8

Bengali	–	1	—	1.4
Cree	1	1	1.3	1.4
Hindi	2	1	2.7	1.4
Korean	–	1	—	1.4
Lithuanian	1	1	1.3	1.4
Portuguese	2	1	2.7	1.4
Slovak	1	–	1.3	—

APPENDIX 4

Further Education Courses

In 1978-79, there were 82 Further Education Councils in Alberta. Through these Councils, general interest courses for the public such as Chinese cooking, pottery, languages, etc. are co-ordinated and then submitted for approval to the Further Education Branch of the Department of Advanced Education and Manpower. Normally, a further education course may not exceed 100 hours, must have a minimum of eight participants and is funded on the following basis:

English as a second language: $14.00 per hour
Other languages and courses: $ 6.00 per hour

Until January 1, 1979, French as a second language was funded at a higher rate, because it was considered part of the Citizenship Instruction Agreement and cost-shared by the federal government. From then onward, French has been funded at the same rate as other second languages.

Reliable files (Further Education Claim Forms, upon which the statistical data in this summary are based, were introduced in 1975) were only available for a three-year period, 1975-1978. The following figures may be of interest:

ENROLMENTS AND FURTHER EDUCATION GRANTS FOR NON-CREDIT FRENCH AND NON-CREDIT OTHER LANGUAGE COURSES

	NON-CREDIT FRENCH		NON-CREDIT OTHER LANGUAGE	
Year	No. of Students	Total Further Education Grant	No. of Students	Total Further Education Grant
1975/76	1,569	$50,064.00	2,656	$30,532.00
1976/77	2,259	$62,009.38	2,820	$36,369.00
1977/78	1,601	$41,422.00	1,920	$21,274.00

ENROLMENTS AND NON-OFFICIAL LANGUAGE COURSES
OFFERED BY FURTHER EDUCATION

Languages	Courses 1975-76	Throughout 1976-77	Alberta 1977-78	Enrolments 1975-76	Throughout 1976-77	Alberta 1977-78
Arabic	2	2	–	17	18	—
Blackfoot	–	1	–	—	11	—
Cantonese	–	2	1	—	28	12
Chinese	10	3	–	87	31	—
Cree	9	7	14	127	82	148
Czech	1	2	–	11	16	—
Danish	6	6	4	103	71	63
Dutch	5	5	3	86	70	50
Esperanto	2	2	–	18	16	—
German	37	47	25	500	586	369
Greek	4	2	1	79	31	21
Hungarian	2	1	–	19	8	—
Icelandic	2	1	–	22	15	—
Italian	4	6	1	66	84	21
Japanese	5	7	5	59	79	54
Mandarin	–	1	–	—	8	—
Norwegian	5	6	1	100	91	21
Polish	–	2	–	—	18	—
Portuguese	1	2	–	8	17	—
Russian	6	4	3	72	47	28
Slovak	2	1	–	24	8	—
Spanish	50	86	53	909	1,223	852
Swedish	9	8	8	135	104	106
Ukrainian	16	12	12	206	158	175
Urdu-Hindi	1	–	–	8	—	—

APPENDIX 5

Accredited Ethno-Cultural Language Schools

The following Alberta ethno-cultural schools offered accredited courses during the past year, 1978-79:

Schools	Students Enrolled
Calgary French School	5
Calgary Italian School	11
German Language School, Edmonton	19
German Language School of Calgary	53
German School Edelweiss, Edmonton	107
Ivan Franko School of Ukrainian Studies, Edm.	81
Lang. School of the German Can. Club, Calgary	73
St. John's H.S. Ukr. Lang. Immersion, Edm.	60
Westend German Language School, Edmonton	77

To become accredited, a school must fulfil certain regulations outlined in the policy made public by the Director of Special Educational Services in March, 1977.

ALBERTA EDUCATION POLICY REGARDING THE ACCREDITATION OF PRIVATE LANGUAGE SCHOOLS

Private Language Schools may be approved to recommend for high school credits in a senior high school second language course provided that:

1. Only teachers with a valid Alberta teaching certificate are employed to teach any course for high school credit.
2. The course of study in the language offered by the private language school is either a provincially or locally produced course approved by the Minister of Education.
3. At least 13 hours of instruction time be given for each high school credit offered (a five-credit course would require 65 hours).
4. The private school has submitted a senior high school registration form (SR1) which has been approved by an official of Alberta Education.
5. At the end of each school year or semester the principal of the private school submits in writing a list of pupils to the Director of Data Processing and Student Evaluation indicating for each pupil the course and the number of credits for which the pupil is recommended.
6. No high school credits obtained through study at a private language school will be entered on a pupil's high school record until the pupil has registered in a high school and has completed the work of the appropriate grade. For example:

Credits Awarded In	Year of High School Completed
French 10, French 11, German 10, Ukrainian 10, Cree 15, Hungarian 15, Italian 15, Polish 15, Russian 15	Grade 10
French 20, French 21, German 20, Ukrainian 20, Hungarian 25, Italian 25, Polish 25, Russian 25	Grade 11
French 30, French 31, German 30, German 31, Ukrainian 30, Ukrainian 31, Hungarian 35, Italian 35, Polish 35, Russian 35.	Grade 12

COMMUNITY AND THE GOVERNMENT: A DIALOGUE

Manfred Prokop,
University of Alberta

I am very grateful to CEESAC for having been given the opportunity to articulate concerns I have had for some time about the state of multiculturalism and its acceptance in our society.

As part of my contribution to this panel discussion, I sought out the opinions of most of the leading personalities in the German community of Edmonton on the question of the relationship between the community and government. I am happy to report that there was, on the whole, a definite feeling of satisfaction with the amount and quality of government assistance and with the extent to which the aspirations of the German ethnic community are being realized. Now, this is not to say there were no criticisms or suggestions for the future, but the attitude of both levels of government was acknowledged as being helpful, co-operative and accommodating. I have incorporated the concerns and suggestions of these people into the following remarks.

Some of my comments will address the larger question of the realizability of ethnic aspirations, but I would prefer to zero in on special approaches to specific problems as they have been perceived by these leaders in the community and by myself. They can be divided into thoughts (1) on the qualitative development of activities of ethnic groups, (2) on the development of communication within ethnic groups, and (3) on the development of communication from and about ethnic groups to the public at large.

Starting with number three, I submit to you that the traditional approach to the preservation and cultivation of the ethnic heritage has put too much emphasis on preservation, on reflecting the community upon itself. What I mean is that activities are arranged, documents collected and festivities organized by an ethnic group for the benefits of its own members or for other subgroups of the same ethnic community. In my opinion, there have been too few systematic attempts on our part to open up to other ethnic communities, to establish communication among the various ethno-cultural identities which, it is claimed, make up the Canadian mosaic. And yet, has not the ultimate goal of a multicultural policy been to get to know one another, hoping that by knowing others we get to know ourselves better, with the side benefit that we may become more acceptant of each other? But we have, in too many cases, encapsulated ourselves by restricting the language in which we communicate to an ethnic language, by organizing activities which are oriented specifically towards our own cultural group.

Now, I am not saying this approach should be completely abandoned, and not for a minute do I propose abandoning the preservation, use and teaching of ethnic languages — it is the emphasis I would like to see shifted towards more effective inter-group communication, away from a reverent staging of folkloristic events that have little to do with the contemporary situation in "the old country," and towards a self-portrayal of the basic values on which our ethnic culture rests.

To all of us, I am sure, culture is more than a collection of folksongs, a dress, a poem, a cathedral — it is much more than that: it is the sum total of ways of thinking, believing, feeling and acting which characterizes a people in addition to physical achievements and appearances. Getting others to know us therefore means communicating our knowledge of ourselves, our values, priorities, our perspectives on life. These are the features which really differentiate among cultures, not just the external trappings. Otherwise we will raise a generation of students who, after having travelled in Germany, tell us upon their return: "Well, they are no different from us, they wear blue jeans, they want fast cars, they eat Big Macs. What do you want — they are like us, just like us." Well, they are not "just like us," as we know. They do differ from the Canadian "mainstream," if there is such an accepted construct, in the deeper strata of their social perceptions, in the way they react to family and friends, to authority and respect, to love and death and so on. And here the "ethnics" can make their valuable contribution. By letting others know how they think, feel and act; how they judge the issues, we are all confronted with a choice between alternatives, a choice of futures from which we can pick the more intelligently.

I should like to suggest as the number one priority, therefore, that the communities as well as various levels of government direct more attention to the *communication of ethnic cultures towards the public at large.* This aim can be achieved in the media and in organized enterprises such as exhibitions, lecture series, extension and evening courses. It can be approached by making materials available in the form of culture capsules as they are produced in Ontario and as they are envisaged by the Alberta Heritage Council for optional use in schools. The print media could offer special sections on other countries, their culture, their economy, their educational and political systems as is done routinely in many European newspapers. The *Financial Times*, some time ago, presented an excellent special section on Germany which many of you will probably have seen.

In conjunction with this plea, government could play a major role in *fostering an attitude of openness, receptivity, even curiosity towards other cultures*, rather than encourage the orchid-like blooming of a culture in some backroom of a museum or community hall.

Thirdly, an ethnic community's self-understanding and projection can be increased by the *organization of conferences and lectures* like those organized by CEESAC where aspects of traditional as well as contemporary culture are critically examined.

Fourth, we need to *prevent the ossification of culture* which results from its being closed off in itself and from the "homeland," the result of which is a petrified piece of folklore that resides, so to speak, in a museum all year, to be taken out and paraded around only on Heritage Day. The goal of avoiding this fossilization of culture in our own communities can be achieved by increased contacts with the "homeland" as they are afforded by lecture tours of speakers who can speak with authority to the ethnic community as well as the Canadian public at large on issues in contemporary culture in the "old country." In the German community, this would mean increasing co-operation with such institutions as the German Academic Exchange Service of the Federal Republic of Germany or the Goethe-Institute, both of which frequently send lecturers across the continent in search of an audience. Co-ordination of efforts here is often very poor indeed.

Additional exposure of German contemporary culture can be obtained by making the many valuable "Internationes" tape program and audio-visual packages available on a wider basis. At present, they are usually buried in some school or university library for use once a year, if at all. If the collection were housed, for example, at ACCESS and were available on a duplicate loan basis, then schools, ethnic organizations and individuals could use that regional institution as a clearing-house or media library like a Centennial Library for the entire province. As regards the expenses involved, the Federal Republic of Germany contributes these programs to all interested and qualifying institutions on a no-cost basis; some assistance in the delivery of these materials and services by our government would represent a fair share and, of course, a borrower would be expected to pay a reasonable user's fee.

Similarly, and this may sound rather futuristic, but it is certainly feasible, the government may consider establishing a pay-TV and radio network via satellite or cable in which the community at large can receive (for a fee, of course) the programs of the *Deutsche Welle* short-wave broadcasts in English and German, and of other ethnic groups on a regular basis. Is there a demand for this service, at all? Well, I have been given to understand that Edmonton, on a per capita basis, has the largest number of students enrolled in bilingual and immersion programs in French, German, Ukrainian, Cree and Hebrew on the entire continent, and I also know there is a consistent demand for a news service: the German Cultural Exchange Association provided a phone service from 1978 to 1980 which, via the number 432-2344, each day played a recording of the latest news from the *Deutsche Welle*. An average weekly rate of about 180 calls was recorded for these two years!

The purpose of a better understanding of other cultures could be furthered by an explanation of travel and study/exchange programs which could offer scholarships and bursaries limited to non-native speakers of the language. Here again, the emphasis would be on getting to know the other culture directly, as for example, was the case with the Contact Germany/Contact Canada program which the Federal Government ran a few years ago.

In my second area of concern, *increased communication among the members of one's own ethnic group*, I would suggest that governments expand exchange programs between German Clubs. For example, on exchange between students from Kitchener who could visit Edmonton for a few weeks in June with a return visit of Edmontonian youths in Kitchener is an excellent means of fostering a better understanding of various ethnic groups within Canada. Similar programs at the university level such as those already in existence in Quebec would also be highly desirable.

The ethnic community's efforts to communicate with its own members and with the public at large also deserve more support, for the production and printing of newsletters or monthly issues of a club paper has become increasingly expensive. Although grants from Alberta Culture are very gratefully acknowledged by the *Alberta Echo*, for example, a distribution formula for grants based on the number of club or organization members up to such and such a percentage of the total costs would probably be fairer than present practice. That way, large organizations with many members and higher publication and mailing costs would receive more money than a small organization with only a one-page newsletter. Precedents for such a distribution formula exist on the federal level (SSHRC). The publication and mailing of a monthly calendar of events to ethnics and the public at large would represent an extremely efficient way of communicating an ethnic group's activities.

I am now turning to my third area of concern, the *development of ethnic activities and programs*, and here much attention should be given to an improvement in the status of teaching ethnic languages in non-institutionalized as well as in institutionalized settings.

In particular, increased effectiveness of ethnic language schools or Saturday schools could be obtained by encouraging their merger. This coming-together would allow streaming of children according to backgrounds and abilities and therefore would facilitate more effective instruction. I realize the community itself would have to take the initiative here, but government could help the process along by increasing grants to consolidated schools.

The problems associated with the greatly varying enrolment figures in these ethnic language schools from year to year, especially in the area of materials, could be alleviated, for example, by establishing a central library at the Department of Culture, from which schools could borrow a certain maximum number of books every year when required. These would be returned for use by others when their own enrolment declined. The same Department could also encourage the more uniform and therefore efficient use of textbooks by sponsoring workshops at which representatives of the various ethnic groups would discuss a mutually agreeable selection of textbooks. Furthermore, the Ethnic Language School Branch could serve as a clearing-house of cultural information from which ethnic language schools without direct access to the Department of Education could borrow up-to-date materials.

The establishment and operation of bilingual and immersion programs in German and other third languages could be facilitated by increased grants for materials, development and transportation. Clearly, transportation in such programs should be the major responsibility of parents, but at present, the burden — especially for a small program which has only a few schools in a city like Edmonton and needs to bus children from all over town — is extremely expensive. The Alberta government, in 1978, is paying only about 25% of the total cost of about 80 dollars per month and *pro* child in the English-German Bilingual Program, the remainder to be raised by parents and the parent association. This represents a real hardship for some. A new formula could be established that would raise the ceiling to, say, forty percent of total costs incurred on the basis of student miles.

In the same general area, there is a dire need for increased assistance to teacher education programs in the third-language bilingual and immersion programs. At present, teachers are being hired who are, first of all, qualified elementary school teachers and who also happen to know German reasonably well. So far, these programs have been lucky, because the teachers' enthusiasm and dedication have made up for what they themselves consider to be gaps in their preparation for teaching, and we are very happy, indeed, with them. But what will the future hold, in view of the fact that the university, in 1980 does not have the funds to offer primary school teachers a sound program in the methodology of second-language teaching in immersion and bilingual programs at the elementary level in third languages, not to speak of the secondary level?

Since the reading of this paper, the funding problem for transportation has been resolved, and the Faculty of Education of the University of Alberta is offering courses for teachers in bilingual and immersion programs.

In the area of cultural activities, representatives from the German community have entered a plea for increased assistance with out-of-pocket expenses, such as contributions towards travel expenses of a choir to Barrhead (but not for entertainment, food and lodging, just for receipted travel expenses), expenses for hiring a conductor, or for the purchase of music sheets and the like. These should all be eligible for increased grants — to be matched by funds raised by the ethnic community and capped with a ceiling, of course.

I hope I am making it quite clear I am not suggesting for a minute (and neither were the leaders of the German community) that ethnic organizations be given a free ride — on the contrary, strictest financial accountability should be an absolute must — but I think government, with relatively meagre additional funds, could be of tremendous assistance in the qualitative expansion of existing activities and services available in the ethnic community, from which a greater number of people would be able to benefit. In the pursuit of a positive multicultural policy the role of government should not only be the role of purser: it should serve as the catalyst, the agent of change that provides ideas, brings people together, helps to set a course for people and helps them to follow through. Clearly, ethnic communities should be allowed to develop their own initiatives, but government should not have to feel content to remain in a perennially passive, reacting role! A closer and more active co-operation between the two partners should result in the development of a truly vibrant multiculture in Canada.

DIALOGUE: CENTRAL AND EAST EUROPEAN COMMUNITY/GOVERNMENT

J. Stribrny, President,
Czechoslovakian National Association

The main aspirations of the Czechoslovak community in Alberta, which I have the privilege to represent on this panel, are the same as those of any other ethnic group: to preserve our language, culture and traditions here in Canada, our new homeland. I believe everybody will agree with me that language must be on the top of the list; culture and traditions can hardly be maintained without preserving the mother tongue.

In this respect the situation of our group is somehow special, because it is not just one language we have to preserve, but two, namely Czech and Slovak. There is no such thing as a Czechoslovak language: Czechs and Slovaks speak two different tongues. True, not very different ones: members of both nations are able to communicate with their countrymen from the other group without any special training, and there is no difficulty even in reading newspapers and books written in the other language. This is not the case, as far as I know, for any other two related languages, such as German and Dutch, and this makes our situation even more unique.

To add to the confusion, there is another catch: Slovak is spoken in Slovakia — quite logically — but Czech is spoken in Bohemia, Moravia and Silesia. Therefore, Czechs have sometimes been referred to as "Bohemians," confusing them either with Parisian artists or with gypsies. Actually, the name "Bohemia" is a very old one, dating back to the times, when there were no Slavs in the area, which was inhabited by a Celtic tribe named Boii. This was the state of affairs about 2,000 years ago, when the Roman Empire flourished: the Romans, therefore, named this region "Boiohemum," from which the form "Bohemia" developed. You will probably be surprised to learn that in Czech there is no equivalent to the expression "Bohemia": we call our country "Čechy," which means Czech lands. Thus, there are some expressions and sentences which cannot be correctly translated into Czech. For example, the Bohemian nobility (both Czech and German) issued, at the end of the eighteenth century, a proclamation, in which they stated that they are "nicht Deutsch, nicht Tschechisch, aber echt Boehmisch" — neither German nor Czech, but truly Bohemian. Such a sentence, believe me, is virtually impossible to translate into Czech.

As far as Czechs and Slovaks are concerned, there are more than just language differences between them. Even the character of the two peoples is not the same, Czechs being more stiff and formal, Slovaks on the other hand more carefree and gay. This is reflected in their folk songs: the tune of the Czech songs is usually slower and somehow more grave, but Slovak melodies are more dynamic. Actually, this difference is older than the one in their languages. As a matter of fact, Slovaks were using a Czech translation of the Bible until the end of the eighteenth century, and it was not before the mid-nineteenth century that a written form of Slovak was established. But even before that, the Slovak national character was undoubtedly the same as today, and thus distinct from its Czech counterpart.

Outside Czechoslovakia, especially in America, there are many people who do not realize that the name Czechoslovak is actually composed of the names of two nations. They suppose that the word "Czech" is simply a shorter form of the word "Czechoslovak" in a way similar to the shorter form "Newfies" for Newfoundlanders. This is not the case. Slovaks, of course, do not like to be referred to as Czechs. As a matter of fact, they feel offended, much in the same way as the Irish are if one calls them English. Please, keep this in mind when speaking to or about Slovaks!

From the roots, now I would like to go back to aspirations — that is the theme I mentioned at the start of my paper. As I already stated, I believe the preservation of our languages is the first condition for the rest of our aspirations, namely, the preservation of our cultures and traditions. I do not think having to preserve two, instead of one language, could be considered our main problem in our effort to start and maintain a Saturday language school for our children. We are facing — at least here in Edmonton — a more difficult problem. Unlike some other ethnic groups, members of our community are not concentrated in special areas. Consequently, it is very difficult even to choose where such a school should be located with sufficient convenience for the majority of pupils.

Language preservation, of course, is just the first step towards the preservation of cultural tradition, which we consider to be our ultimate goal. But we do not feel it is enough to keep our culture alive just for our children and grandchildren — we would like to make this treasure accessible to our fellow Canadians as well. In past years, we have tried to promote better understanding for our culture and a deeper knowledge of it among the public at large.

We have done so with exhibitions, concerts, radio and TV programs, and we would like to continue our effort. We have also provided materials about Czechoslovakia and about Czechs and Slovaks in Alberta to different schools for their multicultural projects, and to people engaged in research into

Alberta's past.

One of our achievements is a Czechoslovak library, which we maintain both for readers from our community and for other people interested in our culture. We have acquired — partly by purchase, partly by donations — about 250 books, mostly in Czech or Slovak. We also have English translations of some Czechoslovak authors. I would like to express our appreciation and gratitude to the government of Alberta for a generous grant which made this possible.

We would like to continue our endeavour, perhaps even by organizing something like a Czechoslovak Book Day, in order to attract more readers. There are many outstanding authors still living in Czechoslovakia who are not permitted to publish there, because their ideas do not conform to the official point of view of the present communist government. Fortunately enough, their books are published both in Czech and in translations in Canada, West Germany, Switzerland, and so on. Many of these books we have in our library, and we would like to continue to obtain new titles from these editions. Unfortunately, our financial means are very limited, so we do hope the government will once again support us.

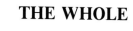

THE WHOLE

ROOTS AND REALITIES: SYNOPTIC COMMENTS

M. L. Kovacs,
University of Regina

Roots

Canada's connection, through her immigrants and their descendants, with Central and Eastern Europe, is perhaps not always readily or gladly remembered. Nevertheless, this connection, throughout Canadian history and, in fact, a long period before it, has been in existence. The pursuing of this connection or, rather, contacts with various sociocultural entities in the vast eastern expanse of Europe, would fill numerous volumes and be beyond the scope of the present study. Nevertheless, properly interpreted, the chapters of this volume reveal a colourful panorama of backgrounds, roots, aspirations, programs and realities that have been joined with the relevant discussion of the migration of individuals, groups, religions and ideologies from one continent to another.

An East-European country of immigration

Many people, when thinking of Russia, would often envisage an overpopulated country emitting one group of emigrants after another. While this image may have been true at certain later times, it was not so during the 100 years beginning in the early 1760s. Indeed, the eighteenth century witnessed the acquisition by Russia of vast areas in her south and west, often without any appreciable settled population. It may be claimed, with some degree of justification, that a veritable "population vacuum" arose in what contemporary administrators preferred to call "New" or "South Russia" and what has been renamed, at a more recent stage, the Ukraine. It might even be asserted that Catherine II, Gregory Potemkin and their immigration agents were only tools for the removal of that "vacuum" by inviting, to the Ukraine, settlers representing different religious groupings, whose common denominator was their German background and industry.

The Russia in which the newcomers arrived was a strange and bewildering country, whose conditions were to leave an imprint even on the late descendants of the new arrivals. It was definitely one of the backward countries of Europe, in which the Czars could have served as emancipators, leaders and educators of the people, had their traditions and personal inclinations not dictated otherwise. Nevertheless, at least some of them noticed the desolation

299

and emptiness of the newly-acquired vast expanse in the southern part of their country. One of the great enterprises of the eighteenth century was the organization and administration of a population movement mainly from the Germanic countries of central and western Europe into the vacuum existing in the new Russian territories. This went on for about a century, the second half of which was characterized by the emergence of a society in Russia that was full of tensions and contradictions.

As an eccentric medley of would-be social reformers, religious zealots and mystics, romantically-minded poets and writers became spokesmen of the demand for a happier era. Hryhory Savych Skovoroda, the "Ukrainian Socrates" of the eighteenth century, did not directly influence such sects as the Doukhobors and Molokans, nor was his world view affected by theirs. Nevertheless, Skovoroda's teachings and lifestyle contributed to the shaping of a set of ideas that was to inform the way of thinking of the social philosophers of the next century and later. Thus, Leo Tolstoy displayed a strikingly similar striving for a simple life, and both he and Skovoroda were strongly inclined towards moralizing. Both despised worldly possessions and individual property. Nor would they recognize ranks or offices. Not surprisingly, some Marxists of later times became interested through them in the communal living of Russian peasants in general and Skovoroda's influence upon it in particular (Buyniak). Even if Skovoroda's potential significance was great, Tolstoy's writings and example were enhanced by the greater sophistication of nineteenth-century life and their integrated views were spread more quickly and broadly through the improving technology of the time.

Along with the realization of Russia's insufficient technological advancement and need for general modernization along the lines of Western Europe and America, it was probably the vision of people like Skovoroda and Tolstoy that prepared the way for the social reforms of Alexander II. However, some of the social reforms were not at all regarded as blessings by practically all classes of German immigrants. Perhaps the most important initial inducement for the immigration of the original settlers had been a set of privileges additional to the grant of a comparatively large amount of land; however, exemption from military service, education in one's native language and freedom of religion could not survive Russia's increasing nationalism. By the 1870s, it became clear the choice was between compliance with changed public opinion as expressed in new legislation, or the search for another country with greater tolerance and less interest in militarism (Yedlin).

The first group to act was, not surprisingly, the Mennonites, for whom abhorrence of violence, even when a result of military service, was a basic tenet of faith. Besides, they were well equipped to become pioneers in a new exodus. They were not only farmers during their stay in Russia; they had acquired significant capital as well as a number of worldly skills connected with trade and commerce, which enabled them to negotiate successfully with the government agencies of Russia. These and other traits, developed in Russia, became lasting qualities for the Mennonites to such an extent that they may be causing mental anguish and conflict in some present-day Mennonite communities (Vogt). Nevertheless, the willingness to compromise, deriving from those worldly traits, contributed to their ability to reach agreement, to a large extent under their own terms, with the Canadian government.

The approximately 100,000 colonists invited to Russia in the early eighteenth century settled in the Volga area, the Black Sea region and Volhynia after the partitions of Poland. Because the settlers were very prolific, their numbers had increased mainly through natural growth to 450,000 by 1870. This growth is indicated by the establishment between 1853 and 1863 of more than 100 branches of earlier colonies. Some groups of them, such as the Volga Germans, multiplied by 16 times within 140 years.

Inasmuch as major political, cultural and economic reforms were being introduced in Russia during the 1860s and 1870s, the German settlers felt their culture, religion and education threatened. The last straw was the introduction of compulsory military service in 1874 (Yedlin).

Peopling the Prairies

From the European angle, the Canadian prairies had long been regarded as an enormously underpopulated area. It was only after the peopling of the plains of the American West that the vacuum aspect of the prairies north of the border came to the fore. In fact, the first Mennonite settlements in western Canada came about at a time when the government was desperate for settlers and willing to agree to conditions for the Mennonites, which tended to constitute privileges not granted later on to other groups.

Their emigration and propitious resettling were to set a precedent both for the ethnic groups of Russia, with particular reference to the Germans, and for the Canadian immigration authorities. Thus, although the immediate connection is not clarified yet, the Lutheran Finns tended to place similarly great emphasis on the value of education in their ancestral language and increasing literacy. They also got into a conflict — at a later stage, it is true — with the autocracy of the Czar. But their response was twofold; in addition to increasing emigration to the New World, they were adopting political radicalism. By the time they were arriving in Canada in greater numbers, circumstances no longer favoured bloc settlements and, in any case, they were more attracted to industry, especially logging. Handwritten newspapers formed a symbol of the Finns' interest in their ancestral language, general education and curiosity about the past and present. The writing and distribution of these papers was both a pastime and a means of maintaining contact among the similarly minded. These journals were often tools for forging new acquaintances and bridges between the converted and those still to be convinced. All the same, both the handwritten newspapers and the lifestyle that necessitated them were dated and, in due course, they disappeared (Lindström-Best).

One of the early groups of continental immigrants to Canada was the Hungarians. The arrival of the first representatives of this category had been connected with the desperate attempt in 1849 of Imperial Russia to stop progress in its tracks and help in the subjugation of Hungary. It was through the exiles of the War of Hungarian Independence that a trickle of emigration from Hungary developed later on into a torrent. Until 1885, Canada had not been recognized by Hungarians as a potential emigrational objective. It was due to the joint efforts of the Canadian immigration authorities and an expatriate of the debacle of 1849, P. O. Esterhazy, that the first Hungarian settlements on the Canadian prairies came into existence.

One of these, Esterhaz, and its market town, Whitewood, were the scene of the tragedy of Julius Vass. His untimely end by suicide would have been insignificant, had the case's investigation not provided a glimpse of the working, the problems and shortcomings of the administrative machinery of the time as a whole. History shows the almost patriarchal nature of early government when federal ministers were still forced by circumstances to interfere from Ottawa in the petty affairs of obscure settlements in the North-West. When the hiring of a minor official and the spending of $200 constituted the subject of long and complex discussions between two powerful ministers, in the course of events, the plight of the man, the candidate for the position, was largely disregarded. With the self-inflicted death of the first Hungarian-Canadian government official, the whole matter could conveniently be shelved. However, the story involves aspects of life in an early prairie settlement as well, including inadequacy in the care of new arrivals. The background to all this is Canada, as part of the British Empire also, characterized by the contrast between the avowed conservatism of the government and its adoption of laissez-faire liberalism and free competition, the application of which in practice had left a young peasant settlement in upheaval and disarray. Its settlers, only about a generation removed from the bonds of serfdom, were still desperately in need of an educated leader and the frighteningly large measure of freedom left them at first bewildered and disconcerted. Julius Vass, while he apparently had the knack of arousing confidence to a surprising extent in members of the government of the time, failed as a leader of the peasant community (Kovacs).

The German Influx

However, the largest inflow of early immigrants from Central and East Europe was supplied by Germans in Russia. It was from this reservoir of quickly multiplying population that settlers of German background began in the 1870s to pour into present-day Saskatchewan, either directly or via the United States, and establish mainly bloc settlements in which they could receive from and give each other material, spiritual and intellectual support. This was the beginning of the process that was to leave Saskatchewan inhabited within 50 years by almost twice as many settlers of non-British as of British origin.

Two traits of German immigrants was their more favourable financial situation and more thorough education — compared with some other arrivals from eastern Europe. But the more striking mark of German settlement on the prairies was the conglomeration of their settlers more according to religious affiliation than to place of origin. Owing to this circumstance, settlers from diverse areas of Central and Eastern Europe were brought together in one "colony".

These settlements could be categorized according to religious or regional homogeneity, or both. In other cases, these elements and their states of being homogeneous or mixed must be interchanged or permuted to describe their ethnocultural conditions more adequately. Thus, the religious factor constitutes the measuring stick for establishing the respective identities of settlements of German origin.

In the more distant past, bloc settlement, alike in ethnicity and religion, compact in population, would contribute to the formation of communities often capable of surviving — complete with their ancestral languages and cultures — for many hundreds of years.

Settling of this type had been a characteristic of German immigrants in many parts of Central and Eastern Europe and many such newcomers to what became Saskatchewan followed this traditional pattern. However, the ethnocultural development of even the most sizable, religiously homogeneous and ethnically compact bloc settlements, the two principal groupings of Catholic colonies in Saskatchewan exhibited a surprisingly sharp deviation from the traditional pattern. This happened despite their continued expansion and the relative completeness of their institutional organizations. By the early 1970s, the results of an extensive survey revealed that only 73 per cent of the first-generation respondents favoured the retention of their ancestral identity, while the percentage in this respect of second and successive generations dropped to 34.6 and 10.5 respectively. Moreover, almost 46 per cent of the first-generation respondents, 72 of the second- and 82 of the rest preferred at this stage the use of English in their everyday lives as well. That these data are not anomalous or exceptional is confirmed by related statistics in respect of Saskatchewan as a whole, where the population of German extraction who were still German-speaking declined from 73 per cent in 1941 to 42 in 1971, with only 10 per cent using German even at home. While their adherence to German ethnicity had become much weaker, an average of about 93 per cent of the respondents were found to be regular churchgoers and 90 per cent had German Catholics as spouses. Consequently, they were speakers of different German dialects, thus making the seemingly strong ethnocultural homogeneity of settlements in fact greatly fragile.

Since the ethnocultural traits discussed so far had been developing in some of the strongest "colonies" of German origin, it is perhaps no exaggeration to assume that the same trends of ethnocultural modification have prevailed, frequently in a more pronounced manner, in most other German bloc settlements.

Examined from the viewpoint of religious affiliation, the variety of denominations in Saskatchewan is representative only in part of Germany itself, with German Lutherans and Catholics being the almost exclusive religions in the latter. The determination of the places of origin for the German followers of such faiths as those of the Mennonites, Hutterites, Baptists, Adventists and Jews is more complex, but as a rule, it has ties with eastern Europe (Anderson).

Also, Alberta began to have her share of German settlers. The German Catholics began settling there in 1896 and set up some seven colonies. German Lutheran immigration was on a larger scale and better organized. Starting with a settlement in 1889, this group had established some ten colonies by 1897. Arriving from Volhynia in 1894, the Moravian Brethren founded four colonies within three years.

In the decade from 1895, additional arrivals from Russia settled south of Edmonton. Volga Germans north of Edmonton and in Calgary quickly established themselves. As in Saskatchewan, the congregation was the most important communal institution. While the Moravians and the Baptists had, as a rule, arrived led by their own spiritual leaders, Lutherans would obtain advice and ministers from the German Lutheran Synods in the United States.

On the other hand, Catholics had to rely for priests on German American Benedictines or Oblates. After the First World War, immigration from Soviet Russia began with the arrival of Mennonite and, later on, Lutheran and Catholic groups. The total number of immigrants from the Soviet Union to Canada did not exceed 10,000, with half of them settling in the prairie provinces. During the Second World War, some 100,000 Russian Germans were evacuated by retreating Nazi armies. Since the end of the War, nearly 100,000 Germans have entered Canada. According to the 1971 census, Alberta's population included about 230,000 Germans or 13 per cent of the total population. Owing to the church-centred nature of the German settlements, their historical sources have tended to deal mainly with congregational matters.

The gradual withdrawal of the communities from public life is attributed to the interruption of cultural activities and to restrictions on the public use of the German language during the Wars. But this passivity of ex-Russian Germans might also be due to their forbears' isolated existence in Russia and to deeper religion (Yedlin).

Warfare and Immigration

Actual wars, or their threat, contribute to the release of waves of immigration (Anderson, Yedlin). The proposition is tellingly illustrated in the successive stages of Hungarian immigration to Canada. The earliest had been released by the consequences of the unsuccessful War of Independence from 1849 and the 1885-1914 wave was initiated through the threat of an Anglo-Russian War. This latter population movement largely consisted of peasants in search of land (Kovacs).

The interwar immigration, with considerable urban elements, was enhanced by the effects on Hungary of the First World War, one of which was the Great Depression. As a consequence, many large Hungarian communities arose in the urban areas of Central Canada. The first important Hungarian organizations there were congregations and self-help societies and one of their members' pressing social problems was a skewed distribution of the sexes, with a large surplus of men.

The wave of Displaced Persons, in the wake of the Second World War, contained a majority of urban, skilled, well-educated individuals. Many mature political refugees had to accept diminished social status on arrival. They were politically the most conscious group among Canadian Hungarians. They also established several important institutions, including newspapers. Since initially many of them regarded themselves as émigrés intent on ultimate return to their native country, they greatly emphasized transmission of their ancestral language and heritage.

It is an inexorable law of immigrant life, that successive waves take over social, cultural and institutional leadership from representatives of the previous influx. In this respect, the 1956 arrivals, refugees from revolution, were no exception. In contrast to the other two groups, young, unattached single persons prevailed among these newcomers. Compared with previous arrivals, they were exceptional in that the authorities looked upon them as special arrivals to whom special consideration was due. Because of this as well as their comparative youth, the refugees adjusted well to their new environment. Another noteworthy leaning of this group, participation in creative cultural organizations, also found expression with them in creativity itself. Each wave had its particular trauma: the Great Depression, the DP camps and loneliness respectively (Papp-Zubrits).

A closer examination and comparison of divergent features of pre- and post-Second-World-War Hungarian society identified categories of emigrants as products of two stages of development in the same society and, consequently, attributed many tensions between the two waves to their contrasting qualities. Different social origins, ages, occupations and such dissimilarities in sociocultural expectations as derive from disparate training, education and socioeconomic circumstances were some of those qualities. The conflicting attributes, were lined up in confrontation. In a final act, the resolution of the conflict was attempted through a higher. and more comprehensive reconciliation. The new insight involved the awareness first that both groups benefited in their respective ways — the Canadian Hungarian community on the one hand, Canadian society as a whole on the other — and second, that "strength lies not only in their shared aspirations, but also in their obvious differences" (Bisztray).

Another side-effect of warfare — besides releasing migration — was its impact on certain categories of immigrants and citizens of Canada. This corollary is shown in the awkward position not only of the Austrian Canadians, but also of Mackenzie King's government in connection with the issue.

In the years after the Third Reich's collapse in 1945, there existed an apparently strange contrast between Mackenzie King's reluctance not to regard Austria as an ex-enemy, and the official Canadian position on Austria, publicly stated in 1948, that "Canada was never at war with the political entity of Austria ... " Even if the status of Austrians had inauspiciously been declared as "enemy alien" in September 1939, certainty of the action's correctness was never complete throughout the rest of the War. Thus, to boost morale, anti-Nazi activities were organized by Austrians in Canada with official blessings. Archduke Otto was allowed to enter the country, and ex-Empress Zita and "the headquarters of the Austrian monarchist organization" were located there. The Canadian government had been unwilling in the first place to become involved in the affairs of Europe, nor was it quick to plan for post-war Austrian policy. It might have been King's consistent refusal in the early post-War years to dispose of the Austrian question that he used as a device to keep Canada out of the occupation and control of Central Europe (Keyserlingk).

Political antagonism is not necessarily expressed by the wielding of weapons. In the opinion of one contributor, it may also take place through the manipulation of university curricula. Thus, the fundamental absence of Russian prose writers of post-1956 vintage from university courses may, in that it handicaps students in becoming up-to-date in Russian studies, fall into that category (Polowy).

A third consequence of warfare is territorial, socioeconomic and political change. A forceful example of such rearrangements is available in the emergence of the vastly altered relationship among the Comecon countries in Central and Eastern Europe.

The Central and Eastern European Sphere

It would be wrong to ascribe all difficulties of the area to the belated aftermath of warfare; many of them derive from the clash of political wills, from the excessive tempo of modernization and the concomitant and inordinate growth of socioeconomic expectations. While all countries in the sphere exhibit more or fewer symptoms of these phenomena, it is Poland that has recently attracted, in these respects, the most consistent worldwide attention.

A more structural analysis of the subject would reveal a number of positions arranged in hierarchies dealing with the same problems according to the same rules in the same processes and procedures. Expressed differently, the countries constitute something of a revolving stage on which simultaneous performance goes on. The 'script' being the same, the 'roles' are likewise, yet the developments and outcomes vary because the 'actors' are different.

Descending to a less structured level, the real-life drama can be seen as carried out between the 'establishment' or 'the elite' and the opposition. While the former is made up of the more or less continuous layer of high and lower administrators and office-bearers, the opposition seems to be in flux, often depending upon economic and other external circumstances. The elite is the product largely of sociocultural innovation, often through accelerated transfer from the lower ranks by means of sped-up education, with the opposition naturally including the dispossessed and overlooked ambition. However, by far the largest number of the opposition's recruits are occasional and linked with unsatisfied expectations respecting such prosaic matters as bread, potatoes and meat and long queueing up at shops.

It might be generalized that the popularization of the elite and the system they represent was attempted by what was intended to become a large-scale and accelerated modernization of every aspect of life of both the individual and the group. A part of it was the intention to uproot and destroy the old and, thereby, to strengthen the new, but another part was the desire to experiment, on a tremendous scale, with the construction of a new social order. One aspect of experimentation was the extension of modernization and its principles in technology to social, cultural and economic life. To achieve this, it was necessary to promote the growth of industrialization at the greatest possible rate. This in turn was only feasible through the utmost mobilization of resources, which processes could be effected only by means of the broad introduction of long-term planning at all levels. In this process, heavy industry as the basis of technological advancement usually received the highest priority. Thus, the resources of the country were concentrated in this sector. Inevitably, consumer goods and the consumers became the losers. Until recently, the peasant farmers had been the strongest, most conservative, but least organized, segment of society. Their interests and traditions clashed in great measure with the modernizing tendencies of the new era. Their independent lifestyle did not fit into the projection of a socially-minded society; their small holdings were too small for the introduction of mechanization and their farming methods were well behind the times. Nevertheless, their political potential and tenacity were so great as to preserve to a large extent, at least in Poland, their small-scale farms, but only at a price. Due to a lack of investment in new equipment, the growth of their productivity was at best limited, which fact, combined with the greater availability of higher education and training, resulted in their sons' and daughters' leaving the farms for cities in droves. Altogether, the numerical decline of independent farmers in the last two decades has been staggering, as, of course, has been the decrease in their influence. Furthermore, this tendency has not promoted greater food production.

Most of the sons and daughters of farmers tended to augment the ranks of blue-collar workers, who, because of this, replaced the peasantry as the largest and potentially strongest political factor. This development was tied to the modernization of the role of women as workers outside the home. One of the important aims of modernization in the social sector was equality for all. This expectation was particularly strong in respect of women and between blue-collar workers and their white-collar counterparts. Educational institutions, books, newspapers, radio and television were used on a huge scale to make the innovations attractive.

However, planning and actual life can only be brought together imperfectly. Thus, quick industrialization, while it indeed brought about accelerated socioeconomic transformation, had its drawbacks, as for instance, external female employment that was meant to replace housework and minding children, but which became a combination of factory or office work and domestic chores, inclusive of looking after the children. More and higher education was designed to produce more enlightened men and women, but the more educated and sophisticated the Poles became, the more difficult it was to manipulate them. Furthermore, as the workforce became larger and better trained, it grew more eager for consumption. Besides, the large-scale use of mass media unavoidably brought along the unintended presentation of richer and more colourful lifestyles, which was an additional impulse towards larger and more varied consumption. Another source of pressure derived from the impact of full employment; yet, while industrial production and investment per head grew tenfold, agricultural yields increased by only one-and-a-half times. Expressed differently, income growth — for instance, in Poland of the 1970s — did not prompt a proportionate increase in the supply of consumer goods, particularly food. Similar disproportion between supply and demand could be observed in other fields.

The mass media were also decisive factors in the continual power struggle between opposition and establishment. For their good graces, the government was willing to make concessions, because they represented the means of controlling public opinion and the unions. Yet, in some countries, the opposition and establishment were able to coexist (Matejko).

Neither their centuries-long incorporation in the Habsburg empire, nor the traumatic effects on Austria of two World Wars could reduce the vitality of the Slovene speech community. This little-known world of sociocultural relationships of the speakers of a minor Slavic dialect in Carinthia, was the site of an experiment based on the "matched guise technique." The study, carried out by a University of Alberta researcher, has reached a finding that may be significant in other contexts as well. It is the high rating allotted to dialect- as against standard-language speakers on "likability" and "sociability" scales. Very properly, attention has been directed to the need for similar research in Alberta. Such research would reveal "the critical matter of attitudes in the communities concerned" in respect of bilingual or ethnic language programs, and would illustrate the importance of the nexus between ethnic languages and the social climate that surrounds them (Priestly).

Jewish Immigration to Edmonton

In some cases, not only conflict, but also ethnocultural identity may be a major factor in emigration. Thus, the latest wave of immigrants to Edmonton from Eastern Europe gave a combination of "Jewishness," political reasons and economic factors as well as a concurrence of close friends, close relatives, favourable job circumstances and availability of "solid information" as reasons for leaving the USSR and choosing Canada. Of the 5,424 Soviet Jewish immigrants to Canada between 1973 and 1979, as many as 286 individuals in 122 family units came to Edmonton. In order to better understand their adaptation, the immigrants were approached with a questionnaire drawn up in Russian. About forty per cent of them were in the 30-45 age brackets, with a preponderance of males of about 10 per cent and with an average of 1.5 children per family.

Even after only seven years or less in Edmonton, they as a group showed signs of fragmentation and an increase in socializing with native-born

Canadians. Yet, 90 per cent needed further training in English; in fact, almost four-fifths thought knowledge of the language indispensable in their occupations and attended language classes, and practically all the remainder viewed English language proficiency as useful. More than four-fifths of the respondents displayed signs of ties with Russian culture in the Ukraine, thus revealing a frequent tendency among minority groups to identify with the prevailing culture and its language.

Members of the grouping had attained unusually high levels of qualification with more than 70 per cent having graduated from a university or its equivalent and with the rest having undergone *tekhnikum* or college training. Almost half of them worked in their field of specialization and another third, close to their specialities. While nearly four-fifths lived in rented homes (mostly apartments), about 65 per cent indicated a wish to own a house.

About a quarter of the respondents reported having two or more cars; three-quarters claimed having one automobile. Four-fifths owned television sets and two-thirds reported listening to radio. In both cases, about one-third indicated topmost interest in news items. Many of them were more or less regular movie- and concert-goers. More than 60 per cent were readers of the Russian emigre press, while about 44 per cent followed the Canadian press and only three per cent claimed to read Soviet papers.

Eighty-three per cent exhibited a strong desire to know more about Canadian history, culture and geography. Only 14 per cent attended synagogue in the Soviet Union; "the casual approach to worship attested to the fact that Jewishness in the Soviet Union has little to do with religion." Yet 86 per cent reported having encountered frequent indications of anti-semitism in the USSR. More than three-quarters of the respondents reported achievement of material success, but only a little more than one-third had realized their non-material expectations. Viewed as a whole, the author interpreted the results of his investigation to be "a basic vote of confidence in Canada" (Busch).

Realities

Not only did representatives of some ethnocultural groups and other organizations of Alberta attend the conference, but they also presented papers. The subject-matter of the presentations is varied; nevertheless, their examination reveals a structure that transcends the individual papers and provides consistency. Thus, it is not only the Czechoslovak Canadians that are weakened by linguistic-sociocultural divergence and spatial distance among the members, but in their case the problem is compounded in that the Czechs and Slovaks represent two different, even if similar, backgrounds. Nevertheless, the members of the group are strengthened by their zeal to create a better understanding for, and a deeper knowledge of, their own culture in society at large (Stribrny).

In actual fact, older groups, such as the Ukrainians, have already seen much advancement in social outlook and government policy from the stage of negativism (before the late 1960s), through "cultural awareness" (no instruction in the ancestral language involved as of the late 1970s), to the level of "third language" (other than English and French) as the medium of teaching. The decisive development in this respect was the setting up of the Alberta Cultural Heritage Conference in Edmonton in 1972. The resultant image of culture placed emphasis on the importance of language. Other attainments of the Heritage Conference included the establishment of the Alberta Cultural Heritage Council, as well as a Cultural Heritage Periodical and a coordinating organ for the Alberta Ethnocultural Program. Even though the movement within the decade had reached, in Alberta, "educational multilingualism," the federal government still has not moved beyond the stage of multiculturalism (Pelech).

Undoubtedly, this advancement has been due in a large degree to institutional pressure from ethnocultural groups. Relevant examples of this tendency were such Hungarian activities as the promotion, through appearing in person before government and church agencies, in a progressive sequence, of the introduction of the Magyar language and Hungarian studies right up to the university level (Duska). An even more striking example of the effects of social pressure as a lever of advancement was the case of the Ukrainian Professional and Business Club of Edmonton, whose achievements included contributing to the successful endowment of a chair of Ukrainian Studies, a bilingual program in Alberta and the Canadian Institute of Ukrainian Studies in Edmonton (Decore).

The relationships of the ethnocultural groups of Central and Eastern European backgrounds formed an issue with the strongest emotional connotations. How could the various sociocultural boundaries surrounding these groups be maintained and bridged over at the same time? This dilemma, expressed in simple, yet complex, terms, added up to the phrase "better communication" (Stribrny) and in the feeling that folkloric exhibitions, dances and the like were insufficient for achieving it. In one view, even the fostering of the ethnic tongue and heritage should yield significantly to the presentation of real ethnocultural "knowing" through interaction at the individual and group levels (Prokop).

However, knowing is based on information. Consequently, lack of knowledge in most cases derives from lack of information. Thus, the disapproving comment on the readiness of governments to rely on secondhand information passed on by civil servants (Buski) is more understandable. Of course, requesting opportunities for members of ethnocultural groups (Gertler) to enjoy reciprocal acquaintance with the past and present of other groups is logical.

But it is not enough to exchange "knowing" with other ethnocultural groups of Central and East European origins. The same ought to be the case with society at large. None the less, this is not so, and a lopsided situation emerges in which knowledge of, from, and by society is distributed and eagerly consumed, with little inclination from the latter to attempt to reach in this respect an equilibrium of reciprocal information. One obstacle in the way of achieving it is the inability or reluctance of scholars in Canadian history to record and utilize, in their writings, evidence of ethnic contributions to Canadian life (Manolakos).

Knowledge of ethnocultural groups is hampered by the inadequate distribution of information about them and their cultural heritage. This fact is clearly attested to by some authors. Third-language speakers are at a definite disadvantage in the allocation of broadcasting time because of the desire of stations to maintain a set audience and attract more money (Charest). Newspaper coverage, furthermore, is unequivocally reduced for ethnocultural groupings. It is allotted to various minorities (ethnic, religious and cultural) according to their newsworthiness. Even then their shares should not be excessive, but proportional to the whole (O'Callaghan). Because of these unfavourable, yet sincere, considerations, not enough information or non-relevant information on East and Central European backgrounds is provided and assimilated; the present insufficient representation for the "third group" on federal and provincial boards and commissions should be altered and made proportional. For the same reasons, third-language education given in the present amounts is not enough. The position could be righted by government subsidies and by its placement within regular school curricula. Polish Canadians would like to see greater stress on human rights and a redefinition of the naming and status of "refugees" (Gertler).

The setting up of special institutions for the preparation and introduction of particular reforms makes their orderly enactment more feasible. Such institutions are the Alberta Cultural Heritage Council and its sister body, the Alberta Cultural Heritage Foundation. The Council is representative of cultural groups and includes government appointees as well. Its subjects encompass liaison, the promotion of identity, cultural preservation, advice and policy recommendations. The Foundation is a funding body for projects (Buski). New reforms would require new institutions; thus, intergroup difficulties could be pinpointed and studied in an "interethnic research institute." A "forum for exchange of views" could presumably provide a platform for sounding out the opinions of ethnocultural groups and the general public (Gertler). According to the precedent established by one of the founding races, the French Canadians, a Joint Commission for Ukrainian Canadians as well should be set up by the federal government (Decore).

The various papers forming this volume have succeeded in distributing the findings of studies, information about population movements, personalities, the present, the past, the ambitions of groups and many other useful views and suggestions. It is hoped the synoptic overview provided in this concluding chapter will have been helpful in showing connections even where they are not quite obvious.

INDEX

213, 214, 230, 232
Giles, H., 86, 95, 96
Gilroy, Sask., 215
Gitelman, Z., 102, 108, 112
Gladmar, Sask., 213
Glan, J.A., 35
Glazer, N., 209
Glen Kerr, Sask., 215
Glenbush, Sask., 202, 215
Glidden, Sask., 195, 203, 216
Gluckstal, 214
Gnosticism, 17
Goethe Institute, 289
Goethe Institute (Toronto), 272
Gogol, N.V., 80
Golden Prairie, Sask., 188
Goldner, Franz, 36
Gönczy, Lajos, 139, 149, 150
Goodeve, Sask., 196, 211, 214
Goodsoil, Sask., 189, 190, 212
Göös, W., 135
Gordon, M.M., 209
Gorky, M., 75
Gorlitz, Sask., 193, 194
Gouldtown, Sask., 201, 215
Govan, Sask., 190, 192, 212
Grande Prairie, Alta., 281
Grassland Ukrainian Language
  Association – Grassland (school),
  281
Grassy Lake, Alta., 227
Grayson, Sask., 189, 211
Great Deer, Sask., 215
Greek Catholics, 157
Greek Community School (Calgary),
  280
Greeks, 7, 255, 260
Greenfarm, Sask., 215
Greenwald, Sask., 210
Gregherd, Sask., 192, 212
Grenfell, Sask., 196
Grosswerder, Sask., 187
Gruenfeld, Sask., 198
Gruenthal, Sask., 198
Guatemala, 273

Guerin, Thomas, 35
Guernsey, Sask., 184
Gull Lake, Sask., 195, 215
Gulutsan, M., vii
Gurdwara Shriguru Singh Sabha –
  Punjabi (Edmonton school), 281
Guru Nanak Sikh School (Calgary),
  280
Gyülvészi, George, 156, 164
H.H. The Agakhan School – Gujarati
  (Edmonton), 280
Haas, Georg, 213
Hackworth, Green H., 35
Hague, Sask., 197, 198, 200, 213
Hallam, Sask., 187
Hamilton, 156, 259
  L.A., 141
Hampton, Sask., 193, 194
Handel, Sask., 188
Handlin, O., 208
Hanley, Sask., 202, 216
Hannover, 196
Haraszti, M., 57, 72
Harris, Sask., 203
Hatton, Sask., 187
Heart's Hill, Sask., 187
Heeney, A.D., 37, 39
Height, J.S., 209
Heimthal, Alta., 228, 231
Heimthal Moravian Church, 228
Heitman, S., 231
Helicon Society, 168
Hepburn, Sask., 198, 200, 201
Heppner, John, 216
Herbert, Sask., 201, 202, 203, 215
Heritage Language Schools, 271
Hermagor, 84
Herrnhuter, 227
Herschel, Sask., 202, 203
Herzl Colony, 205
Hesse, 179, 213, 225
Hesseluene, 182
Hill, George A., 140
Hillcrest, Sask., 216
Hillsvale, Sask., 216

326

Upper Hesse, 187
Urals, 8
Ursuline nuns, 182
USSR, 3, 51, 52, 54, 56, 57, 58, 59,
 64, 66, 67, 68, 69, 70, 75, 80, 99,
 100, 103, 108, 110, 111, 113, 228,
 229, 230, 273, 304
Vähäkyrö, 132
Valley, Sask., 198
Vancouver Island, 132
Vanguard, Sask., 189, 216
Vantage, Sask., 211
Varadinov, G., 15, 16, 19
Vass, Julius, 137, 138, 139, 140, 141,
 142, 143, 144, 145, 146, 147, 148,
 149, 150, 151, 152, 153, 302
Vegreville, Alta., 241, 281
Veiter, T., 95
Velik, F., 95
Verigin, P., 21
Vermilion Hills, Sask., 195, 201, 202
Verulam, Sask., 187
Verwood, Sask., 211
Vibank, Sask., 181, 196, 209
Viceroy, Sask., 211
Vidora, Sask., 195
Vienna, 21, 25, 27, 34
Vietnam, 54
Vietnamese, 260, 262
Vineburg, Philip F., 35
Vinokur, A., 112
Vishenka Colony, 204
Vistula-Nogat Delta, 5
Vladimir-Volynskij, 214
Vogel, Sask., 195
Vogt, R., 12, 301
Voinovich, V.N., 77
Volga, 6, 7, 8, 178, 223, 224, 225,
 226, 228, 301
Volga German Autonomous Republic,
 229
Volga German Colony, 191
Volga Germans, 179, 193, 194, 195,
 226, 227, 228, 301, 304
Volgyes, I., 149

Volhynia, 187, 192, 196, 197, 205,
 212, 213, 214, 223, 227, 231, 232,
 301, 304
Volhynian Germans, 227
Volhynian-Galician Germans, 189
Volksdeutsche, 179
Volksverein, 182, 183, 210
Vörösváry-Weller, István, 164
Wagner, J.F., 209
Wakaw, Sask., 184
Waldeck, Sask., 195, 203, 216
Waldheim, Kurt, 264
 Sask., 197, 198, 200
Waldron, Sask., 196
Wales, 93
Walter, J., 132
Wapella, Sask., 137, 196, 205, 214
Warman, Sask., 198, 200
Warsaw, 71, 72
Waseca, Sask., 203
Washington, 33, 35, 38
Waterloo County, Ont., 202, 203
Watrous, Sask., 195, 205, 216
Watson, Sask., 183, 184, 190
Webb, Sask., 203, 215
Weimar Republic, 229
Welland, Ont., 156, 157
Welland Canal, 156
Welland Hungarian Self-Culture
 Society, 157
Wengrow, 196
West Bench, Sask., 216
West Germany, 66, 229
West Indians, 259, 260
West Prussia, 4, 7
West Prussian Platt, 5
West Reserve, 197
Westend German Language School
 (Edmonton), 285
Westerham, Sask., 187
Westfalen, 190
Wetaskiwin, 227
Wetaug, Ill., 182
Weyburn, Sask., 190, 213
White Bear, Sask., 205

White City, Sask., 181
Whitewood, Sask., 139, 140, 143,
  144, 145, 146, 150, 151, 152, 196,
  214, 302
Wiegner, P.E., 213
Wilcox, Sask., 190
Wilkie, Sask., 188, 195, 211
Williams, H.P., 231
  Maurice, vii
Willmont, Sask., 210
Wimmer, Sask., 183, 210
Windisch, 83, 95
Windschiegl, P., 210
Windsor, 156, 157
Windthorst, Ludwig, 189
  Sask., 189, 214
Windthorst Colony, 196
Winkler, Man., 197
Winnipeg, 135, 140, 156, 191, 197,
  210, 212, 249
Wisconsin, 182
Wishart, Sask., 216
Wölck, W., 95, 96
Wolff Valley School District, 212

Wolffton, Sask., 212
Wood, S.T., 36, 37
Woodcock, G., 21
Woodrow, Sask., 203, 215
Wrong, H.H., 35, 37, 38
Württemberg, 224, 225
Wurttembergers, 214
Wymark, Sask., 215
Wynyard, Sask., 216
Yedlin, T., v, vii, 223, 300, 301, 305
Yellow Grass, Sask., 190, 194, 213
Yorkton, Sask., 193, 194, 205
Young, Sask., 183, 211
Younge, E.R., 208
Yugoslavia, 83, 156, 182, 245
Yugoslavs, 260
Zaduban, George, 161, 162, 164
Zaporozhe, 8
Zaporozhian Cossacks, 5
Zehner, Sask., 194
Zelma, Sask., 183
Zenkovskii, V.V., 21
Zimmermann, A., 209
Zita, Empress of Austria, 30, 306